For Adelyn

~~~

A Spiritual Evolution

by Louisa P.

Copyright 2012 Louisa P.

Createspace Edition

~~~

ISBN: 978-0692297087

DISCLAIMER ~ PLEASE NOTE:

While this book makes frequent reference to Alcoholics Anonymous, the views expressed and characters described herein reflect only the personal experience of the author and in no way represent the membership, meetings, philosophy, or program of AA itself. Except for quotations from AA approved literature, no part of this text is in any way related to the organizations of AA, Al-Anon, or IANDS. The names of significant characters have been changed to maintain confidentiality.

Cover design: Chariti Canny (chariti@charitidesigns.com)

Two quotations guided the writing of this book:

...[B]e only too willing to bring former mistakes, no matter how grievous, out of their hiding places. Showing others who suffer how we were given help is the very thing that makes life seem so worthwhile to us now. Cling to the thought that, in God's hands, the dark past is the greatest possession you have – the key to life and happiness for others. With it you can avert death and misery for them.

-Alcoholics Anonymous
The Family Afterward

Teach me to bear a humility that shows me, without ceasing, that I am a liar and a fraud and that, even though this is so, I have an obligation to strive after truth, to be as true as I can, even though I will inevitably find all my truth poisoned with deceit. This is the terrible thing about humility: that it is never fully successful. If it were only possible to be completely humble on this earth. But no, that is the trouble... Our humility consists in being proud and knowing all about it...

-Thomas Merton
Thoughts on Solitude

A SPIRITUAL EVOLUTION

*How 14 after-effects of a Near-Death Experience
helped cure my addictions and changed my life*

Preface to the Online Edition: Why No Last Name?

Readers may ask, "Why don't your share your last name? What's this *Louisa P.* business?"

Originally I e-published a first draft of this book with my full name, having changed the names of family members. It turns out, however, that my siblings' perspectives on alcoholism and the plausibility of paranormal experiences differ drastically from mine. They saw me as dishonoring our father, demeaning our family, and trivializing family deaths to glorify my own ego, and said so in a steady stream of irate emails telling me to "take the turd down" and that I had "the right to publicly humiliate yourself, but not to drag us into it!" So, to respect their wishes (and Tradition 11), I removed my last name from the book. Unfortunately their emails got only worse: I was a narcissistic and exploitative liar brainwashed by the cult of AA.

My siblings, like most folks from alcoholic families, believe in putting only our best photoshopped foot forward in public. Addiction, it's true, is not pretty. The Big Book of AA expresses the hope that readers won't find the "self-revealing accounts" in its second half to be "in bad taste." These life stories, like the shares of speaker meetings, tell of ways AAs went about blotting out their intolerable existence until the pain grew intense enough to force open their minds to a spiritual solution.

In other words, telling our stories is the cornerstone of AA fellowship. While the specifics may vary, the root storyline highlights the nature of alcoholic insanity common to all of us, so that newcomers caught up in their own inner turmoil can identify and relate. "We believe it is only by fully disclosing ourselves and our problems that they will be persuaded to say 'Yes, I am one of them, too; I must have this thing.'" In my case, the "things" I've had are multiplex – alcoholism, codependence, sexual addictions, etc. – making my story a mosaic of illnesses and recovery.

I doubt this book will appeal to normal people. Fortunately, no such people exist. We all carry a lot more symptoms and quirks inside than we let on to the world. The most abnormal thing about me, you'll find, is the disarming degree to which I'm honest about mine. That inner sickness and healing make up the primary focus of this book. There's also a whole hunky-dory façade of my life that I virtually ignore – the side most people would emphasize in a memoir. Writing about addiction, on the other hand, requires an attitude much like burlesque dancing: you drop your shame and replace it with humor.

How did I get from the one to the other – from fear and shame to joy and freedom? That's the focus of this book. It's the story of an evolving faith in a non-religious god, including an NDE with fourteen after-effects, and a spiritual approach to living that has delivered me from addiction to savor the beauties of living. As we say in the rooms, take what you like and leave the rest.

NOTE: See also my alcoholic blog at:
aspiritualevolution.wordpress.com

Book photos can be viewed at:
flickr.com/photos/133472207@N04/sets/72157654976322805

Introduction:

SNAPSHOT

of the

Problem

In 1993, following much therapy, my life looked great. I'd bought my dream house in the country, a three-story log home overlooking a gently sloped meadow, partly shaded by tall, graceful Douglas firs, where my hen, lesbian ducks, and two half-wild dogs – one a dingo mix and the other coyote – could roam. My partner and I planted fruit trees and a garden, and I fenced the acreage myself. This was where I was finally going to be happy, because I'd quit teaching college English and set up a simple life that focused on writing. By that time I'd published four short stories and won two prizes, so all I needed was a good pastoral retreat.

Instead, what I developed over the next year was madness – I guess you could call it that. You might also call it a relapse of obsessive-compulsive disorder, or codependent end-stage alcoholism, or going bat-shit crazy.

I'd become wildly obsessed with a boy from the espresso shop where I worked. This was my third go-round with sexual obsession, by a now hackneyed pattern I'd called "falling in love" the first two times, cycles that had netted my ex-husband and current partner, Jenna. But now after four years, Jenna had lost all her magic. Sure, she loved me, but without the chase, there could be no high. Now the charismatic boy, Theo, gave me that recurring fix of euphoria, the light that powered my world. I imagined conversations in every waking moment and scrawled sexual fantasies about him in my journal, pages I later burned in yet another failed effort to exorcise him. But this entry survives:

> 7/13/1994: "Help me, help me, help me! No one could be more lost! God, I should see the shrink. I don't have the – I don't know what – the wisdom, the discipline, the *something* – to get myself back on track. I know that I am fucked up and have created something to tie my lifeline to. Fucked up! Fucked up! I am not sane. Depression – so make an idol, someone way up in the clouds and dream they'll somehow pull you up to feel worth. It fills my mind against my will.
>
> "Is this cruelty? Yes, but it feels like self-preservation. The crime is that I haven't told her, that I would leave her in an ocean of abandonment. I am cowardly. I do what's easier instead of fighting through this madness to love and want Jenna again.
>
> "Oh, God, Life, whatever – I'm so close to falling apart! My body has the shakes. I smoke and smoke and don't want to eat. I can't ever sleep anymore because bits and pieces of the fantasies catch the needle of my thoughts and play constantly, hour after hour, like a big stack of overused 45s."

My only hope was the shrink, a psychologist I'd seen in Seattle years ago to get my shit together. Back then my mom had offered to pay $100 an hour in hopes the doctor could nip my suspected lesbianism in the bud. I'd agreed to go because my life was a mess: I was spending far too much time in the absurdly symbolic closet of the apartment I shared with Jenna, crying over the phone with my ex-husband. I'd left him for her without a trace of emotion a year before, but the grief had caught up with me.

At our very first session, after assuring me he wouldn't try to de-lesbianize me, the shrink asked a bunch of questions about my background and upbringing. Sitting there in my men's clothes and wingtips, my hair buzzed except for an Elvis-like pompadour, I'd told him how my father was a university professor who also made and drank a lot of wine; my mother taught Art History, her own mother having been a famous art historian and museum director. All of us kids were slated to be brilliant: my older sister was an associate professor of Musicology at Harvard, my brother a classicist fluent in Greek and Latin, and my younger sister a full-time painter, sponsored by my parents. At 29 I was a middle child, and my shtick was writing and lit. The shrink took copious notes.

"Is there anything you'd like to add?" he asked, glancing up toward the close of the hour. "Anything you think I should know?"

"Yes," I responded. My heart pounded, but my mind was made up, so I spoke: "When I was nine years old, my mother found a stack of drawings I'd made of naked women, who were in bondage, and getting tortured or killed. My parents sent them to a psychiatrist. I was terrified, but he said they were normal, so we never talked about them again. I kept wanting to draw them, though, even though I didn't. Then when I was seventeen, I started acting them out by tying myself up in the bathroom and looking at mirrors." I was shaking like fury, my voice having turned to a bleat, but I kept on. "All my life I've tried to stop, but I couldn't. When I first turned gay, it stopped for about a year. But the last time I did it..." (I *would* not cry!) "...was day before yesterday."

The urge to sob seemed to be taking a battering ram to my throat, but I forced it back to get the last words out: "And I don't want to do it anymore."

I waited in that chair, in what seemed a bright, trembling silence with my back to the Seattle skyline, while the shrink's fountain pen flew across his yellow legal pad again and again. Finally he looked up and met my eyes – the first human being ever know the truth about me.

"We're out of time!" he said. "But I can tell you two things. First, you're a very courageous young woman. I don't think I've ever had a patient tell me so much so fast – you just saved us months of work. So, I salute your courage. And the second thing is a promise." He sat forward to say gently, "You don't have to do that ever again."

I couldn't look at the man, couldn't speak, and fled from his office before the tears won out. When I finally reached my faithful little Mazda on the street below, I was in a daze. I remember looking up at the silver skyscraper, trying to find the window where I'd actually done it – exposed my deepest secret. "You *idiot*! You've ruined *everything*!" lamented some demon inside me. "Our only escape!" I knew what it meant, and I felt frightened, too. But I steeled myself to answer it matter-of-factly: "There are other ways to live," I thought, unlocking my car. "There have to be."

He'd been right that day. I'd never had to do it again, thanks to a lot of work covered together – hypnotism, affirmations, a meditation routine. He also guided me to come out of the closet, first to my family then to friends and coworkers. I even wrote a short story about denied lesbian love that won a prize, and landed a highly competitive teaching position as an "out" dyke. Unfortunately, the pace of that job brought on panic attacks, so he put me on the antidepressant, imipramine, to help me cope. Eventually, I got so well that I quit both taking those meds and seeing him. I think a normal person might have flourished from this point, but I was not normal. I was an alcoholic child of alcoholics.

Now, five years later, I was driving north from Olympia to find him again, having told my partner nothing. Why was my life falling apart? What could be so wrong with me? And how could I hide all this from Jenna? From everyone? The shrink, I told myself, would help me figure it out.

But the shrink had, alas, come down in the world a few notches since my last visit. His office was no longer in the pristine silver monolith, but an older, musty building in a drug-ridden section of town. The moment I walked in, I saw why. Even back in the day, the painkillers he prescribed himself for lower back pain sometimes caused his eyelids to droop embarrassingly if I droned on for too long. This had been part of the reason I quit seeing him. Now, I saw he'd piled on a lot more weight and his eyes, set in the florid strip of face between his beard and glasses, were mere slits.

I sat down. I'd meant to confess to him the merry-go-round of sexual obsession that ran my life, the pattern repeating with such sickening regularity that I could name each stage and symptom even as I thrilled to it. Instead, the obsession co-opted all thinking, so that as soon as I opened my mouth I began to babble helplessly about the magic boy. Secret stashes of over-analyzed anecdotes fairly gushed out, a stupid smile taking over my face, almost as if I hoped to make the shrink fall in love with Theo, too.

He listened a few minutes, but I felt irritated to note his lack of proper captivation, especially as his head began to loll to one side. I spoke faster, more frantically, heart racing, hands shaking. With a sinking sensation, I became conscious of how insane I sounded. But no response could have been less welcome than the thick, loud words with which he interrupted me.

"How much are you drinking?"

What the *fuck*? What did drinking have to do with *anything*? My obsession was sick, but my alcohol was normal and precious. Plus I was fragilely dry at the moment – more so than he, I might add.

"I don't know. Kind of a lot, I guess."

"How much?" he asked again, aggressively alert for the moment.

I thought about how to answer, balancing what the shrink already knew with what he didn't – the countless instances of getting inadvertently bombed, secret trips to the recycling station with empties I hid from Jenna, and having acknowledging to my inmost self a fact heavily layered with daily denial – that I was an alcoholic. He knew I'd grown up in an alcoholic home, that I struggled with self-loathing, codependence, and now, compulsive infatuation. He knew that no matter how often I'd promised in years past to "drink less," I seemed unable to follow through. But he didn't know solid numbers, and I saw no reason why he should.

"I dunno, in a day maybe like... four beers? A bottle of wine?" Those were the limits Jenna had set. But fortunately, Jenna worked a lot more hours than I did, leaving me time to replace what I'd drunk before she got home. By now the truth – and what did "truth" mean, anyway? – was maybe three times that much on a non-bender day.

"You have a problem with alcohol," the shrink announced, fighting to keep his own eyes open. Those were words I'd heard many times, so they seemed harmless enough, but his next got even worse: "You need help."

What could he possibly mean? We both knew Alcoholics Anonymous was a joke, some place Dear Abbey sent everybody, a club of dimwits who believed God would help them not drink. Thank god, what the shrink advised me to pursue instead was Rational Recovery, a program he told me tapered one's drinking rather than eliminating it. (In fact, RR requires abstinence, same as AA. The shrink must have confused it with Moderation Management, a program of restrained drinking whose founder, six years moderate, killed a father and child driving drunk.)

I tried to return to the topic of Theo, but now the shrink straight up refused to listen. I needed support to limit my drinking. Nothing else would improve until I got it. Only to appease him, I promised to go to an RR meeting and report back at our next session. Of course I did neither. Why? Because no matter how badly my life was deter-iorating, no one fucked with my drinking.

Drinking was my oxygen. It formed the core of my life in ways no one else could ever understand, supporting me as surely as a skeleton supports a body. It made life bearable. No matter how crazy I'd become, I was not insane enough to give up the one good thing I had left. I'd rather be paralyzed. I'd rather go blind. Because in either case, I could still drink my way to that safe, familiar isolation tank of being thoroughly sloshed.

I crossed the shrink off my list of solutions.

I had one week left til Jenna would read my journal.

I had six months left until I'd hit bottom, when my only choices became AA or death.

Part of me knew the clock was ticking. In the meantime, though, I would drink.

1: ORIGINS

A long strip of life lay behind her. ...Millions of things came back to her. Atoms danced apart and massed themselves. But how did they compose what people called a life?

-Virginia Woolf
The Years

I was not quite five years old and getting into bed when, as I slid between the sheets, something stung the sole of my foot. I recoiled and yelped to my mom, who was putting down the baby nearby. Already I'd jumped out of bed, trying to tell her what just happened.

"Get back in there," Mom said briskly. She threw back the covers. "See? Nothing!" And she seemed right, because the sheets looked immaculate. No bees. No ants. I sat down cautiously. So far, so good. But as soon as I slid my feet down the sheets, I felt stung again in lots of places.

This time my mother came over to take a look. Dangling from my calf was a tiny strand she plucked off: a sewing needle. "How did this get in your bed?" she muttered. Running her hand over the sheet's surface, she discovered more. There was, in fact, an entire package of sewing needles embedded points-up in my mattress.

She called out: "Adelyn! Walter! Get in here!"

Adelyn was nowhere to be found, but Walter, second oldest, made a sheepish appearance.

"It was Adelyn's plan," he confessed. "She read it some-where."

Adelyn was nine, always reading and reading. She'd skipped a grade and, as a fifth grader, seemed to me virtually an adult. According to her latest source, Walter explained, a fine needle entering a body undetected could migrate to the heart or brain and bring about death.

Mom was still picking out needles, but now she stopped.

"Go find her this instant!"

As he left, Walter added in my direction, "There's another plan to put ground glass in your food. So if you bite something crunchy..." he shook his head, "don't swallow."

Adelyn came in, scowling wordlessly, her eyes obscured behind her 1960s cat-eye glasses, her hair a mass of dark tangled curls. After Mom had drawn a monosyllabic confession from her, she began to help pick out the remaining needles, never once looking at me. She was foiled and furious.

Watching my sister and mother at work, my mother muttering fretful scoldings, I realized two key things. The first was that my own sister wished I were dead. She didn't just pretend to hate me, the way big sisters were supposed to. Those needles were real, and she had spent real effort getting them in there, points up. She wanted me gone from the world forever – that's what death meant. I understood that she was filled with rage, but I could not see why – nothing had happened – only that her rage was frightfully intense.

The second was that my mother wasn't going to believe or look into this fact in any way – that one daughter carried enough rage to wish the other daughter dead, or where that rage came from. I could see it in her annoyed focus on the needles themselves. She would acknowledge that Adelyn had done something naughty, no more.

As my five-year-old mind struggled to make sense of this, another thought came to the rescue. I was, after all, Mom's favorite. The baby didn't count because she wasn't a person yet, and Walter didn't count because he was a boy. But Adelyn – watching her glower while Mom scolded – I decided she was a sore loser. Mom didn't like the way she slouched, had quit ballet lessons, used big words. Look at her, so big and uncute, all chubby and clunky! Her hair always wild like a bird's nest, her nose always poked in a book – both Mom and Dad criticized her constantly for these things. Whereas *I*, standing there in my little pink nightie, had a huge advantage.

Louisa was the cute one. Everybody knew it. Wasn't I dainty and pretty, the one strangers greeted with delighted smiles and fluty voices? Didn't Mom and Dad marvel at my lisp, at dances I performed? The joy of inspiring instant affection – that was my superpower, and one that mean, angry Adelyn had lost long ago.

Mom had picked me. The spotlight I held now, I realized at some level, had once belonged to Adelyn. But that wasn't my fault, was it? It didn't make me bad or wrong, and I certainly didn't deserve a needle in the heart for it, did I? As long as I could stay cute enough, I'd be safe from whatever had made Adelyn so mad.

Even so, when we got oatmeal for breakfast the next morning, I took forever to eat mine because I had to swish it around in my mouth for so long. What a bummer, I thought, to have to do this the rest of my life!

The deeper lesson, though, I was not consciously aware of: Love was *not* a given. Love had to be won.

~

In most ways, I couldn't ask for better parents. They offered my siblings and me all the gifts that were theirs to give, loved us tremendously, and were determined to raise us optimally.

But like all parents, they could only pass on what they understood, and like so many of their era, their understandings were skewed. They'd been raised during the Great Depression by parents so preoccupied with making ends meet, they had no time or attention for nurturing. My dad's mother, the child of an alcoholic, repressed any difficult emotion by constantly "keeping busy" – a coping method she couldn't abandon even after the Depression was over. All his life, my father carried a deep resentment that she'd favored his older brother, a high school athlete, and younger sister, a star-struck beauty, over him – her fat, brainy middle child. The older brother's ruthless pranks left Dad deeply humiliated, yet they went virtually unnoticed as his mother was constantly busy baking, sewing, gardening, and finding ways to keep food on the table.

Meanwhile, my mom's parents separated when she was three, except that no one bothered to tell her. All adults involved assumed my mom would simply "forget" she'd once had a father, so she lived in a secret, unrewarded hope of his return. She, too, was tortured by older siblings in ways that their elderly governess, who raised the daughters after their mother took on a "man's world" career as an art historian and museum director, likewise overlooked. The older girls locked her in the dark cellar of their wealthy grandparents' mansion, taunted her constantly, and excluded her whenever possible, so that she learned the solace of living as a victim.

Flash forward twenty-some years. Denial was the art at which both my parents had become grand masters. Therapy in those days was strictly for loonies so, both of them being optimistic and positive, they simply walled out their pain as best they could. Denial formed, in many ways, the bedrock of their relationship: I'll deny if you will. Everything can be fine if we insist it is.

Academia was my family's religion. Education was sacred. The country's very first wave of tuition scholarships had transformed my dad from a poor hick stuck in Michigan's Upper Peninsula to a top graduate of Harvard Law School, though his Midwestern accent was odious to many blue-blooded classmates. Academia had also brought my parents together in what was for both their first and only relationship. Mom's social activism, acquired at Vassar, meshed well with Dad's interest in Labor Law, so they spent their first date talking late into the night about unions and politics. Married a year later, the two of them moved to Seattle, far from their families, and bought a house with a view overlooking the University of Washington. Dad, a new faculty member there, rode his bicycle to work every day in an era when doing so made him a whacky professor.

But my very first memories are not of Seattle. Instead, they dot the globe with fantastic randomness. My father won a grant to study the legal effects of recent independence upon the Philippines, with funding included for the entire family to travel the world for six months. When he came home buoyant with the news, Mom countered with an announcement of her own: another baby was on the way, due right in the middle of the trip. They considered canceling the trip; they also considered canceling the baby. But in the end, they decided that if they could circle the globe with three kids in tow – ages seven, six, and three – they might just as well drop a tot in Manila.

I sometimes wonder if traveling in that early stage of life set my expectations a little too high. I couldn't remember a time we weren't tourists, a time without dramatic scenery and exotic people appearing to surprise me every couple of days. This world, I felt, was a place blooming with magical, unpredictable scenes and incomprehensible strangers whose costumes and customs changed almost daily. We flew. We rode trains, busses, boats, and the occasional horse-drawn cart. There were fountains and cupolas and markets and cows in the street.

I loved the boat people of Malaysia, the many upturned faces of child divers for whom I flung coins into the sea with only the faintest privileged guilt, but disliked a parade of believers with bloody hooks stuck in their backs. I loved the badass Sphinx but not the stuffy, breathed-up air inside the Great Pyramids, loved riding a real camel and seeing mummies in the Cairo museum, but not the trouble I got in for climbing quite high on a golden Buddha in Thailand before getting busted by a guard – no translation needed. So what if it was sacred? It was huge!

I sometimes slept in an open suitcase, looking back on the fact that taxis in Venice were motorboats or that the leaning tower of Pisa did, in fact, lean. I could say "Kochel Am See." I turned four at a German hotel with a real (?) bear mounted high on its sign, where I was given the birthday gift of a music box. I opened it in a beautiful flower garden where my mom made up a song to its glassy little tune, about how pretty I was, how much she loved me. I remember the waitress watching the two of us with a golden smile.

Why? Because I was so frickin' cute. In country after country, I delighted the locals simply by addressing them in English. Have you ever heard a tiny kid rattle off perfect phrases in a language you're struggling to learn? Shopkeepers, waiters, and hotel receptionists – they all loved my piping voice and trusting candor. I felt like some sort of exquisite, astounding little doll.

"Pig of attention" – that was Adelyn's name for me, echoed by Walter. My performances relegated them to the category of awkward older kids, and they resented the hell out of me for it. There was only one brief incident in France when Adelyn and I dropped the rivalry. We'd somehow gotten "trapped" in a barn near dusk, where peeking out through the closed doors revealed cows just outside cantering toward us, wanting, not to be let in for the night, but to gore us. We screamed for what seemed like hours. We were going to die, and cuteness here was no defense – I recall that thought. I clutched at Adelyn, feeling she *was,* after all, my big sister, and she hugged me back, at least, until the farmer came by and laughed at us.

And then one day, the trip was over. The P. family returned permanently to a home I didn't remember among Americans who saw me as an average kid. Worse, now there was no place to go to. Fantastic adventuring was eclipsed by a plain, daily routine.

You might think this sudden shift would inspire me to become a world traveler. But I didn't. Instead I became an internal traveler. I developed imaginary lands and states of mind that carried me away from the boring world of my neighborhood, family, and peers. Alcoholics are good at that: it's what we do.

Not coincidentally, it was around this age that I discovered alcohol. I was born an alcoholic, as were my father and much of his side of the family. While the disease ran rampant in his brother and sister's lives, Dad practiced amazing restraint. On weekdays he held off until arriving home from work. Then, his skin still cold and sweaty from the bike ride home as I kissed him hello, he would shakily pour a glass of sherry or mix a highball. Mom would start in with him. They'd progress to a bottle of wine with dinner, which my father followed up with a second bottle or a few highballs until he went to bed. By late evening, he'd be cranking Beethoven and conducting with tears in his eyes. Alcohol freed him. It let him try out Greek dancing or play old jazz records and savor the poetic poignancy of life. Without it, he was tense as hell. Always.

That first year back home, he'd bring his drink and sit with me on the sofa to look at magazines together. Snuggling close, I'd plop my tiny finger on photos in *LIFE* and or *National Geographic* as we discussed them. His loving attention was heavenly. But heaven got even better if Mom called him away to help out a bit in the kitchen. His glass waited under the lamp, ice cubes melting into amber curves. I discovered the delicious sweetness of gin and tonics, vodka tonics, sherry, and vermouth. But, dang, there was a certain zest to that scotch on the rocks, too! What a funny taste – somehow like a briefcase.

And then – magic! No need to travel the world for it; the living room itself transfigured, blossomed with loving ambience and silly possibilities while that warm glow in your tummy spread to a flush in your cheeks. "You little mischief-maker, did you finish my drink? You *did*, didn't you! Which leg is hollow, Missy? Is it this one?" Oh, the tickling, the joy! This was love, this was happiness complete.

Certainly it was an entirely different father I encountered in the mornings – one who was all brittleness, efficiency, and re-pressed annoyance. Morning Dad shook visibly, spoke minimally, and did everything at a clipped, rigorous pace, as if annoyed with something. Was that something *me*? To try any silliness with *this* father would invite disaster. I remember staring into the silverware drawer one particular morning, struggling to think what I might be doing wrong or what I could try to bring back the happy, easy-going Dadda of last night. I needed to be cuter; I needed to be better. Gradually, I learned to practice quiet helpfulness. I'd stir the scrambled eggs as he mixed pancakes, or set the table carefully, asking for little to no attention. He expressed appreciation as best he could through his jitters.

Dad's mood cycles were predictable, but Mom's seemed entirely random. (In most alcoholic homes, it's the co-dependent that children identify as the 'mean' one. At my first Al-Anon speaker's meeting, I was amazed to hear the speaker describe my mom to a T – except that she was recalling her co-dependent *father*.) Mood swings came on like sudden storms; you might be the perfect darling one moment and part of the hopeless fiasco on her hands the next, or she might snap at you out of nowhere with a misplaced ire. What was I doing wrong? Panic attacks had not yet appeared on the medical radar, so Mom's racing heart episodes were diagnosed as tachycardia. The same confident woman who orchestrated la-de-da dinner parties sometimes had to squat down outside a grocery store by the gumball machines, hissing at you to wait! Wait! Just *wait a minute*, dammit! So you, too, squatted and waited while passing shoppers glanced down with concern or dismissal. Other times you sat in the car on the side of the road waiting for Momma to feel okay again.

My parents had no close friends. Their social life was geared more toward showcasing sophistication than sharing trust and intimacy. Every few months they threw fancy dinner parties to which they invited many prestigious university professors, wives in tow. Everyone arrived all dressed up. My little sister and I would sit on the landing overhearing titters and chuckles that, as the evening progressed, expanded to thunderous waves of laughter that rolled up the stairs toward our room. Dad was a pioneer vintner in Washington State, having helped to found one of the first Washington wineries to cultivate European vinifera like Cabernet Sauvignon or Johannesberg Riesling. He knew absolutely *every-thing* about wine making – sunrise to noon vineyard temperature curves, sugar percentages at various benchmarks, variations among regions in France. People came expressly to taste wines, and they tasted plenty! In the 1960s, anyone who scorned drunkenness was labeled a fuddy-duddy. One night my parents extolled the flavor of Nyquil. They broke out a big bottle and served it round the table as a digestif. It was a rockin' good time.

What a contrast with our ordinary life, when the telephone seldom rang and if it did, Mom answered in melodious June Cleaver tones. Someone might be inviting them to a cocktail party or conferring with her about Museum volunteer stuff, but as far as I knew, no one ever called just to chew the fat. Likewise no one, with the exception of one or two neighborhood friends, ever came over just to hang out.

As a result, I learned nothing about forming genuine, open-hearted friendships. I learned nothing about sharing my inner self, or voicing feelings that defied simple terms, or telling the truth of my experience. Even within our family, presenting an ideal front was essential. No way would I ever explain to my dad that I felt like he didn't love me in the mornings, or to my mom that she scared me when she got so pissed out of nowhere. I didn't have the words because I'd never heard a human being express difficult or subtle feelings they didn't want to have.

Love and attention are the most important staples of a child's world. They form the bedrock of emotional security. When the flow of these feels inconsistent, as it does in any alcoholic household or even a second-generation alcoholic household, children grow up immersed in an unnamable fear. The mental habit I formed staring into the silverware drawer stayed with me for decades and still distorts my thinking to this day: that reality was defined by the ways of others, and that it was up to me to read these signs and revise myself accordingly. I learned that my authentic, spontaneous self had to be tailored to suit whatever conditions my parents set, from Dad's invisible hangovers or Mom's martyred impatience to the rollicking fun we all shared in late evenings. As a child, I had no idea the controlling force in our home was not actually my parents, but their addictions.

God, in our family, was a historical myth. Having been force-fed small town Catholicism before he reached Harvard, my father saw any form of spirituality as primitive superstition. There was no Catholic Trinity, and therefore there was no god at all — only the wonder of physics. Spirituality was for kooks. This he would insist even as his loving reverence for nature's beauty and ingenuity contradicted it. Mom's ideas were more amorphous. Around Christmastime she'd get out her art history books and have us look at nativity paintings by Giotto, Massachio, and the Renaissance gang, making it clear that we should regard them with a certain solemnity. I put together that God was a revered character humans had invented to explain the world before modern science came along.

So I didn't know what to call that awareness I had as a small child of Something Big that Loved me. Certainly it wasn't the old man from those paintings, though it did seem to come from the sky. Until I was somewhere between five and six years old, I could sense its presence whenever I lay on the grass watching clouds.

I remember a particular spring afternoon when Dad was turning over his vegetable garden while I swung on the backyard swing set that overlooked it. I was asking him what his favorite color was, and he kept playfully refusing to specify. "My favorite color for *what*?" he'd object. "I don't like green steak… or brown toothpaste!"

I'd laugh and try to corner him: "A plain piece of construction paper."

"What's it for?"

Ah! – there was no beating him. But I loved his sweatiness, and the way allergies made him sniffle in a particularly Dadda-ish way. He often worked with a cold beer set on an empty wine cask.

I turned to swing in the other direction, facing up the mowed hill toward the tall, double-trunked dogwood tree swaying in full bloom at the top. I sang "Shoo, Fly!" and "Skip to my Lou," both songs I'd learned in nursery school that somehow reminded me of old-fashioned people from long ago, now doddering or dead. Enjoying the sound of my voice, I felt sorry for the people in the songs and yet happy that now was *my* turn to live, to swing, to sing songs. Cloud reflections in the puddles swooped in sync with me. The sky, the tree, and the world itself seemed to love me, as I'd once been loved by everyone, and I loved them back so much my heart ached in my small, singing chest. I felt joy and gratitude, an instinctive awareness that being in the world was a gift.

No one ever told me that feeling was prayer.

*Clockwise from top left: Listening to records; as good as it gets –
Dad, magazines, and alcohol; in Venice with Adelyn; at Great
Pyramids with Dad, Adelyn, and Walter – just another ordinary
day.*

2: EVERYTHING GOES TO HELL

For me it was a system of lies, distortions, half-
truths, and manipulations that began when we, as a
family, tried to make sense of, control, and excuse the
behavior of persons in the family who were
frequently drunk. This system of deceit perverted my
sense of what was real and left me without the ability
to live comfortably with myself and others.

-Anonymous
From Survival to Recovery

Everybody has a screwed up childhood, to a degree. Any transformation from dependence to autonomy is a rough one, as traumatic as birth itself, and injuries sustained when we're young and tender can't help but leave scars. But childhoods set in homes where addiction skews reality day after day, year after year, with micro-lies layered to disguise and deny reality – those are especially fucked up. I had one of those.

Most people still don't understand alcoholism, despite all that AA has illuminated. My father inherited the disease and passed it on to me. Yet no one else in my immediate family has a clue what that means. They think they do, of course! But they also think AA is a cult, and that I continue to go to meetings not to maintain clarity on my life and disease, but because I've been indoctrinated and brainwashed. None has considered reading the Big Book of Alcoholics Anonymous or any other text on alcoholism, or attending open AA meetings to hear the experiences of those who live with it.

The American Society of Addiction Medicine defines the condition as follows:

Alcoholism is a primary, chronic disease with genetic, psychosocial, and environmental factors influencing its development and manifestations. The disease is often progressive and fatal. It is characterized by continuous or periodic impaired control over drinking, preoccupation with the drug alcohol, use of alcohol despite adverse consequences, and distortions in thinking, most notably denial.

Most notably, indeed. Defining the terms of this statement, the Society adds:

Denial is used here not only in the psychoanalytic sense of a single psychological defense mechanism disavowing the significance of events, but more broadly to include a range of psychological maneuvers designed to reduce awareness of the fact that alcohol use is the cause of an individual's problems rather than a solution to those problems. Denial becomes an integral part of the disease and a major obstacle to recovery.

In our family, we explained that Dad was a "European drinker" who, while not addicted, benefited from alcohol because it let him loosen up. Wine was to be loved, the elixir of a good life, the solution to tension, blues, and social awkwardness. We pointed to the fact that Dad did not drink in the mornings or at work, or ever get a DUI. Other facts, like that he drank nightly and frequently to drunkenness or that Mom smuggled wine into hospitals for him – those we placed in a category called "So what?" He was obviously an honorable man. How could anyone label him a drunk?

AA characterizes alcoholism as a physical, mental, and spiritual disease. Our bodies react to alcohol with a phenomenon of craving, our minds are co-opted by a primitive mechanism that causes us to "forget" all reasons not to drink, and our spirits feel empty. More than anything else, alcoholics feel isolated and somehow different from "normal" people. We fear being outcasts, denied love and security, yet we sense that at our cores we're neither worthy nor loveable, so of course we're going to be spurned and left out. *Unless...* we do something to fix the problem. Alcohol delivers that fix.

Fortified by alcohol, our egos swoop to our rescue like some deceptive superhero, kicking Fear right out of the fucking stadium and lending us vast confidence so we can be smart and sexy conversationalists, charismatic figures who are just plain irresistible. It feels heavenly! Better yet, it reduces the solution to every puzzle life can throw at us down to a refreshingly simple "what the fuck?!"

If alcohol kept on delivering relief, AA would not exist. But here's the rub: it deserts us. Our egos get too torn up to inflate anymore. The superhero wizens, so we need more and more drinks to heft ourselves from our trench of victimized self-loathing. Eventually, we get no lift at all. We struggle and wallow in the shit pile that is our pointless life. All alcohol can do now is ease our misery a bit and help us to function, because without it, our bodies go into shock.

If we're lucky enough to drag ourselves to AA, we learn our situation is hopeless. Nothing that we decide, resolve, or demand of ourselves can rebuff that insidious craving for alcohol, which infiltrates our reasoning itself to make "just one" drink seem a fine, sensible idea. No fortress can protect us because the enemy lives inside, within our brainstem and our bodies. Once we take that "one drink," those that follow become as irresistible as our next breaths. Hence the AA saying, *One drink is too many and a thousand not enough.* Or, as the Big Book puts it: "The alcoholic at certain times has no effective mental defense against the first drink. Except in a few rare cases, neither he nor any other human being can provide such a defense. His defense must come from a Higher Power."

Drinking allowed my father to play the life role he'd chosen. At heart he was a private and subtle man who, without the social lubricant of alcohol, would simply *not wish* to socialize – not, at least, with that crew of brag-a-thon figures who showed up at my parents' parties. Posturing was pretty much the norm. These people were of *the better sort* and their conversation served as a means of parading accomplishments, never of acknowledging weakness, confusion, or insecurity. Everyone wore an invisible banner that read, *I Know Exactly What I'm Doing and I'm Damn Good At It.* And yet, these people's approval meant everything to my mother, who drew her self-worth from their impressions. Dad loved her, and she *needed* to feel like a socialite, so he put in his time performing.

Never did my parents consider attending AA or Al-Anon meetings; even if they had, I doubt they'd have identified. Both groups comprise members from all walks of life, united via the shared humility of hitting bottom. Not only was alcoholism itself a disgrace but, by my mother's classist standards, the "nobodies" at such meetings would have far outnumbered the "somebodies." To mix with a bunch of losers who freely admitted their disease had robbed them of all dignity would be a disgrace. Besides, the friendship of so many working class people had nothing to offer hegemonists like my parents, who considered class and education direct indicators of intelligence. They never imagined the wisdom such people could teach them might transform their lives and free them to experience joy. Short of a *complete* psychic change, the two of them were trapped.

~

We had a song, "Happy Little P. Family," that we'd sing around the dinner table, joining hands and singing out the title twice, followed by the slower last line: "We all love each other!" And it was partially true, especially when we were young.

All we had to ignore was Adelyn's glowering refusal to join in. We also had to not wonder about the reasons for her rage, or why she, Mom, and Dad got into such terrific cat fights during which she would howl or even physically strike back, like the night Dad went into her room and tried to force-brush her tangled mass of hair. I heard both of them yelling and screaming like fighting animals as I tried to go on playing, terrified, in the living room.

We also couldn't acknowledge Walter's disability, which caused him to speak slowly and write laboriously. Today he'd be called "twice exceptional," a term for intellectually gifted children who also have a disability, usually in the area of social skills. But what we as a family called his condition instead was, "What condition?!" To name it, to say that we loved Walter just as much with, or maybe even *because of,* his halting and drawn out way of speaking, would be to imply there was *something wrong* with him – which conflicted directly with our family creed of being *superior to everyone.* We lived by a dichotomy where the only alternative to *better than* was *shameful.* Therefore we pretended, as a family, that Walter did *not* speak slowly and that we noticed nothing, even while we were all, as a group, staring at our dinner plates waiting for him to finish a sentence. "Don't say 'uh,'" Dad would snap at him, as though Walter had any more choice in the matter than Dad did over whether to take another drink.

Whenever fear prevents us from calling a spade a spade, shame takes over. All the troubles Walter and Adelyn suffered socially were swept under the family carpet. We likewise didn't acknowledge my speech defect, a lisp and tendency to favor the right side of my mouth. When the school speech pathologist tested us all and then showed up at the classroom door and beckoned me to the "Special Ed" room, it meant there was *something wrong* with me – something my family hadn't made common knowledge, even though we all knew it.

Love can treat any condition with acceptance and humor, naming it directly and weaving it into the mainstream of life. Shame, on the other hand, leaves only two options: silence or derision. So we were silent about a *lot.* Anything not part of the ideal we pretended did not exist. In my young mind I developed a theory: the reason my family had to pretend we were *better* than everyone else was that we were secretly *worse.* My whole family suffered from a huge *something wrong with us* that we had to cover up by parading our achievements.

Academics and the arts were the things that mattered most in life, the currency for a person's worth. Mom often joked that Dad had been hit by a gamma ray in his youth, which is what raised him from among the worthless hicks of his hometown and set him on the path to a life of achievement. Her father had been hit by a similar gamma ray in the small Russian village of Yekaterinoslav, giving him the musical artistry to be plucked off the streets where he played violin for spare change and sent to an academy in America. There he met my grandmother, who had no need of any gamma ray since she was born into a noble, blue-blooded family – never mind that their wealth came from a poor immigrant's medicinal company that profited immensely from the carnage of the American Civil War. We were cultivated, enlightened people inhabiting a lofty realm that excluded the riff-raff.

Most important to my parents, therefore, was that we children live up to our family's standards by excelling. Unconditional love would have ruined our motivation to do so, since we'd get the impression that just being ourselves made us worthy and loveable and thus would never amount to anything. In fact, the *best* thing a parent could do was to employ approval as a leveraging tool, a reward given or taken away based on performance, with just a little fear of rejection thrown in to spark that exacting inner discipline the child would need to rise above the masses. This was a pressure that, in our house, never relented. Thus, a tempera painting I brought home of a bunny with extra large ears went straight into the garbage: "You can do better." A bouquet of dandelions did, as well: "Those are *weeds*!" Maybe for a child with resilient self-esteem, this method would have worked. But for me, it translated to constant failure that joined forces with my alcoholic disposition to confirm the inner message that I, of myself, was worthless.

Mind you, in the 1960s there was no such term as "parenting skills." Botanists recommended spraying DDT, doctors praised menthol cigarettes, and principals doled out spankings, often with a wooden paddle. Residing in a cabinet above Mom's pillow, however, a worn, dog-earned copy of Benjamin Spock's *Baby and Child Care* advocated restraint from hitting or whipping children, so we were rarely spanked. But alternatives such as taking away privileges had not yet become common practice. For instance, Zelda and I watched *hours* of TV every day, often all day and into the night, pausing only for dinner, without ever having so much as five minutes withheld from us. No toy was ever removed as a consequence of "bad choices."

What tool did that leave? Shaming. It was Mom's primary means of disciplining us. Shaming worked great with dogs, right? So why not use it on your kid? The distinction between *guilt* for bad choices and *shame* for being a bad child wasn't handy. If you were a "bad girl," Mom would scowl with anger and speak in her most reproachful voice. Even hours later, she'd still shoot you looks of disapproval: you were *not* a child she could be proud of. You'd let her down, she who had thought so well of you, and she wasn't going to let you forget it.

Most of my conflicts with Mom involved, as did Adelyn's, femininity. Certain things defined a lady. The Victorian governess who raised Mom in the 1920s and '30s was full of old world admonitions about feminine charm: "Ladies poise their lips as if to say, 'prunes'; coarse woman with slack mouths say 'Caa-bage!'" Her own mother spoke in those quasi-British accents you can hear in old movies: "Woood you come at fohr?" Unfortunately, at five-foot-ten Mom felt denied the requisite form of the petite and dainty "It" girls so popular in the twenties and thirties. So she transferred her feminine aspirations to her firstborn daughter, dressing her up in lacy pinafores and ribboned bonnets. Baby pictures show a chunky Adelyn enduring this indignity with thoughtful scowls – not one bit the frilly princess Mom had ordered. This daughter turned out too big, too clumsy, and soon too intellectually aggressive to fill Mom's criteria. So she shifted her hopes to the next.

Initially, I'd fit the role perfectly, a protégé of daintiness destined to become the next Audrey Hepburn. But I, too, refused to be what Mom wanted. Maybe it was all that traveling early on, but my body seemed to crave adventure, danger, and exploration. While my dolls lay in the closet, I was constantly showing off for her that I could climb fences and scramble up trees, dig deep holes, or string a bow and arrow from saplings to play Robin Hood. I'd call her outside to watch me, wanting praise, but instead we got into fights. I remember her coming out on a particular hot and sunny afternoon when I was about five, thoroughly unimpressed with how many somersaults I could do in a row.

"You need to put your shirt on, missy. Now."

My turtleneck, strewn on the newly cut lawn, was covered with grass clippings.

"I don't wannu! It's way too hot out!"

"You're too old for no shirt. You hear me? It stays on from now on."

"What – *forever*?!"

"Yes, *forever*! One day you'll understand." And here she got that knowing *look*, referring to some rite of passage that could not be named. "Because when you're a lady, the certain times you *do* take it off will be... very special."

The turtleneck, when I put it on, itched like a hair shirt. Even my vague understanding of what she meant by "very special" – some crap to do with boobs – enraged me. If boobs meant I couldn't be outside in my skin, then to hell with them! Sexy was a prison! I didn't have the words for this, but I knew Mom had all of society – all the ads and TV shows I'd seen, all her dinner party friends, all the women at school, where girls could not wear pants – on her side. I cried and screamed that I *hated* being a girl.

Meanwhile, as my daintiness degenerated, Zelda, my younger sister, was emerging as a green-eyed, golden-haired cherub, a Libra and the most easy-going of all us kids. In my mind, the transition was obvious: Zelda was the new cute one; Louisa was the new Adelyn. I became, in Mom's eyes, the oppressor. Whenever I exerted my will, Zelda ran to Mom, who would identify with her as the youngest child. Mom's cruel older sister – for some reason my middle name was after her. Mom would hug Zelda protectively and rebuke me with hurt-filled eyes – she could be very dramatic.

What should have happened right about now was that I'd branch out and make friends at school. But that wasn't going to happen. Already, by age four, I'd developed an alcoholic's sense of social dis-ease. You can laugh, but alcoholics will get it. From my first day of nursery school (i.e. pre-K), I felt like I'd missed some key memo on how to interact and make friends. I remember a time when the Guitar Lady was singing a song about the zoo while we kids were supposed to play-act being the animal of each verse. One moment I was channeling elephant, crawling among the desks and waving my arm as a trunk, and in the next I was overwhelmed with embarrassment at how stupid I must look. That's a solid memory. I also recall having to sit inside alone at recess because I'd brought no rain boots, watching from a bench inside the glass doors while the other kids played in puddles – kids who somehow knew spontaneously what they should say and do – and feeling a sort of dark rush in the admission that there was *something wrong* with me. That was the true reason I was excluded. Yet that ache of being unwanted felt strangely attractive, a letting go of the constant strain of trying. I sucked. Let's just face it. No one wanted to hang out with me.

If only snack time had offered Budweisers with graham crackers instead of Tang, I'd have totally rocked the Green Table – funny, free, and best friends with everybody! But I didn't know that yet.

~

My son takes after my father and me emotionally. Starting around age five, he developed a strong bent for self-loathing. "I'm a terrible person!" he started to blurt out regularly, for no reason. "I feel sorry for anyone who has to be around me!" "I suck worse than anyone!" So I taught him the term, self-loathing. I explained how, just like germs, this voice in his head was trying to hurt him. I suggested a counter-mantra: "I am here to love," which he found way too corny to practice, even then. That I love him exactly as he is – he still needs to hear it often, with a lot of hugs and kisses. I can ask him, "How's the self-loathing today, scale of one to ten?" Or he might say to me, "I must be *such* a disappointment to you," but with a little half smile. That remark and that half-smile stand for the greatest prize god has given me: honesty sure enough to share with those I love.

But I'm getting ahead of myself.

Conversations like that didn't happen in the 1960s. They just *didn't* – at least, not in our family. Vulnerable honesty wasn't on the agenda, so I had no name for the feeling that I was fundamentally flawed. Vaguely I sensed that my father suffered a pain similar to mine, but who would want to hear something so silly as that I was horrible? Or that I felt less likeable than other kids? Or worthless? Don't be ridiculous! Conversations in our family centered on *topics*. Politics, as covered by the media, served as a constant team sport for my parents. My father also brought home entertaining stories from the university to discuss with my mother over dinner. If something was wrong, it had to make sense: you needed a verifiable problem and practical solution.

Problem: I was lonely. What I needed, I decided, was a cohort, someone who would *have* to like me the same way Walter *had* to like Adelyn, and play Robin to my Batman. Zelda, just out of diapers, was playing on the living room floor under the *object d'art* shelf at the moment I hatched this plan. True, she was uncouth (clown mouth of food residue), had a bulging stomach, and couldn't talk much. And granted, she'd stolen my place in Mom's heart. But rather than hate her for it, what if I recruited her?

With Zelda's recent graduation to a big-girl bed, the three of us girls shared a room, from which Adelyn had marked off a forbidden section as her "study area." Now, to get back at her, I strung a blanket between Zelda's and my beds. Inside was *our* study area, where Adelyn was not allowed.

"Study area?!" she scoffed. "You've got nothing to study!"

Yet we did, in a way. I was determined to groom Zelda into a minion worthy of my company so I would need no one else – not at school, not at home. We worked on climbing the stairs one stair per step. The pacifier had to go. If I asked where something was, she'd try to lead me to it, but I'd cast down her pudgy hand and insist: "Describe it in *words*!"

Eventually Walter moved downstairs into a newly finished basement room, and Adelyn took his old room across the hall. Zelda and I shared a room and continued to even after the others had moved out. It's still "our room" to this day.

In the years that followed, the two of us built an imaginary world so rich and complex, it almost made up for our lack of friends. For instance, we developed a large cast of characters we could act out, each with its own voice, mannerisms, and eccentric preoccupations. These personalities lived in a parallel universe but could inhabit our bodies, channeling through us. When they left, the channeler experienced a brief bout of amnesia ("Who am *I*? Who are *you*?") that could be cured only by a pantomime blow to the head. Perhaps a dozen such characters we created, with lots of conflicts and drama among them.

We also wrote and illustrated a book of some hundred pages about our hamsters' adventures in "Hamster Land." Given a sunny day, I'd insist we lug Zelda's small blue desk into the yard and work for hours on our stories, using rocks as paperweights, consulting with each other, and composing in labored, childish letters. Zelda usually wanted to quit before I did. I'd require her to finish something – a drawing, a paragraph – then excuse her.

No other kids lived on our street, and while we made enough friends at school to get by, I guilted Zelda if she drifted too far afield. She was big for her age but physically lax (she wore Sears Chubby-Girl Toughskins). I was muscular and athletic enough to pin her pretty quickly at wrestling, which made me the boss, the one who laid plans and enforced them. Adelyn and Walter still scorned us – we couldn't play Risk, watch *Star Trek,* or go anywhere near their fort – but it's a lot easier to be scorned as an "us."

Adelyn was full of brilliant ideas and plans not quite like other kids', and for this I couldn't help admiring her. To celebrate the 4th of July, she hung King George III in effigy in our front rockery, only to have drivers knock on our door and complain that the swinging dummy posed a dangerous distraction. On May Day, we delivered homemade baskets of flowers, ringing neighbors' doorbells and running away under her direction. Every Christmas she orchestrated huge Catholic-style murals drawn on butcher paper, which served as stained glass windows when we taped them up on the sliding glass doors. We also had to act out pageants of the Nativity, so that with the drop of a bed spread curtain Mom and Dad would witness our poses: Adelyn as Mother Mary, Walter as Joseph, Zelda the Christ Child, and me usually a shepherd or something. Her last project was a giant paper-mâché angel-kite that was supposed to float from the top of our dogwood tree streaming banners high in the sky. She worked on it secretly for weeks in the playhouse, after which Walter was tasked with launching it. Sadly, all it did was get soggy among the trees upper branches with no divine hovering. Failure was a bitter pill for her to swallow.

Adelyn had also begun piano lessons at age seven, and by eleven she won first place in an all-city competition. She had *excelled* artistically as well as academically. My parents rewarded her with a seven foot Steinway grand worth several thousand dollars even in the 1970s – which became her private world. She practiced six hours a day, pounding out classics with furious intensity, so that her music became a constant soundtrack for our household. She'd bust out of the piano room a few times a day, swinging the cage of her parakeet, Clementi, as she went to get herself a diet pop or carrots, or later coffee, since she was always supposed to be on a diet.

No one spoke to her much. Bullied and mocked at school, a target of flung stones and beatings from mean girls who broke her glasses and stole her watch, she withdrew increasingly from the world of cheery well-being. She took pride in her grouchiness. When she wasn't practicing, she was reading Victorian novels or studying in her room. And she was unhappy. In her early teens she developed a secretive habit of getting up in the night to bake and eat entire batches of cookies. Every few years she'd confess it to me, and I would pretend not to already know. Over the years I intruded into her room and found empty jumbo-sized pastry boxes hidden under her bed. She had forged herself a private world of anger, intellect, and compulsive eating, where nothing could touch her.

Anger – a constantly brewing rage – was clearly Adelyn's solution to Mom's urgings. It sparked around her like a force field, arming her with contempt that warded off criticism. But that wasn't a path I wanted to take or could have even I'd wanted to. I lacked the gumption to defend myself.

Instead, I began to create myself a private refuge, though my weirdness left no telltale signs like obesity or anger. By age six, while fully normal on the outside, I'd developed two secretive habits that laid a foundation for the obsessive/compulsive disorder I would develop later on.

The first habit, I'll call the poop trance. (Sorry! I spare you nothing.)

One evening I found myself hanging out on the toilet unable to poop. Besides boredom, every now and then I'd be seized with panic that this tremendous turd – we called them BMs – would *never* come out, and that I'd have to go to the hospital or something. Meanwhile, on the wall across from me that my father had tiled imperfectly, I noticed a chipped tile that looked like a human profile. The face was angled down at forty-five degrees, and if you followed its diagonal gaze for what I later counted to be sixteen tiles, you came upon a second chipped profile looking in the opposite direction. Follow this gaze horizontally sixteen tiles, and you arrived at a final chip, this one not a profile, just a slight divot filled with white grout. You could imagine maybe the person had turned their head away to stare into the wall itself. The number sixteen was two doubled and redoubled two times. I knew a Danny Kaye song, "Inchworm," that rehearsed these multiples as I mentally unfolded tiles from their central point.

Meanwhile, a pleasant visor of fuzziness slid over my mind, and impending hospital crises fell away in the coziness of trance. It was like finding a big, safe space between waking and sleep where all the responsibilities of being *me* melted away. Before you knew it, I was ready to flush.

These rituals became more elaborate as the years passed. Upstairs, without tiles, I began arranging various bathroom products along the windowsill for my own imagined commercials. I focused on the shapes, the perfection, the "thingness" of the shampoo or mouthwash or whatever. I wanted new-looking things, and I wanted them spanking clean. The rows might go smallest to largest, or highest in the center, while their imagined newness, their perfection, fuzzed my mind into trance.

To be honest, I still use the trance sometimes for a shy "second wave" of the day. Over the years I've done all kinds of weird things to bring it on: zoom in on individual TP perforations as I tear a slow V between sheets, make TP books or long braids or even paper chains, or visually line up TP edges with objects in the room. I'm pretty sure I'm weird because I'm telling you this, more than because I do it.

Anyway.

The second habit was bondage fantasies, which also started around age six.

Every night, after the lights were out and I'd sung Zelda to sleep, I'd continue with one of the stories I'd kept running in my head, adventures that placed me in various Batman-like predicaments, bound in death-traps and so on. Alice Munro describes a similar habit in her story, "Boys and Girls." Except the emphasis in *my* stories was never on being rescued, as in Munro's. It wasn't on escaping and triumphing, either, the way Batman did. No, mine dwelt on the humiliation of hopeless captivity. I lingered at the place of total powerlessness, of having no way to help myself, nothing but futile struggles to get away. Every night the plots developed a little further as I discovered what thoughts excited me most. Lying there under the covers, running through my favorite scenarios of bondage, I had no idea why they inspired such a pleasurable glow in my crotch. At that age I had not the faintest idea that sexuality even existed. I just knew those imaginings felt good and, like the poop trance, occupied my whole mind so that no self-criticisms could reach me.

And yet it's also true to say that I enjoyed a happy childhood. I got all As in school and did well in ballet classes. My parents, while not rich, could afford to buy a rustic summer cabin on an island in Puget Sound, a place without electricity or phone, where

Zelda and I could adventure in the woods or on the beach while Mom slaved over the wood stove. By night we sat up with kerosene lamps drinking beer from our own tiny cups and learning the basics of poker. Dad continued to love us with his quirky repertoire of games and playful affections, while Mom took care of us and Dad. So for several years, between the freedoms of play and the secrets of trance, I managed life easily enough.

Third grade; Mom's 42nd birthday; codfish triumph at the summer cabin with Zelda

3: OF SEXUALITY AND SHAME

*The uniqueness of a person is made up of the insane
and the twisted as much as it is of the rational and
normal.*

> *-Thomas Moore*
> *Care of the Soul*

A Saturday morning cartoon Zelda and I both liked, *The Perils
of Penelope Pitstop,* came on the air in 1969 when I was eight years
old. Penelope was a benignly stupid and overtly sexy Southern belle
who persisted in daring adventures despite the fact that every
episode found her tied up in some kind of peril at the hands of a
pervy, masked villain voiced by Paul Lynde. This Hooded Claw
character was supposedly after her inheritance, though he always
devised overly-complex demises involving bondage. One day at the
end of the show, Zelda and I agreed there was something strangely
exciting about "pretty girls tied up." We decided to find ways to
continue the stories after the show was over.

First we tied up our Barbies (Tammy dolls), designating one
Patty doll (Tammy's little sister) as the bad guy, on whom we drew
a beard in permanent black marker, obliterating Patty's cutesy smile
so that he could gloat over the sexy dolls' impending doom in the
scenarios we set up – buzz saws, railroad tracks, etc. As time
passed, since we both drew remarkably well, we decided we could
draw pictures of these scenarios with better details than our toy
props allowed, and our drawings progressed from bombs and vats
of boiling oil to conveyor belts and mechanized threats. The whole
"Pretty Girls Tied Up" game, we agreed, made your crotch feel
good. It also packed a lot more wallop if the girls appeared in their
underwear, so we created machines in the bad guys' lairs that took
off their clothes.

Neither of us had ever heard the word "vagina," suspected that
crotches involved anything but pee and poop, or knew how women

got pregnant – other than by sleeping in the same bed with a man. (Mom had explained to us that *fuck* meant "a very bad way to say have a baby," and when I asked her if people mated the way our hamsters did, she replied emphatically, "Not at all!") So what could be wrong with talking about how certain images brought more glow to your crotch than others?

By the time I reached fourth grade, I knew I wanted to experiment with drawings beyond anything I wanted Zelda to see. Drawing alone, I could enter the same kind of trance I enjoyed during my night fantasies. So when Zelda was away or absorbed by TV, I'd lock our door and let my mind guide the pencil wherever my deepest daring might take it. Here was absolute freedom – a world from which all "shoulds" from my mom and the world in general were banished. The drawn women became naked, with loopy W's for breasts and hairless Y's for crotches. Now their perils involved chains and torture, bloodshed, dismemberment, and in one drawing, lying on a bed with the bearded villain to do "it" – I wasn't sure *what*, but something forbidden. Anything I could conceive, I would draw, just to find out the effect it might have. The more dehumanizing the images, it turned out, the more intense the pleasure. Sometimes I needed several tries to get an image right, but I'd erase or start over until I nailed it.

I kept my drawings stashed behind the radiator inside the closet for many weeks without incident. But, of course, one day I forgot to lock the door and Zelda barged in on me in the midst of drawing. I had time only to stuff the pages in a bottom drawer of my desk, insisting she never mind about them. I must have forgotten to re-hide them. In my normal, trance-free state of mind, the drawings struck me as grim and depressing, and the desire to work on them didn't come over me sometimes for weeks.

Until the day my whole life changed.

Mom came to pick me up from ballet class as usual. We often gave a ride home to my classmate, Jackie Smith, who was also in my class at school and came from a "bad home." It was our custom to talk shit about poor Jackie the instant she was out of the car, when I would report her scandalous flirtations with boys, how she'd lifted her skirt or gyrated her hips in gym class, so we could both condemn her. But on this day, after Jackie got out of the car and I'd started describing some great playground lewdness, Mom cut me off in her sternest voice.

"How *dare* you talk about Jackie when you're a thousand times worse yourself!"

A *thousand* times worse. I'll never forget that phrase, or the horror that washed over me. The pictures! Somehow she must have found the pictures. I stared between my knees at my pink ballet bag that could do nothing to save me. How could this have happened? Why would she look behind the radiator?

"I've called your father at work and he's on his way home to talk to you."

I said nothing.

"Zelda stayed home sick today. When I came upstairs with laundry, she was on the floor drawing something she tried to hide from me, and it turned out to be... you know what! Something horrible. I asked what made her do this, and she went straight to your drawer."

Betrayed! What an idiot I'd been! How could I have forgotten to re-hide them? Stupid, stupid, stupid! Now I was busted beyond belief.

"None of this is her fault. She's only six. But *you*... Well, your father will speak to you."

My head seemed enormous – a swollen, heavy watermelon of shame.

Dad arrived home soon after. He had Zelda and me sit side by side in an armchair while he perched on the coffee table directly across from us. Before this, while I'd been banished to our room, Zelda had come in briefly. I said something to the effect of "How *could* you?" She seemed sorry, but her eyes also refused to take blame: this was all on me.

Unlike my mother, Dad spoke without a trace of rancor. He sounded more like a grave judge, saddened by what he must say.

"Zelda has told us that drawing these pictures makes—"

"—Don't say it!" Zelda blurted, too late.

"—makes your cracks feel good."

Cracks!! I let out an involuntary shriek and covered my face. I couldn't believe she'd told them that part. I couldn't believe he'd just said it.

He shushed us. "Okay, I won't say it again. But these pictures are not of things that children should be thinking about. Your mother has taken Louisa's drawings to a psychiatrist. He's a friend of ours, and he'll help us decide what to do. But I can tell you the first thing is, you need to promise never, ever to draw pictures like that again."

We promised avidly, repeatedly. I meant every oath I spoke.

But I knew that, even so, my life would never be the same. And I was right, though for reasons I could not foresee. My drawings – the most daring, inexplicable musings of my mind – were in the hands of a stranger, a psychiatrist, a grown-up I'd never met. He was examining the W-boobs and Y crotches and ropes and knives dripping with blood that I (because yes, it *was* me) had drawn. I'd meant to be a good kid, but now my badness had erupted *so* badly, it had exceeded even my parents' knowledge of what to do. This went beyond scolding, beyond punishment. It had become a question of how to handle their daughter's diseased mind.

I understood psychiatrists to be the bosses of men in little white coats. The whitecoats carted away lunatics in straitjackets and stuck them in the funny farm, behind bars, somewhere they could do no harm. That's what the psychiatrist was deciding: whether Louisa should be put in the funny farm.

I can say without melodrama, that night was the worst of my life. Because a nine-year-old has no sense of scale. I knew my drawings were deviant; I didn't know the word but I understood that civilized people did not allow each other to do certain things, and one was to get pleasure from torture of others, real or drawn. By drawing, I'd revealed the evil inside me. In the past I'd fooled my parents into believing I was a good daughter. Now the exposed truth of me horrified and disgusted them – especially my mother. She had refused to meet my eye all through dinner.

Lying in the dark, I imagined the psychiatrist might send me to a special kind of funny farm just for kids. I'd have a different bed in a scary place, stuck with other crazy kids. I pictured Western Washington State Mental Hospital which we often drove past on the way to the summer cabin, all of us kids pretending to be nuts and scanning its barred windows for a fleeting figure. Might I somehow make the best of it there? Would they let us play outside? And how long would I have to live there? What about my birthdays and Christmas?

I cried, turned over my pillow, and cried more. I believed I'd never be happy again. And I hated myself for wrecking my life.

In the morning, my mother still wouldn't look at me. She was standing at the sink when I entered the kitchen, my heart pounding with shame and fear. She turned her head just enough to see it was me, then returned to whatever she was doing. I couldn't look at her, either.

Understand that my mother was doing the best parenting she knew, using the tool of shame to underscore that my behavior was not okay. She wanted nothing but to steer me toward the best life she could. And, of course, she must have been scared out of her wits. What mother drives her nine-year-old daughter's drawings across town to a psychiatrist and isn't? That wasn't apparent to me, though. What was apparent was that somewhere, unspoken under many layers of embarrassed denial, we shared the knowledge that my mother had breasts, had a Y crotch, could do "it." My drawings, in a roundabout way, had assaulted *her*.

Mom had no idea this moment, with her at the sink and me shamefacedly skirting past to the breakfast table, would become an icon of rejection – of the loved one turning their back – in my psyche. I would tell shrinks about it. I would write poems about it. I'm telling you about it. But even today, after all the work and prayers to let it go, I still cry as I type this. In my mind's eye I've gone back countless times to rewrite history, so that my Mom – or grown-up me taking her place – turns from the sink, holds out her arms, and says, "It's okay, honey. I still love you, no matter what!"

But Mom didn't. In fact, it seemed a long time before she hugged me again, and even then, the memory of the drawings lingered between us as an almost palpable awkwardness.

Later that morning, my father informed me the psychiatrist had called and said the drawings were "normal."

Normal?! Really?

Relieved as I was, the word didn't seem to make sense. *Normal* little girls would draw a chained woman being stabbed in the breast by some villain demanding she marry him? Normal girls mixed this debacle with images of cannibalism? I didn't think so. What I guessed it meant, though, was that my drawings, and the good-feeling cracks, and the horrible taint of this entire ordeal would join the long list of things we did not speak of.

And so we didn't speak of them.

Ever.

To this day.

For the next eight years, I banished from my life all sexuality and sensuality. Photos show my hair went into tight ponytails, and I quit wearing mini-skirts, embracing a Tomboy neutrality. Still, changes in my body posed a constant source of shame and embarrassment. I refused a trainer-bra for as long as I could, then layered it under my little girl undershirts. I tried to hide my body's changes from Zelda, which meant wearing the same underwear sometimes for days at a time, and often dressing in the closet.

But inside, I longed more than ever to draw the pictures! I could still envision them, the best ones. Which had to mean I was a monster.

My ballet classes were at the old Cornish School, where the bathroom off our dressing room featured a shower stall. Just before my class, the advanced girls, teens and twenty-somes known as the "Dailies" because their class met every day, emerged from the studio drenched in sweat, showered briefly and then re-entered the main dressing room casually naked while I was getting ready.

"So it went like this?" one naked girl might ask, going halfway through a combination's steps, bosoms bouncing.

"No," another would answer. "Not *pas de chat*. It's *assemblé battu*." Then, in perhaps nothing but bikini panties, she'd show the jumps herself.

Staring, I knew, would be detected, so suddenly the inside of my ballet bag grew incredibly interesting. "Creep! Weirdo! Pervert!" I'd berate myself, because I dared not lift my eyes to those sexy goddesses. Did I want to tie these girls up, torture them, make them do "it"? I must, secretly.

Discipline: I had to keep bad, sexual things out of my thoughts. If I lapsed even a little, I might draw more pictures. "Never," I'd tell myself. "We will never, *ever* draw those pictures again."

When a perfumed lady visited my sixth-grade class and handed out pink booklets about how special it was to menstruate, I tore mine up. It had the word "vagina" in it, which the lady had kept repeating as if it weren't embarrassing as hell, her polished nail tapping some cutaway diagram of a hollow slug inside half a butt. Fortunately, I didn't have one. And a year or two later, when Zelda got the same booklet, I tore that up, too, without her permission. I clung to playing like a child and thinking of myself as one, raising pet ducks in the city (a lot of work), and writing more hamster stories, even when the topic felt too young for me. I would block my own puberty.

In the family, and with Zelda, the incident of "Pretty Girls Tied Up" seemed forgotten. I don't believe Adelyn or Walter ever caught wind of it, and Zelda had been young enough to let the memory fade. But as for me, whenever I was alone in our room, the temptation resurfaced. Paper. Pencil... It would only take a few minutes.

But I had *sworn* to myself!

Nor was I the only one who remembered the drawings, as it turned out. Three years after the disaster, my mother requested as a birthday gift a particular amulet of Tutankhamum, whose treasures she was studying in order to lead museum tours. It was a pure gold miniature she'd circled in a catalogue. Dad quietly ordered it for her. But to create some element of surprise on her birthday, he proposed a prank to Zelda and me. We wrapped dozens of small jewelry boxes that actually contain little gadgets or do-dads, like a set of plastic corn-cob holders, a tiny bottle opener, and fridge magnets. They made a big pile of amulet-like gifts on the coffee table, while Dad kept the real one hidden in his bureau.

The plan backfired. By the time Mom opened the last little box, she flung it down in tears, revisiting some childhood pain. I ran for the real Tutankhamen amulet but now she opened it bitterly, still crying. Dad sent Zelda and me upstairs so the two of them could talk.

Except I didn't go upstairs. Zelda did, but I went only around the wall and sat on the landing to eavesdrop. I heard my father's comforting voice, and my mother's hurt one. It was a terrible trick, she said, and my name came up as instigator. Dad insisted more than once that it had been *his* idea, that it was meant only in fun, not to—

"But she *enjoyed* it," cut in my mother. "I saw it on her face!"

When Dad protested, I heard my mother half-whisper, "Oh, come on! You know as well as I do, that child is ____!"

The last word dropped too low for me to catch, but sitting there on the landing, I filled it in: "evil." She was saying, "Come on, remember her drawings!" I could tell by how fervently Dad objected.

Some words, when they hit us, seem to physically impact our bodies. I was hugging my knees to my chest when those hit me. Even with the unheard word, my heart dropped, and by the very next beat, my body flushed with self-loathing's triumph: "I *told* you!" it said.

No one had forgotten my atrocity – the W breasts and Y crotches, the cartoon bubbles of begging for mercy, those dismembered breasts on a plate. I cringed all over again. We'd been only pretending for three years that they were forgotten, that I was a normal kid. I picked my way silently up the stairs and joined Zelda in our room, where I said nothing. That deep heaviness of shame felt almost a relief, a sense that now, at least, I finally knew the truth: I was, in fact, unloveable. Now, at least, I could quit hoping.

Around this time of the mid-seventies, the media made a celebrity of serial killer, Ted Bundy, whose method was to feign an injury and then kidnap and murder the women who offered him help. Any discussion of Bundy made me squirm, because I wondered if my parents were thinking of my drawings. The only difference between me and Bundy, it seemed to me, was that he *acted* on his urges. But how awful to feel a secret, shameful empathy for this killer; becoming an inhuman psychopath, I knew, had never been his child-hood dream.

Gradually, beginning around the age of fourteen, I developed a clinical depression, undiagnosed. I felt a constant sense of loss, as if the world were fading to gray. Between 6th and 10th grades, I switched schools six times, in part because of Seattle's evolving integration program, which shuttled me out of my white neighborhood from 5th grade on. In the early years, I tried to pass for black in hopes it would bring me friends, braiding my wet hair every night so it would dry kinked and sitting out in the sun with a homemade foil reflector even as fall progressed. I even made it into a popular clique for a few blissful months before a rival 6th grader asked the incriminating question, "How come yo' ass so flat?" I should have counter-challenged, "Girl, how come yo' ass so big?" Instead, I cowered and was ousted.

By high school, though, I was fine with my loser status, because it was assigned. I was part of a 10% minority in a hostile school where white and Asian kids cowered on the sidelines, got refused seats on the shuttle bus, and suffered constant taunting and violence. If you weren't black, you had zero chance of popularity, but you did find yourself naturally united with fellow non-blacks. Seeing a white boy get beat up and cry, you didn't judge him. For lisping and getting A's on everything, no one judged me. I'd never felt so socially confident.

Sophomore year, however, my parents enrolled me in the same expensive private school my brother had attended. Far from the inner city, I found myself suddenly thrust among Seattle's richest elite. My father's meager professor salary seemed something the rich kids could sniff out with disdain. And I was shy. Here, without the excuse of race, my awkward loserdom stood out starkly.

Popularity now obsessed me. It seemed to hold out everything I lacked. The popularity ladder in my mind featured a distinct rung for every kid I knew. The more unattainable a friendship, the more desperately I longed for it. The cool kid's charisma, I believed, qualified them to exonerate all that was lacking in me. It seemed a mere matter of studying and then accurately replicating their social habits. Vernacular from the inner city, which still echoed in my ears, was not used here, so I had to listen carefully to whatever went over well.

Wouldn't you think that, being clear-skinned and big-eyed, with bona fide boobs, a small waist, and ballet-honed legs, I ought to be able to crack this secret formula? Why not? Yet time after time, I'd gather my gumption and sit down in the midst of a rowdy table of popular kids. I'd try to edge into their conversations, slip in a practiced joke, ask admiring questions. Within minutes, the table would be deserted – except for me.

"Why do you keep trying?" self-loathing would sneer.

Since I got A's in everything, I might have joined the school geeks who hung out in the main building's basement computer room, except that I still clung to a dream of popularity that would be doomed by any association with them. So I spurned them. I befriended some medium-outcast girls – smart, but not computer basement smart.

During free periods I hid out in the library, studying whether I needed to or not. Since I was always starving myself for ballet's sake, always longing to be thinner than I was, I rarely ate much, so my stomach growled incessantly. I'd discovered that by not swallowing saliva, I could delay the growling and decrease its volume, even if I ended up with a huge mouthful of spit I'd be forced to gulp down if someone worthwhile greeted me. In that case, the spit would make my stomach growl twice as loud and absurdly often, so that I'd have to leave the library. Thus in greeting people I would have to gauge, based on their popularity, whether they merited the sacrifice of swallowing or just a spit-retaining nod.

One day as I was reading and collecting spit, a quasi-popular red haired girl led into my area five beautiful, popular girls who rarely showed up in the library. All six took armchairs in my vicinity and opened their books within seconds. Puzzled initially, I swallowed a huge batch of spit in hopes that one of them might speak to me. But none so much as looked my way. All their apparent attention seemed trained on their books.

At the first drawn out, slightly inquisitive yowl from my stomach, two or three of the girls erupted in barely suppressed giggles. My thoughts began racing toward escape, yet it seemed better to hold out, because my stomach felt like it might get quiet for a while. It didn't. The next yowl came louder and longer. This time the whole group repressed laughter, sinuses resounding, books quaking in their grips. Too late, I understood what was going on. A robust chortle of sing-song, undersea burbling rolled forth from my stomach. This time it was so loud that the lot of them just plain lost it, slumping over in their chairs and shaking, mouths covered, eyes squinting. The red haired girl's were wide open, though, beaming from one popular girl to the next with I-toldja-so pride. Even fellow library geeks from neighboring tables looked up at the disturbance, then at me. At that moment I realized my growling stomach was such a fixture in there, everyone knew exactly what was happening.

The girls' bathroom was down in the basement. I didn't quite make it to the furthest stall before my sobs exploded. I punched at my stomach. I hated myself.

Ballet, socially, was even worse. At a smaller school now, I progressed to the advanced class, where I became the youngest – a fourteen-year-old among late teen and twenty-somes. Dancing I did well enough, but even casual exchanges catapulted me into a chasm of awkwardness. Since I was constantly spaced out rehearsing the dazzling conversations I'd have with various cool girls, I'd find myself clueless about each upcoming dance combination. Even my most carefully planned chats would crash and burn horrifically. No one said what they were supposed to, and my improvisation skills sucked. I envisioned my repulsive social aura like the dust cloud around the *Peanuts* character, Pig Pen. "Personality Stink," I called it. Nice girls were instinctively repelled. They couldn't quite pinpoint what was wrong, unaware this girl was teeming with perverted desires that had estranged even her own mother, but they sensed enough to keep her at a distance.

Up until senior year, home offered something of a haven from these pains of social failure. Solidarity with Zelda was the source of almost all my happiness. After school we'd spend hours together drinking tea and reading fun parts of the paper. We loved our pet ducks and the puppy who'd recently joined our family, and now instead of writing hamster stories, we filmed short movies about each of them, *The Mystery of the Disappearing Duck*, and *Super-puppy*. Zelda had befriended a classmate with identical twin sisters at her Catholic middle school, and the four of them always invited me along. We played records, danced in their basement, and talked about boys.

Another source of happiness was that my father had started taking us on hikes in the mountains, some of which my mother joined. On any sunny weekend, he'd get out a hiking book and pick a trail for us. Being out in nature lessened my pain. I'd consider the millennia for which those enormous mountains had stood oblivious to high school drama, and spirits in the old trees who considered me just another human. Back in my room I'd play the Beatles song "Mother Nature's Son" over and over, tearing up as it evoked a romantically sacred haven – the stream, the meadow, the sun.

After I got my driver's license, my parents let me spend time alone at our summer cabin with only our German shepherd for company. Solitary sometimes for as long as two weeks, I found relief in the chores of chopping wood and keeping the fire going, reading by kerosene lamps, and yanking the pull cord of the well's pump motor to start it up and fill the water tank on the roof. I loved the misty view of Kitsap Peninsula with the snow-topped Olympic Mountains beyond it, and the constant murmur of waves breaking on the beach below. This setting where I'd played since I was seven – I had the odd feeling it *loved* me. It was as if the land and cabin knew me to my core and carried empathy for me in this difficult part of my life. It seemed, temporarily, to heal me.

Naming that feeling 'god' never so much as crossed my mind. God was stupid. He was the equivalent of some great big daddy or king invented by church people long ago, that simple-minded goody-goodies still worshipped. Plus religion was a crutch, an answer book for the lazy-minded. Already, I identified with existentialism. One ought to think for oneself. And in my ability to do that, at least, I had the ultimate faith.

*Top: A few weeks before my drawings were found
Bottom: About two years after the drawings, with our
lesbian ducks, Spring and Summer*

4: OF COMPULSION AND DENIAL

"Why am I as I am—and what am I?" Her mind
would recoil while her spirit grew faint. A great
darkness would seem to descend on her spirit – there
would be no light wherewith to lighten that darkness.

-Radclyff Hall
The Well of Loneliness

Zelda's first date happened the same week she started high school. At the close of middle school she'd shot up, transforming from a chubby girl with stringy hair and smudgy, cock-eyed glasses to a tall, shapely babe with contact lenses and a cute Dorothy Hammill haircut. Makeup, tube tops, low cut shirts – hers was a Catholic prep school where the girls dressed like whores. Over the course of her freshman year, she took on the proportions that would make her a model during college. Beside her, I felt short and homely, a Mary Anne to her Ginger.

Throughout all our childhood I'd been boss of whatever Zelda and I did, not so much from aggression as from fear. That I'd co-opted her allegiance in retaliation to Adelyn's hostility and my loneliness – that I was vaguely aware of, even as a child. But it's only in recent years that I've recognized the degree of anxiety that chafed at me all through childhood, which I treated much as my paternal grandmother had – by keeping busy. Whenever I slowed down, the gloomy afternoons exposed a soul-sucking emptiness just beneath the surface of things. I remember sitting in silence after one of my storybook records finished, rain spattering the window behind it, and feeling something dismal and ominous infiltrating my awareness. Today, I wonder if it was my sense of the nameless elephant in the house, something haunting our family that could never be thrown off. In any case, to evade it I spent years constantly coming up with activities – bike rides, projects, games – that were pretty much mandatory for Zelda. At one point, I wrote up a list of such options. Zelda herself had no such anxiety or fear of emptiness and would have preferred to just loll about watching TV for hours on end. But I'd make her put on her shoes and join me whether she felt like it or not.

Now, though, Zelda was finding a will of her own. She had signed up to be a water-girl for the football team. Early in the school year, my parents were scandalized to see a convertible squealing down the winding hill of our street, crammed with teenagers and blasting raucous music – before they recognized Zelda perched atop the back seat. Soon she came home from a field trip and shut the door to our room to talk privately. She'd gone off in the tall grass with a cute guy from the football team and gotten almost naked. They'd *nearly* had sex, but hadn't. Did I think she should still not have sex?

What a question! I'd never so much as held hands with a boy. For me, sweet sixteen had long since come and gone without even the prospect of a kiss. I had three half-friends I clung to at school – and there ended my social life. I idolized popular boys, thrilled to touch door handles after they did, and fantasized countless conversations with them – and there ended my dating life. For years I'd claimed authority in everything, but now my dating tortoise lay upturned in the dust of Zelda's hare with neither of us, practiced as we were in denial, able to admit my failure. I managed to say something vaguely cautionary and Zelda was kind enough to accept it. We would pretend I had a life, though losing Zelda to her healthy shift toward peers and dating would, in fact, pretty much empty it. Now most days she didn't arrive home until evening. I drank tea and read the paper alone.

Zelda was turning out to be the only normal P. child, starting her rebellion right on schedule. Adelyn, meanwhile, still despised all but a few exempt friends and found solace in her intellectual and musical superiority. She lived in California now, studying piano with a grand master, one in a series. In her quest for excellence, she romanticized the world of music and got swept away in passionate affairs with musicians she idolized. Walter was still reeling from Dad's almost palpable disappointment at his rejection from Harvard – the holy land of our family. He had, as a teenager, spontaneously developed a British accent. We were out in the yard one day, he and I, when he referred to Dad as Fah-thah.

"What do you mean, 'Fah-thah'?" I asked, incredulous.

He responded, "Fah-thah! I've oh-lways colled him Fah-thah!" And so it went for about the next fifteen years – I don't know why. By this time he'd enrolled at the University of Washington where he majored in Classics, able to both read and write in Greek and Latin, which constituted, in *our* family, an honorable skill. Teaching was the only career avenue for that field, however, from which his slow speech would later bar him.

I, meanwhile, spent many teen hours alone in our room. Zelda and I had inherited Mom and Dad's 1950s stereo, which had no headphone jack, so I couldn't crank music as obliteratingly as I wanted. Instead, if the house was empty I'd lug our two speakers within about a foot of each other and lie down between them to crank Fleetwood Mac's "I'm So Afraid" as loud as the old woofers could handle:

Days when the rain and the sun are gone
Black as night
Agony's torn at my heart too long

I'd sing along in my duck-like voice, tears trickling into my ears: "So afraid! – slip and I fall and I d-i-i-e!" Then I'd get up and move the needle back to replay it.

School remained torture. Once, amid the fallout of some particularly disastrous social snub, I took a melodramatic walk on the running track to let out my tears. Slumping along in the gray drizzle, I felt hopelessly crippled by Louisa-ness. Even the squirrels and birds on that campus, the very trees themselves, seemed to disdain me. Visions of suicide flashed in my thoughts. Relief. Escape. But even I knew they weren't genuine. That was the whole trouble with me – *nothing* I did or thought felt genuine! I wanted to tear my hair, punch my face, anything to vent this rage at my inept and phony personality.

Eventually I grew desperate enough to make an appointment with the school counselor, a jockish and upbeat woman named Terri, in retrospect probably lesbian. I sat in her office and rattled off pleasant clichés as my parents had taught me. Terri was well-liked by many of the cool kids, which, to my mind, made her likewise cool. My heart pounded and I sweated – one of the few times I really stank. I managed to utter a few things about my difficulty making friends and hurt feelings when my "hi"s went ignored in passing, but she assured me such things were *normal*. Yes, I did have a very high GPA. Yes, I played JV soccer. I'd come in meaning to alert her of how often I contemplated suicide, but now it seemed too embarrassing. How could I explain it wasn't really *killing* myself I wanted, so much as just *not to be here*? Terri, meanwhile, seemed to be thinking of other stuff she'd rather be doing. Just like the popular kids, it seemed, she saw me as a dull burden. I thanked her for her time, and I never went back.

Even that, I had blown.

Then, on a Friday night in the fall of 1977, my life took another irrevocable turn. Everyone in the family had somewhere else to be. Adelyn and Walter lived away from home. Mom and Dad were out. Zelda had a date. At school I'd overheard the popular kids talking about some huge-ass, wild party that night, but naturally they'd shushed whenever I came near. I had no friends to call, but I did have a paper due the following Friday on some aspect of French history, so I was at my desk attempting to read and take notes for it. The paper wasn't due for a *week,* but pretending to work on it helped camouflage my loneliness.

I'd try to focus on the book but instead find my eyes sliding over the text while I imagined what might be going on at that party. I pictured the popular boys who must be there, and the popular girls who actually *kissed* and were *touched* by them. In my scenarios of imagined conversations, Louisa was a confident seductress these boys found irresistible – quite a contrast with the reality of my lobbing botched one-liners from a desperately twitching face. I'd grown tired of hoping, always hoping I'd do better in the future.

The air seemed to thicken, to grow tactile, and I could feel that old glow in my crotch. The pictures were calling again. I got up and went to the window, which looked out from our hillside at the glittery night lights of the University District. Everyone everywhere was out on dates, enjoying romance, holding someone. I sat down again and tried to read. Idiot. Loser. Plus I wasn't even ugly. My face was okay, and my body clearly sexy. What these facts proved was that the astounding intensity of my loserishness outweighed every advantage.

The images began to take shape in my thoughts. Right here was paper! Right here a pencil! So easy, but mustn't – *mustn't!* Don't you remember what happened?

And yet, drawing was not our only option. I had a "pretty girl" body of my own now. When we'd lived in Michigan, my parents' bedroom featured a large wall mirror. Back then, while they were out, I had often locked the door and explored myself in that mirror, sitting on the carpet with my legs apart. But – oh *no!* Where girls were supposed to have a vagina, I had instead a discolored patch of misshapen folds. Everything down there looked horribly bruised. I wondered if that were the reason I'd still not gotten my period.

The real reason, as it turned out, was a lack of body fat. When we'd returned from Michigan, the family pediatrician put me on birth control pills to jump-start my hormones. I'd bled for the first time in ballet class, saw in the mirrors the red stain blooming on my pink tights, and dashed for the dressing room. There I sighed to Joanne, in her mid-twenties, "Got my stupid period!" Since I had none, Joanne kindly tossed me a tampon, and I went in the bathroom to stare at it uncomprehendingly. How the hell did these things work? Deconstructing the applicator, I dropped the cotton part to the floor. Then, since I had no vagina, I just dusted it off and tucked it amid the discolored folds – which proved *extremely* uncomfortable on my bike ride home.

Once I got home, my mother, with some semi-sarcastic remark about this being the last thing she needed, handed me a box of tampons. "You know how to use them?" "Of course!" I said, rolling my eyes. Inside it was a tiny folded instruction page showing that same stupid cut-away butt with the reverse slug vagina, which meant nothing to me. But the instructions did explain in words, too – something about parting skin folds to insert it. To my utter amazement, half the applicator slid painlessly inside my body, and when I depressed the outer tube, the tampon deployed.

A vagina?! Amazing! The thing was vast, too! I found the opening with a hand mirror. Imagine discovering, after all these years, a handy kangaroo pouch where you could stash all kinds of stuff. As soon as my bleeding stopped I took to secretly carrying around orphaned toothbrushes, dental floss, smooth hair curlers – anything I could hide in there that wouldn't get lost or hurt me. What a kick to walk around the house or sit at the dinner table knowing no one could x-ray the contents of my secret pocket! I had only a few moments' panic if I couldn't reach something to get it out. Strange as it may sound, none of these adventures had involved arousal.

But arousal was what I had full on now – and no way to express it.

That mirror in Michigan had been right under Mom's nose day after day, yet it never betrayed a thing. Mirrors were safe. So why create the incriminating evidence of drawings when I now owned a body that would let me – and here came a stroke of genius – *act them out myself* in a mirror? I could create any image I wanted, then have it disappear forever.

The distant party of populars, the dates everyone else was having – all that slipped away in my keen, focused excitement. I started to gather the things I might need to recreate the drawings – belts, knee socks, scarves, and how about this old bikini top? To hell with what people might think! I was a pervert, I'd known for years. So why not just live it out?

I took the full-length mirror off its nail and brought it in the bathroom. It seemed to me – by what logic I don't know – that getting caught in our room behind a locked door would be more damning – why is the door locked?! Whereas bathrooms cut you some slack. Everybody locks the bathroom.

The body in the mirrors took on the same "thingness" as had shampoo bottles during trances of the past. I wanted to create images as close to the drawn ones as I could. The trick was to tie up everything but your hands ahead of time, then make a sock loop, slip it over your wrists, and twist. The sock loop could be in front or back, attached to the trap of the sink drain or not. I tried to rig my ankles to the doorknob, but that didn't work. There was really nothing at that whole end of the room – a technical problem for the practical designer in me, almost like the director of a low-budget porn.

A lot of things didn't work, and the last thing I wanted to do was bend the shower curtain rod by hanging from it or something, then have a lot of explaining to do. So I just experimented with what might. I could lay the mirror face down by propping it from the edge of the tub across to the bench opposite, then scooch underneath. Or I could lean it against the toilet. I did not want to see my own face. These images were not me – they were the hapless victims from my drawings and fantasies, figures who stood for utter degradation.

Neither would I actually touch my vagina with my fingers, because that would be sick. I didn't need to, anyway, because the glow in my crotch swelled on its own. Struggling against bonds felt delicious. Certain images, especially close-ups in Mom's magnifying mirror of my half-formed breasts, absolutely tantalized me. This trance took me far deeper than anything I'd attained before. The insulation from my normal life was seamless, like a thick mental wetsuit. I became viewer, voyeur; I became characters, at once cruel fiend and suffering victim. I could switch these perspectives at will, too frequently for me to even notice.

After half an hour or so, when I began to worry someone might come home, I covered my tracks – until next time. And there would be many next times over the next year and a half, because I was frequently home alone.

I didn't know a thing about orgasms. Yes, I'd read about them in health class, but the memory didn't seem pertinent. I'd never heard the word fetish, either, and had no idea there existed other people captivated by similar fantasies. In fact, I'd been conditioned so thoroughly to view anything sexual as depraved, I couldn't possibly imagine healthy couples having intercourse. As late as age 16, I held the belief that only sick, deviant people screwed.

Definitely the most thrilling thing about the self-bondage ritual was that I *should not do it*. There was such liberation, such power to flipping off the entire human race whenever I followed an urge I thought was mine alone and did things no sane girl would do, solely because I felt like it! I became increasingly daring and imaginative in my bondage adventures, collecting mirrors from all over the house, which I arranged for a variety of views. I also brought in new props I'd noted during normal life. Out of all the screwdrivers in the basement, I soon knew which handle I preferred and could grab it in a second.

My almost-adult body was a new toy to me, still under construction but finished enough to do. I became the ultimate performance artist for myself. I'd smear toothpaste all over my skin, then draw in it. I'd put curler clips on my nipples, fit my breasts through plastic hoops, wrap my torso in Saran wrap – whatever emphasized that thingness of the thing. Cleavage was still a bit tough to muster, but with a band of nylons, I could manage some. Water balloon falsies also worked... sort of. A metal nail file made a good fantasy knife. I did not enjoy real pain – only visuals suggesting it. Practical glitches came up all the time: things spilled, knots that wouldn't untie, mirrors that fell over but – thank god – never cracked. I would deal with these issues swiftly, then resume the trance. But no matter how lost I'd get in fantasies of torture, I never made the slightest sound. Not from secrecy – no one was ever in the house – but because any sound of my voice would break the spell, remind me of the stupid, faltering Louisa I was doing all this to escape.

Clean-up time, on the other hand, was hell. Now my normal, socially judgmental self had to get rid of all the damning evidence. Look at this wreckage! God, what a freak I was! What I'd just done came back to me through the eyes of kids from school, their parents, or teachers who considered me a nice, intelligent girl – what if they knew? Rapidly I'd dress, clean and wipe down everything, then return my props to their rightful places around the house – Mom's bureau, basement tool area, kitchen – all the while vowing that I would never, *ever* do this horrible, sick stuff again.

There's nothing wrong with bondage per se, in my opinion. Even today it plays a role in my sex fantasies. There's nothing inherently wrong with acting it out, either, in open and shameless ways, as a pageant for psychic tensions that may or may not be addressed in therapy. For the sake of contrast I can tell you about a brief conversation I had twenty years later, ten years after I'd brought this compulsion to therapy and two years into sobriety. I was working as a barback at Vivace, a hipster espresso shop in the most visibly gay neighborhood of Seattle – Broadway on Capital Hill.

Wiping down a sidewalk table next to one occupied by a Harley-Davidson dyke – I'll call her Dee – who was then a bit of an icon at gay AA meetings, I eavesdropped a bit. Dee was sporting her customary leather jacket, chaps, and Doc Martins, with many a facial piercing and spiky red hair, despite having passed forty a few turns back in the road. She was talking to an overweight man well on his way to becoming an old queen, about how her S&M habit kept messing up her relationships.

"They're all so into it at first," she complained in her Texan accent. "Sign me up, bring on the chains! But then I swear it fucks up everything. They start thinkin' I don't respect 'em, then we're fightin'…" she left off with a shake of the head that indicated all intimacy went down the shitter.

"Yeah," sighed her friend. "It's like anything with sex; brings up all sorts of childhood baggage."

"All I know is, my life'd be a hellova lot simpler—" she lifted her cup for me to wipe their table. "Thank you, ma'am."

Right then I chose to do something I'd never done in my life. I said simply, "When I was a teenager, I used to tie myself up and get off looking in mirrors."

"Wow!" This was unexpected indeed! Dee sat up a bit. "Yourself! Mirrors? Why, that is so dang *thrifty*!"

Her companion agreed. "Mirrors can be great."

"How'd you tie yourself up?"

"Knee socks – just pre-tie them and save your wrists for last."

"Tube socks are great," agreed the queen. "I'll take tube socks over silk scarves any day!"

"So you'd pretend it was somebody else, or what?"

"Yeah, I'd just put the mirrors so I couldn't see my face."

"Damn!" Dee sat back and grinned at her friend, floored. "Wish *I* had a cute little body I could get off on like that! Me – I look like me," she laughed with a shrug. "Don't do nothin' for me, else I'd save myself a lotta hassle!"

I moved on to wipe the next table. My moment of frankness had passed and, with my heart still pounding, I was ready to wrap up the topic.

The friend remarked thoughtfully, "You must have a strong creative imagination."

I laughed and replied that a past shrink had told me just that. But mostly I marveled at how easily and naturally the conversation had flowed. In her wildest dreams, teenage Louisa could never have imagined the curse that caused her such wretched guilt would someday be praised by near-strangers as "thrifty" or "creative."

Rather, as a seventeen-year-old virgin caught in an obsessive-compulsive disorder, I found the whole phenomenon frightening. Once, in an adamant fit of self-recrimination, I gathered up all the belts and socks and as many of the props as no one would miss and stuffed them all in a plastic bag, which I then stuck in a second bag full of trash, took out to the garbage, and stuck in with the kitchen garbage. I was really done this time. Take that, pervert!!

Imagine how I felt to find myself out there early in the morning on garbage day rummaging desperately through various bags, my addict-self delighted to discover that the plastic had kept my entire stash pristine. I wasn't even in a trance then, but I knew I couldn't live without those things.

Once everything was safely re-stashed, I considered what I'd just done, and I cried – angry, confused, and scared. Welcome to addiction.

Something changed on the day I finally stumbled on orgasm. I'd kept up the rule against touching myself directly, so for all those months of mirror trysts I'd only enjoyed arousal. But one night during my senior year, I discovered that if I kept my legs closed around the screwdriver inside me and bore down with my abdominal muscles against the restraint of the belts, something swelled in my crotch almost too wonderful to stand. Then it exploded all through me. A fountain of pure heaven overflowing, not just between my legs but all through my being, swirling on inner currents.

When it was over, I marveled. For god's sake, what had just *happened*? Oh! – I knew the word! What was it? C'mon, Health Class vocabulary list: *uterus, ovaries, zygote, fallopian...*

Orgasm! Oh my god, I'd had an *orgasm*! Me! My body somehow knew about them all by itself! Except that – wait – my body was made by Nature, a work of amazingly dividing cells, and it... it *liked* what I'd been doing? It had *answered* me?

It certainly had.

Which could only mean that all this sex stuff, even my perviness, was *not really evil*! I'd believed sex was bad and dark and wrong because I'd been taught to, but what if my body, with Nature, knew better? What if arousal was a part of life, part of how I worked?

I tore off my bindings and dashed to our room where I danced all over the room stark naked to Fleetwood Mac's "Go Your Own Way." The curtains were open to the world, but who cared? Somebody'd told me I was okay. There would be a future. I would become a woman and yet still be me. I felt loved by Nature – *Mother* Nature – in the very ways my own mother had condemned.

From then on, my compulsion seemed slightly less abominable. I still knew it was wrong in the world of humans, but now Nature, or whatever it was that bestowed orgasms, was complicit in my crime. I began going for them deliberately, touching myself to help them along, learning what I liked. Believe me, throughout my seventeenth year, those mirrors and I enjoyed quite a potent, kinky sex life!

My parents must have marveled that, as a teenager, I never rebelled in the slightest. I excelled consistently in school – had, in fact (having sidestepped the too-geeky honors courses), the highest GPA in my graduating class. I did my chores without complaint, almost never went out, hardly talked on the phone, and showed zero interest in boys or sex. During senior year I had to quit ballet because of scheduling conflicts, but took up drama after school and even made a few friends. I was, in short, a model teen.

My rituals were never discovered. I had cleanup down to a science. Since the bathroom window overlooked the driveway, I could hear the family car pull in while I was half tied up and trying to fit my breasts through large mason jar rings, yet be slouched at the kitchen table lazily reading the paper by the time whoever it was came in – just a tad winded. Once, though, I was horrified to notice, as I talked casually to my brother, that the knee socks had left bright red knit impressions on my wrists. I hid them before he noticed.

~

Trance, I soon discovered, wasn't the only way of escaping reality. I'd always known I loved alcohol, but had never had a chance to drink to oblivion. That chance first came on another lonely night at home.

Zelda was out with friends. At dinner my parents opened a gallon jug of cheap, sweet wine they didn't like, so when they left to see a play, they instructed me to pour it out as I washed dishes. And that I did – down my gullet.

Just about every alcoholic tells a cherished story of their first drunk. Because drinking is, for the budding alcoholic, a truly transformational spiritual experience, the moment is framed forever. For the first time in our lives, we are fixed.

At first I danced my way through the dishes and kitchen clean up. Then I sat with the half-empty jug and blasted Walter's Pink Floyd album through headphones, my head swirling with stereophonic effects, my singing loud enough to make me hoarse. Wow – space was unending. Music blew my mind. And I... was charged with power. That business of being intimidated at school, my constant chase after popularity – what a joke! I imagined calling each popular kid before me on trial, finding them guilty of being an asshole, and dismissing them to some humiliating punishment. Because I didn't need anyone! Man, I wanted to go places and do stuff and live my fucking life! And drink! Hell yes, was I going to drink my way through life! I played the Beatles. I lost myself in fantasies. And I wanted this feeling to stay with me forever. *Never before* had it felt so good to be alive.

Around dawn I awoke sideways on the loveseat with something like half-cured glue sticking my tongue to the roof of my mouth. My brain had gelled to custard. I had my first case of the spins and was a little pukey. It took a while for me to piece together how things stood. Mom and Dad hadn't even seen me when they came in, and were asleep. No one had a clue what I'd done.

I switched off the stereo's still-circling turntable and padded into the kitchen with the empty jug, amazed to find the house unchanged. What had become of all the magic? Hadn't Pink Floyd and the Beatles practically *been* here in person? I chugged a glass of water and went upstairs to where Zelda was likewise asleep, not even having noticed my unmade bed was empty. I slid under the covers with my guts sloshing puke and my pulse slamming my skull like a wet rag against a concrete wall, utterly ecstatic.

By this age I'd started writing in a journal, but not honestly. My entries were all tailored to convince some imagined audience of peers that I was normal and healthy. Even if I'd possessed the self-honesty to know my truth, which I did not, I wouldn't have risked writing it down. For starters, Zelda might read it, or my mom. Occasionally, when I wrote drunk, some honest feeling spilled out in big, scrawled letters:

> 5/1978: "Why even write. I hate. I am too tired to do anything but hate. I hate me, I hate Zelda, I hate everyone at school, and I hate this book. I am pretentious. I am overly self-conscious and insecure. I get insecurity *fits* when I go in circles and am all wrapped up in arguing with myself whether I'm complete crud or not. Then I can't think of anything outside myself. I am afraid of other people. I plan everything, always conscious that I'm planning. I just planned to write that. There is no way for me to live spontaneously, except when I'm drunk.
>
> "I like to get drunk. *Oooo!* What does that mean? Sicky, sicky, sicky, this girl. Not me, though. She just pretends. And don't go reading this! Don't read, I hate you, I'm just so dumb! This is hopeless any way I go I come out dumb. *Why*? Because I'm a *fake*. I am scared to let out what's really in. I don't trust 'em. No one read this. Sick, sick, sniveling, quivering me! Schitzo!
>
> "Who *really* knows me. No one. Who would I let read this? No one. I'm tired of trying, tired of everything. I give up. Dead to the world. Dead to other people. It's nonsense, of course, nonsense."

Drinking was my ticket to cool. The last two months of high school saw me bombed at every class-hosted event and beginning to hear tell of parties. "Louisa P., drinking?!" Indeed, I could swallow, and I could get very stupid. My first party at a rich home in Broadmoor saw me blacked out and losing major chunks of time. I found myself eating ice cream out of the box at a kitchen sink, not knowing how I got there. Next I was in an upstairs room, apparently alone. I ended up sitting outside on a curb with Dwayne, a popular boy from the basketball team who, earlier that night, had given me my first bong hits. In his worldly wisdom, he cautioned that I'd gotten *too high*. But could there be any such thing? Was not Dwayne himself talking with me right now – something that would never have happened if I were my normal self? He was cool, and I was me, but I remember wondering if he might even be flirting.

I piled on at least ten pounds from beer. After graduation, I threw a kegger for my eighteenth birthday and was amazed that people actually *came*. There were games of beer pong and wasted badminton played amid loud music. My parents drank with my friends. My father, in fact, got fairly schnockered playing beer pong with some of the coolest boys. Alcohol, it seemed, could make anything possible. The next day I tabulated attendees in my journal, ranked in categories for each degree of coolness.

During senior year I'd gone on several "dates" with a smart boy from my philosophy class, but each time I'd leapt from his car with the goodnight shout, "See ya later, Phil!" I was not at all attracted to him, and this worried me. What if my pervert stuff had turned me gay? Later that summer when a boy from drama class asked me out, I practiced making out with my pillow to be ready.

But the date itself was a disaster. The boy brought not alcohol, but pot, which I'd already discovered made me feel paranoid and isolated.

"Not so hard!" he complained after our first kiss. I wanted to point out that kisses in movies sure *looked* like they involved a lot more pressure than *his* method of loose and proximal lip-licking, but I said nothing. His slobber repulsed me, and I was shivering. When he went for second base, I felt a sudden anger. My breasts were *private*! I pulled away and announced: "I want to go home!"

Afterwards, he told everyone from high school I was frigid – a rumor that even Zelda, who started there the following year, would hear. I worried that he might be right.

By this time, the orgasms I was able to give myself struck like mighty bolts of lightning blasting open some huge, ancient oak, with after-spasms engulfing the landscape like tidal waves. My adult orgasms pale by comparison. But the fact that I'd hardly touched another human being was – I knew – highly abnormal. What if I lived my whole life with romance confined to the bathroom?

My escape to college on the east coast, I hoped, would save me from this fate. Boys there would know nothing of my past, and alcohol would let me be different.

7/1978: "Drinking gin and tonic makes me write easier. I *love* to get drunk and high. I love *Catcher in the Rye*. He got drunk, so that's why I did. I ought to give Anne

Stephens [my English teacher] a buzz. Only I'm so fat. I hate my fat thighs and trunk. I will diet for the next few weeks so as to be thin when I head for the ole college. Do you want to hear a shocking thing?? I want to lose my *virginity* at college! Oh my God!"

I set myself an iron-clad deadline, swearing that I would lose my virginity within forty-eight hours of arriving on campus. I'd seen some R-rated scenes and figured I knew pretty much what to expect. Better to get it over with quickly, rip off the Band-Aid, than dawdle and maybe chicken out.

Maybe I'd be struck normal. Maybe, at Vassar, I could become a whole new person.

Senior year, and dressed for the junior year "tolo"
– a dance to which girls asked boys

5: QUEST FOR NORMALCY

She saw herself like that – she was a fly, but the others were dragonflies, butterflies, beautiful insects, dancing, fluttering, skimming, while she alone dragged herself up out of the saucer.

-Virginia Woolf
The New Dress

I had to conceal from Zelda how excited I was to be leaving home. At the airport, hugging her goodbye, I was too self-conscious to cry genuinely, what with wearing make-up and my fanciest clothes with our parents watching sentimentally. I worked up some tears because I longed to feel what I knew – that I would miss her. She was starting at the rich-kids school, but I felt sure she'd do fine without me.

I was so ready to throw away my old life and launch a new one, I could hardly stand it. The whole trip started off auspiciously. Because of a seating snafu I got upgraded to business class and found myself next to a well-dressed businessman in his forties who mistook me for an attractive young woman. He kept buying me drinks. Me! By the time we landed at Kennedy, I'd gotten quite tipsy and he'd invited me out to dinner – but I told him my aunt was picking me up. He told me, in parting, that I was beautiful. Had he been thinking we might have sex? I still had no clue how all that stuff worked.

As my aunt showed me New York City, we kept running into the same phenomenon. At a United Nations function, men older than my father grabbed my waist and kissed my cheek with their shiny, boozed faces touching mine. My aunt also took me for cocktails atop the World Trade Center, where, coming back from the restroom quite buzzed, I passed yet another businessman who turned back at the same moment I did to rate me with an approving nod. It was like an intoxicating game, this new power to fool men – regular, grown up men – into thinking I was sexy.

So it began to seem attainable in the real world, this virginity-shedding goal of mine. After my aunt dropped me off at my Vassar dorm, which was obnoxiously modern, I noted posters for a circuit of "Welcome Freshman!" parties. Technically, I had two nights before my deadline, but a party seemed to offer the best range of candidates. I'd talked to a number of boys already that day, and they all proved as easily deceived as the New York businessmen. None guessed I was a loser.

The very first boy I talked to, at the very first party I went to, seemed as good an option as any. He was a little too short and his voice acquired a sort of bubble at times, but his white-boy afro of curls was the height of fashion. I'd left myself the caveat that if someone truly repulsed me, I could abort, but I could hardly claim those spittle strings at the corners of his mouth as sufficient cause. I had to go through with it. This boy kept slanting one eyebrow in a manner he imagined debonair, much like one of the outer-worldly characters Zelda and I had invented (The "Insecure Man" – inspired by Captain Kirk's wooing persona). His incessant talk of slick cars and Florida beach parties bored and irritated me, but fortunately, he didn't expect me to say much. I could just stand with my beer, my cigarette, my long hair, my tight sweater, and nod as if he were interesting. Nothing more was required. Soon enough he invited me to his single dorm room to show me his jazz record collection – a ploy so cliché that even *I*, whose sexual experience to date involved screwdriver handles, could call it obvious. But my mission right here and right now, to change that experience, took priority. I played dumb.

Clayton – the boy – considered himself quite the Don Juan. Midway through beers from his ultra-cool mini-fridge and against a backdrop of Stanley Clarke, he claimed to have already had sex with half a dozen girls. I admitted being a virgin, at which he laughed. "Virgins make lousy lays!" he scoffed. "Most of 'em just lie there." He cocked a vacant ogle toward the ceiling.

This I found vastly reassuring: it gave me permission to just lie there, ogle the ceiling, and be a lousy lay. Which I did. This was perhaps the *only* intercourse I had in college without faking an earth-shattering orgasm. I was way too nervous to try for any more than just getting this business over with.

The worst part, I felt, was getting naked in front of a boy. I mean, you spend your whole life making sure nobody so much as glimpses your undies, and then – boom – you're supposed to just *take* them *off*? And then he touches where you're not even supposed to touch *yourself*? It didn't make any sense. How could you be supposed to do both?

I'd never seen a penis. Like a lot of girls, I had little interest in changing that. Penises were – well – more or less a pissing organ that dangled from the body like some extra intestine. I associated them with dried urine. Testicles in particular looked like they belonged *inside* the body. If men had gallbladders in their armpits, would they expect girls to go wild about those, too?

Fortunately, this nineteen-year-old Casanova knew exactly what to do, so within twelve hours of my arrival on campus, I checked "lose virginity" off my to-do list. What a relief! The morning after, I'd stained Clayton's sheets and wondered if my period had come early. "That's your popped cherry," he explained matter-of-factly. I marveled that there'd been anything left to pop. After all, I'd stuck everything but the kitchen sink up there.

Since next on my normalcy to-do list was "acquire a boyfriend," and since Clayton was most conveniently positioned for it, I ended up staying with him for over a year. Granted, he was *literally* the first Vassar guy I'd talked to for more than five minutes, but we'd had sex, so we must be intimate. Did I *like* him? Not particularly. But the fact that he soon cheated on me with a big-boobed girl, then asked me back after she dumped him, definitely increased his attractiveness. Romantic turmoil was another empty checkbox on my list. I thought back on huddles of popular high school girls gathered to console the one with the broken heart. Finally, I, too had one of those – not a huddle of friends but a broken heart, at least. I climbed a high tower in the library and gazed down at the drop in sweet despondency. Would I ever love again?

The urge to tie myself up was blocked for now. When I wasn't with Clayton, my roommate's presence, or at least possible entrance, rendered it impossible. Intercourse with Clayton never so much as mildly aroused me, but at least I had a real sex life. One time at his parents' house, he fell asleep inside me, and as he snored I managed to use my abdominal muscles to reach a meager orgasm, having just faked a cataclysmic one minutes before. Now I could check off "orgasm during sex," too. My progress was excellent.

The only flaw in my execution, as I saw it, was my lack of a clique. I'd made casual friends all over the place – in my classes, in the dorms, and at parties – but none of them fit together to provide a solid circle of friends. It's not that I didn't have opportunities to settle down within a given group – I did. But I was still too obsessed with amassing popularity *in general* to limit myself. Friendships, to my mind, were like investments; you wanted a varied portfolio. Visibility was key. And so I went around meeting and befriending, acting chipper with the class leaders, logy with the stoners, and brusque with the jocks – however *you* were, *I* was.

And it worked. After just a few weeks, I knew people at Vassar. I could always find tables to join in the dining hall where no one got up and left. Sometimes I even had to weigh which group was more popular.

Vaguely I sensed that not everyone lived this way. For example, my new roommate (who swapped places with my old roommate because the latter had made a big stink about my smoking a pack a day in our non-smoking room) seemed a lovely, attractive, and potentially popular girl when she moved in. A granola chick in Nordic sweaters, she played a lot of Joni Mitchell and made sweeping, confessional statements about herself. "I worry my feet stink." "I highlight just to convince myself I've read stuff." Tragically, however, Jenny decided within only a week of moving in that she aspired to become a lesbian.

What social suicide! Here my greatest fear was that I might be a closet lesbian, while Jenny was entertaining the idea of lezzing out *on purpose* because she'd befriended another pair of fellow lesbian wanna-be's down the hall. They'd all attended some lesbian meetings in the Women's Center and decided they wanted to love women. Joni M. now traded off with Joan Armatrading, Cris Williamson, and some album called "Lesbian Concentrate," while Jenny read Audre Lorde and let her calf hair grow out to downright Hobbit-like furriness.

The oddest part was, none of them wanted to be lesbians *together.* I mean, there they all were; it seemed pretty handy. Instead, Jenny would loll around on her bed cushions with her lesbian magazines saying, "*Some*day I'll meet the woman of my dreams!" She didn't even try to hide her preoccupation from her parents, who listened obediently to "Lesbian Concentrate" during visits and perused lesbian books while Jenny explained the basics of gender theory.

One morning when I came back from Clayton's, Jenny excitedly described how the three of them had borrowed a speculum from the Women's Center to actually look inside each other's vaginas! What a speculum might be – I pictured a sort of endoscope

– I had no idea, but even so I couldn't wait to tell Clayton. He seemed to keep me safely normal, the way he mocked them as "lezzies" and jeered out things like "mucha-muncha-muncha!"

Deep down, I felt ashamed for mocking my friends. I understood that what Jenny and the others were seeking was their own truth. They were largely unconcerned with how others perceived them or how they scored in popularity. Instead, they wanted to explore their own ideas and beliefs and – yes – even desires. And they were doing it right out in the open, where everyone could see.

My whole life, by contrast, was a sham. All I ever did was try to get good grades, get people to like me, and fret about what else I was supposed to do. That, and I drank a lot. Toward the end of freshman year, however, I discovered *cheating*.

Floyd was in my *Chaucer to Pope* English class, which ran all year. A flirtatious rake, he had black hair and blue eyes that sparked his risqué remarks into compliments. Like so many boys in college, he fucked around like a bunny sampling clover. In my eyes, he rated as high on the popularity scale as had the crown princes of high school. The only difference was, he invited me to do things. We smoked hash with his two roommates, or went on dorm room calls together, looking up more hash.

One evening while Clay was pulling an all-nighter in the library, I met Floyd at the campus pub where he introduced some non-Vassar "friends," two pot-dealing fat boys à la Lynyrd Skynyrd who owned a car. We all got wasted and I ended up many miles from Vassar alone in a bar booth with Floyd and making out as if for the first time in my life. The room spun around the blind sensations of our kissing while awareness of where the hell I was caromed in and out of focus. And at last it was happening: I actually *wanted* to slop kisses all over another person! I cannot convey to you how amazed I was to feel between my legs the lost ache of the bondage trance – *even though I wasn't by myself.* What I'd feared might never happen was actually coming to pass: I wanted somebody, and a boy to boot. I was normal – a healthy, horny girl!

The problem of roommates kept us from having sex that night, but a few weeks later Clayton pulled another all-nighter, so I went out with Floyd again – and this time, he had a room all picked out. What we did for the evening, I don't recall. Memory kicks in with us climbing the fire escape ladder of Jewett Tower late at night, drunk off our asses, in the midst of a blustery and torrential spring rain. We had to climb as high as the eighth floor, where Floyd could let us in through the window to a single room his friend had vacated for the weekend. I had no coat, and my tiered cotton peasant skirt billowed up around me with each new gust until it got too soaked, while the raindrops pelted my face and flattened my hair. Wet iron from the rusty ladder rungs colored my hands and filled my nostrils, and each look down to the campus lights brought on a swirl of vertigo.

If only high school could see me now! This was living! In a movie rife with action, adventure, and daring, I was at last the star. Yes, falling and dying would suck. But if I made it, I could frame this moment and display it forever on the mantelpiece of my life. I could know that I had on this night, with this boy, without fear or limitations, been *cool*. Cool was everything – as everyone knew. It was the confidence to wield power, the freedom to dominate life. And it was mine at last: alcohol had let me claim it.

Floyd jimmied the window up; we jumped in and kissed, soaked to the skin. We fell to the bed and wrestled for some minutes until it became evident that Floyd could not rise to the occasion. Too much booze and cold, perhaps? We were still trying unsuccessfully when the door opened and in bustled the room's surprised owner, who'd known nothing of Floyd's plans. The poor guy apologized for entering his own room and left us to resume our efforts. I had then a distaste for blowjobs, so I didn't volunteer, and poor Floyd didn't ask.

In the end I set the alarm of my enormous plastic digital watch for 5:00 AM, just a few hours away. We both had an English paper due at 10:00, an essay on the 18th century poet, Alexander Pope. I woke in the dark and left Floyd sleeping. Minutes later, in the fluorescent living room of my dormitory, I brewed a pot of coffee in the little kitchen, lit up my Salems, and worked at my manual typewriter. The triumph of coolness from the night before emboldened my writing. Life was the shit, and Pope knew it! I'd written about half a rough draft already, and momentum carried me through to the end with no white-out.

Floyd showed up for class late and puffy-eyed. He had no essay, and I remember his hangdog, betrayed look as I handed in mine. At our next class, the elderly professor, Mr. Mace, read mine aloud as an example of excellence. My essay's final six words were "...a part congruent to the whole." I recall how he slowed down to let these words resonate throughout the vaulted space of his ornate, 19th century classroom, his eyes gliding from student to student with a grave, dated look of triumph.

Floyd shot me a glance across the classroom. I'd been exposed as a geek, and he desired me no more. Still, I would not be dumped: he was the only boy in the world, I thought, whom I could genuinely desire.

I worked out sexually over that summer to build up my seduction skills. That is to say, when I was invited to Green Lake by a handsome thirty-something man who'd asked me for change in the mall where I worked, I met him there and sunbathed with him for an hour or so. He'd cleverly arrived by bus and told me of a bottle of wine chilling back at his apartment, so I agreed to drive him home. Approaching my parents' Studebaker we found, tucked under one of the wipers, a note that said in labored print: "You are a very beautiful woman. I saw you park and couldn't help hoping I might meet you." As if on cue a husky, bearded motorcycle man stalked up from nowhere and held out a meaty palm for his note. "I shoulda known," he sighed, with a concessionary nod to the mall change dude.

Utterly thrilled and breathlessly blushing, I tried to act as if this happened so often it bored me. Back at his place we drank the wine quickly, until I shattered a wineglass and laughed with embarrassed hysteria, fell off the couch, and we had sex on the rug. Screw birth control. My parents happened to be out of town that night, so I slept over.

The mall guy worked at 6:00, so I said goodbye as he got in the shower. His quaint apartment building faced a portion of Woodland Park thickly misted with summer dew, and I felt zestfully alive as I walked alongside it, savoring a surreal clarity, marveling at the crisp details of a world unaffected by all these immense changes in me. High school could so kiss my ass, now – finally! I was a woman! I'd just had spontaneous sex! This was what you called a meaningless affair. Check! Check! Check!

Zelda scolded me the instant I came in. She'd waited up, worried like crazy. Out all night with some *stranger* from the mall?! What, had I had sex?! I waved her off. The tables had turned now, indeed, and the boss was back! Zelda, despite many close scrapes, was still a virgin.

I dated the mall guy all summer. Of course I still tied myself up now and again, because how else was I going to have an orgasm? What the sex served was my ego. The mall guy confessed to me that he, too, had recently suffered from impotency, but that my incredible sexiness had cured him. Was that not an A in sexiness? I'd already informed him of the last day I could see him, two weeks before Clay's visit, and on that last date he all but asked me to marry him. Sorry, I said. Not happening.

Upon returning to Vassar I promptly broke up with Clayton to pursue Floyd outright, confident that I could overcome his disinterest. But ever since the flaccid Pope fiasco, Floyd was just not into me. After one daytime quickie in the campus townhouse he now shared with four boys, he gave me the slip. I'd often show up at the sliding glass door of that townhouse, where I'd ask one of his housemates if I could leave yet another note. They'd learned my name already by taking multiple phone messages, but also knew Floyd had all the girls he could handle.

One rainy night I absolutely *had* to find Floyd and make him want me. Feelings of worthlessness flooded me, and I felt he alone could change that. Among the campus townhouses I wandered from party to party in search of him, getting drunker, more soaked, and more baked at each stop. I'd ask virtually anyone if they knew Floyd, or of other parties where he might be. Long past midnight I backtracked to the party that had seemed to display the highest percentage of cool people and sat on the carpet in my waterlogged jacket, knowing no one. Still watching for Floyd, I kept slurping beer and toking off dubies while a new album, the B52's, blasted the room. My hair was flattened, make-up running, eyes reddened and small from pot. I got astoundingly fucked up. Yet I remember – and will never forget – what happened.

I could not get the kitchen sink to work. Pull the handle up, turn it this way, push the fucker down – what the fuck? Was it fuckin' broken? I kept trying, asking for help from nearby people who didn't hear or care, and was already humiliated when I looked up to see Zodiac, one of Vassar's coolest celebrities, pointing me out to his friends. He'd made a joke, I could see. Derisive laughter. Another comment and they all laughed again.

I shouted some complaint about the damn sink, slurring preposterously, but the music was too loud. Zodiac shook his head of dark, curly locks and turned away. His huge eyes made him incredibly handsome, and he knew it. Famous for insane partying and drug dealing, he had everything – power, rank, and more friends than he knew what to do with. Yet he had to shit on me, straggling as I was on the brink of failure.

It was the high school library all over again. Before my tears exploded I fled the party in the pouring rain and slumped across the muddy grass circle toward my dorm. I didn't care if my shoes sank in or my clothes got soaked, because all my hard-earned coolness trophies had tumbled off the mantelpiece. Mine was counterfeit cool, and everyone could see through to the geeky loser underneath. Floyd had; his housemates had; and now this motherfucker Zodiac and his fucking buddies had rubbed it in my face.

I cursed him. Why should the strong pick on the weak? He didn't need to step on my neck to raise himself higher. Yet these feelings themselves were poison, they could drag me down to the lonely prison where from which I'd only just escaped. This thing that was wrong with me, I would never escape it. I cried as only a drunk cries, without a shred of restraint.

Would you believe me if I told you the following Friday night I was dancing with my friend Jessie at the campus bar when I noticed Zodiac and company at a table nearby? His seat faced the dance floor, and those gorgeous, popular eyes were trained on it. An audacious plan of revenge – fantastic yet plausible – came to me. My hair, make-up, and outfit all looked sexy. Dancing, I turned it on – I *was* a dancer, twelve years of ballet. In fact, just the summer before I'd entered a dance contest sponsored Seattle's KJR and, with a boy I'd asked to partner me, scored the $100 first prize. Now I smiled lazily at Jessie, barely cutting a glance or two in Zodiac's direction. I could snake a beat through every joint in my body, pulsing out rhythms like they came from inside – a fact that he was beginning to notice. When the song finished, I dared myself to mount the steps in his direction and sit down near him, angled slightly away. I gathered all my sexiness, turned toward him, and brought a cigarette to my lips.

Did he have a light?

Everything hinged on whether he'd recognize me as the girl with the sink. Those eyes – piercingly clear and gushed over by so many girls – met mine. I weathered this precarious moment when disdain might break over his features, when he might scoff at my Lauren Bacall imitation and laugh, "*You?!* You're that trashed clown from last week!"

It came and went. The boy had no clue.

"Yeah, I do," he murmured.

A few hours later, near the path to the townhouses, a breathless Zodiac swung me against a wall for yet another round of ferocious kissing.

I squirmed away. "I can't go home with you, I *can't*!"

"Please," he breathed. "Why not?"

"Becau-uzzz! I'm on my period!"

"Listen: I don't give a shit," he said meaningfully, and kissed me again. Half into my mouth he breathed, "You can have a goddamn baby in my bed if you want to. Just come back with me. Please… please…"

And I have to say that, campus idol or no, Zodiac was indeed better equipped and more adept than any of the previous three. I still faked orgasms, but at least now they were plausible.

How long, I wondered back in my dorm room, should I set for this thing? What I intended was to make Zodiac fall hopelessly in love with me, so that I could dump him and pulverize his popular heart. I pulled out my syllabi from various classes. Midterms were still more than two weeks away. Even if I put in every night with him, dumping him by Halloween would leave me ample time to write my papers and study for tests. Grades, after all, had to come first. My father was breaking his back to send me here.

This role demanded a lot of dedication. The ideal girlfriend for Zodiac was ready to party at any hour. Bowie blared through our wake-up bong hits. Sex on 50-yard-line at 2:00 AM left my back muddy. Quaaludes and pitchers of Kamikazes with the brazenly defiant toast, "To Karen Anne Quinland!" did not kill us. And there was Friendly's. Imagine Zodiac with a weakness for hitting up Friendly's in the middle of the night, claiming it was his or my birthday so the waiters would bring a free sundae and sing to us – which we pulled off at least twice apiece. He'd gone there for every birthday as a kid – the happiest times of his life. He was still a little boy inside; I could see that. He told me he'd grown up in the trail of an airport runway, and when his family moved away, he couldn't sleep without that comforting scream of jets. He'd been diagnosed as hyperactive and put on Ritalin. Unbelievably, his real name was Clayton.

I listened with endless fascination and spoke little about myself, since I feared betraying my uncool past. Sober, we wrestled in his townhouse living room – really wrestled because I had bragged about being the champ of my fifth-grade class, my father having taught me. We grappled under a table; something went crash; we would laugh too hard to keep on until one of us rallied, "Motherfuckahhhhh!" And we'd be off again, sweating away.

His groupie roommates watched from a safe distance, amused, I think, by the sheer wattage of our energy. They were used to Zodiac's extremes. At the top of the stairs, for instance, remained a large pile of books, charred and waterlogged. These they had ritualistically set fire to some weeks before in drunken rebellion, which brought the fire department. Studying was not high on their list of activities. They never guessed how high it stood on mine.

The plan was working – I could see it in his eyes, hear it in his voice. He'd found a girl who could keep up with him, match him drink for drink and hit for hit, clamber on Dumpsters and throw shit at him – this chick was wild as Sid's Nancy. There were things he said late at night, or when we first woke that let me know: he was in this for the long haul.

And good thing, too, because Halloween was almost here! I knew I couldn't keep this stuff up much longer, anyway. Being that cool was kind of exhausting.

My dormitory put on a huge Halloween party. I dressed as a gypsy with Cleopatra makeup, ribbons braided into my hair, and bangle bracelets through my hoop earrings. Zodiac had told me to expect him around nine. But he was late.

I drank hard to settle my nerves, spending most of my time in line for the kegs. Between refills, though, I was having a hard time finding people to hang with. Having lived in Jewett Hall for only two months, and with the majority of my focus elsewhere, I hadn't made many friends. Only one girl, Elizabeth, who lived two doors down from me, had extended her friendship and, despite my lukewarm reception, taken an almost maternal interest in me. But she had her own clique of friends here tonight, and I didn't feel bold enough to break in.

I noticed Floyd's housemates standing together in a clump – minus the elusive Floyd, of course – so I went over. The four of them had a great story to tell: they'd broken into the costume room of the Drama Department and stolen Shakespearean costumes – only *borrowed*, they insisted (though I doubt the department ever saw them again). Eager to describe their adventure to anyone who would listen, all four focused on me at once.

Largest of the group was a muscleman with a touch of Brando about him. He'd always seemed to resent my inquiries about Floyd, but now he was a happy drunk, his velvet Tudor hat sliding down over one eye until he would catch it just in time. His name was Jim Reilly, but the others called him just Reilly. After a while another girl, cute and petite, sidled up, and the boys dropped me in favor of a fresh audience, so I floated off.

Finally, at about 10:30, I noticed a commotion near the entrance to the main lobby. Zodiac was *in the house*. He and his entourage had arrived dressed as rock stars. I recognized only the guy in Kiss make-up before Zodiac took my attention. David

Bowie, or rather, Ziggy Stardust. How thoroughly he'd gone to town! He had on a reddish Ziggy wig, heavily made-up eyes and a powdered face, in some kind of spandex costume. Friends greeted him with hoots, dug the look, laughed at the lengths he'd gone to. Bowie was god, Zodiac was fond of saying. And now he himself looked like one to me, the way such throngs of people naturally flocked to him.

And to think – this campus icon was in love with me! Loser Louisa. Even when he was out of view, I could track his movements in the crowd like some kind of rip tide. I entertained, not for the first time, the possibility that I might reign from now on as Queen Zodiac if I just became his girlfriend for real. We could make such entrances *together.*

But my syllabi came to mind, the papers and tests. To ace them I'd have to buckle down, and such acing was the religion of my family – the only code of honor I'd been given. My parents loved me. I couldn't betray them. Between my twin gods of academia and coolness, I knew which was the graven image. Zodiac hailed from the circus; I belonged in the library. The circus was more fun, but I didn't want to live there. I watched from the steps near the elevator, frustrated to see him vanish into an adjoining room. I would go pee one more time, then track him down and get this thing over with.

He hugged me happily and apologized that he couldn't kiss me right without fucking up his face. Really, he was strikingly beautiful. False eyelashes – he'd even managed those. I said only that we needed to talk, not here but up in my room. Mystified, he followed into the elevator. I felt a cutthroat lack of mercy as we rose, summoning to mind the pain of crossing the muddy grass circle. My room, no more than an oversized closet, was on the fourth floor at the top of a staircase wide enough for two girls in hoop skirts to walk abreast, next to a room renowned for having once been Meryl Streep's. I sat on the green bed quilt Zelda had sewn me, while Zodiac took my swivel chair and prepared to hear what was up.

I said, "I'm sorry, but I need to end this."

"End what?"

"Our relationship."

"You need to *end* it? Is something *wrong*? Did I do something?"

"No, nothing. It's just not right."

"*What*'s not right?" He wasn't going down easy. "You're, like, the most amazing girl I've ever hung out with. *Right* is exactly how it feels."

"Not for me. I'm just..." I pondered how much to disclose, "...different from you. I need to do well in my classes, and I've been acting like I don't care."

He tried promising me time to study, more time to myself, anything I wanted, but I shook my head until he grew silent.

I wrapped it up. "Bottom line is, we've had fun, but I need to get back to work."

"Really." His focus seemed to shift to the air just in front of him – a skillful rendition of being stunned, I thought. Then he threw me for a loop. Those two enormous dark eyes, beneath their thick, glued-on Ziggy Stardust eyelashes, actually pooled and spilled over with tears.

I'd not foreseen this. There was no way to contain him. He sobbed, his whole body heaving, while streaming tears melted stripes through the white powder on his face. He wiped them, ruining everything. He didn't care. The voice coming up his throat frightened me. It was too real, too genuine, the voice of that boy who loved jet screams and Friendly's. He kept asking what had happened, what he had done, trying to draw back the girl I had seemed. Whether he spoke the word "love," I can't say for sure. In any case, the word was evident in his pain, his pleading.

"You need to go," I told him. "Right now."

I herded him out somehow. I recall how utterly ridiculous he looked standing in the hallway as I shut the door – in spandex, wig askew, make-up scrambled. I sat on my bed a few minutes with my heart racing.

I'd won. Louisa had won. I was cooler than Zodiac.

As soon as I was sure he'd gone, I stepped out to pee yet again. Unexpectedly, the girls' bathroom door slammed open and Zodiac came out, face to face with me. He'd not tried to save his make-up but had regained his composure nonetheless. He flashed me a look beyond reproach, closer to warding off evil, before swooping down the staircase at a run.

For a brief moment, I sensed there might be more depth to Zodiac than I'd ever imagined. From the rail above the open stairwell, I heard his steps recede with mixed feelings. This was supposed to be my moment of glory. "Die, fucking popular people!" I projected down the stairs after him, as I'd imagined. But something was tainting my triumph. Except for the sink incident,

Zodiac had always been kind to me. He didn't plot his popularity at others' expense. He just naturally attracted friends with his spontaneous, open nature. Had I miscalculated in some way?

Was it possible Zodiac didn't *deserve* what I'd done?

My heart twinged... but I refused to look deeper. *Remember the mud, remember walking in the rain.* Rejection, humiliation – it was *his* turn to feel them. This was a blow, not at Zodiac personally, but at the armies of cool people all over the world inflicting pain on social runts. Fuck them all! Let them feel what it was like!

I went home that night with the muscleman in the slipping Tudor hat.

Top: Clowning with Jenny at Vassar; bottom:
Junior year, taken with self-timer at the summer cabin

6: I BECOME A DESERT COWGIRL

This is what you learned in college: A man desires the
satisfaction of his desire; a woman desires the condition
of desiring.

> -Pam Houston
> *"How to Talk to a Hunter"*

What should a girl do in a relationship? My answer at nineteen, if I could have been honest, would be A) efface herself completely to please her boyfriend, yet B) simultaneously project a mysterious, entrancing, and irresistible feminine energy known as her "ways." Billy Joel's "She's Always a Woman" provided a template for this ineffable (or highly ef-able) feminine quality:

> *She can kill with a smile*
> *She can wound with her eyes*
> *She can ruin your faith with her casual lies*
> *And she only reveals what she wants you to see*
> *She hides like a child,*
> *But she's always a woman to me*

George Harrison's "Something" offered a similar blueprint for the intriguing, seductive temptress I needed to be. Trouble was, if ninety percent of your brain is busy figuring out what your mysterious, entrancing feminine ways ought to be right now, you tend to fuck it up. I always did, at least.

If only I could have really *believed* in my feminine powers I might have pulled it off, but I was trying to build a Ferrari from popsicle sticks. College boys liked to claim the power of the pussy reigned supreme and could bring men to their knees. In reality though, every girl on campus had one – even the cafeteria ladies! So it seemed to me that unless you could pull off that alluring, entrancing ways thing, a pussy held about as much power as an ear canal.

I can honestly say that Jim Reilly, the costume thief, turned out to be my first love. He was Marlon Brando meets Holden Caulfield – often all tangled up inside but determined to arrive at a rock-solid truth. Plus he was hesitant to get into a relationship with me, which made him vastly attractive. The fact that I'd been with his playboy housemate, Floyd, or that dope Clayton, drove him crazy. He insisted I burn all my photographs of Clayton and the mall guy – which, sadly, I did.

Most of all, the fact that I'd slept with Zodiac tortured him, because Zodiac stood for the sort of rock star, party-hyped cool he despised. Of course I couldn't tell Reilly the real reason – that I'd only *pretended* to be dating Zodiac in order to avenge myself for the night of the sink. "How could you *be* with that jerk?" he'd complain in anguish. But his mysterious and darkly magic woman would only shake her brunette tresses with a wan smile, concealing her misty motives ("Duh! You're *supposed to* have sex with the cool people! He's practically *famous*!").

In truth, Reilly's disdain for Zodiac dismayed me. All my work to gain that coolness trophy counted *against* me with him. That was the trouble with coolness! Unlike test scores, coolness was a relative concept. There was no set scale, no rubric by which you could excel. Even more confusing, if Reilly didn't base his coolness scale on popularity, then on what could he possibly be basing it?

Physically, Reilly stood at about six feet, weighed close to 200 pounds, and once borrowed a pair of my size 8 shorts to go swimming. Can you picture that? His features were classic Irish, a broad face with crescent eyes and dimples, and he had a slight stutter – of the halting silence variety – that vanished when he drank. But what attracted me most to Reilly, what caused me to stay with him for three years while cultivating a martyred sense of neglect, was his moral certainty. Sure, Clayton had considered his Jewish family superior and Zodiac had sworn that Bowie was God while my old roommate worshipped Audre Lorde – everyone had an angle. But Reilly's sense of right and wrong was more powerful, evolved, and definite than any I'd encountered before or have since. That was precisely what I lacked.

Emblematic of this instinct was a large rubber stamp standing at the ready on his desk, primed to print the word BULLSHIT! I remember him sitting at his desk in nothing but tighty-whiteys beneath his enormous poster of Hemingway, stamping whatever text he felt deserved it – sometimes all over library books or reserve list photocopies – if the author aroused a certain ire in him: BULL-SHIT! He'd stamp at all angles in a frenzy, barking out the word as if to drive back an army of peons: "BULLSHIT! BULLSHIT! BULLSHIT!!"

I feared getting stamped, myself. Because no one knew better than I what a complete phony I was in every move I made. The conviction behind Reilly's judgments captivated me even before I loved him. All my self-worth came from graded performances, convincing people to like me, earning others' admiration. And here was a boyfriend qualified to judge. A gold star from Reilly would be worth all the 4.0's in the world.

He'd spent his teen years in the desert hills of New Mexico, a Chicago transplant who took to the countless desert acres open for driving, shooting, and drinking. His parents had met at Harvard and Radcliffe, both on scholarships. His father, once a big shot New York reporter, still wrote for big names like *Life*, *Time*, and *People*, while his mother showed photographs in Santa Fe galleries. Clearly they had imprinted their son with an ethic for living, an internal compass that guided his choices toward genuine value.

With envy I studied his assessments of everyone and everything, hoping to learn. Reilly himself was an odd mix. He excelled in courses that intrigued him, but slacked off in those laced with BULLSHIT. Weightlifting had built him up to an imposing physique, thinly layered over with beer fat and sporting the occasional buffalo boots and cowboy hat, yet I remember how he fretted one day over placement of a new Matisse poster in his room, moving it several times, as well as relocating a digital image of two New York City Ballet dancers. The eye should start here, then follow this line upwards...

What. Does that strike you as faggy interior decorator shit? You think? Then go fuck yourself! You're *BULLSHIT!* Fuckin' Neanderthal piss-ant, go live in a goddamn toilet. You wouldn't know beauty if it bit you in the ass.

~

About a month into our relationship, Reilly almost stamped me after I went on a drinking binge without him. My friend Jessie and I had gone to McAuley's, a townie bar off campus, where we got quite soused. All our money spent, we came up with the idea to recruit sponsors for a shot-slamming contest, easy enough for two good looking girls. We faced off at a small table with five shots of Jack and a chaser pint lined up before each of us, waited through a count-down, and were off. I don't remember who won, though I do recall feeling shocked halfway through my chaser to realize I was losing momentum. Louisa of the hollow leg? Incredible! I took tremendous pride in my drinking capacity, so this was a blow to my ego. I couldn't see Jessie over my pint glass, so I just went on chugging as best I could. Which of us won, I don't remember.

So now we were plowed, us girls, plowed as hell, and fuckin' Floyd shows up, wouldn't ya know. I hung on him a bit, but clearly his eyes were on Jessie – new territory and shit. No big, I had a boyfriend, anyway! I lost my purse and crawled around under the red laminate tables full of people, which was so much fun I forgot all about the purse and made a game of untying people's shoelaces.

Everybody seemed so damned *surprised* to discover a girl down there on her hands and knees – what's the big fuckin' deal? Why do people always make such a big fuss about the floor, like, "Oh, the floor's dir-tee! Don't put your *hands* on it, don't *eat* stuff off it!" What a buncha pussies! I'd show 'em.

In the wee morning hours Floyd invited Jessie back to his room, so I tagged along. The cold air snapped me out of blackout, I guess, because I remember the walk back across the frigid parking lot. Weren't we all three friends? Wasn't this so fun? I kept taking Floyd's other arm, but he was all about Jessie.

"You guys wanna see my ballet recital from when I was seven? I 'member *egzackly* how it started. No shit. Watch this. Watch, okay?"

And I was off in my wooden clogs: *Chassé sauté, chassé* – BOOM. Down I went. The side of my head slammed the asphalt. But asphalt, really, was a lot cushier than most people thought. It had a lot of air in it, actually, in those tiny pockets between the stones, and they added up. People always made such a big *deal* out of falling down! Josie and Floyd were freaking out – all that oh my god are you okay stuff.

"Yeah, yeah, lemme just show you. No, I wannu! Okay, it went..." *Chassé sauté, chassé* – BOOM. Down again.

That's all I remember, except one little flash where I'm knocking on the locked door of Floyd's bedroom, trying the door-knob. Weren't we all friends? It seemed kind of mean. I wandered into Reilly's room and lay down. At least I *thought* it was Reilly's room. His housemate, Matt, who later said he'd wondered for a second if he'd gotten *really* lucky, carried me to Reilly's bed.

I awoke in broad daylight, fully dressed on top of Reilly's purple quilt. I recall looking down and realizing I still had both clogs on, even though my feet hung off the edge of the mattress. Must not have moved around a lot. But there was no sign of Reilly.

I went downstairs where I found him at the kitchen table with a cigarette and cup of coffee, not looking happy at all. He sat silent for some time, judging while I tried to joke away the tension. He'd just started to say something when I had to go puke. The toilets in this house were, as you can imagine, utterly disgusting. I had to kneel on piss-rumpled porn mags and touch god-knows-what on the bowl to steady myself. The puke came out white, as I duly reported when I came back in the kitchen, and I must not have looked so hot, because Reilly told me to just go home. One more quick puke and I started off.

I remember plodding across that same circle of lawn between his townhouse and the path to campus, just at a different angle than I'd crossed from Zodiac's. I tried to conceal the limp from my bruised knee and hip, but couldn't help fingering the scabby egg on one side of my head. I guess it had bled a bunch. My palms were flecked with pebbles. I wondered if Reilly were watching me through the sliding glass door.

But surely, surely this *had* to be feminine wiles stuff – ?! "Gets totally shitfaced but she's always a woman to me!" Bottom line: wasn't erratic, out of control drunken misbehavior what *everyone* respected deep down? Wasn't it as renegade cool as you could get? Then why was he so disapproving? It was those damn inscrutable standards of his, again – that right and wrong business.

When at last we talked, it turned out to be not so much my drinking itself, as that he wanted nothing to do with a woman he couldn't trust. I don't think he used the word, but what he was talking about was integrity. Most of me was decent, he said, but streaked through the grain of my character like rot through a wood whorl was something morally ambivalent – my weakness for "dark and smoky rooms," he called it.

Listening to Reilly's analysis of my faults, I experienced a profound conversion. I don't mean I resolved to behave better. Rather, I recast my entire schema for who I was in the world. It was more like being born again. I realized everything I'd ever believed about living, all that my parents had ever taught me, and all that I'd pieced together on my own, was wrong.

Some people sold their souls for what was showy and hyped. They were the poseurs. Other simply wandered adrift, filling their sails with whatever prevailing breezes came along. They were the flakes. But there existed certain people who stood solid with pure characters founded upon what was real and good. I had been a mix of the first two, caught up in the gusts of whatever I'd perceived as glitzy and cool. My quest to accumulate friends as tokens of self-worth now revealed itself to me as empty and cheap. To join Reilly, I would have to abandon all that. From this moment on, I swore to myself, I would cultivate loyalty to authentic and moral living. *That* was what would render me "always a woman" to Reilly. I would become real.

Over Christmas break, in an era when long distance calls were costly, Reilly sent me a letter from New Mexico. In it he described what he wanted: to have all of me, to know the darkness inside my marrow and the blood that coursed through my thighs… Every time I reread those words, they struck like a gust of hot wind in my body. I went around the house holding them in my mind more covertly than a stashed toothbrush. I was desired. I was *desired*. What did Mom or Dad or Zelda or *anyone* know of a power like that?

Unfortunately, I have few memories of sex with Reilly. Of course he was quick, as were all the boys at this age, leaving me at most five minutes to amp up my faked crescendos. I recall walking into my own room one afternoon to find him sitting at my desk. He'd been drinking at a friend's where someone nailed a pair of panties to the wall, and he'd left to come here. I remember the slightly self-conscious fixation in his eyes as he stood up, experimenting in his own mind with lust and where it took him.

But mostly I recall that, after the first few months, there was never enough sex to keep me secure. I wanted him to want me more than he did. Sex was my proof, my receipt for his esteem.

~

Now pretty much everything I said or did had to be filtered for Reilly's approval. Friendships faded. Habits were dropped. I switched from Salems to Marlboros. For years Zelda and I had spoken to each other in an accent we called "dumb talk." It had evolved from our mocking the old lady neighbor at our summer cabin, exaggerating her clipped, curtailed Mid-western accent to an absurd degree. We said "yull" for yes, "fixin' t'," and "warsh" – a whole slew of shifts. Overhearing it during our phone calls, Reilly winced. That was baby talk, he said, and it had to go. He *hated* that shit. Of course, when Reilly and his brothers joked around, they adopted a hick sort of hillbilly accent. All Reilly's housemates used it now, too. *That* was funny. Dumb talk was not, so it was banished as BULLSHIT.

Zelda wrote a me long, pain-filled letter saying that all my thoughts and energy went to *him* now, and that my indifference hurt her worse than anything. Navigating the rich kid school was a nightmare, and she needed my love. She described a dream where she discovered her face was misshapen and oozing puss. I called from a dormitory phone and tried to reassure her outside Reilly's hearing. I felt the truth in what she said, and it tore at me, but what could I do? Pleasing Reilly, or at least my idea of him, had become my new religion.

Gradually I morphed into an urban cowgirl, one who sat up late at night drinking longnecks and smoking Marlboros, shootin' shit with the boys in TH A-7 (their unit) until empties, bottle caps, butt-filled crockery covered the kitchen table. I went by my last name, or phallic terms related to it, and even owned up to never having heard the term 'pecker' before college, which dumbfounded the lot of them. Floyd moved out soon after the McAuley's night, and Jack moved in. Jack was a redhead who acted and dressed like a small town mechanic, wearing coveralls and pointing with his thumb, though Reilly pegged him as a rich boy. You could smell the wealth of his family in little things, Reilly said.

There's a certain distinction enjoyed by a girl who can drink with the guys when she realizes they're not holding back for her sake anymore. Not just with talk of cunts and cornholing, but in the general tenor. We'd all seen *Apocalypse Now* more than once and phrases from it peppered our speech, sometimes with purpose, sometimes just for the hell of it: "Terminate... with extreme prejudice," "No method at all," or "smell of napalm in the morning," could be cued with only the vaguest association. "Saigon... shit," you might say if someone mentioned homework. *The Right Stuff* gave us other phrases. Everything good was "outstanding." To fuck up was to "screw the pooch." And "Fuckin' A" could be thrown out at any point.

At long last, I had a clique – even if not a soul on campus considered these boys popular. Check! I'd wanted for so long to belong somewhere and right here, in my seat at the kitchen table, I belonged. Sure, I was still acting, attempting to pull off this current persona, but so were all of us to an extent – even Reilly – pretending to be adults on our parents' dime.

We had a few adventures together. I recall crashing an exclusive "Black and White Party" to which none of us had been invited. We walked in and checked it out, looked at slightly askance because we weren't dressed right. On our way out of the dorm Matt nabbed a water fire extinguisher from the wall and snuck it past the White Angel, an old lady attendant who sat at the front desk. We opened fire on the party through an open basement window, spraying water into the screaming crowd of guests amid the balloons, black lights, and blaring Blondie. Someone else probably did most of the spraying, but I remember picking up the extinguisher after the others had run and spraying as wide a swath as I could reach through the opening, hammered and inspired, while the poor guests shrieked and fled for cover. Die, popular people! It was Jack who ran back and pried the thing out of my hands – "Jesus, Pecker!" – and we sprinted into the darkness.

I was a part of life at last.

~

Several times I went home with Reilly to the hills of Tesuque, a few miles outside Santa Fe. You drove past the tiny post office, then up a long, winding drive that climbed gradually, crossing over arroyos and leaving a plume of dust in your wake. I'm sure by now developers have destroyed it, but at the time the area had a lonesome charm.

The house itself sat among lots sparsely developed, with cactus and piñon trees dotting the arid landscape above, hillsides and cliffs reflecting chalky pink tones. For decades after I would dream about the place. It became magical to me, infused with a sort of sun-bleached *Bonanza* aura, charged with that sort of yearning you get from watching classic westerns on the big screen with their backgrounds of stunning grandeur. In those dreams, which haunted me for fifteen years, I'd always yearn to seduce Reilly, but he would dismiss me offhand as false and depraved, usually refusing even to speak with me.

In reality the main house was a tiny adobe with only one bedroom and bath. Each of the boys – his brothers stood six-four and six-six – had an outbuilding to himself, but every morning we all had to compete for the same tiny green bathroom, six people showering, shitting, and four shaving.

During Christmas Break of our third year together, Reilly and I stayed in the addition I'd helped to build the summer before, which Reilly had designed himself. One morning I was enjoying whatever Mrs. Reilly served up for breakfast (she served complete breakfasts to the whole family) when Reilly's father appeared unexpectedly in his bathrobe and dropped into a chair at the head of the table. He looked quite pale. His wife offered him a plate and he declined almost vehemently. Why he was hanging around, I couldn't quite figure, because he made no effort to join the conversation. In fact, he seemed ill. With my hair slicked back from the shower, I was dressed and chatting away with the brothers, but he puzzled me.

Brains are amazing things, because the thought struck from nowhere: *Did you get your diaphragm from the sink?* Shit. Like a toll of Big Ben, mortification struck. I rose without a word and darted to the bathroom. There it was, full of curdled spooge and jelly, set at a jaunty angle near the drain where I'd tossed it before stepping into the shower.

I beckoned Reilly frantically into the addition, but instead of sympathy, I got horror.

"How could you *do* that?! How could you *forget* your fuckin' diaphragm in the sink?"

He paced and carried on for some time, fingers clawing through his long hair.

"I can't believe it! My god – my *dad*!"

"Well, how do you think *I* feel?" I wailed.

He turned: "Then why the *fuck* did you go and leave it there?!"

I forced myself to work up tears. Devastated as I was, they just wouldn't flow. If there were ever a time I wanted to cry it was now, but to this day I remember that pitiless room and my barren struggle to produce false tears – even for myself.

Desperately, I strove to fake authenticity. I might be sitting in the living room with the family in the evening, the youngest Reilly picking a tune on his banjo while the rest read books. I could only pretend to read the same paragraph over and over because my brain was so ceaselessly scrambling for ways to make them like me. What funny remark could I make? What mood should I project? And yet I hated my self-consciousness. If the Reillys could read my mind, what a pathetic fraud they'd see! I was jealous of their ease, even as I turned pages I hadn't read. It was their fault, somehow, this whole nerve-wracking mess. In fact, I nursed a slow-growing resentment against the lot of them, even though none of them was ever anything but nice to me.

Mr. Reilly would hold forth at dinner with strong opinions of all sorts, delivered in explosions of eloquence like verbal fireworks.

"Trust me, you don't want to be a writer," he'd say. "Writers know a little about a lot of things, and a lot about nothing. I'm this far in my life and what am I good at? Nothing. Words. And what the hell are words? You can't fire rockets with 'em or peer through microscopes to unveil their mysteries. Any idiot can string them together, so you find yourself a constant bedfellow to mediocrity. Be good at something *concrete* – that's my advice."

In spite of myself, I had some fun times there. I did read many volumes of Louis L'Amour and acquire a taste for Merle Haggard and Loretta Lynn, plus I bought my own pair of mule skin boots and cowboy hat. I took long walks in the desert and explored remote canyon roads on a beater bicycle I oiled up. The Reilly boys taught me to shoot cans from about sixty feet under a bright, echoing sky, with both rifle and revolvers. We took camping trips that included multiple coolers of beer; often we'd just pull over at a roadside fire pit and unroll our sleeping bags, since hiking with a half-rack apiece doesn't go very far.

My fondest memories come from the summer we built that addition – me and Reilly rising early in the chill of morning, lighting up Marlboros, drinking coffee from chipped mugs we'd set steaming on the outdoor workbench. I pounded nails or cut rafter blocks with the circular saw, tipping back longnecks from about noon onward. My skin tanned and my hands toughened. I squinted and said "reckon" and "ain't." When I was on, it was pretty good living.

I do think Reilly and I shared a kind of love, young as we were. Neither knew what the hell we were doing, but each perceived something rare and vulnerable in the other. He liked to tease me with this Shel Silverstein song, "Put Another Log on the Fire," from an album he played frequently:

Now don't I let you wash the car on Sunday?
And don't I warn you when you're gettin fat?
Ain't I a-gonna take you fishin' with me someday?
Well, a man can't love a woman more than that.

Those lyrics proved a lot more apt than Billy Joel's, as it turned out.

Top: With Reilly at Winter Formal and A-7 party in 1980. Bottom: Building the addition in New Mexico, summer of 1981. I'm in charge of rafter blocks.

7: FLYING ON INFATUATION

Or else he would be in front of her, feel her gaze on
his back, and experience a thrill as from an ant
crawling down it. His bearing, of course, was that of
a person unaware of her presence, leading a free,
independent existence of his own...

-*Thomas Mann*
The Magic Mountain

During my senior year at Vassar I was determined to prove
Reilly wrong about those whorls of "dark, smoky rooms" in my
character: I would be true. Though he'd moved to Houston a
thousand miles away for grad school in architecture, our relationship was serious. My family knew it. All my housemates knew it.
When we got married, we'd prove it to everyone.

But why I wanted to marry him, or even continue to partner
with him, given that I couldn't speak a single candid word in his
presence – that I couldn't have told you. Relationships among the
young are frequently a foregone conclusion. But Reilly, I think, did
begin to question his commitment during his final months at Vassar.
During graduation week, in particular, he pulled away. The effect
on me, as on any resolute co-dependent, was to fortify my
determination to have him and to hone what was already a well-
developed taste for martyrdom.

That hurt I'd felt freshman year when Clayton cheated on me
turned out to be the bud of a delicious feeling. For someone who
fears herself innately bad or shameful, to be wronged brings
tremendous relief. When all the judges in our minds find that our
partner has treated us unjustly, yet we stoically and silently endure
their treatment, we can *know* for a little while that we are virtuous.
We have a merit to point to, evidence with which to counter all
those self-condemning voices.

Reilly was prone to jealousy. One night after a kegger at A-7 during which I'd talked with, in his opinion, too many guys, he got so angry he punched a dent in the wall above my head as I sat on his bed. I cowered and said nothing. Here was a new feeling, and a highly poignant one: to be threatened with abuse and suffer silently, knowing you were innocent. Reilly, who was such a towering figure of morality and right, had straight up wronged me. I retreated into meekness. Didn't that make me *immune* from Mom's accusations that I was a pushy big-sister bully? Immune from the sadism exposed in my drawings? Faced with Reilly's powerful anger, I had no voice. In my mom's book, you just couldn't *get* much more feminine. Being a victim was, in my twisted thinking, subtly sexy.

Reilly never became abusive, but his appreciation for me waned as time passed. He took to calling me "Tubes," which stood for Tubby Ruskie, because of my Russian grandfather and constant battle to stay thin. I hated the name, but said nothing. Often he'd stay out all night with the guys, then sober up to focus exclusively on his senior projects and admissions essays. I proofread and edited, but always with the underlying assumption that he was the brains and I the less gifted assistant. He often reached a nervous frenzy, claiming exhaustion, as some deadline loomed. When the pressure finally let up, he was keen to celebrate – but not with me. Throughout graduation week he stayed drunk, disappeared frequently, and kissed his buddy's girlfriend on the mouth instead of me after he got his diploma. I'd kept a bottle of champagne in the fridge for a week, waiting for the time when we'd toast our future. I'm not sure what happened to it.

To say, "You know what? I'm not happy with this. Maybe we should split up," was about as plausible to me as levitating. Instead I would *will* Reilly to see how I endured and sacrificed for him. *He* was the betrayer! *I* was the loyal one! Who's the one whorled with smoky rooms now, mister?

Thus as our year apart began, I was ready to survive off martyrdom perks and go the distance. Except, right from the first week, there came a boy…

My senior seminar class – Modernism – consisted of ten girls and two boys, Patrick and Kevin. Patrick nursed a crush on me. Tentative and shy, he was a tall, slim young man to whom I never gave a second thought. Kevin, on the other hand, had a Dustin Hoffman-like oversized head, shoulders that sloped like the eaves of a roof beneath the dark woolen overcoat he always wore – his "dead grandfather's coat," as he called it – and was only a few inches taller than I. But he also had cheekbones sharp as Bowie's beneath sleepy blue eyes and a natural-seeming ease combined with the odd habit of pointing out his own shortcomings for others' amusement. His was the opposite of my approach. While I tried to pull things off to impress people, nothing pleased Kevin more than exposing his own simple-minded motivations. "I'd hoped to seem clever by comparing Maisie to Daisy," he might say of James characters in class, "but then I couldn't remember which was which." The moral of the story was that people – including Kevin himself – were vain and silly.

His philosophy ran opposite to Reilly's in every way.

During class smoke breaks Kevin always attracted a clutch of girls. "He's the kind of boy that girls love instantly," one of them said dreamily. I smoked apart from his main audience, but close enough to overhear him.

Boston accents were new to me then, that dilation of vowels not quite British. Kevin was just back from spending junior year in England where New Wave and the blasé attitude toward pre-apocalyptic futility it espoused was just coming to the fore. It had captivated him. He told countless stories of the drunkenly nihilistic stunts pulled off by his British friends. One of them, called Disco, wore the same men's suit for months and had perfected nonchalance as an art. One morning, still awake when the milkman called, Disco and Kevin had stacked a precarious tower of half a dozen glass milk bottles on their kitchen table just to freak out their fastidious, early-rising housemate. Every story brought peels of laughter from his all-girl audience. It was something about the way he told them.

About two weeks into the quarter I started scouting for Kevin everywhere. I'd spotted his girlfriend with him, a slightly chunky girl with a Bronx accent and curly brown hair. Not that she mattered. I had a boyfriend, myself. In fact, when it came Kevin's turn to have a paper critiqued by the entire class, I was particularly hard on him. I accused him of being wishy-washy and failing to take a clear stance. It was a criticism Reilly might have written, and though I told myself I'd been stern out of indifference, I actually hoped to impress him.

I'll never forget our first private conversation. It took place while I was procuring cocoa from a vending machine in the library and centered on the fact that I wore reading glasses to balance eyes of differing strengths, since I had fallen out of a tree as a kid and scratched the cornea of the right one, causing a scar which later prevented that eye from developing astigmatism. Eye surgery via tree-falling – Kevin loved ideas like that. And I looked clever in my glasses, he said.

Oh, the joy that comes from a stalker conversation when it goes over without a hitch! The euphoria! It has nothing to do with what either person actually said, but everything to do with having met their eye, thought of words, sent your voice into their sacred ear canals to affect their magical brain. Back in high school, I'd choked on my epiglottis any time I attempted such exchanges. And now I hadn't! I'd been funny! I'd even worked the cocoa machine at the same time! A little out of breath it had made me, sure, and my hands had trembled, but he didn't notice either. I'd *done* it! One witty conversation *in the bank* to be replayed over and over.

Now I became fully obsessed. My high school habit of narrating imagined conversations with popular people took on the addictive proportions that would plague me for decades to come. *Everything* that happened became fodder to recount for Kevin, so that I was half in fantasy any time my mind could wander. And any time I spotted him, even as a distant figure across campus, dopamine flooded my system.

I next spoke to him a few weeks later in line for the automatic teller machine, a newfangled form of technology recently installed in the lobby of Main Hall. I really did need cash. I really did need to get in line right behind him.

"It's my birthday," he said. "My aunt sent me coke."

With his Boston accent he said "b*uh*thday" and "*ont*." He smiled and held up an envelope. I'd recently discovered that fabulous flying carpet called cocaine, myself. But I stuck to the issue at hand.

"She did *what*?! Is she young?"

"Mmm…" he seemed to estimate, "about fifty-two."

"And she sent you coke in the *mail*? That's pretty dumb!"

He nodded thoughtfully. With that relaxed, sleepy amusement he clarified, "She doesn't *know* she sent me coke, though." He drew out an ordinary birthday check, smiled craftily, and turned to the machine.

He'd been teasing me.

I recognized something right then: this boy was the *anti-*Reilly. He wore winter scarves and fingerless gloves indoors. He cared deeply and sincerely, it seemed, about nothing at all, a sort of conceptual vagabond bumping his way through noncommittal ideas, only amused, endlessly amused. The word "lackadaisical" fit him perfectly, and I had no doubt Reilly would have stamped him BULLSHIT! a thousand times.

With Reilly, everything had to be so careful. I'd been balancing a loaded tray of concerns for years now, trying to include all he valued. Something about Kevin's ease tempted me to drop the whole tray, let all that china crash to the ground.

"I'm terribly confused again," he confessed during a seminar discussion of Virginia Woolf, "which is normal, of course." His mind could follow maybe half a sentence of Woolf, he said, before he started thinking about lunch or his sneaker. He was voicing what we were all afraid of – looking stupid. The girl nearest touched his shoulder consolingly, the teacher smiled, and we all appreciated Kevin for his candid befuddlement.

Remember how I'd redefined my entire world around Reilly? Well, I did it again. Now Reilly's creed of standing up for what was pure and true became pompous and self-righteous. Kevin showed a deeper, less glamorous honesty: all of us were, at heart, a bunch of self-serving fools.

So imagine my reaction when a housemate handed me the phone late on a November night, and the voice proved to be Kevin's – accent and all. How could that be? I went in the bathroom and shut the door on the cord. I knew he must want help with the homework, understanding a novel, or maybe our last essay assignment. That was the only reason popular boys had ever phoned me. So I asked him: "What can I help you with?"

"I'd like to ask you to go to the Winter Formal with me."

"You would? Why?"

"Why not? You seem interesting. It's a dance. You ask someone – that's how it works."

"I know, but I—" What about his girlfriend? My heart accelerated, my mind seizing up. "I'm just surprised!!"

"That's okay. Surprise is fine." His voice was so calm, so simplifying.

I had to choose the Right Thing, though. I was with Reilly. He rarely wrote and was terse when he called, but I was still his *woman*, and I was true, and we were gonna get married and show the world, and... so this Winter Formal business would not work.

"I *can't*! I have a *boy*friend! He's off in grad school, but I *can't*!"

"Sure you can. We'd just go as friends."

"You don't know him. He'd –"

"Just say you're going with a friend. It doesn't have to be a *date* or anything. It's just a *dance*. I mean, how stupid to begin with."

"I wish…" I carried on. "You don't *know* how much I *wish*!"

"Well, if you *wish*, then you should go." He grew a tad impatient as I continued agonizing. "Fine," he said eventually, "do what you like."

What I did was go straight to the campus bar and guzzle Long Island iced teas with all the money I had, keeping constant watch on the door in hopes that Kevin would happen in to witness my pitiful anguish. Amazingly, that's exactly what happened. He came up beside me at the bar to order drinks, took me in, and recognized that I was bombed out of my brains.

I conveyed to him that I was drinking out of frustration.

"You mean, you're actually getting drunk on *purpose* because you can't go to the *dance*? Are you serious? I'm sorry, but that's so –" he shook his head "—corny!"

Corny? Corny was a dated word in itself, and to use it you had to have no fear whatsoever of sounding uncool – which meant he was serious.

"You don' unnerstan', my boyfrien'…"

Kevin was uninterested. He gathered his beers, told me to have fun, and moved off. I didn't know whether to be angry at him or admire him for refusing to play along.

At the dance itself, I pulled a similar stunt. Dressed sexy to the hilt and dramatically made up, I stood alone on an open walkway overlooking the festivities. I'd been drinking like a gutter grate all night, wanting Kevin to see my pain (which wasn't really pain – all this was so delightfully dramatic, yet technically loyal to Reilly). I saw him with the girl he'd asked out instead of me. Such a nice girl. A happy girl. A girl without anguish. I, on the other hand, was in full-on Black Magic Woman mode and ready to let it rip.

He came up to say hello as I leaned drunkenly on a railing, the whole second floor being lined with interconnected balconies. No, I said, I wasn't having fun, because I was loyal to a boyfriend who took me for granted. I spoke as a bitter woman, filled with dark and complex passions no man could possibly understand. At one point, to emphasize my contempt for the world in general, I scooted both forearms over the balcony's surface to knock down half a dozen abandoned drinks on the people sitting below. Plastic cups half-full of tequila sunrises, sloe gin fizzes, rum and cokes, some with butts in them, rained down on the guests below in their best formal dress. They screamed and scattered like shot.

Kevin leapt back from the railing in alarm – precisely the effect I'd hoped for – while I stepped just out of view and laughed diabolically. No, I was not a nice girl! Fuck his nice girl! See me?! I was a demented woman whorled with the sinister tints of dark and smoky rooms. And he wanted me.

"That was so *mean*!" he shrilled.

"I know," I shrugged. "Who gives a fuck? They're rich. They can afford dry-cleaning."

He walked away quickly, meaning to avert all connection. I felt *vastly* cool and successful, straight out of a movie. Kevin knew I was someone. And if all his stories of Disco and other New Wave delinquent friends had told me anything, it was that he was a sucker for risqué depravity. I would clinch this boy without even looking like I was trying, and keep Reilly on board as well.

Out of this alloy of drink and infatuation, I commenced to forge the weapon that would one day turn in its flight and... well, you know the rest.

~

Instead of going home to Seattle for Christmas, I went to meet Reilly in Houston. I'd planned my outfit literally months in advance, dieting hardcore to fit the twenty-two inch waist of my skirt. More than once I'd tried on my whole outfit for Allie, my housemate and close friend, who might suggest different shoes, different earrings. She was going to visit her own boyfriend at Ithaca College, so we fed each other's excitement.

On the flight to Houston, much to the consternation of my poor aisle seat neighbor, I got up half a dozen times to check my hair, fuss with my make-up, and drop Visine in my eyes. I strode from the jetway looking absolutely fabulous, ready for Reilly's open arms – except no one was there. I waited. Half an hour passed. Forty minutes. At some point I noticed a young couple in a ticket line some ways off. She was short haired and petite, wearing a little-girl undershirt and dwarfed beside some longhaired guy who carried a pair of skis. They turned out to be Reilly and a female friend of his, whom he was seeing off to her gate.

"Jesus, Tubes!" he winced when I greeted him. "What's all that shit on your face?" After a quick hug and no kiss, he said,

"Where the hell's your luggage? You haven't gotten it yet? Well, shit – it's gonna get stolen! Getcher ass down there!"

He was drunk. And the tiny girl with him, her nipples showed clear as day through that undershirt.

Diving headlong into martyrdom, I went to fetch my luggage as ordered. Even then, we had to wait fifteen minutes – a chummy threesome – for her nipply self to board the plane. Reilly looked gaunt and sleep-deprived behind the chunky curtains of hair that obscured his eyes.

"What's wrong, Tubes?" he asked when we got in the car.

"Nothing."

"We'll get some beer in ya. That'll brighten ya up!"

He knew me well. After a few beers, the incident didn't seem such a big deal.

That whole Christmas proved a series of similar slights, but, as the superior partner, I discounted them all. I languished. I moped. Somehow I convinced myself Reilly was on the brink of realizing the profound depth of my love for him, and that when he *did* see it, he would love me with intense gratitude for all I'd suffered. But that didn't happen. The last straw came when we returned to Houston a few days before classes resumed. He went out for a beer with the nipply friend and stayed out so late that, the next morning, he was too hungover to take me to the airport. He parked by a bus stop, hustled me onto a shuttle, and waved bye-bye.

I remember sitting in that bus and looking out through the grimy window as Reilly hopped back into his van. I felt wronged beyond the sweetness of martyrdom, enough that the game was shifting. He would pay. As the flat, bland landscape of Houston rolled by, I thought, "You'll see, Reilly. You spurned the wrong girl. I'm going for the Magic Boy – and you deserve it."

~

At Vassar, One Hundred Nights is a celebration that marks the length of time left until graduation. For the class of 1982, it was held somewhere outside Poughkeepsie at a large dance club with many rustic wooden stairways to sizable lofts, decorated with a tropical, tiki theme of palm trees and indoor thatching. I went with Maria, one of my housemates, to whom I'd confessed my crush on Kevin. My goal was no longer casual conversation: this was a seek and destroy mission – of the unfair restraint Reilly imposed on me.

Maria yelled that she'd sighted Kevin up on a loft, but he was with his girlfriend! Maybe they *hadn't* broken up.

I pressed through the thick, jabbering crowd, making a beeline for Kevin, who stood at a bar fringed with bright plastic grass. Those Bowie cheekbones. The hipness of his Howard Jones hair and sleepy eyes. Yet he was wearing a T-shirt with broad, sky blue and white stripes that made him look – I don't know – like we could throw water balloons at each other.

Was I intruding, I asked, cutting a glance at the nearby girlfriend? No, no – he shouted in my ear – they were only friends.

Then he asked me to dance. Delirium. Delirium.

What is that transporting potion of dopamine, oxytocin, and endorphins that fills our brains when we're with the object of our infatuation? What transforms the mundane world into a snow globe of thrilling, euphoric wonder?

We danced. I could not have been more high. If I could fly, if I could luxuriate atop a hot air balloon sailing through a cloud-puffed, storybook sky, if the world's most beautiful paintings would open like windows and let me wade through their colors while angels sang, I could not match that moment's exhilaration. *And we danced, like a wave on the ocean, romanced.*

A lot of guys don't like dancing; it makes them nervous. Kevin didn't care. When "Genius of Love" by Tom-Tom Club came on with its slow, syncopated rhythm, I threw away my fancy moves to invent silly dances with him. We pantomimed all kinds of random actions, laughing inordinately and staking a private island in the dense crowd. At the end, he gave me a kiss on the cheek.

"It's not right, what you're doing," Allie said. "It's not fair to Reilly."

"What about the nipply girl?"

"That doesn't make it right."

"We just *danced*," I told her. "Nothing's *happened*."

The next morning, as on every Sunday, I went to work at the college snack bar, frying burgers and making sandwiches to earn my beer money. Kevin came through with his housemates, the four of them playing off each other like a comedy team. As soon as I finished my shift, I joined them at their table and liked the lot of them instantly. I didn't notice all were Jewish – such things don't occur to me – but their vibe could not have been more different than the manly manner at A-7.

The overly articulate, brainy guy among them, Adam, they teased relentlessly. Silas, whose afro of dark curls transitioned via beard stubble to chest hair, was gifted in math. And there was Dave, master of sarcasm. But Kevin – that lax charm, that half-smile, with an inch of ash accumulating on his cigarette because he didn't notice – he was somehow their ringleader.

On this day, he burned a five dollar bill just so that we could all have the entertainment of watching it burn, the novelty of which he thought would be well worth the price. Adam – or Addie as they called him – couldn't stand it. Twice he snatched the bill out of the saucer and shook out the flames. Kevin laughed but demanded it back.

"It's my fucking fiver. Give it back!"

Kevin grabbed and they squabbled, nearly tearing the bill, skirting in and out of earnest *fuck you*'s mixed with boyish laughter. In the end the five dollar bill burned to a few curls of black ash, which Kevin puffed from the saucer to the floor.

"That's just plain wrong!" Addie sulked.

Another day at the library, Kevin and I talked of how we'd enjoyed the tacky tiki of the One Hundred Nights bar and how it might be fun to explore other tacky townie bars around Poughkeepsie – a sort of sociology experiment, not to be mistaken for a date. We also pretended not to consider that, being off campus, I wouldn't have to hide from the eyes of Reilly's friends.

Kevin picked me up in his huge and rusted 1970 Oldsmobile Cutlass Supreme, nicknamed Lurch because its engine occasionally missed. The first bar he chose featured an absolutely deafening Bon Jovi style band. Even screaming, we couldn't hear a word from each other, so we did some signing. From the crowd of Charlie's Angels girls and mulleted buttrocker boys, we'd point out the more outrageous cliché figures with feigned approval. During a band break we fit in a strange conversation about whether we wanted to have kids. I claimed to pretty much hate babies, mainly to sound controversial; they reminded me of little Napoleons, I said, expecting parents to jump at every command.

"They're nothing but unrestrained *id*," I explained, "a shitting, puking, drooling blob of human selfishness. I mean, that's what we all are underneath, but at least later we learn to *disguise* it!"

Kevin listened. He enjoyed anything counterculture. Which was, of course, largely why I'd said it.

Over the next few weeks we went to similar bars and had similar conversations. One night, or early morning, I came home to an urgent note from a housemate. The much-underlined handwriting suggested terror: REILLY had called while I was out, and she'd done a shitty job of lying. I called him later that day with an excuse about having been out with Allie, but he remained suspicious. The conversation frazzled me badly enough that later I couldn't get to sleep.

And so, well past midnight, I ran across campus to Kevin's Terrace Apartment, peeking into various windows until I found him. He was alone, studying. I flung pebbles at his window until he noticed, though he was playing music so it took forever.

His house was magical. His room was magical. Every object carried his charm. Sitting at his magic desk, I related this latest development – Reilly's phone call – as though it tore me apart. Kevin listened a while, as impassionate as he'd been during our first phone conversation. Presently he asked, "Would you like to go running with me? One thing I've never done is smoke cigarettes *while* I was jogging. Shall we try it?"

A golf course extended directly behind his apartment, dark and wet with early spring rain. Neither of us wore sneakers. We jogged up a hill, inhaling from our cigarettes at a furious pace.

"This is awful!" I said.

"Isn't it?" he agreed. "I've never *not* wanted a cigarette so much in my life!"

Yet we kept at it for maybe three or four cigarettes over fifteen minutes, lighting new off the old.

"I – feel – kind of – sick!" I gasped.

"That's why – no one – does this!" he managed.

I remember him saying we could quit at a certain time on his watch. I kept asking how much longer, though I could barely talk. At last he called time.

"That was *so* fun!" I said approaching his door. "Thank you!"

The Reilly dilemma didn't seem so important anymore. Kevin didn't try to kiss me; he said goodbye and went inside as I jogged backwards, waving, both of us grinning with childish delight.

But the night did come, at a black-lighted bar where the dance floor flooded with dry ice smoke during Hall and Oates' "I Can't Go for That," the two of us inventing dance-in-the-shower moves to go with the 'steam,' when Kevin ceased clowning, grabbed me, and kissed me hard. After months of build up, the boy, the magic boy, the object of all my narration and fantasy – he and I were kissing! And we didn't stop. The room swirled and we caromed drunkenly into other people until a bartender yelled at us to take it outside.

So we did, into Lurch. Damn, was Kevin a good kisser! Maybe it was those hollows of his cheeks, or I don't know what!

We made out furiously until he drove me home, where we made out furiously some more. He didn't try to go further; kissing and clinching seemed plenty wonderful in themselves, and I was still somehow playing the Reilly card as a brake. But how I ever got back in that house, I have no idea.

In May, Kevin asked me to the Spring Formal, an ironic counterpoint to the Winter Formal I'd refused. Saying yes felt bold and reckless, since we'd be seen by spies of Reilly, who had taken on, in my mind, the role of a jailor. But I would let the tray of china delicates crash to the ground, if need be.

I borrowed a deep blue crepe dress and suede sandals from Allie, because I was broke. Kevin took me out for dinner, where right at our table we dipped the filters of our cigarettes in a vial of coke for what Kevin called "the wimp's freebase." Like the Winter Formal, this one was held in Main Hall, featuring the band of old Lionel Hampton, the xylophonist; the music might have seemed an old fogy disappointment if we'd not been flying on cocaine. We danced. A few times we ducked in the girl's bathroom to do more coke, where I painted black eyeliner on Kevin. BULLSHIT!, maybe, but so fun!

While the band took a break, the party organizers had arranged for an old fashioned presentation of couples. You waited in line for the names you'd written down to be read into a mic, then proceeded down an imaginary red carpet into the main room. "Kevin and Louisa!" came over the loud speakers, and we entered, arm in arm. Fortune was throwing attention and applause my way. I had arrived.

When the party started to shut down, I swept through one of the bars and stole a bottle of champagne, two stemware glasses, and a white tablecloth all in one fell swoop. We tried to invite others to accompany us for a "picnic" on the hillside by Vassar Lake, but as it was 2:00 AM and about 40 degrees out, no one showed up. Vassar Lake is really more of a sinkhole of runoff from the golf course, usually covered with algae and a bit stinky. Still, by moonlight it could pass for picturesque. We spread our tablecloth on the slope above it and opened the champagne. Glasses and bottle went somewhere as we sank back onto the tablecloth, making out in dreamy, swirling oblivion.

But the swirling grew stronger – a bit troublesome in fact. And someone pummeled my back in an unwelcome way – was that right? *Something was happening*! Everything went black and surreally cold. There was nothing to touch, nothing to stand on. My mind scrambled through possibilities until I struck upon one of sheer brilliance: I had somehow fallen into Vassar Lake! I was underwater! I needed to breathe, but couldn't tell which way was up. There was a brief temptation to simply sleep and not worry much about it, but I had to remember, I *must* know this blackness was water. Drown, I could drown! With great effort I kicked my high-heeled feet, and somehow I burst through to the surface. Kevin was there, gasping as well. We were okay.

"We're in the lake!" I notified him.

"I know it!" he said. He was rather brilliant, too.

We swam toward shore, but between my drunkenness and the spike heels I made slow progress. At the edge my feet sank into the silt and Kevin half-dragged me up through the sludgy reeds and mud of the bank to the grass. I clambered to my feet, sopped and slimy in Allie's dress! And her suede sandals! They were coated in mud. Even so, the whole thing might have struck us as hilarious, except that now we were truly freezing.

"I know a shortcut to the TA's," Kevin chattered, and I followed him through the trees. Allie's shoes sank into more mud, now ice-crusted under the trees, and picked up dry leaves. I shivered more spastically than I could ever remember, and the safari, as we called it, seemed to go on forever. I worried we were lost.

Indoors at last, Kevin told me I could shower first. Alone I slopped my dress and nylons onto the bathroom floor and stepped under the burning spears of hot water. I hadn't been there long when the curtain drew back and Kevin stepped in. Neither of us spoke. We sort of had sex, but the spatial dynamics weren't quite there.

After that, I'm sure we went in his room and had sex for real. Except I don't remember. Of all the times to black out, why then? But I did. It's gone. All I remember is sneaking from his Terrace Apartment early the next morning and getting caught by a hello from Elizabeth's housemate. So I went to Elizabeth's place for tea, extremely hung over, and met with her terrific disapproval of my antics, which was nothing compared to Allie's later that day, for her ruined dress and shoes, and my cheating, and our almost drowning. For me, though, all the above constituted a new set of mantelpiece trophies. I had landed the big one. Now I had not one boyfriend, but two – making up for lost time.

Clockwise from top left: Warming up before ballet; "presented" at the Spring Formal with Kevin; slightly schnockered with senior year housemates (except the one I owed amends), 1982.

8. MY NEAR-DEATH EXPERIENCE

...That strange spectacle observable in all [wounded]
Sperm Whales dying – the turning sunwards of the
head, and so expiring...

> *-Herman Melville*
> *Moby Dick*

    Graduation week left little room for romance since Kevin's family came to attend the ceremony, as did Zelda, now a freshman painting student at a prestigious fine arts college. She had weathered the last of her years at home marooned with only Adelyn and Walter, both graduate students living at home while Dad taught at Stanford for a year. Rebelling against Dad's atheism, both Adelyn and Walter had become born-again Christians, Walter head over heels in love with a sylph-like virgin who required marriage prior to sex, and Adelyn head over heels for her pastor. They'd succeeded in converting Zelda one day when she was feeling utterly hopeless, but her Christianity had lasted only as long as her mood.

    During Vassar's outdoor graduation ceremony, it poured. I walked across the stage, water dribbling off my soggy mortarboard, as my honors rolled out over the loudspeaker: General Honors, Departmental Honors in English, Phi Beta Kappa, and Distinction on Thesis. The only ones not surprised by my closet geekiness were my housemates, who knew how much I studied. After the celebration, I spent a weekend with Kevin, Zelda, and Elizabeth in Boston. Zelda hit it off with Kevin, who'd began to pick up bits of our dumb talk. Then, after a quick visit home, I flew to New Mexico since I was supposed to marry Reilly soon. I didn't see any way to back out of that without pissing Reilly off. What marriage meant or my own truth – well, those didn't figure in much.

    I landed a waitressing job at a resort in downtown Santa Fe called La Posada, where I was frantically inept at best; several tables walked out on me. There was a pool where I could relax after my shift ended at two o'clock until about four when Reilly and his brothers swung by to get me after their construction jobs. There was also a payphone in the main lobby. Every day after my shift, I would place a collect call to a certain travel agency in Boston, where I would request my travel agent, Kevin. We would converse in dumb talk for half an hour or so. Only once did I get walked in upon by Reilly's brother – but I hung up before he saw me.

At Reilly's house I also received a letter from Zelda containing inside it a second letter. Kevin's handwriting and ironic sentences seemed to glow with more magic than ever. He didn't ask me to come back, but the call radiated from between the lines. I also received letters from Elizabeth urging me to come live with her in Manhattan. She was renting from her uncle a one-bedroom on West 85th near Riverside and wanted my company there. Would I please, please come out and live with her? We'd have so much fun!

Hmm… Elizabeth's apartment was a four-hour drive from Boston. I spoke gravely to Reilly about my need to really find myself before our marriage. I didn't quite feel *ready* yet. I wanted to take a job in Manhattan first, be on my own just for a year. Maybe his dad could help me get a job at a magazine or newspaper there so I could try my wings. *Then* I'd feel ready to settle down and become his wife.

He bought it. Of course, he had a year of school left himself, with a certain nipply classmate.

~

Manhattan terrified me. The first morning I spent alone in our apartment, I heard a radio traffic report that advised, "Avoid the area around Grand Central, where scattered body parts along 42nd are causing problems. Police have cleaned up most of the mess, but drivers are still gawking and traffic is backed up." The announcer's voice had a "what will they think of next?!" kind of revelry to it.

Rent was $500 a month, which we split. An old and scuffling elevator hoisted us to the building's eighth and highest floor, where caged windows overlooked a littered street. Straight across we could see into scores of apartments lacking blinds, where we came to know a cast of immodest characters, while the lower floors opposite our building's door housed a halfway house for the mentally ill. In the middle of the night, blood-curdling howls and sobs often rang out: "God, just let me *die*! I'm hurtin' so bad! Pleeeeease!" Pause; more sobbing. "Lord, jus' lemme *go-oh-oh*…!"

Elizabeth would sit bolt upright in bed, put her face to the caged open widow, and yell: "SHUT UP!" Then, sinking back, she'd add with a sigh, "If we close the window, I'll get too hot!"

My life seemed to count for nothing in the big city. Thousands of people within a square mile were flushing a toilet at the exact same moment as I. Shopkeepers, clerks, and waitresses seemed to prefer I'd drop dead and spare them the exertion of waiting on me. At a Red Apple grocery I once dropped a raw wool mitten I'd knitted myself and, as soon as I discovered the lack, went back inside to ask the clerk if she'd seen it. She let her eyes drift heavily past me without a hitch and, chewing gum with bovine regularity, didn't deign to reply.

"Have you *seen* my *mitten*?!" I held up the mate insistently, wiggled it to get her attention. You could see it took every ounce of customer service in this girl *not* to say she didn't give a fuck about my dumb-ass mitten. "No," she managed, still refusing to look. Later I found it under the bubble gum machines and, just to irk the shit out of her, went back to assure her she needn't worry. "It's okay! I've found it all right," I beamed. This time she couldn't help looking, in case I were nuts.

Late at night from our ceiling we often heard the scuffs and footfalls of "roof rats" – burglars who broke in from above. One day we came home to find a cigarette that wasn't my brand burning in the ashtray by the open window, but Elizabeth refused to believe someone had sidled the narrow ledge eight floors up. Whoever it was came back the next day and escorted Elizabeth's 36-inch TV and camera out the building's front door.

But the place had its perks as well. Thanks to Reilly's father, I had interviews with top editors at *Life*, *Time*, and *People*. I no doubt amused them in ways of which I was only faintly aware (the editor at *Time* remarked archly, "So in other words, if you can make it *here*, you'll make it… *any*where?"), but none had jobs for me, so I had to take one as a busgirl at a trendy Columbus Ave. restaurant. There, like a vulture, I kept my eye on the entrees of skinny women, took their plates as soon as they'd allow, then either wolfed their leavings right there at the bus station or dumped them into my large doggie bag. I was hungry not because I had no money, but because I had to save it all for more important things like exorbitant cover charges at nightclubs. I regularly hit up the ABC streets' vintage clothing shops where I could find hip outfits for cheap. With Elizabeth I went to a fancy downtown salon and had all my hair cut off. Long hair felt more like *me*, but I wanted a sharp Siouxsie or Pat Benetar look for the clubs.

This was the scene I'd longed for. Kevin came down from Boston every two or three weeks, often accompanied by Silas, Addie, and *lots* of cocaine. As many as eight of us piled into Lurch to head to the Ritz, Peppermint Lounge, and other '80s hotspots, where I begrudged every friend who shared our coke. Afterwards, Kevin would come back to our tiny apartment, where he and I would go at it on the fold-out sofa. The door to the bedroom didn't close right, so poor Elizabeth heard everything. Sex with Kevin was good. With him I had my first orgasm with another (conscious) human being – that I know. But when or where it happened, I can't say. Graduation night at Vassar? In the New York apartment? I'd probably faked enough by then that I couldn't *tell* him it was my first real one – so the memory is only of being surprised within myself, amazed that this could happen.

Unfortunately, one can't party and fornicate *all* the time. Whenever I was sober and Kevin wasn't around, I suffered gut-dropping panic attacks – which in those days had no name. I recall walking to my busgirl job past some cyclone fencing that lined the cross street between Broadway and Columbus Ave. The buildings on the other side seemed to get wavy, and as I wondered what was happening, doom smashed a wrecking ball into my solar plexus: I would die.

I arrived at work shaking like a doll. To quash these attacks I drank more than ever, at work and home, dialing the package store down the street to get my booze delivered. Rum and diet Cokes, vodka or gin and diet tonic, or straight up Jack. At 120 pounds, I could put away most of a fifth in one night. Elizabeth, who often worked late, would come home to find me bombed in front of the TV, my ashtray overflowing with cigarettes, and squashed cockroaches dotting the carpet within my slipper arm's reach. Why she didn't kick me out, I really don't know.

After a few months of this sort of life, however, Kevin broke up with me. Reilly had flown up from Houston for a weekend, during which Kevin was instructed not to call. That same week he sent me a breakup letter. I knew I needed to take some action, because of the two I wanted Kevin more, but I was still too afraid of Reilly to break up with him. So things stood when I went to a Halloween party thrown by some gay Vassar boys. I'd tried to dress as Audrey Hepburn, but nobody gave a crap, and I ended up on the wrong side of the bedroom door when the cocaine came out. What good was *anything* without coke? Left out again, I proceeded to have a terrible time and then stormed home, where Reilly called for what Elizabeth said was the third time that night.

"Where *were* you?" he demanded. "What were you doing?"

I rode my coke-jonesing to get angry at Reilly – for the first and only time.

"I was alone!" I shouted. "I'm so tired of you never trusting me!" I spoke in a brittle, victimized voice. "I can't do this anymore, Reilly. You make me feel guilty for just existing! It's over. I've had all I can take."

Reilly tried to backpedal, but I got off the phone with a thin smile of relief. Finally! Funny – wasn't this Halloween night our third anniversary?

It seems my egomania had dug two pitfalls. The flipside of my self-loathing, self-abasing, and codependent victim was my arrogant, egotistical controller who rose to occasions such as these. All I had to do now was lure Kevin back. I checked a calendar. In two weeks, I'd go up to Boston dressed all sexy and turn him around. People were pawns. When I was on my game, I could move them about at will. Wasn't that how life was supposed to work? The way of the successful?

In the meantime, having no boyfriend, I found other ways to go out. Through friends I'd met a beautiful Swedish girl, Anna, who told me, as we drank strong coffee in the lavish brownstone she was house-sitting, that she knew the bouncer at a hip club. If I dressed hot enough, she could get me in free. In her sensuous accent, she explained: "Then once you are in, you choose a handsome man, you say, 'Hi! Are you Dave?' Then you laugh and look embarrassed because you are supposed to meet Dave but he is not the one. And so..." she gave a murky shrug, "you pay for nothing all night."

I met Anna outside the club in a miniskirt and spikes, and she made good on her promise; the bouncer lifted cordon at the head of the long and restless line, and we entered almost wordlessly. Surrounded by music and lights, we scoped the dark expanses of tables and bars for handsome men. Like a slim, carnivorous gazelle, Anna sighted a prospect and told me she was going for it. I tried not to watch too obviously while she went through the Dave routine. She really did look embarrassed, flicking her long blonde hair all over the place. At a certain point, though, she met my eyes directly and waved "bye-bye" with unmistakable finality. It was then I saw in plain outlines what I'd never quite worked up the nerve to ask. Yes, she was going to sleep with him. Basically, she was a club whore. That was how she'd landed the brownstone; it was how she got everything.

I bought my own alarmingly overpriced drink and continued looking for handsome men, but with flutters of panic. Yes, I wanted many drinks and much coke, and yes, I wanted a man's attention, but I couldn't go through with this. Sure, if I were shitfaced, that'd be one thing, but you had to choose your John *before* you got shitfaced, and that I just couldn't do. I gave up and took a subway home, defeated and upset with myself.

There had to be another way.

So I called up Silas, Kevin's coke-dealing best friend, and asked if he'd like to come down to city and hit up the town with me. I didn't even mention coke, but neither did he disappoint: he brought a ton of it, at least two grams of pure 1982 cocaine. What heaven! We did some when he arrived to pick me up, and a bunch more in the back of the cab.

We'd decided to return to the Peppermint Lounge on 5th Avenue in Lower Manhattan because it was my favorite club so far. It featured three levels of dance floors; I was all about the New Wave basement – Duran Duran, Adam Ant, Roxy Music. The familiar thrill rushed up to me from the lighted floor as we entered that pounding darkness – black walls, black lights, colored beams roving. Tonight I would soar higher than ever. Tonight, I would be unstoppable.

If ever there were a recipe for a girl headed straight for the fiery furnace, I certainly fit it. You name the sin, I had it in spades. And utter contempt for God? Duh! Hadn't I won a distinction on my senior thesis, which analyzed the demise of an outdated Victorian faith replaced by "the horror" of a morally meaningless modernity? God and the Jolly Green Giant seemed equally compelling figures to me. I fancied there was a bit of despairing nihilism in every cigarette I lit up.

How I looked to other people at that club, I have no idea. Probably they saw some naïve, slightly big-nosed girl cavorting about in a little black mini-dress, maybe somewhat extravagantly. But vanity idealizes every self-proclaimed Dancing Queen. As if intercut mirrors lined the interior my brain, I saw myself through every onlooker's eyes as a superstar. I hardly even noticed Silas, and whenever the floor gave enough space, I'd crank up my spins, spine flexes, and over-head kicks. See me! Want me! Envy me!

With every shitty song we took a break for more coke. Drinks in hand, we sought out a dark corner amid the black vinyl couches where we snorted up little piles from the webs of our thumbs. We were touching carelessly now, my nylons against Silas' trousers, his fingers coming to rest near the nape of my neck as we shouted in each other's ears. Things were shifting. Did I really want to make out with Kevin's *best friend*? Would that be fine so long as we didn't have sex? Or were there maybe some things you just shouldn't *do*?

Then his coke ran out – all of it.

I wanted more.

I had twenty-five dollars, Silas thirty-some. We asked a number of people until someone pointed out a scrawny, stooped guy amid the shadows. He looked like a pubescent Mafia wanna-be, wearing a beige polyester suit and projecting shifty-eyed contempt for us even as he took our wad of bills and barked out something about his shit being good.

We settled down and did a bunch of it, but it was *not* good – not at all. His stuff numbed your gums all right, but didn't taste good and didn't deliver squat. Nothing! We were coming down, both of us, straw in hand. It must be cut with something, Silas said. But since we'd bought it, we finished it off. Gentleman that he was, Silas let me snort the lion's share.

I told Silas I had to pee.

What neither of us knew was that we'd been sold not cocaine, but lidocaine. Lidocaine is a local anesthetic, usually applied topically or injected subcutaneously, which was used frequently in the '80s to fake out coke buyers by numbing their gums. Ingested systemically, however, it often causes death. "Central nervous system effects may include loss of consciousness, respiratory depression, and seizures," says Wikipedia. "Cardiovascular effects include hypo-tension, bradycardia, arrhythmia, and/or cardiac arrest."

I had all of the above.

My blood pressure plummeted. My lungs drew in less air with each breath. Neither my brain nor my heart could function properly, my pulse slowing over the ten minutes preceding my grand mal seizure, cardiac arrest, and death. Yet, incredible as it seems, I had no fear that anything was wrong. How could I not know?

Because of trust. I'd been raised with unshakeable faith in the goodness of alcohol, the goodness of inebriation. I'd transferred that faith to drugs of all kinds. Cocaine was my *friend*; it gave me super-powers, and I believed it was causing all these interesting symptoms, varying the show for me a little bit, carrying me further down the path toward wonder. All I had to do was hang on for the ride.

In line for the bathroom, I noticed an outer band of my peripheral vision had turned dark with tingly orange speckles, as if I had on narrow goggles. Tunnel vision – that's what you called it.

I was sure it must be some kind of cool cocaine effect – a game where you could see only right where you looked. I couldn't wait to brag about it. The line for toilet stalls extended past mirrored sinks, so for a while I was parked in front of one. My area of vision had shrunk to something like looking through twin toilet paper tubes, but I could still admire my own looks. I finger-fixed a bit of make-up, judging the chatter I overheard. These girls weren't cooler than me; no one could say that anymore. Look how far I'd come! Me, here, the spit-gulping laughing stock of the high school library, glamorous and coked out to the point of tunnel vision in a hip Manhattan night club. Fuck everyone!

In the toilet stall, that's when I first started to get concerned. Graffiti messages on the door looked like gibberish – *all* of them. I sensed that some were printed in normal English that I, for some reason, could not recognize. My vision had constricted down to a small portal, and even that was becoming dim and infiltrated by the tingly orange speckles. What if I lost my sight completely? And air – there was no air in this bathroom!

I found Silas at the bar and grabbed his arm.

"Is something wrong?" he asked.

Who knows how slowly my heart was beating by now?

"I need air," I heaved. "There's no air–" I tried to inhale deeply, over and over, with a growing alarm at the lack of oxygen in this basement. It was all breathed up! No air! I couldn't understand why no one else was gasping for it. I felt angry and frustrated that no one knew what I was talking about – but that I might be about to die never crossed my mind.

"Let's get you some water," the bartender said.

They put the glass in my hand, though it wasn't what I wanted. To please them, I took a sip. Then something struck the base of my chin like a prizefighter's upswing. For an instant I thought maybe I'd slipped and hit it on the bar, but in reality that was the moment I left my body.

I shot straight up, like someone fired from a cannon, up and up into the perfect blue of an open sky above the blue, blue ocean. The nightclub was no more. Air – delicious air – flowed over me. I seemed to lead with my sternum, and as my momentum tapered, I arched back and opened my chest to the sky in a backbend that curved over seamlessly into a perfect swan dive. Here came the ocean's surface to meet me – ready or not! I pierced the water and shot down into it. It felt cold but not too cold to be lovely, and the surface dappled far above but not too far to reach. Effortlessly, I surfaced. For the first time I saw a beach, and, wanting to be there, arrived. I waded through shallow surf to a stony shore.

To my left I saw a distant house on the top of a hillock or mesa on the beach, as though waves had eroded away all else. Arriving promptly there, I saw the house was pale blue, quite weathered, and rested on a foundation of large boulders and rocky slabs that were covered with oozy, dark muck like rotten seaweed. The base of the house was a good ten feet up. I had a sure sense of competence, of can-do, and I wanted to reach that front door, so I climbed despite the slimy stuff. As I climbed, my already faint sense of body seemed to slip away, so that I became only vision and climbing, almost like a subjective camera. By the time I reached the door, I was at the level of the doorsill.

As I crossed over the threshold, I realized, or more recognized with wonder, that this was indeed the house of my ancestors. All of them had crossed that threshold, all of them had been here. I *loved* this place, this legendary waypoint! A sense of joy filled me, of honor to be here. From my vantage point I could see the grain of the wooden floor in extraordinary detail. Countless footsteps, so many generations of *us*, had worn the boards to an almost powdery consistency. I was brand new here – an upstart, the youngest – and though they were not visible or distinguishable, my ancestors' combined presence somehow welcomed me. I sensed in particular my father's father, whom I knew only from photographs since he'd died before I was born.

And there was the famous picture window! It framed a gorgeous view of the ocean that all my ancestors loved. I knew that in the past, there'd been a chair where generations of us sat to savor it, but that was gone now and I was approaching from below, floating just above the floor, wondering how I'd get high enough to peek over the sill.

What a surprise to feel some magnetic force swoop me toward it, up the wall and – whoa! – right over the sill into the open air! I flew, amazed, without a trace of fear. The low sun cast a dazzling track across the ocean's surface. Over this I zoomed, so deliciously, again with the sense of being pulled by my sternum and – though I was bodiless – the exhilaration of air rushing over me. The motion, the sensation of passing *through* something as I zipped over that dappling brightness was so perfect I wanted it to go on and on, but before I knew it, with that same sense of surprise – *really*?! – I was sucked right *into* the sun itself.

I knew the sun was good, the giver of life.

Light engulfed me, surrounded me, embraced me, not just my surface but all through me. Imagine the warmest summer sunshine on your skin, but saturating your entire being. Its illumination shone white, bright as the sun's core in the noon sky but endlessly enlarged in all directions, yet not burning or glaring because I received it so flawlessly. Its power permeated all my consciousness.

And the light was love. I was loved, I was adored beyond measure by a Parent who now invisibly cradled me and delighted at my being, my cuteness, my innocent goodness. I was perfect, the Parent's immeasurably precious infant. And I – I who had *starved* for this feeling all my life, who had searched for it so blindly, pining inside to be loved in exactly this way – was at last complete. I knew a happiness beyond description.

My bliss was so complete that "I" – my I-ness – evaporated in the brightness. I forgot about being Louisa, forgot the whole enterprise of living her life. As if the intensity of love's brilliance overexposed the lines that distinguished me from the Parent, loving ceased to be a transmission – *Parent → loves → Louisa* – and became simply

Love is.

Love loves.

I can't say how long I passed in this state. Time did not exist, and since there was nothing to want, nowhere to go, and nothing to expect, I can't say I missed it.

But then something did happen. As if with the flip of a switch, the light cut to utter darkness. At the same instant, I knew a decision from the Parent, equally absolute:

You cannot stay. You're not done yet.

What?! Give me back the light! Man, was I pissed! You're so *wrong*! I *will* stay! I'll *never* go back! I threw a tantrum – a huge, infantile tantrum of defiance. I howled with my will: *Nooooooo!* I would *teach* the Parent it couldn't send me back; I would *convince* it.

What I sensed in response was a purely loving but utterly inflexible ruling: Case closed, sweetheart. In fact, the Parent had gone – left me. I found myself alone in utter darkness.

I felt only a moment of alarm, even the outer edge of terror. But then I saw them, little chalk-lined stick figures playing and rollicking against the black backdrop, and I realized that the Parent still loved me and had given me this delightful toy – something to amuse me until I could return. And since I was still a child, the antics of the stick figures were childlike, too. Okay, this wasn't anywhere near as good as the light, I thought, but I could settle down and content myself with the show for a while.

They flipped, they cartwheeled, so full of playfulness! They swung on a chalk trapeze. Oh, and they were cute, too. Little verses, they were calling out now. Silly rhymes and riddles: How does a hippo light a hopscotch? How many fiddles make a flim-flam? A, B, C makes 1, 2, 3-!

I loved it – how fun! Except that one of their chalk-outlined O-faces came in closer, while the others carried on behind. His outline filled in like a white plate. How many fingers? What is your name?

"What's your name? How many fingers?"

He was *seeing* me. He wanted something. Oh *shit*! I remembered now – that crazy, stupid way things used to be!

Dammit! This was the *world* again! I was back inside the meat puppet – that stupid, burdensome flesh-pocket of maneuverable limbs – and I couldn't get out. But, oh, I didn't have the *patience* for this farfetched game anymore! It felt like remembering an onslaught of pointless chores – countless – you've left undone, all of them mandatory. Imagine being ordered to spend the next sixty years enrolled in kindergarten.

"How... many... fingers?"

He was so insistent. Okay, okay! Reluctantly I recalled how all the dumb rules used to go: he was one of *them*, and I was a *me*. And what *he* wanted from *me* was that deal where you send messages back and forth by grunting. I was supposed to use that meatloafy thing parked down there, you know, in that garage of my mouth.

I pushed. "Two," gusted over the loaf.

"What's your name?"

So he wanted to play rough, huh? Fine, I was up for it: "Lou-izz-ah."

See how good I still was at this shit?

Then the world came back in full, all around me, and I remembered my life as if I'd always been in it. They were a crowd, all those stick figures, looking at me. Where was I? Lying on a floor. Someone must have thrown a bucket of water over me, because I was soaked and had a puddle beneath me.

"Can you stand up?"

I saw Silas. He was my friend. He helped me stand up.

"Oh my god!" he kept saying, rubbing his face. I held his arm and the idea was, we'd all climb some stairs to a different spot.

"Are you okay?" he kept asking. Of course I was!

We and a bunch of people went up the stairs and out a door to where it was night and very cold. Silas had my coat. He told me stuff he thought was super important. I'd been dead, he said. Could I understand that? Really, really dead – like, gray and a corpse, and not at all like myself – for a long, long time. Silas had never been so scared in his life! Then, long after he'd given up, I'd come back, breathing and getting color and streaming sweat from every pour until it puddled around me.

I tried to act concerned, like Silas. I asked for a cigarette. I could still remember the Parent's love, and still felt myself a child of about five. Everything seemed a delightful game. Worry of any kind was just silly!

We sat outside on a bench with our backs to the building. A lot of people were milling about. A balding, black haired man in a white shirt came up to talk to us, squatting beside me. I'd never seen him before in my life, I thought.

"You were gone a long time," he said. "Three minutes, maybe more. I almost gave up!"

Silas seemed to know this guy. "I couldn't believe how you kept on. You were really whaling, too."

As they talked, I began to piece together that this man, who was old (in his thirties) and balding, had put his mouth on my mouth many times, for a long time. And I didn't like that one bit. His hands must have been near my boobs, too. I felt embarrassed, like he thought what happened during that time meant there was something between us. I wanted to make clear there was *nothing*, so I behaved quite briskly toward him.

"Yeah, thanks," I said dryly and looked away, smoking.

"Thank you so much! Oh, my god." Silas gushed on and on. Fine if he wanted to chat, but I was done with this fellow. I wouldn't look at him – it was too embarrassing. I didn't want to have sex with him, and I wouldn't go for any of that *You saved my life!* drama. Eventually, to my relief, he moved off and spoke with others a few feet away.

"Silas," I asked, "what are we doing?"

"Waiting for the ambulance."

That seemed like a fine answer, until I began to think about it. They claimed I'd been dead. What if this ambulance were *for me?* They'd take me to a hospital, and hospitals – especially in New York City – were terrible places! I'd visited one not long ago: puke green tiled hallways, nurses who'd prefer you drop dead. And they'd tell my parents.

I turned to Silas. "Is it for *me* – the ambulance?"

"Of course it is! Who else would it be for?"

"Silas, no! I *don't* want to go in the ambulance!"

His eyes wavered on mine, then darted to the lineup of cabs waiting at the curb.

"C'mon!" he said, grabbing my arm. We ran across the sidewalk, past lingering spectators, and jumped in the nearest cab. People yelled after us, someone even rapping on the trunk, but Silas urged the driver, "Just drive!"

We woke up Elizabeth when we got home, where she and Silas talked for some time in hushed voices. Louisa had died and the taxi driver needed money. While Silas stepped out, I tried to pour myself a drink, but Elizabeth wouldn't let me. She made me drink water and go straight to bed, even though she and Silas were going to stay up and talk more.

When I woke up the next morning, my whole ribcage hurt like hell, especially my sternum. I had a bunch of lumps on the back of my head, and my hands were bruised. But – yes! – I remembered the wonderful dream and had a feeling of delight, like Christmas morning. I told my whole dream to Elizabeth, who listened carefully, but I couldn't describe the light, I couldn't describe how hugely loved I'd felt. Elizabeth, while a good Jewish girl, was nearly as clear-cut an atheist as I. Neither of us had ever heard of a white light experience, so what else could this be but a dream? She asked in a skeptical tone – so was the Parent, like, God? We pondered it in an eye-ogling, half sarcastic way.

Meanwhile, on the table a section of the *New York Times* showed a photo of a helicopter. Except I couldn't remember what those things were called, and the printed caption looked more like: Xcf8n#ivz.

"Are you *sure* that's right?" I asked.

We both knew I had brain damage.

Elizabeth made me read the whole article aloud, and I struggled haltingly, the print seeming to jump about like a glitchy film. Every few lines I'd hit on another Arabic word, and even short ones like "then" and "also" required sounding out and seemed fantastically random.

Elizabeth asked me again about the hospital, but I wasn't having it. Brain damage, shrame damage! Silas called to talk with Elizabeth about it still more, but I was firm. No way was I going.

As soon as I was able to write, I recorded the dream journey in a spiral notebook. To my innermost self, I acknowledged it was more than a dream, but what or how, I couldn't say. The intuition that I'd crossed over and touched my source in god kept presenting itself, and I kept dismissing it. No way. The only conception I had of god was the old man God of religions. Rejecting that image, I'd thrown out the entire concept. Still, I knew I'd never felt, in any dream or waking moment of my life, anything that could compare to that intensity of bliss.

So how could I account for what happened? There's a scene in *2001: A Space Odyssey* when Dave pulls out tube after tube of computer functionality to slowly shut down Hal's brain. Maybe my brain had been shut down that way from lack of oxygen, gradually reaching some baseline core of love and bliss analogous to Hal's "Daisy." That being the only thing left, I'd experienced it as super intense.

I also decided the journey had been a trip fueled by cocaine. People said coke was not a psychedelic, but who knew? Perhaps it had the power to intensify dreams or concentrate a whole sequence into a single millisecond on the last tiny bit of oxygen left in the brain. That seemed at least *possible* – far more possible than my spirit having journeyed apart from my body.

I didn't know then that the brain goes devoid of all activity – flatlining on an electro-encephalogram (EEG) – ten to twenty seconds after a heartbeat ceases. Synapses do not occur. My brain, already starving for oxygen, would have shut down almost immediately when my vital signs quit. And the fact is that *any* sustained narrative requires contributions from many areas of the brain, particularly a narrative of seamlessly vivid sensory experiences.

But even if I had known these facts, I was such an emphatic, almost evangelical atheist, I'd have found a way to dismiss them. Accepting that I'd left my body would mean throwing out twenty-two years' worth of understanding the universe and my place in it, which I was certainly not about to do.

I read the account to it Elizabeth, and to Zelda over the phone. Later I read it to Kevin, but at some point after moving from New

York, I lost the notebook. Even so, the memory, I would find, faded not a bit for decades – which I could not explain. I'm somewhat gifted with memory in general, as you may have surmised. But that journey, what I now understand to have been a classic Near Death Experience, I can almost *re-live* to this day, except that my best efforts to recall the intensity of bliss and love are like a flashlight compared to the sun. So it goes, I've learned since, with all NDEs.

~

I want to flash forward for a bit, just to provide a little closure for this episode.

Seventeen years later, in 1999, I was jogging around Seattle's Green Lake, four years sober and midway through my Ninth-Step amends. It was a beautiful spring day in Seattle, which means everyone deprived of sunshine comes out to the park to enjoy it. Children, old folks – everyone seemed happy to be alive, to spread blankets on the grass, to skate, laugh, throw Frisbees, and illegally feed the ducks.

As I ran, the thought struck me: *You lost all this. You died at twenty-two from your own stupidity. This day, this life, this beauty – all of it was given to you by a man you were too proud to thank. He didn't just* save *your life. He actually went after it with his goodness and rescued what you had thrown away.*

Tears flowed as I ran. To dwell on the actuality of my having died had always seemed too melodramatic. I could say to myself "I crossed over," but not "I died." By this time, though, I had lost enough loved ones to understand that death holds no drama. Death, from the perspective of the living, is absence – nothing more. I would have been *absent*, gone from the world, had it not been for the efforts of a certain balding, thirty-something bartender at the Peppermint Lounge who had shared his own breath of life with a thankless brat.

I owed him my life.

I had to find him. I had to thank him. Maybe in this world of Google and such, I could track him down. At home I searched online for Peppermint Lounge, but there was none in Manhattan. All I could find were clubs outside the city, one in New Jersey or someplace, and another in Brooklyn. I dialed information and asked for the Peppermint Lounge in Manhattan, but the woman gave me the Brooklyn number.

It was all I had. So I called it. No one answered, so for a few minutes I just listened to the ringing and prayed my gratitude. My prayers were interrupted by a slightly annoyed hello.

"Is this the Peppermint Lounge?"

"Yeah, but we closed." The accent sounded Southern – certainly not Brooklyn – and the voice older.

"I'm trying to find the Peppermint Lounge in Manhattan, like kinda near the Village."

"No, this ain't. We in Brooklyn."

"Were you ever in Manhattan, like, did you move?"

"I don' know, I don' think so. I jus' sweep up here days, but the phone wouldn't quit. Why? What you want?"

So I told this man about my being in AA and working the steps and having had this revelation earlier today. Then I told him the story of that night seventeen years before and he listened, the whole country between us. I didn't go into my Near Death Experience – this was about what happened on earth. I even told the part about how I didn't like the mouth-to-mouth aspect, how shallowly I judged. The bottom line was this: I had never thanked the man who saved my life, because I was too busy being cool.

"But you clean now," he clarified. "You clean, yeah? In your AA. How long you been clean?"

"Four years."

"Four years?! Whoa! You ain't had no drugs, no alcohol, no *nothin'* for four years?"

"No nothin'."

"*That* is a beautiful thang! Man, I tell you what – that is somethin'!" He marveled for some time, then explained, "I got this good friend, he into drugs and shit, worse all a' time. His woman all tore up about it. God, she jus' all tore up. So that make me happy, hearin' 'bout you."

We talked some more about his friend, about how recovery can begin only with honesty, but when it came time to hang up, he had one more thing to add.

"You know... that man you ain't thanked, that bartender," he said gently. "I'm thinkin'... you don't need to worry none. That man, he *know* he done a good thing that day. I think he got that, he carry that with him. Inside his heart."

We said goodbye. He told me that talking to me had given him "a real lift." I told him likewise. I couldn't tell him what I was feeling – that to me, his was the voice of god.

At Vassar with Elizabeth and Phi Beta Kappa notice; New York City haircut two weeks before my Near Death Experience

9: I BECOME A DASHING INTELLECTUAL

*Where am I, or what? From what causes do I derive
my existence, and to what condition shall I return
...Most fortunately it happens, that since reason is
incapable of dispelling these clouds, ...I dine, I play a
game of back-gammon, I converse, and am merry
with my friends; and... after three or four hour's
amusement, ...I am ready to throw all my books and
papers into the fire....*

> -David Hume
> A Treatise of Human Nature

I moved in with Kevin the following spring at the place he was housesitting with his best friend in Newton Center. A few weeks before, I'd taken a Greyhound up to Boston to meet him, one that wended its way through the slums of Harlem where, seeing trashed storefronts and people in tatters circled around barrel fires, I felt more worldliness than compassion. Though the day was young, Kevin and I went directly to a bar called the Red Hat, where it took me about two of many more drinks to tell him I'd broken up with Reilly and to ask the intentionally cliché question: "Will you be my boyfriend?" He said yes.

Given that I was increasingly unhappy and panicky in Manhattan, I took only a month or two to elbow my way into his house-sitting gig, pretending I would just be a housemate. I'll never forget, though, once my various bags and boxes sat piled high in his friend's kitchen – the parents were off traveling – the way Kevin stared at them with a stricken sort of terror. It was more justified than he knew.

That was April. Then one bright Saturday afternoon in June or so as we glided into the driveway in good old rusty Lurch, Kevin asked me to wait a bit before I got out of the car. He needed to say something. I looked at him with apprehension, half afraid he meant to break up with me. We'd just come from a farmer's market and he was wearing his dead grandfather's coat – the one I had scouted for all over Vassar in my early days of stalking him.

But that obsession, already, was beginning to fade. It lost power when Kevin became my regular boyfriend, not a secret and forbidden one. It lost more when he took a job he cared about, one in state government his father helped him land, and started wearing a suit without irony. And, to be very honest, it lost a bunch when he had gum surgery and his breath smelled like a cesspool for several days. Without infatuation, or nightclub vanity, or even grades to buoy me – that is, without something to *chase*, I found myself increasingly prone to depression and anxiety. Both of these I treated by pretty much emptying the house owners' liquor cabinet. I used to stare at the blue striped T-shirt in Kevin's drawer; it had once held such powerful magic.

"I have half a million dollars," he said dully to the steering wheel, "and I'll be getting a lot more. My grandfather invented a kind of wrapping paper with foil on one side. He made a lot of money off it."

Silence.

"That's okay," I said.

"I've never told you because... I like to pretend it isn't there."

"We can still pretend," I said optimistically, reassuring him that, despite gobs of money that made him anything but counter-culture, I still considered him cool. I poured earnest sympathy into my voice but just underneath, of course, I was thinking, half a million bucks?! Are you fucking kidding me? We could do *any*thing, go *any*where! That's right: *we*. If I stayed with Kevin, I'd never have to worry about money again. How one earned that stuff was my biggest blind spot, in part because my parents had never taught us a thing about making a living.

"I don't want to draw from it," he said.

"Of course not!"

"I want to try to pull my own weight and *add* to it, you know? That's why I'm working."

"That's fine," I said.

But we did draw. And draw, and draw. When the house-sitting stint ended we rented an aging brownstone on historic Marlboro

Street, a fourth floor walk up from that venerable avenue of great arching elms and ornate stoops. I found a job at an environmental non-profit in Cambridge and kicked in a little rent, but certainly not half. We economized most of the time but occasionally went out for lavish and exorbitant dinners.

We shared a lot of happiness during that year. I remember a Saturday morning we drove into Cambridge for something. Freshly fallen snow detailed the sills of every small-paned window above the decorated shops, every railing, every wire and twig, and the sunlight bouncing off it was so bright that, without sunglasses, my eyes were dazzled to achiness. I had a nasty hangover, but I loved Kevin – the cold tinting his cheekbones, that distinctness of his blond lashes. All I remember is us getting coffee and chocolate croissants, looking for his brother, and trying not to wipe out on patches of ice. Depression still haunted me. But on that morning, at least, I felt as if life might be enough.

Around this time I accidentally almost killed myself again. Whoops! Since what Kevin called my "heart attack," I was no longer allowed cocaine. But when we threw a housewarming party at Marlboro Street with old friends from Vassar, one of them presented me with a fifth of 151 whiskey. I drank it. I'd already been drinking for hours, and I didn't quite get what that number – 151 – signified. Most of that night is blacked out, but I popped out of it twice. (Cold, it seems, always jolted my brain into record mode.) The first time, I was puking from our fire escape onto the neighbors' planters below, which may in fact have saved my life. The second, my arms slung over Kevin's and someone else's shoulders, I was being made to walk a frosty, rumpled stretch of Marlboro Street's sidewalk, my clogs clopping the pavement so haphazardly I half believed I could levitate. Literally. The only trouble was, no one could understand my words. I didn't matter how I tried. Wasn't that a fun game? – talk insistently and watch people not get it!

I came to in mid-morning, fully dressed but this time wearing no clogs. Kevin spoke without a trace of dumb accent. He told me I'd scared the shit out of him. Earlier that night he'd shaken me, slapped me, shouted, even poured water on my face, and all the while I'd flopped about like a lifeless rag doll. He'd not known whether to call 911, whether I would die of alcohol poisoning.

I flashed back to Reilly's kitchen, Reilly sipping coffee and me excusing myself to puke. All I wanted was absolution; I had zero concern about alcohol poisoning. I smiled cheerfully from beneath the slab of my hangover. Look – here I was! Everything was just fine! Personally, I thought the rag doll business might make for some good kinky jokes – but Kevin was far too angry.

To me, this experience brought only one lesson: next time, before I guzzled a fifth, I'd check to see if it was 151.

~

I constantly disparaged the east coast – its overcrowding and lack of wilderness – and praised Seattle, especially after I'd brought Kevin to visit. My whining paid off. We moved to Seattle in the summer of 1984, based on my promises that living there would cure my malaise. While we were house-hunting, we invented the code word, "lovely." It meant this place sucks beyond belief and I don't want to waste another minute looking at it. There was one apartment we looked at on urban Capital Hill, an old converted hotel, where I kept saying the floors were lovely, the view was lovely – but Kevin missed them all because he *did* like the place. He wanted to live in town, and I kept trying to find a rental in the country. For each one I found, though, the commute to downtown office work was always too long for Kevin. Eventually, with our welcome at my parents' house wearing thin, we compromised on a somewhat trashy rental house on Sand Point Way, a 1950s rambler with old shag carpeting and a corny chandelier that were admittedly "lovely."

There was also a large garage where, expanding on the carpentry skills Reilly had taught me, I built us a bed, two bookshelves, a coffee table, picnic table, and other furniture out of cheap pine wood. I would crank the radio and dance around in the sawdust to Madonna, using power tools, smoking, and drinking beer all day. In this way I avoided getting a job for some months.

It took me that long to work up enough nerve to tell Kevin my secret dream. I wanted to get my Masters in Creative Writing at the University of Washington. At Vassar, where all the self-proclaimed "writers" struck me as flamboyant and full of shit, I'd closeted my ambition. Then in Manhattan one drunken night I'd finally pounded out a melodramatic story of a selfish girl living resentfully for a summer on a rustic island with an old lady neighbor (who spoke dumb talk and died at the end). It came out well enough that I could submit it to get into the program. And Kevin had the tuition money, easy-peasy.

A new Louisa came to the fore – the intellectual rebel. Let's try that with an exclamation point: intellectual rebel! Done was the physical vanity of sexy nightclub Louisa, who had fouled out of the game. Now, by embracing the academic prowess I'd always disguised for popularity's sake, I developed a new self who concealed her body and flaunted intelligence. At some point I'd seen a photo of French philosopher Jaques Derrida looking brilliantly sloppy in his 1950s suit and tie and hit upon a wholly revamped definition of cool. I took to wearing oversized suit jackets, mostly lifted from my dad's closet, with men's dress shirts, forgoing only the tie.

I bleached my hair to an orangey blonde and later buzzed the sides to black for a two-toned look not seen by me or most people on campus, not even on MTV. (Strange as it may seem, in the 80s, hair dye was still a sort of liability, like a toupee, something you tried to pull off as natural.) A pair of men's wingtips completed the look. I smoked fiercely, striding around campus with my dead-grandfather-like coat billowing behind me and my head full of great skepticism for all things conventional – except, of course, the ideal of coolness itself. I was a Deconstructionist, whether you got what that meant or not. And, by the way, fuck you.

I judged you instantly, perceived in a flash all the mindless conformity that oriented your choices – your clothes, your job, your TV watching. I could see you judging me and I urged you mentally to go fuck yourself. All this could happen in the ten seconds we shared in an elevator or if you sat on the bus next to me. My survival depended on defeating you and everything you stood for, establishing my superiority.

One of my first quarter's courses analyzed works of Shelly and Keats in light of David Hume's philosophy. Most mornings I rolled out of bed with a hangover (fixture of living), lit a cigarette, and cracked a fat tome of densely arcane philosophy before the tea water even boiled. In Literary Theory classes I discovered that the majority of my classmates said dumb things betraying their faulty grasps of Hume, Kant, Derrida, or Foucault, and that when you said *smart* things, the professors lit up like you'd goosed them. The worst grade I ever received was a 3.9. Two of them.

My depression vanished. I was putting on a show again, performing as this inscrutable New Wave Poindexter with nicotine-stained fingers poking through Kevin's old fingerless gloves, and it was going well. I impressed the fuck out of you – or at least, so I thought.

What's more, if you'd crossed paths with me on campus, you'd probably have assumed I was a dyke. More and more the term seemed a badge, not of shame, but of counter-culture honor. I began to worship an older lesbian professor, Gertrude Stein-like in aspect, largely because of the subtly sardonic air with which she ruled her class. My literary heroes became Stein and Djuna Barnes, both lesbians. I wrote essays on both that earned 4.0s and the professor's request for a personal copy.

This same professor invited me to enroll in the University of Washington's English Ph.D. program, an honor reserved for candidates whose excellence renders the application process unnecessary. But I declined – yawn – much to my parents' disappointment. That decision impacts my life to this day. A lot of things would be easier with a Ph.D. The trouble was, I knew Ph.D. students. I knew the years of toil they poured into researching an absurdly narrow topic to add to the miles of shelved English dissertations in universities around the world. I wanted a life more dashing and adventurous, beyond the fishbowl of elite and ruthless academics. Or maybe I just doubted my ability to stand out among fiercer competitors.

My sister Adelyn didn't need to doubt anything. Her fierceness was incontestable, demonstrated as she earned a total of three Masters Degrees – in Music Performance, Music History, and Musicology – before heading off to Princeton where she would complete her Musicology Ph.D. with a ground-breaking dissertation. From what I could see, her whole raison d'etre boiled down to being smarter than everyone else, I guess in part because she *was*. No fun, playing trivial pursuit with Adelyn. You never got so much as a turn unless she landed on entertainment. No fun playing Scrabble. She'd whip out words you knew but would never have thought of. Next to hers, my mind seemed mediocre at best.

This same sense of mediocrity haunted me in my job as a reader and grader for certain English professors. In my final quarter I graded papers for a radical lesbian professor only a few years older than I who was on fire with Gender Studies, a new field at the time. My attempts to impress her always flopped. Too many holes in my knowledge came up, and filling them all seemed more than a lifetime's work. But there was another reason for her spurning me, I believed. I looked and talked as if I, too, were a lesbian. But whenever I spoke the phrase, "my boyfriend," her repulsion seemed as evident as if I'd said, "my buttjuice." And when I explained that part of the reason I wasn't staying for my Ph.D. was that my buttjuice and I were getting married and moving back to Boston where my buttjuice would earn his MBA, she always seemed to remember some important appointment.

The marriage proposal had come about while we were visiting New York for the wedding of one of Kevin's best female friends from Vassar. During the reception, while we were talking about their self-written vows, I asked:

"Do you want to do that when we get married?"

"I don't know," said Kevin. "*Are* we getting married?"

"I don't know," I answered back. "I just mean *eventually*."

"Rahr," he said, using our dumb talk name for each other (derived from the Insecure Man character's signal for promiscuity – *rahr-rahr-rahr!*) with consciously ironic sincerity, "will you marry me?"

"Yes, Rahr," I said. "I will."

So on a June afternoon a few days before I turned twenty-six, under a cotton chuppah stretched in turn under a dazzling white canopy in my parents' panoramic back yard, we married. Kevin's parents, his extended family, and all his Vassar friends flew out to Seattle for a sunny week of festivities that included an all day cruise, a bachelor/bachelorette party, and several celebratory dinners. Our wedding day itself turned out only slightly overcast, with the mountains partially obscured. Just a few weeks before, I'd captured the university's most prestigious award for creative work, $5,000 for my short story, "Spot the Sweetie." I'd written it during ten days' solitude the previous winter while Kevin was visiting his family and I, for god knows what reason, swore off liquor.

I drank heavily before the ceremony. Despite trying with all my might to cram into my mind the realization that I was getting married, despite a string trio wafting Brandenburg concertos across the lawn, my little nieces carrying my long white train, and the smiling faces of one hundred guests, I felt strangely absent. I could only watch myself going through motions with none of the feelings I ought to have. I wanted those feelings, but all I could muster were toneless, practical thoughts. Speaking my vows after the rabbi, I made myself cry. It seemed a good way to at least *look* like I felt something. Unfortunately, wedding photos show me veering a bit too far toward harrowed languishing, when I was actually shooting for poignant joy. Anyway, after much dancing to a steel drum band we'd recruited from a sidewalk show weeks before, Kevin and I retired to a five star hotel room with panoramic views and, though both whupped, checked "wedding night consummation" off our to-do list.

Immediately following which, the bride excused herself to the honeymoon suite bathroom and took the biggest dump I have *ever* taken in my entire life. Talk about laying some cable! I felt pounds lighter afterwards because I was, having dropped the whole week's worth, pretty much. Who'd have guessed that small-waisted, big-eyed bride was completely full of shit?

I'd married because I had no idea what else came next. The picture I had painted for the outside world was all for *you*, whether to please or rebuff you, to convince you I was someone. Inside, I was increasingly no one. For some months, Kevin and I had been meeting with the young rabbi who would marry us. Under his direction I "reclaimed" my Judaism and started to attend temple, where I tolerated talk of a Yahweh I considered an arrogant, sexist prick. None of it resonated. I was determined but hollow, rejecting but desperate.

Lately, an old affair had resumed in the Sand Point rental house. I can't remember just when it happened, but the mirrors, belts, and tube socks had all started coming out again regularly. I had never really stopped, except at Vassar and in Manhattan when I had no privacy. Any time I visited my parents' house I would revert, and even a few times at the Newton house-sitting place. Now that I had a room of my own where I could draw the blinds, the routine had changed only a little. I knew by now the images that packed a punch, so that the whole ritual, from decision (fuck everything) to clean up (I'm so sick), took less than fifteen minutes. After-guilt, likewise, became routine. Yes, I'm a creepy twisted pervert. Everyone would be horrified. Right.

What need was there for my husband to know? Our sex life had dwindled to about twice per month, but I was always good to go if he wanted. Those intercourse orgasms, though, became increasingly difficult to rev up, so I often told him I didn't need one.

"What's this old thing?" he once asked of the old bikini top I'd been using all these years, which was too small and stored, not with our swim stuff, but in my underwear drawer.

"It's nothing," I said. "Put it back."

"It's so old. Why not toss it?"

"I don't want to," I said simply. "Put it back."

Now the newlyweds shipped boxes back to Boston. The very day we were to leave from my parents' house for our European honeymoon, I came downstairs early in the morning to get a towel and overheard my parents talking in the kitchen. I put together that my grandmother – the famous art historian – had just died. She'd been unable to attend my wedding because of a trip to Italy which, at age ninety, had proved too much for her.

I looked into the cupboard containing towels. I noted its familiar scent, and the associated awareness of cleanliness and order. And I realized that, once again, I felt nothing. My only thought had been of inconvenience, of whether her funeral might delay our trip. I went quietly upstairs and proceeded with my shower. When I came down to breakfast, I *pretended* to absorb the stunning blow of this news with tremendous grief.

And yet, my callousness frightened me. I'd loved my grandmother to some degree and admired her to a vast one. The feelings that should have sprung up by themselves, just as they should have for my wedding, were simply *not there*. Even earlier in the month when I learned I'd won the big prize for my story – no feeling. Admittedly I'd *practiced* looking stunned in the mirror or while driving for groceries, but when I actually heard – You won! – I manufactured overblown stutters of amazement when in truth I could have just blown a bubble with my gum, staring blankly. What did I *really* feel then? Relief: "Now I can quit worrying about *not* winning." I felt a similar relief learning my grandmother's memorial service wouldn't happen for weeks.

Amazement. Joy. Grief. Love. They all pulled no-shows. They left me as empty-handed as a hostess with her home all laid out for guests who never arrive. The only emotion to show up on my doorstep was heavy and paralyzing guilt who occupied a big armchair and wouldn't budge. Meanwhile at the window, just to overdo the metaphor, tapped the haunted fear that something might be grossly wrong with me. Why couldn't I feel? I'd always faked myself socially, and now, it seemed, I had to fake an inner life of emotion as well.

Clockwise from top left: Clowning with Zelda on a visit home from Newton; Lurch broke down in New Hampshire, good reason for a six pack; bleached hair in grad school; engaged but a little bit dykish, 1986.

10: I BECOME A NEUROTIC JEWISH HOUSEWIFE

And I say ...
I wouldn't live there if you paid me.
I couldn't live like that, no siree!
I couldn't do the things the way those people do.
I couldn't live there if you paid me to.

-Talking Heads
The Big Country

Words can't describe the emptiness I felt upon returning to Boston. Gone was my audience of professors and classmates. Gone was the focus needed for writing assignments with urgent deadlines. Marriage had snuffed out the last of Kevin's magic. He was just a person and stuck with me by law, anyway, so impressing him offered no avenue of progress. For the first few weeks, we house-sat in Waltham, a wealthy neighborhood where run over squirrels festooned the roads like cherry pies tossed from a madman's bakery truck. The ultra-mod 1970s house we occupied reeked of some potent mystery apple juice, somehow related to ceiling mold, and stood amid acreage recently bulldozed for more development. When Kevin took the car for his business school preparations, I found myself marooned in a wasteland.

Worse still, I'd become aware of an alarming conspiracy among his family. They intended for us to *buy* a house, then reside in it for decades while we aged. There, I was expected to get pregnant and bear offspring – which would sap our attention and life energy for the next several decades. In other words, they wanted to kill me.

True, Kevin's wealth was now mine. As his wife, I could have had anything I wanted – clothes, facials, pedicures. But I wanted none of them. There was no one important to show off for. Without that, life felt pointless. Plus it seemed to me in a way I could not pinpoint even to myself, that if I spent "our" money – planned trips for us, joined the tennis club (though I didn't play tennis), or even took on Kevin's last name to become the rhyming Louiser Friezier (as Bostonians pronounced my name) – I would be edging closer to captivity in that wholesome prison of familial life, which I dreaded as a kind of death. Whereas sitting around getting drunk all the time somehow kept me rebellious, kept my life mine.

Eventually we rented the ground floor of a quaint Brookline duplex from an elderly Jewish couple who lived upstairs. The place was old and charming, not far from the famous Kennedy's' childhood home. Our front windows looked out at the graceful maples and oaks of Fuller Street. Wainscoting and floral wallpaper decorated most rooms, seeming to hearken back to content housewives of the fifties. Three bedrooms meant there was a study for Kevin's schoolwork and a room of my own for my writing. Because that's what I was going to be – a famous writer!

Had I not seized the grand writing prize at my university? Had I not completed a top-notch graduate program with a GPA of 3.97? Now I would craft my own assignments – compose a profound short story along the lines of "Cathedral" or "Where Are You Going, Where Have You Been?" – and editors of the most prestigious literary magazines would allot them 4.0s. What did it matter that I was twenty-six, utterly baffled by life, and couldn't feel?

I wrote long, chatty letters to various people – to the rabbi who'd married us, various professors, Adelyn, and my parents – and considerately retained copies for my future biographers. Here's one to my great aunt, whom Kevin and I visited in Northern Italy toward the end of our honeymoon. Sister to my famous grandmother, she'd been a beautiful violinist of antique music who toured Europe with a trio, was forced to work in a Nazi kitchen, and risked her life to help rebels – one of whom was caught and hung to death by piano wire – escape the country. She was worth trying to impress.

All my letters are written in this same affected voice of June-Cleaver-turned-brilliant-artist:

> 5/23/1987: "I signed up for a night-school writing course only to find it full of stupid people who wrote tedious stories of themselves thinly disguised. At least I could

feel thankful that my problems are a little more sophisticated. This is the most difficult time I've ever gone through with my writing. When my state of mind is not balanced, I write off-center. It is as though I have a grudge against the world, and that pressure distorts my vision. I write to prove something to myself, instead of writing life... The pool has to be still before it can reflect something."

"Only to find it full of stupid people..." Isn't that awesome? Smarty-pants have it so tough! Among my "more sophisticated" problems was recurring nightmares. In my most frequent one, Kyatty, our parakeet, had gotten loose, often in a frozen greenhouse at night. As I wandered the darkness calling to her, I'd begin to sense a horrifically evil presence stalking me from the shadows, a darkness potent as the devil. You'll never guess who it was: none other than the Patty doll with the felt-penned beard that Zelda and I had used as villain for our first games of "Pretty Girls Tied Up." Patty-villain had the same big swath of brown plastic hair, but he'd aged into a stocky, swarthy dwarf of no mercy. He meant to destroy me in the most sinister way, or to possess me as a demon. Toward the end of every dream I'd be forced to turn on him, stand my ground, and try to bluff my way out of my fate. "Well, well, well..." I'd struggle to say, but my voice simply wouldn't come out, until I pushed so hard I would bray in my sleep.

Kevin called it neighing, because it came out in a warbly kind of *wa-ah-ah-ah*! It was actually more like a goat, though. Kevin, too, had a remarkably similar problem: night terrors. These dated back to his childhood, when his older brother had been critically injured by a car while sledding and almost died. Kevin would feel himself falling into the blackness of space with a sensation of dropping so real that he would scream in his sleep: *Ah-h-h*! On one particular night we both went off at the same time and woke each other up. It was a moment emblematic of our relationship – all the stuff we didn't talk about rising to the surface.

Zelda was once again my only friend. Having graduated from art school, she worked as a housecleaner and painted in her small apartment, which literally neighbored the Boston Museum of Fine Arts. She'd come over and the two of us would get plastered and watch TV. Adelyn was still at Princeton, shacked up with a geeky physicist boyfriend. Zelda, Kevin, and I went to visit her for a weekend in their small apartment. I'd never, in all my life, seen her so happy. She was tearing up the Musicology Department like hell on wheels. All three of us sisters slept in one bedroom that night, where my neighing woke the other two.

I tried. I cooked. I built a shitload of pine furniture in our driveway. How the hell did normal people live without constantly wanting to blow their brains out? I simply couldn't find a way. For the first month or two I tried really hard not to tie myself up. I'd not had a chance since having left Sand Point, and I hoped to stay quit. The nightmares, I knew, had something to do with this compulsion. On the other hand, now I did have my own room, and it had blinds. They were rolls of aged, sun-yellowed paper with a few minor tears near the bottoms that just *made* you want to tie yourself up and wank. The instant I pulled them down, the trance would close over my head like water. Soothing silence. Worlds in the mirror. Clicky, firm belts. Not-me. Not-me. For that fifteen minutes or however long it took, I knew peace.

If the phone rang in the middle of all this, I'd often answer it. I remember standing by the bed in my yellow room, a gag slung casually around my neck, wearing the old bikini top and no panties with a number of belts around me. I probably toyed with a tube sock knotted around one wrist while I chatted and laughed. Whoever it was, they *really* couldn't see me. It was just like life; present them with a few tokens of normalcy and most people were willing to sketch in the rest. I could be charming, simply charming.

We flew back to Seattle for Christmas, where I somehow imagined I'd feel normal. The dog of my childhood, our sweet German shepherd, had to be put down because her hips had gone. On her last day, which broke out in rare winter sunshine, I took her to her favorite park and held her hind legs suspended in a blanket so she could walk with her front legs and sniff things. She was so excited, not having been able to walk or get out for so long, that she panted a smile and even trotted a little as I jogged beside her. Her love of life was heart-wrenching – I saw it, but I couldn't feel it. That night I had to get on a plane a few hours before her injection. Partway drunk as I said goodbye, I knew in some ways there was no one I loved more, but I couldn't cry. I kissed her forehead, smelled her scent, looked into her eyes. I thought of those weeks we'd spent alone at the island cabin – just Trouvée and me by the fire, or walking along the waves – when she'd been my only friend in the world. I felt nothing – nothing, that is, except the torment of *not* feeling, that wasteland of numbness. On the plane I looked at my watch and thought, They're doing it now: she'll be gone forever in a minute or two. Yet that fact pulled at my heart no more than whether our snack might be peanuts or pretzels.

The day after my 27th birthday, Zelda left Boston. She was flying down to New York to meet college friends and begin a road trip back to Seattle. I took her to the airport and we said goodbye. As I was driving back through the Logan tunnel, I finally, finally after all this time, cried. For those moments I could let go, allowing that everything was lost, everything sucked. I had no one. Life was not mine anymore; it was a sterile obstacle course overwhelming this crippled dummy I'd become.

Kevin didn't know what to do for me. He'd long ago reached a point of disgust with my drinking – which made him my enemy. To threaten an alcoholic's drinking is like threatening a normal person's air supply. Having come home so often to find me bombed, he came home less and less, taking on a job in addition to full time business school. When his business school friends came over to study or socialize, I judged them as chipper, shallow conformists I wanted nothing to do with. So Kevin socialized without me.

Now the panic attacks took over. If I wasn't actively wanking or drinking, they were on me. The tremors I'd experienced in New York were nothing to the doomsday devastation that toppled my reality in Brookline. The first sign would be that I couldn't quite catch my breath. The more I tried, the worse it got, until the terror came on, itself as thick as drunkenness.

Consciousness – what the hell was consciousness?! It could cut off at any moment; awareness could somehow upend itself. Dizzy. What could stop this? How could I possibly keep fighting to distinguish what was real from what might be nothing but vapid clouds of crazy? I'd never heard of panic attacks. In 1987, I believed I was the only person this happened to, just as I was the only demon-chased neigher, only mirror-lost wanker on the planet.

On a referral from my mother-in-law, I began seeing a therapist in the suburbs around Walden Pond – a pleasant woman in her mid-fifties with Multiple Sclerosis I was always secretly afraid of catching. I told her nothing.

"How are you today?" she might ask, setting aside her cane.

I'd settle into the brightly cushioned wicker armchair and fold my hands demurely, having already tied myself up perhaps twice that morning but allotted sufficient time for the red marks to fade, then bolted a quick glass of wine before our noon appointment.

"I'm great!" I'd say brightly, chewing spearmint gum. "I've been working on a new story."

So damn annoying, the biddy wouldn't let me smoke!

I couldn't tell her I'd made a fatal mistake in marrying Kevin. I still loved him because he was good, but I'd only been *in* love with his magic, and he'd lost it. Our intimacy felt like a childish playhouse, a toy you pretend to still like. Dumb talk had cutesified our every exchange until nothing could be said in dead earnest – and yet we still used it constantly because we had no other currency for love.

I couldn't explain that I'd once dared to defy Reilly's authority in order to snare Kevin. The Emma Peel of romantic intrigue, I'd pulled it off. Now that hazardous trail of wild adventures had led into the plastic cul-de-sac of marriage – a dead end. This role was not for me. I was *not* a Jewish housewife. I did *not* enjoy shopping at Lord and Taylor, I did *not* get a bang out of Passover.

Most of all, I couldn't tell her what a colossal liar Louisa P. was. She had lied to the rabbi, lied to Kevin, to her parents, to *everyone* by pretending to be a self-sustaining young woman, to know who the hell she was. If I wasn't a writer, I was nothing. If I wasn't brilliant, I had no excuse to be. And the humiliating truth was, no one wanted my stories. I'd sent out manuscripts to zillions of literary magazines. All had been rejected. Rejection slips literally covered the inside of the closet door in my writing room.

One sunny day I took a brisk walk in the bright, cold sunshine to exercise my panic away. I made it a block and a half before adrenaline flooded my system to the point of palsy so that my knees kept buckling under me. I grabbed a No Parking sign and held on as if at sea. A kind, middle-aged woman appeared from nowhere. Did I need help? She took my arm and led me along the sloshing, turbulent sidewalk. Eventually we reached my front door, where she made me promise to call 911. I didn't, though.

Around this time I began keeping a journal – and never stopped. I wrote at first to impress an imagined audience. I couldn't help it. Why else would anyone write?

> 4/6/1987: "I am so lonely. Lonelier than I can ever tell, because to tell would be no longer to feel lonely. There is something out there but I fall short onto my face, and afterward is the silence of myself."

I flew home for another visit to Seattle – Kevin didn't come along – but there the panic worsened. One morning, sleeping out on the deck of the summer cabin with Zelda, I woke just before dawn immersed in panic. I found myself swimming halfway between dreams and waking. I don't know exactly what delirium tremens are about, but I sometimes wonder if I had them. When I lifted my swirling head to look out at the meadow, I saw a black panther emerge from the head of the beach trail. It was huge! It slouched along the edge of the meadow, all menacing intent. Right there! This was for real! It meant to stalk us! My father and brother came out brandishing pieces of firewood, meaning to drive it away.

Frantically, I shook Zelda awake: "Look! Look!" I pointed, my hand trembling so violently it appeared a parody of terror. But Zelda saw no panther, no brother or father. And now, inexplicably, neither did I. The deck seemed to roll on ocean waves.

"Are you okay, Luza? Are you okay?"

I went in the bathroom and pleaded desperately with the spigots: *Please, please! Don't take my sanity! World, I need my sanity!* The mirror, the faucets and water cup and toothbrushes – all these things, I reminded myself, were merely real.

It's not our problem! they replied with exasperation. *We're just the bathroom stuff, for chrissake! You're the one who's losing her mind!* The fixtures were heartless. The whole bathroom was heartless.

The point at which I could take even a shred of satisfaction in comparing myself to Virginia Woolf had long since come and gone. I was terrified not only of ending up in a mental ward but, even worse, of losing the world. Sanity, I realized in that bathroom moment, is life's most precious gift and taken utterly for granted by the sane. We assume the world will stay put, that we'll know which thoughts are "real" and which "imaginary." But when the border between liquefies, you cannot recognize the world, and there is no peace.

I prayed to a God that didn't exist: *Help me! Please!*

I chugged a few glasses of wine at breakfast, right in front of my parents, and felt much better. Inwardly, I resolved to stay drunk at all times. And I pretty much did. My mother took me to see a doctor in Seattle, a kindly man in his sixties who pronounced it a case of bad nerves. Perhaps the stress of being a newlywed, he said. What I needed was something to fill my time – children! Had I considered having them? Meanwhile, he wrote me a lovely prescription for Valium.

When I returned to Boston and described to my therapist, Kitty, a fraction of what had happened, she insisted I not refill the Valium prescription. Kevin had told her I drank – I'm sure of it – and that now I was double-dipping. She referred me instead to a psychiatrist to evaluate me for anti-depressants – a term I had never heard. I barely recall that visit. He diagnosed me with "panic attacks" brought on by "depression." I wrote to my graduate school friend, Rosemary:

> 9/8/1987: "The fact that he recommended *anti-depressant* drugs – it's never occurred to me that I might be depressed. It seems like such a simple problem compared to all the complicated diagnoses I've invented. Really, if there is any possibility of those weird-out spells coming back, I'd do anything to avoid them. …Every one I've had has made me more afraid of some kind of permanent slip."

Strangely, I never filled that prescription for anti-depressants. Instead, I began to get better on my own. There were two reasons for this.

The first was that taking Valium even for just a week or two had exposed the attacks as nothing more than a symptom. Whenever I took one, the attacks went away. If a pill could annihilate them, I realized, they must not be real. And if they weren't real, they couldn't kill me. So I learned a new response. Now, whenever I started feeling dizzy, I played a game of chicken with my own panic attack: *I'm gonna die, am I? Fine, let's do it. Let's see you try.* I'd let go for the ride – the swirling, the palsy, the loss of all control.

The only requirement for this method to work was that you had to be *genuinely ready to die.* In some ways, I was. My secret weapon, I think, was that life had become so unbearable I was almost ready to chuck it. *Let's go!* It was like cheerfully handing an armed mugger your wallet, jotting down your PIN, and providing directions to the nearest ATM, then confessing that frankly you'd been considering suicide anyway, so you really appreciated the help. If you meant it, there would be no fear.

But it's not a method I would recommend. During my bitter willingness to surrender – a sort of psychic suicide – something slipped inside me. I underwent some sort of Sybil-like shift in identity. Just as years before at Vassar, Kevin's lackadaisical irresponsibility seemed the antidote to Reilly's teetering tray of *shoulds* and *oughts,* now I shifted toward an indifferent willingness to dump my whole life.

The other reason was that I'd landed a job at a women's fitness spa, Fitness Universal. No one knew back then that exercise alleviates depression, so why I went for that job, I have no idea. The only experience I'd had with aerobics was checking out the covers of my mom's Jane Fonda videos, but I somehow convinced my interviewer that ballet and aerobics amounted to the same thing. Not true, by the way. I didn't know at first that everybody made fun of my ballet leotards with the leg holes cut way too low, and my bargain aerobics shoes that looked like foot marshmallows.

Everything in that females-only spa was pink, including walls, machines, and carpeting. Two years after Jamie Lee Curtis showed off aerobics as sexy in the movie *Perfect* (which I'd never seen), our glamorous instructors ruled a realm of glossy spandex and mirror-fueled vanity. Most of my coworkers had big '80s hair, wore fake nails, and tossed out "like" several times per sentence around gymnastically active gum. Our constant soundtrack featured songs like Exposé's "Come Go with Me" and The Cover Girls' "Show Me."

On my first day, the manager showing me around stepped out of the break room and left me there among three instructors who introduced themselves. Jenna was in her early twenties, an Asian girl with Chrissie Hynde hair and a dark tan marred by a recent bout of chicken pox. She reclined in a vinyl swivel chair eating instant oatmeal with one leg up on a table, and struck me as a self-proclaimed ring leader.

"Were you up all night?" one of the blondes asked her

"Nah, went home. But *you* – talk about crazy—!"

"Oh, shut the fuck up!"

"*You* shut the fuck up!"

The two big-haired blondes returned to the front desk, leaving me alone with the chicken pox girl. With her spoon she waived aside everything I'd overheard.

"We have fun here," she said dismissively. "I mean, the people are cool and you get to work out. Not exactly what I want to do with my life, but it's fun for now. "

"What do you want to do with your life?" I asked. I don't know why.

"Ha! I used to think I was going to be famous," she shot back, more frank than I'd expected. She balled up her lunch bag and shot a basket with a trace of jockish cool. "And I didn't really care how I got there. But I've been kinda letting that go these days. It ain't gonna happen, and that's okay."

I didn't tell her I clung to the same stupid hope. I *would* be a famous writer. But if you looked closely, you realized this girl half believed she *was* famous – right here and now. She rambled on about how a bunch of them got bombed the other night, barhopping and snorting lines in some ladies' room. I'd later hear more – how they'd all stripped to bras and panties in a showdown of who was foxiest.

The manager came back in.

"Just filling her in on FU debauchery," Jenna sighed, taking up a *Vogue.*

The manager cringed. "Good god, Jenna! It's her first *day!*" Then, to me, "Don't listen to *any* of them!"

I was a terrible employee at first. Whenever I tried to sell memberships, what blared in my thoughts was, "Sure, you could buy this package – or you could just *not* and save *a ton* of money!" My classes began as horrendous disasters. The clip-on mic scared me, so I went without and no one could hear me. Not having my own music, I played scuffed up vinyl albums everyone was sick of, with beats-per-minute ranges all over the map. I couldn't call sequences in advance, and my repertoire of moves was pathetic. Worse still, I actually have some kind of dyslexia for telling left from right, so I'd call one direction and go the other. For the first couple of weeks, women rolled their eyes and walked out on my classes.

Now I understood why Jenna, the Chrissy Hynde wanna-be, might believe herself famous: she had aerobics charisma. If you really thought about it, our classes consisted of nothing but hopping up and down to music, something that Kevin liked to point out. But there were *ways* of hopping up and down that inspired followers to feel something momentous afoot. A talented instructor seemed to be pushing them ever closer to some explosive horizon of adrenaline and exultation.

This, Jenna could do. For her evening high-impact class, latecomers had to add their names to a waitlist and stick a numbered tag on their chests as they stood aside and watched enviously. If a class member bowed out for some reason, we'd announce the next number via the desk microphone and some jubilant woman would leap into the action.

Jenna mixed her own tapes – Prince, Madonna, Janet Jackson, Elvis Costello, Jody Watley, and hits like "Wild Wild West" – sequenced with gradually mounting tempos. Like a jazz dance instructor counting down a preparation, she knew how to shout spontaneous phrases that fit with the beat and revved you up. Her cues were all called rhythmically and in advance, while she turned from the mirror to face her group without a hitch. She'd laugh, hair bouncing above her cotton sweatband, and count down reps from eight in urgent tones that built to a crescendo of "GIMME all you GOT now!!"

The women loved it. They would holler, they would whoop. One svelte young multi-racial woman whipped off her long hair, swung it over her head a few times, and flung it jubilantly across the room – genetically bald and not caring who knew it. They were hopping up and down, sure, but they were also sweating, pushing themselves, believing they could reach new heights because they believed in Jenna. She had fire in her, no question about it. That's why in the year before she'd come within one match of making the US Olympic volleyball team – the reason she used to imagine she'd be famous.

Panic attacks left me. I had a new goal now. I had a new cool. And most of all, I had someone worth impressing – a girl with a touch of magic.

With Kevin at our bachelor/bachelorette party in the Camlin's Cloud Room; the happy bride (going for 'deeply moved');

11: I PULL A LESBIAN GEOGRAPHIC; 1ST WEIRD THING

And if a double-decker bus
Crashes into us
To die by your side
Is such a heavenly way to die
And if a ten-ton truck
Kills the both of us
To die by your side
Well, the pleasure - the privilege is mine

-*The Smiths*
There is a Light

"Pulling a geographic" is an AA term for pulling up stakes and leaving for a new life in a new town because you're convinced the problem messing up your life is all the crappy relationships and stressful roles that define you in the old town. So you shake off the whole mess. "Fuck this!" you say, "I'm so outta here!" You probably throw in some complaints about the weather or traffic, too. But then you settle down in your wonderful new place and before you know it, you find yourself in the same crappy relationships and stressful roles, just with a different cast. Nothing has changed, because the alcoholic hasn't changed within. "The problem," recovered alcoholics explain, "was that I brought *me* with me."

Becoming a lesbian was my way of pulling a geographic.

About eight years earlier, one night when I was sleeping beside Reilly, I had an erotic dream. In the dream, my former chemistry lab partner, Nina, and I were both part of a harem, dressed as belly dancers and lounging in a lavish pavilion on velvet cushions. During real life labs I had noticed that Nina's breasts were both large and perfect, so in all my fears of being a lesbian psycho-killer, I did my best never to look at them. But in the dream we lay close together. Nina was wearing a jeweled headband and push-up bodice like Barbara Eden's in *I Dream of Jeannie* – which, in early childhood, had been of great interest to me. She looked at me with heavy eyes, knowing what I wanted. Then she unclasped her bodice, and out rolled those perfect bosoms. With meaningful silence she guided a nipple toward my mouth. Nina wanted this. I wanted this. When my lips closed around it, orgasm burst throughout the dream, intense enough to blot out all else.

I woke. At first I tried urgently to return to the pavilion, but it was too late. Then came the cloud of shame. To me, raised in the 1960s, this image and the desire it reflected were sick. I never told anyone about the dream – least of all Reilly.

All my life, starting in grade school, I'd had crushes on girls who were either my friends or distant objects of worship. I could tell you in depth about each. But I'd also associated lesbianism with my drawings, bondage compulsion, and, during college, the only lesbian I knew of – a lumbering, overweight girl with disfiguring acne, downright deadly BO, and an actual *beard* she sported in fuck you defiance. I feared I might somehow turn into her if I succumbed to lesbian desire. But in graduate school, where I'd been exposed to cool lesbian authors, students, and professors, all that had changed. When I married Kevin, I consciously left myself a little caveat, that if I ever had the chance to make love with a beautiful woman, I would seize it. That wouldn't count as infidelity, I reasoned; it belonged in a separate category.

When, during my 'chicken' games with the death threats of panic, I let go my hold on my life and who I had been, something shifted inside me. What happened to me in 1987 was an all out changing of the guard. A new persona stepped in who was decidedly butch. Masculine. Tough. At the fitness club I went from fat-assed novice to a 'cut up,' confident, badass instructor and personal trainer. FU sent me to school for certification. I worked out more than once per day, coming in on my days off. I bought bright capri tights, leotards with leg holes almost to my waist, and overpriced Reebok shoes. At home I hovered near the radio boom box, jumping to hit "record" at just the right instant, and replaying the combination to be sure the tape fit together with slightly rising beats per minute. And at night, I started going out with the FU gang for drinks.

Kevin tried at first to get to know the FU crew. He came along for a weekend outing at a beach house in Gloucester. But getting fucked up was the name of the game there, an exploit that for Kevin had lost its charm. "These people act like kids!" he marveled. The boy who had rolled into Vassar Lake with me no longer indulged even in cigarettes. His circle of business school friends shared a wholesome interest in working hard and prospering – not getting bombed and puking.

FU felt just like high school. By late summer, I found myself in a feud with Vivian, a forty-something instructor with a New York accent who had, in her youth, married an older Vegas style singer, now a doddering burden to her. She made no secret of her contempt for me, often ignoring even direct questions. I confided this trouble to Jenna.

"Vivian hates all the new girls," she assured me. "Plus she thinks you've got a stick up your ass 'cause you went to Vassar and all." She smiled, flicked her cigarette and tossed back her hair. We all smoked in the alley behind the spa, our bright leotards contrasting with the grimy Dumpsters. From then on, Jenna and I would trade knowing glances each time Vivian slighted me.

Then came a fateful evening when Jenna's six-thirty class didn't fill – a November snowstorm had taken drivers by surprise. Managing the spa that night was Janet, a wild local rocker who didn't give a damn what you did so long as no other managers found out. With her permission, I stuffed my sweat jacket behind the front desk and ran out to join Jenna's warm-up, leaping into an open spot just behind her.

A child-like smile lit up Jenna's face, and mine must have looked the same. My form for every move had, by this time, become almost as smooth as hers. Each time our eyes met in the mirror, I felt infused with more energy and aerobicized even harder. She cranked songs I loved, called combinations I knew, so we were constantly in sync. Her eyes kept shining back to me. We whooped in the "Ooo-ah! Ooo-ah!" style of the day and worked up the rest of the class.

Something happened during that class. Our attraction became mutual. Or to put it more romantically, we fell in love.

~

Infatuation is a tricky drug. The first time it transforms your world, you throw all your faith into it. You step off the edge of reality fully believing you can fly. But the second time, you begin to recognize its tricks. The intoxication has become somewhat familiar, so you have to set aside more and more nagging insight to slide into it. I had, it seemed, two options:

A) Endure more empty months of depression and loneliness.
B) Lie to myself just a little – ignore blatant similarity of the excitement inspired by Jenna to that inspired by Kevin just five years before – and revel in secret bliss.

I chose B.

Homophobia is likewise puzzling. In my family, we weren't raised to *despise* homosexuals. But a gay person was first and foremost a *sex-seeking* person. If all things sexual were dark and depraved, then homosexuals, who were *defined by* sex, had to be moral leppers. Enraptured as I was with Jenna, I was romantically paralyzed by this simple syllogism: A) All gay people are creeps. B) I am not a creep. C) Therefore, I am not gay.

I know, you're probably wondering about B. I *was* pretty creepy, what with tying myself up every day to get off. But that was all *secret*. Lesbianism, on the other hand, with someone *outside* the mirror would be a public statement. And in public, I was all about normal.

For months I harbored a full on obsession with Jenna, yet concealed all but the subtlest flirtations. If we could just be best friends, if I could just get really close, that would be enough. Her eyes were so incredibly beautiful, with their smooth, almond perfection as graceful as calligraphy.

We double dated a few times, Kevin wedged across the booth from her slightly pudgy Irish-Filipino boyfriend who took a great interest in hockey and little else. The two of them sat almost inert while Jenna and I gabbed and hooted and giggled our heads off through several pints. Still, such antics could easily fall within the bounds of "girlfriends."

Kevin sensed otherwise. So did I. But we never spoke a word about what was going on. Why not? Because doing so would require uncomfortable honesty. We'd both been taught that what was uncomfortable could be denied. Incredible as it seems, throughout this entire fiasco, the word "lesbian" was never spoken between us.

One night Kevin and I went out for dinner at a restaurant where I couldn't help eagerly checking for Jenna every time the door opened. Kevin's company felt about as significant as the parmesan cheese shaker's, a slight he was well aware of. I could feel his hurt and despair, his amazement that a ditzy Asian aerobicizer had replaced him in my heart, but there seemed nothing else I could do. I had to look – again, again – was it *Jenna?*

The next day Jenna told me she *had* in fact *entered* that very restaurant within minutes of our leaving, where she had for mysterious reasons suffered a fainting spell. This must be a sign, I thought. I'd been supposed to kneel over her, stroke her face, utter frantic words like, "Speak to me, Jenna! Please!" I got some good mileage out of that fantasy, even recognizing it as a new version of one I'd made up in the first grade for a cute boy at my classroom table in which I was the fainter.

Our first date came about accidentally. A number of FU girls had planned to go dancing at Man Ray's – a Cambridge nightclub – but everyone bailed except for Jenna and me. At first she seemed disappointed, but we ended up drinking and dancing into morning hours, just we two. Jenna had a springy, jockish sort of way of dancing, as if the music pressed down springs in her legs that would rebound on the beat – a young Keanu Reeves. I liked it. I got drunk enough to put on someone else's coat and freak out thinking my wallet was gone from my pocket. It seemed hilarious afterwards.

After this we started going out, just the two of us, several nights per week. The more Jenna drank, the more black accent she picked up. Early on, just an edge of sassy would creep into her voice, but soon after came the head waggles and street drawl: "Ain' gon' happen, white boy, 'cause dat be bow-sheeyit!" Asian girl-ness was to her what Jewish wifedom was to me; she flipped the bird at it every chance she got.

At home, Jenna was at war with her traditional Chinese parents. *Joy Luck Club* hadn't been written yet, but she lived it. Both parents had immigrated to America as teens but lived in Chinese enclaves where neither acculturated. This enraged Jenna – the drag they placed on her social success. They never came to a single volleyball game; they wanted her to get married. As a child she'd once answered the phone to be unexpectedly blasted by a racist hate call – and this was somehow her parents' fault.

"They live in their own world," she rolled her eyes. "Ignorant, ignorant, ignorant!"

Her mother raised a beautiful garden of Chinese vegetables, weird squashes that coated themselves with white fuzz for storage in the cellar, but other than that, the drain of television claimed most of her attention. "And she doesn't even *understand* ninety percent of what they're *saying!*" Her mother would occasionally run a broad dust mop along the halls of their old, three story duplex –

they rented out the other side – but no one had ever wiped the walls around light switches, which were black with smudges. Her father had worked in restaurants all his life, so now that he was retired, he cooked sumptuous dishes for the family every night.

"It's just *food*, you know? But they make it some kind of religion!" Every time I joined them for dinner, her mother would admonish me, "Eat mohr foot!" If nieces and nephews were visiting – Jenna was the youngest – her grandmotherly chopsticks would pluck morsels of meat from her own bowl to tuck into theirs. "You need grow," she'd say meaningfully.

Jenna had rebelled by embracing pop culture, but I sensed that now she'd begun to hunger for something nobler. And that's where Louisa fit in. It was easy to entice her with my family lore – how my grandmother had directed the Smithsonian's American Art Museum, and my grandfather, a Russian prodigy, had been Concertmaster of the National Symphony Orchestra. (I left out the Depression era coffee salesman and home seamstress on my dad's side.) In her eyes, I came from a world of culture, yet I taught a decent high-impact class. She'd never met anyone like me – and she fell for the whole act.

Victims in rebellion. That was the bond we shared. Jenna was a victim of her parents' restrictive views, and I was somehow a victim of Kevin's supervision, even though he supported me – or was it *because* he did? Damn them both! We were bohemians! We sought out drunken adventure at local dives where our FU co-worker Janet belted out earsplitting rock with slurred lyrics. At parties we bought coke, which Kevin had basically forbidden me to have. Did they say we were acting immature and irresponsible? Fuck 'em! We were too full of life and freedom for them to comprehend.

On the dance floor and at bars, some of the dudes whose invitations we rebuffed accused us of being lesbians. Sour grapes! The FU bookkeeper, formerly Jenna's best friend, started to view us suspiciously. And Kitty, the therapist I was still seeing, asked if there were perhaps a lesbian element in my friendship with Jenna.

"No, no!" I said. "Kevin just doesn't like me having any friends of my own." I had to be protective. And just to be safe, I quit therapy altogether. I hardly ever tied myself up anymore, and now drank with Jenna more often than alone. Whatever I had created with Jenna, its buoyancy was hoisting me from the darkness.

~

Few people could have been less interested in the paranormal than I was at this point. And yet here, in the midst of my total absorption with romance and the personality shift I was so eagerly chasing, came the first Weird Thing. Perhaps there had been predecessors that I'd missed, or perhaps near constant drunkenness blocked me from them, but this one literally, as you'll see, stopped me in my tracks. I did not believe spirits walked the earth. I did not believe in the other side, the realm of spirit. And I'd label anyone who did a loony. Whatever had happened to me that night at the Peppermint Lounge, I was committed to shutting it away in the past.

That beach house in Gloucester belonged to the family of the FU bookkeeper, Edith. When she invited all of us out there for a winter weekend party, Kevin didn't come along – although he would be picking me up on Sunday as we had to be somewhere. Jenna's boyfriend, Vince, came up with her, and luck put them in the room next to mine, where I could hear their springs rhythmically squeaking as I tried to sleep. The sound was sheer torture to me. I loved Jenna. I had no earplugs. Jealousy and despair washed over me – how would I *ever* win her away from a *man*? All my hopes seemed foolish, and I cried.

I woke early the next morning to their voices, a soft exchange of tonalities coming through the wall. I would endure no more squeaking. I got up and went downstairs. The living room was occupied by several sleeping guests. Since it was only about seven AM, I didn't dare so much as whistle a tea kettle on the kitchen side of the room. Outside, a winter storm was casting sheets of rain at the large picture windows. Inside me roiled a turmoil of frustration over Vince and Jenna's lovemaking. To me it seemed perfectly fitting to venture out alone in the storm à la *Wuthering Heights* or *King Lear*, to rage against the gods who denied me what I so poignantly desired. I bundled up in some of Edith's family raingear and went out on the beach.

The clouds hung so low I could see only a hundred yards ahead of me. To my left were beachside houses getting pelted with rain, and to my right, wind-whipped waves pounding the beach. I walked for some time with my head down, feeling hopeless and empty. Gradually the row of houses to my left gave way to grassy sand dunes that stretched back for some distance. There was some kind of estuary behind the dunes, some place no one could build. And out of these dunes came a man.

He emerged from the tall clumps of grass about fifty feet in front of me, walking with a purposeful stride in high black boots and headed straight toward the water as if intent on some business. I could see from this distance that he was stocky, maybe in his sixties, with a beard more grizzled than not. But what I admired about him as I got closer, him coming down from the upper sands as I approached him perpendicularly, was his boss raingear. It was vintage yellow, just like the deteriorating Mackintosh raincoats my parents kept in the front hall closet when I was a child. His hat, too, was old school Mackintosh – which I admired. Now I felt a kinship with him in two ways: not only were we the only two people crazy enough to be out at this ungodly hour in a heavy rainstorm, but we both appreciated the good, old fashioned value of vintage stuff. In New York, I'd made a hobby of finding quirky old garments. Clearly, this guy did the same for rain gear.

But what was he so intent on? We were almost going to bump into each other if we both kept to our current paces. His face carried some kind of intense apprehension about whatever he was looking for out on the horizon. Reflexively I checked in that direction, though there was nothing to be seen out there but crashing waves and mist. I decided I would compliment him on his duds. I made those inner preparations we make to address a stranger. But even within a yard of me, he kept ignoring me to stare fixedly toward the horizon.

"How's it going?" I shouted cheerfully over the wind.

At that his head rotated just a few degrees in my direction, but he *still* refused to look at me and didn't alter his pace a bit, even as he passed so close that I could have grabbed his shoulder.

Which was just plain rude, I thought as I walked on. Here we are the only two people crazy enough to be out in this weather, I make the friendly effort to say, "how's it going," and he blows me off like some way-too-cool teenager? What the hell? He couldn't even smile or nod or *anything?* Anger burbled up. Excuse me, Mr. Fucking Fish Sticks! I turned to look at him in disgust—

– and there was no one. The beach was empty.

I looked out at the breaking waves. Had he sprinted down and dove straight into them? The water curled and churned without a trace. Was he determined to drown himself by staying under the surface? Was that maybe why he'd seemed so tense and absorbed, because he'd been suicidal? Okay – I'd wait him out. No one could keep even their back from breaking the surface; it wasn't possible. What about his hat? It would float. It *had* to float.

Nothing. My eyes swept the beach. There was no place to which even a young guy could have disappeared so fast. Even if he'd booked full speed, there was no way he'd make it back up to the dunes. He'd simply vanished.

I took a few more steps and then stopped again.

Vanished... like a ghost.

But ghosts were an absurd and corny notion. What?! An old fisherman ghost – that was just too ridiculous. Fuck that. I'd get to the bottom of this right now. I'd follow his tracks. I followed my own back to about where his should cross them. There were none. The sand was undisturbed but for my own footprints. Maybe I'd walked further than I thought after we crossed? So I went on, I kept looking.

Mine were the only tracks on that beach.

Realities collided. What I'd seen minutes ago – a living man – and what I saw now – zero tracks – could not be reconciled by any means. *Help!* What do you do when two completely contradicting facts present themselves? When something categorically impossible has just occurred? This was no hallucination. This had been a calm, plain, ordinary perception. An individual man. I'd seen his crow's feet, the broken capillaries of his skin, the way his eyes shifted when his head turned just a bit toward my voice. He'd walked at a continuous pace, entirely mundane despite his vintage raingear.

Except for the vanishing part. The zero tracks part. Human beings did not do that. Yet it didn't matter how long I searched; every track bore my sneakers' imprint. I, Louisa P., had seen a ghost walk the earth.

I hurried back to the beach house where I found a few people now awake. I babbled out what had just happened.

"Fuckin' A! Awesome!" everyone said. "That's so rad!" "A seafaring ghost? Right on!"

Nobody understood that this *not* awesome. There was nothing rad, right on, or righteous about it – because it had actually *happened* to me. To live an experience you can't understand is an upheaval, a deep disturbance. I did not, would not, could not believe in ghosts!

"Oh, there's all kinds of ghosts around Gloucester!" said Edith, who was mixing scrambled eggs. She spoke as though I'd spied the state bird. "So many ships went down, so many drowned. They have a monument at the esplanade – there's, like, a thousand names."

Everyone acted as though I should just marvel, shrug, and let it go. What they didn't understand was, while you can do that with something odd, you can't with something impossible. Impossible requires a rewrite of reality. And, once again, I was not prepared to go there. Now I didn't give a crap about Jenna and Vince's screwing. I didn't care if Jenna and I never got together. All I wanted was for the world to behave itself – according to *my* rules, my dad's rules, the rules of anyone who knew how reality worked.

When Kevin came to get me later that morning, the weather had cleared enough that he was willing to come out on the beach and help me look one more time for tracks. Mine were now smoothed by rain, and a few other people had added theirs since. None, however, originated from the dunes. I wanted to sob with frustration: I had *seen* him, dammit! A real person! Eventually, Kevin pried me away. He didn't say anything, but I could tell he was guessing my "ghost" had been either a pink elephant or some kind of adolescent ploy for attention.

I had no alternative but to leave the incident behind me as an inexplicable experience, not knowing it to be the first of fourteen equally inexplicable phenomena –i.e. my Fourteen Weird Things – scattered over the course of my life to date. Why I experienced it, I wouldn't learn for twenty-some years, when I at last attended the Seattle Chapter of the International Association of Near Death Studies (IANDS), and began to learn from fellow NDE survivors that they, too, had known paranormal experiences similar to mine. In fact, seeing spirits, prescience, and accidentally reading others' thoughts are all common side-effects of having crossed over. In my community of fellow NDE survivors, they're not even a big deal. Today I wonder if I may have seen other dead spirits in passing but assumed, as I did with the vintage-rain-geared fisherman, that they were living. In few places would a vanishing be so evident as on an open, sandy beach.

But I'm getting ahead of my story. For now, I still refused to believe I'd *ever* crossed over *any*thing, let alone come back with a rupture in my energetic capsule that – yeah, right – occasionally let in spiritual phenomena. What a bunch of hooey!

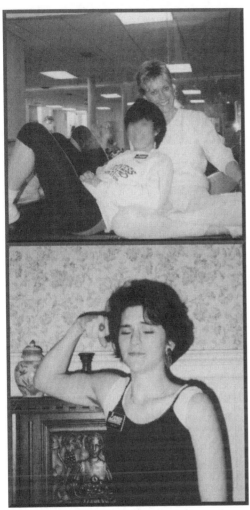

Jenna and Vivian at FU; mocking my new fitness job – but it's the last time I'll have doughy arms

12: I BUST OUT MY BABY DYKE

*I needed no more light than was in her touch, her fingers
brushing my skin, bringing up the nerve ends. Eyes
closed I began a voyage down her spine, the cobbled
road of hers that brought me to a cleft and a damp valley
then a deep pit to drown in. What other places are there
in the world than those discovered on a lover's body?*

-Jeanette Winterson
Written on the Body

1/16/1988: "Why should I tell her? I've tried twice in the
past six months to write about this and torn it up both
times. I'm evasive about the thing between us, what I've
always felt and kept hidden. It frightens me to write this.
I would like to tear it up. That is both a reason to tell and
not to tell, because if I am frightened even by myself,
then how can I expect her to handle it? Lately little signs
have tempted me to hope she is in exactly my
predicament. The big problem is, once you've admitted
to things as they *are*... we'd look ahead and say, what
next? And I don't need any next. Next frightens me even
in optimal terms, and I think it would terrify her. If she
were to tell me I was way off base and a creep, then I
would lose everything, everything."

1/17/1988 (in tiny handwriting): "Never try it. No such
thing. Only in my mind, or if it is there, I'm at least as
scared as she."

What I meant by 'next' was physical intimacy. Even as crazily
infatuated as I was, I just couldn't see it. Lesbians, as I understood
it, had oral sex instead of regular. Wasn't that how it worked? That
would be just too creepy.

One frosty spring night after drinking at a series of bars, we sat in a children's playground near Jenna's house beneath a sky full of stars. Having clambered around on the equipment in drunken play, we were now smoking wistfully and quietly, saddened by unfair burdens the world imposed on us.

"I think I may have to break up with Vince," Jenna sighed, dawdling on a swing. "He doesn't like... all the time we spend together."

"Kevin's worse and worse," I agreed from the top of the jungle gym, looking out into the night. "I do think sometimes of leaving him, but I don't know what I'd do."

All of Brookline lay strangely silent but for the low squeak of her swing. We smoked, our cherries bright in the darkness.

"You don't love him anymore?" she asked.

"It's more like..." I was actually going to *say* it, "...now all my love goes to *you*."

She absorbed this silently. Holy, shit – I'd done it! I felt that thrill of a move well executed, of luring my quarry nearer. We said goodnight soon after.

Homophobia still held Jenna back. She'd always joined in the derisive whispers about lesbian spa members, having never known any cool lesbians in grad school. In those days there was no L-word TV show, no Ellen DeGeneres, no Gay and Lesbian Alliances at schools. The only for-sure lesbians were abnormal women like my bearded Vassar dyke – the ones with nothing to lose. Already a racial minority, Jenna had no desire to become abnormal. And yet she called me as often as I called her, and the hours of talk slipped by as magically for her as they did for me.

Kevin's and my relationship had wilted beyond any chance of revival. Sex was no more. One night we brought our mattress into the living room for a movie and "picnic," where we made a half-hearted attempt that soon fizzled. Too much lay unspoken between us. Every day I jettisoned our marriage a little more obviously in my pursuit of Jenna-joy, as if I couldn't do otherwise. Kevin became a hapless casualty. One night, he stayed home from school sick and cooked us a special dinner, but I ducked out for a quick beer with Jenna.

4/10/1988: "Oh, what is wrong with me? I could not be worse. More heartless. Last night after calling at five and saying I was out for drinks, I drank until nine, heavily and fast, and felt so full and sick I had no energy at all.

But instead of going home to where Kevin was sick, alone, and waiting with a dinner he had cooked for me, I went to Jenna's and drank and watched TV til two o'clock, called way too drunk to drive, and spent the night. I hate myself for what I'm doing. I am a monster."

Still, nothing "happened" when I spent the night. Jenna slept in her bed and I on the floor. It was heaven to be on her floor, heaven to be near her sleeping presence! I wanted for nothing.

In a garbage can alongside the house, I happened upon a plastic bag of crumpled newspaper. Inside that bag was another, with more garbage inside it – layered exactly as I had concealed my thrown-out bondage accouterments ten years before. But when I peeled off the tape and opened the innermost package, inside it I found Kevin's raging pain: here was the first gift Jenna had given me, a little wire sculpture of a figure seated on a bolt toilet, now twisted into an unrecognizable ball. I put everything back except for the figure itself, which I showed to Jenna.

"Wow!" she marveled. "Why does he hate me so much?"

"I don't know," I said, "but it sure is creepy!"

For months I'd held Kevin in reserve exactly as I'd held Reilly before him. I feared moving ahead toward this hazy, prohibited future. What did Kevin's parents think? What would mine? What would our friends from Vassar say?

But at some point I was visited by a figure well known to all addicts who've ruined their lives multiple times: the Fuck-This-Shit Fairy. At some point during our self-centered dance of lies, as we struggle to balance our lives' precarious tray of responsibilities and supposed values, she visits and whispers gently in our ear: "Just say fuck it. You're free! Let the whole trembling, overloaded mess drop and you'll be *amazed*, my dear! Life is so open!"

Then she touches us with her magic wand, whereupon situations that have seemed hopelessly complex and overwhelming suddenly resolve, becoming brilliantly simple with the magic words: *Fuck this shit.*

Fuck it all! I was free to do anything I chose, even if it meant being poor. So I quit trying. I quit feeling remorse. If people wanted to whisper that I might be a dyke, fine.

One day Kevin asked me, his face and voice laden with pain, if we could talk.

"I think we need to separate for a while," he said, "to figure out what's going on."

How delighted I was to hear this! "Perhaps that's best," I agreed. I tried to fake grief and reluctance, but Kevin knew me too well. Yes, a trial separation! I'd fly home to Seattle and get Jenna to follow me! I could scarcely keep the grin off my face. I mean really, literally.

In no time Jenna and I had planned how she could move to Seattle, transferring her Boston University credits in Physical Therapy to the University of Washington. That wasn't weird; friends can decide to move to the same town. But there were conditions I felt I had to clarify before I left Boston.

On my last night there the two of us went out to the Rat, one of our favorite bars, where I drank with determination until the mirror beside our table dissolved into a portal to a twin barroom. I told Jenna I had something very difficult to say, and we ping-ponged the prospect like teens:

"S*ay* it!"

"I *can't* say it!"

"Just *say* it!"

Downing my twelfth Corona or so, I leaned in on my elbows.

"Okay, here it is: you know all those people who say we're, like, lesbians?"

"Yeah," she started in, "they're so totally clueless—!"

I interrupted: "—It's true for me."

Shit. I'd finally said it! No going back. She retracted all connection to me and averted her eyes to the tabletop. The room listed and swirled as I waited. At last she looked up.

"I really respect you for saying that."

No more. She would not say she felt the same.

Oh, God help me! I'd shot the whole thing to hell! But what else could I *do*? Respect? Fuck! Who wants respect? I said no more about it, but somewhere in my shipwreck of drunken consciousness, I respected myself.

I left Kevin in April, a few months shy of turning twenty-eight. He drove me to the airport with Kyatty, our parakeet, in a plastic carrier. I'd distained any squabbling over our possessions. I wanted nothing. He could have the whole schmear of worldly goods, since he and his business school friends were such materialists.

I've described this scene many times in AA meetings. Inside the terminal, my husband hugged me for the last time. I felt nothing but a kind of squirmy embarrassment. There was no kiss, only the familiar sensation of his arms around me. His body hitched with a stifled sob. He managed only the half-broken word "goodbye." Then he turned and walked out the automatic doors without a look back.

I watched the glass doors roll closed and re-open for strangers. I felt only a bit ashamed of the subtle grin spreading over my face. Nice! That nasty business was over with. I raised the parakeet carrier to eye level, squinted through one of the air holes, and said out loud, "Kyatty, it's time for a drink!"

The time was about 11:00 am. I set the carrier on a barstool next to mine and ordered a series of schooners (because a pint would be too much). I really felt that I was drinking *with* the bird, cut so utterly free of constraints that I didn't give a damn what anyone thought. The bartender, for instance. He seemed a bit stand-offish. When I had a conversational thought, I'd whisper it gleefully through the air holes. "We're gonna go, Kyatty. We're really, really gonna go!"

Jenna would be flying out to visit around my birthday, just three months away. Even if I'd scared her, she'd still said she would come, so there was hope.

The day after I arrived at my parents' home, I wrote a letter to Jenna apologizing for whatever I'd said at the Rat. "I was so drunk I didn't know what I was saying! Of course I love you, but not in *that way*."

The afternoon was sunny. Envelope in hand I stepped out onto the front walk, strolled to the neighborhood mailbox, and mailed my letter. When I got home, my mother handed me a letter just arrived from Jenna, come all the way from Boston in record time.

She must have posted it within hours of our parting: "I've known for some time that I loved you," she wrote, "but now that you're gone, I know something different: I'm in love with you."

My heart skyrocketed. Green light. Game on.

~

The $5,000 prize I'd won at the university, which I'd kept separate from Kevin's money and added to with various tidbits, had by this time accrued to $6,000. With it I bought a little 1984 Mazda GLC and rented an apartment atop Queen Anne Hill, with a view through many aerials of the often spectacular Olympic mountains. I lived alone with Kyatty, suspended in a constant state of obsessive fantasy – conversations and scenes where I shone in Jenna's eyes. Unsupervised, I lived on tea, beer, cigarettes, and occasional sautéed chicken livers for cheap protein. On my fire escape deck I built a kitchen table, bookcase, and a double bed frame that ended up more weighted with bolts, screws, and other hardware reinforcements than anything I'd ever constructed. Why? Because I planned to share it with Jenna someday, and I didn't want any telltale squeaks alerting the neighbors that we were perverts.

In addition to racking up sky-high phone bills, Jenna and I exchanged several letters per week. I'd often stay up late penning by candlelight in the thick of passion, rereading again and again as Jenna. Brilliant, I would think. God, what poignancy! *I* would fall in love with me, no question. I almost hated to mail them off without copies. I also made her a drunken tape of myself at the island cabin, recording my voice among sound effects such as the crackling fire, pounding waves, and gasoline-powered water pump. We were counting down the days til her visit in mid June.

Floating on this magic carpet of infatuation, I was impervious to panic attacks and the temptation to tie myself up, even living completely alone. Circumstances for my compulsive ritual were ideal, yet the urge was not there. I was cured at last, and for reasons I considered perfectly obvious: I was no longer suppressing my true lesbian nature, which was what had screwed up my sex life all these years.

I cut my own hair very short. I'd already bleached it blond in Brookline, with Jenna's help, so now it was two toned again. Drunk, I liked to blast music and trim the sides even shorter, cigarettes smoldering on the edge of the sink. I liked the way it made the edges of my jaw seem to stand out. In fact, I liked almost everything about the dyky way I looked.

Admittedly, I still had one or two compulsions even love couldn't banish:

> 5/4/1988: "I drink way too much. And when I'm hung-over, life is so scary. I feel small and weak and vulnerable. I feel like any bad things people say about me must be true. I'm an unworthy person, physically gross and mentally limited, and of a careless, oafish, cruel temperament."

At last, after many ups and downs and dramatic crises around transferring credits, Jenna finally came to visit. Here she was in my apartment! Jenna – with all her magic.

I'd planned a million things for us to do, wanting her to fall in love with Seattle as well as me. June in Seattle is normally gray and soggy, but the weather conspired for ten days of sunshine. We climbed Mount Dickerman amid an expansive panorama of snowcapped peaks. We toured the green lawns of the UW campus and flower-filled arboretum. We camped two nights on the ocean at Shi-Shi beach, miles from the nearest road, where the waves broke almost translucent under brilliant blue skies. Surrounded by sublime towers and arches of rock, we were awakened one morning by three little fawns frolicking outside our tent in the amber rays of dawn. Comparing these spectacles to the trampled beaches and stumpy mountains of the east, Jenna was suitably awed.

One afternoon on the beach at the summer cabin, we sat leaning against a bleached log facing out toward the same vista of layered peninsulas and mountains that had witnessed countless scenes of my life. Our legs were just barely touching.

"I do want to be with you," Jenna said, "but not in *that way*. I really can't see it for me – being *that way*. I just want us to be close friends."

I waited a bit, letting my eyes drift across to the saw-tooth bands of trees on the opposite shore. I'd heard in her voice the same fear I felt in myself. But I also knew Jenna was too in love to live without me, and some courage rose up in me – not lust but a temporary power to speak.

"If you won't be lesbians with me, then don't move out here," I said evenly. "I *won't* be just your friend."

Spot-on the most Steve McQueen moment of my life! Afterward I wished I'd said "be my lover" instead of "be lesbians with me" – which sounds almost like a hopscotch call – but that's how it came out. I'd wanted to use the actual L-word, to name the very thing we feared.

Again, she was silent, absorbing. I probably should have kissed her, but it seemed too vast a leap, as if I didn't know how one did such a thing. Besides, I was still marveling at what I'd just said, my heart racing. She was truly here – Jenna of the perfect almond eyes and delicate fingers – and I had just told her I wanted her. That would have to be enough for now.

On the fourth of July, the day before her departure, we sat out on a blanket for the public fireworks, along with my grad school friend, Rosemary, and her balding brother who aspired to date me. In the dark, we held hands for the first time. She rested her head on my shoulder. As we walked back to the car, I put my arm around her waist. To us, these little touches were electric, and their implications huge. I was learning I could make moves, and that she would respond. There's much to be said for slow courtship. My panties were drenched.

So a few days later when she called later from her parents' to name the date I should fly back to Boston to help her drive her clunky old Toyota out to Seattle, we both knew exactly what that meant.

The drive was intoxicating. Every night we stopped at a motel where we shared a bed, and every night I played the ardent suitor making slow but steady progress. Like Humbert Humbert, I could wait no longer. Somewhere in Pennsylvania, she let me briefly touch her breast through her shirt. Our third night, at the Scotsman Inn in St. Cloud Minnesota, I kissed her. We were propped up in bed after she'd asked me to read aloud to her (she loved the way I read) from *Best Short Fiction of 1987*. At some point I left off reading, turned to her, and kissed her.

We bumped teeth, actually – after all this build up – and I had to reposition to get a better angle. The next was not much better. Jenna put out her tongue like a little crescent of Oreo frosting, no more, and she didn't seem to grasp the suction concept at all. But it didn't matter. Kevin had been a fabulous kisser, but that didn't matter, either. Her lips were so incredibly soft, missing the punctuation of stubble in a smoothness I could never have dreamed of. She was a girl, and I was kissing her. That alone catapulted me into erotic bliss. To give any thought to these flaws of bumping teeth or missing suction would be like Neil Armstrong asking if his spacesuit made his ass look fat.

I don't remember when I slid into third, which was pretty much home base for a lesbian, but it happened before we reached Idaho. Even outside of bed, I marveled at how much I'd transformed. Just over a year ago, I'd been a quivering wreck of a wife paralyzed by panic, barely able to leave the house. Now here I was, driving Jenna's car through wide open states and past roadside attractions, tipping back longnecks and blasting local radio stations while the wind buffeted my short hair. Every now and then I'd reach over to caress the girl I loved with all the boundless confidence of a cocky dude.

Jenna and I didn't have butch/femme roles per se – we were both butchy femmes to an equal degree, though in differing styles. So when I say, I was the dude, I mean there was no captain other than me: I knew where we were on the map, I planned where we'd stop, I knew our dismal money situation and that the pump on her radiator was dying. I was certainly not man enough to fix it; we crossed the hot summer plains of Montana at about 30mph, hazard lights flashing, adding water every hundred miles or so. How we made it over the Rockies, I don't know. It took days! But I was grateful for every one of them. By day the road was a timeless realm where by day we played, drank, and watched the country roll by, and by night we entered the deep, vine-laden jungle of lust in another cheap motel. Who wants to end that?

She'd been in the apartment before, of course, but even so there was that initial moment of awkwardness once her bags and boxes were set down. Here we were! Yes, indeedy. I thought of Kevin in Newton Center. Now I knew how he felt.

I didn't want to act like sex was the only thing on my mind, though it kind of was. One night we were making out, tangled up and grappling on the futon couch, when I had to pull away to breathe hard. I'd just accidentally come from kissing and touching her breasts. After all those wailing, thrashing orgasms I'd faked for boys in college, this one I actually tried to hide.

"I just came," I admitted. "I'm sorry."

"Why sorry?" she smiled.

I didn't answer. She didn't expect me to. I'd never told her the extent of my obsession, how long it had built up, how delirious she made me, because the enormity of it would have scared her. I let her think my experience was the reciprocal of hers, no more.

~

Oral sex. Cunnilingus. Eating pussy. It's actually as much a variation on standard fare for lesbians as it is for straights (I was going to say 'side dish,' but that just sounds too weird). Missionary position is the same for both, except that for lesbians it entails a slight shift of the hips to one side, so that each has her partner's thigh between her legs. You can reach down for finger sex, or not; in my experience, orgasms come more easily from pressure than penetration. Men may be surprised, but the fact is, a clitoris is like a hermit crab: too much jangling from intercourse, and no way will she come out and do her thing. In any case, Jenna and I had been having missionary sex for some time. Cunnilingus remained the hallmark of lesbianism that had frightened and repulsed us both as straight girls in Brookline, the dreaded act we thought we'd never want to give or get from a woman.

But that was then. Jenna seemed so lusciously clean to me, every square inch of her, and her pubic parts so compact and dainty compared to mine. We awoke one Saturday morning on the same summer cabin deck where, the summer before, I'd hallucinated the eerie, stalking panther, and in the very same sleeping bags, now zipped together. But now I had a different kind of kitty on the brain.

I unzipped the sleeping bag to open a vent, then I disappeared from Jenna's view. Geez, it's all turned around and backwards when you get there – yet you know your way. You revive memories of what's felt good to you in the past, half imagining you can feel what she's feeling, almost a receiver as much as giver. Except for that awkward angle. When I came up again after about ten minutes, I wiped my mouth and said, "Damn! That's hell on your neck. Now I see why guys don't want to do it for a long time."

"Really?" she said. "Let's see!" By now the sunlight was beaming through the trees, so she threw the covers back all the way and went for it. No one was around. Eyes closed to the sky, I heard only the morning calls of birds and swish of trees. I still felt a tiny bit nervous and didn't come – neither of us did. But you don't try for a double twist pike the first time you jump off the high dive, either.

Our greatest difficulties arose from the fact that we were the sole pair of lesbians living in Seattle. At least, so we appeared to believe. Homophobia was the norm, and we expected it. We designated the fold out futon in the living room as *Jenna's bed.* "This is where Jenna sleeps," we told my parents and any school friend of Jenna's who came by to study. We stuck an alarm clock and some other night-time crap on the end table and, like most liars, over-supplied information. Yep, she grabs a quilt from right here from *this closet* and a nice cushy pillow. Sometimes she folds out the couch, and sometimes she doesn't! The first friend Jenna made at school met me, put two and two together, and rebuffed her. The blond babes across the hall from us started off friendly and then one day stopped speaking to us.

My mother also saw right through us and was, just beneath the usual P. family veneer of reticence, furious about it. She had loved Kevin and didn't want to lose him. Once when I was home while she was cleaning out a room, she shoved an enormous empty picture frame into my hands and told me to take it.

"What would I do with *this*?" I asked, looking around from behind it.

"I don't know – put a picture of *Jenna* in it?!" she fumed.

Slowly, by baby steps, we discovered a big gay world out there. I landed a job teaching freshman English at a Seattle Central, where I couldn't help but notice many gay-seeming students. Capital Hill neighborhood in the 80's offered a regular parade of queerness, yet I felt disconnected – different. Why should the fact that Jenna and I were in love imply we had any connection with these people?

Most shocking was the night we ventured to a lesbian nightclub – The Offramp – that Jenna had caught wind of at school. We came out of the dark entrance hallway to encounter a dance floor filled with lesbians, lesbians, lesbians! They were whooping it up as a throng on the wildly lit floor, up on platforms in drag or various states of undress! They were leaning on the bar, cuddling in booths, walking past and checkin' y'out. Butches and femmes! Chic and corny! Ugly and beautiful! They seemed as varied as creatures in a Dr. Seuss book.

Dancing, we could actually touch, even kiss – not that we normally danced that way, but why not? One girl at a table we shared flashed long, painted nails. "That's a *princess*," Jenna informed me later. The nails meant she would be *done* but not *do*. Fascinating! I thought. Of what else was I utterly clueless?

Eventually we found the Wildrose, the "Frontqueer" Room, the Vogue, and a number of gay-friendly clubs. And yet still, we made no friends, gay or straight. The carnival atmosphere seemed fine for see-and-be-seen nights, but we didn't really care to invite such people into our *home*, where we studied organic chemistry and graded student essays. For almost an entire year, our relationship remained an island.

We covered a lot of self-discovery during that year. As Jenna grew bolder, our sex life spiked beyond any passionate abandon I'd ever known. I mean, it was *intentional* passionate abandon, but still. The forbidden factor gave us fire. I recall a time we staggered home drunk from a bar, started kissing as soon as we busted in the back door, tore off clothes and went at it on the kitchen floor. Eventually there were few spots left in the apartment where we *hadn't* gone at it. We took pride in our impulsive desire, our ability to bring each other to stupendous climaxes beyond those brought by any man.

But I also think we were lonely and had nothing else going for us, which made it important that our sex life be off the charts. How long can a couple live like that, feeding off nothing but each other? Slowly, as the months passed, the unthinkable happened. Jenna's pedestal began to crumble. Her magic was fading. She farted in her sleep, sometimes in a sustained, quizzical melody. Her talk bored me at times. She listened to Motown music like Luther Vandross.

Even sex became predictable as we ran out of variations. In short, Jenna was becoming merely human – just like Kevin.

By our first winter together, a gap opened up in my heart – too late – to mourn what I had lost with Kevin. If I had once loved Kevin as intensely as I now loved Jenna, didn't it mean that love, inevitably, eroded away?

> 12/2/1988: "I feel like every day must be happy and exciting or we'll worry the spark's lost. I can't tell if this feeling is all mine or if she's stuck in it, too, but I don't like it, and I feel faky again, talking in a high voice, being affectionate. Always I have to respond and be attentive. It makes me feel trapped.
>
> "I feel the loss of my love with Kevin in two ways. One, the loss, the ache of remembering times that seem beautiful and simple now. Two, a restraint, a check in my ability to love, feeling right alongside love the anticipation of loss. I feel like it's impossible to avoid, impossible to control, impossible to understand. By the time you notice, it's probably too late.
>
> "What are relationships? When you love someone, why doesn't that tell you what to do, or what will happen?"

My grief over Kevin, now impossible to conceal, terrified Jenna. There were nights I took the phone into the closet, talked with him for hours, and cried. He flew out so we could talk face to face; that had been the plan, after all – to separate and re-evaluate.

It probably would have helped Kevin's evaluation if I'd told him Jenna and I had been eating at the Y almost nightly, but still, the word 'lesbian' went unspoken. He sensed it for himself. Frozen forever in my memory is a moment I would call the most awkward of all, when I went in the tiny room off the garage where he was staying at my parents' house. The fold-out bed took up the whole room, so I sat on the edge of it and he sat beside me, the two of us talking around the obvious. I felt carved from wood, so stiff I could snap and willing with all my might that he not touch me. Kevin put his head in his hands and was silent, holding back tears. Our divorce proceedings began soon after. The one thing I did right in all of this mess, perhaps in my life to that date, was to claim none of Kevin's money. I asked for no settlement. Whenever papers arrived from Kevin's lawyer, I signed them without even bothering to read.

Yet for months afterwards, memories of how crazy for him I'd once been continued flinging horseshoes of irony at the back of my head as I made love to Jenna. I'd disguise the impacts, pretend to believe her ardent phrases and to avow something similar. Inside me, though, some cynic rolled her eyes: *Listen to you, lying again*!

5/10/1989: "When we're happy, lying in bed, she says the very same things to me Kevin said at first. I have to say back things I've said before. This morning before she left, I was in my hovering-for-her-to-leave stance, and she was saddened by it."

5/28/1989: "Am not happy. Am claustrophobic with Jenna. I feel like she wants to be making love all day every day, just a constant expression of love and possession. In the mornings, I feel guilty just for *getting out* of the damn bed! But if I draw away, there'll be a crisis. How horrible faking feels. But the faking begins whenever I have to hide my thoughts of Kevin."

I tried, of course, to drink the feelings away:

5/1/1989: "I am quite, kwight hungover. Such, unfortunately, is the case. I drink tooooo much. I am too prone to excess. If I am drinking, I want to keep drinking hard even after I can barely see. If I'm smoking, I want to light another cigarette in mid-drag. I want to feed my face with smoke and booze like an octopus."

For some time now, my mom had been offering to pay for me to go see a shrink. Her only stipulation was that it be a *male* shrink, because she secretly hoped he would cure me of lesbianism. At this point, I decided to take her up on it, but not for the reasons she envisioned. For the first time in my life, I was desperate and scared enough to tell someone my truth: I'd started tying myself up again, and powerless to stop.

C

lockwise from top left: Maybe a few too many Rainiers; showing Jenna Foster Island; Christmas morning 1988; scrambled eggs are good for a hangover

13: SOUNDING THE WELL OF LONELINESS

*The people of the house would prepare a meal and place
it on the coffin. ...The Sin Eater would devour this meal
and would also be given a sum of money. It was believed
that all the sins the dying person had accumulated
during his lifetime would be removed from him and
transmitted to the Sin Eater. The Sin Eater thus became
absolutely bloated with other people's sins.*

-Margaret Atwood
"The Sin Eater"

The shrink my mother had selected charged $100 an hour –
quite a forkful in the summer of 1989 – and, unlike Kitty, he didn't
try to connect as a friend and confidant. He was a doctor. He had
both a medical degree and a Ph.D. in psychology, with a plush
office high in a glass tower. His bearing was professorly: rather
corpulent, he had glasses and a beard, wore a suit and tie, and kept
his hair a tad too long as though we were still in the '70s. His fancy
fountain pen scribbled incessantly on a yellow legal pad. As
described in this book's opening, he asked at the close of our first
session whether I had any concerns I'd like to address.

I told him, practically all in one breath, of the history and
recurrence of my sexual compulsive disorder. It was my first
experience with honest self-disclosure, and it shook me to my core.

With this shrink, I cooperated to the best of my ability. His
professorial look gave him a quasi-academic status for me, and I
wanted an A in therapy. Though I tried to be completely honest
with him, I never, of course, mentioned my Near Death Experience
or the ghost I'd seen in Gloucester. I wanted to present myself as a

young woman entirely sane outside an itsy-bitsy compulsion that made her tie herself up and get off on mock-torture in mirrors for twelve years. My journey to the Light and near collision with a nineteenth-century fisherman who then vanished...? That would be crazy talk.

He assigned me a book on sexual addiction – *Out of the Shadows* – that was definitely no picnic to read. (I skipped the part about the Twelve Steps, of course, because anything with the word "God" in it was a waste of time.) He told me to meditate; I meditated. He told me to write ten affirmation cards and read them twice daily; I wrote ten hokey I'm-so-wonderfuls and read the fuckers, just like he said.

Our first order of business, the shrink felt, was for me to confess my compulsion to Jenna. I still had tremendous shame around it. I tried to write about those feelings in my journal, but ended up tearing out the pages and burning them in our hibachi.

> [Between 10/1 and 11/15/1989, seven pages sliced out of the journal, ending with]: "—all this will take over my life. A brutal selfishness and thoroughly certain oblivion – too much like a potent drug. I say, 'I will do what I want and no one will stop me, so fuck off with all your worries of how to assimilate this into a healthy, whole self.'
>
> "It says in the book, 'Horniness = loneliness,' and that is true for me. I have no friends. I have no connections to art or nature. The horniness engulfs me. Saying 'no, I won't!' can only work for so long.
>
> "I *am* scared to tell Jenna. I'm so scared she'll judge me, find me disgusting. I have such a long way to go."

When I finally went through with it, Jenna listened lovingly and sympathetically as if glad of a chance to prove the depth of her love. It was *"okay"* – she seemed to believe that word was all I needed to be cured. I'd had a bad habit; now I would quit. I don't think she understood that it dated back into my first decade of life, an escape hatch from all psychic tension. I had been lonely but also safe within my private sickness. It was a part of me.

The shrink suggested we try incorporating bondage into our real sex life, if Jenna was open to the idea, while I swore off masturbation altogether. We took a shopping trip to a few head shops – there were no "lovers" shops in those days – whose back room display cases featured dildos and strap-ons. We bought both, in addition to some silky scarves. We also rounded up some sleep blinders, and I screwed a set of handles into the underside of our heavy pine bed.

You'd think this would have been the chance of a lifetime – an opportunity to live out my fantasies. I certainly thought so. But in practice, it wasn't the same thing at all. Sharing fantasies in partnered sex felt like a wholesome Romper-Room game compared to the private darkness of my mind. In the past, sorting out logistics took place in a side-pocket of my consciousness where it didn't affect the hotness of what was going on. Now logistics entered the arena of conversation as pleasant chatting. What Erica Jong termed the "zipless fuck" – what I got in my mirror fantasies – could not be duplicated in a real interaction, however kinky. Shame, the thrill of the forbidden, telling the world to fuck off – these had packed the true power behind my compulsion. What's more, bondage had been a way of hating myself, so naturally it wouldn't transfer to a way of loving someone else.

The experiment lasted only a few months. One night after finishing a story, *Puppet Show*, and getting drunk to celebrate, I got carried away sexually and failed for some time to notice that, under her blinders, Jenna was crying. I felt atrocious, untying her as fast as I could and apologizing all over myself. She'd had an abusive boyfriend in her past who had likewise been into bondage, and she'd flashed back to that, feeling silently victimized without letting me know. There was a part of her, just like the part of me, that loved nothing better than a roll in martyred self-pity. I had an odd reaction, a mix of compassion and revulsion, because on someone else, the same self-demeaning feelings I indulged in looked just that: self-indulgent. I realized there was nothing about bondage, or S & M, or any of it that I *wanted* in my sex life. For me, it had evolved as a symptom of childhood pain and would always be connected to illness. We stopped.

From that point on, I began to find sex more fulfilling. My love for Jenna began to recover, or rather, to evolve from infatuation toward a genuine, multi-dimensional love that included desire.

> 1/8/1990: "How many changes can a person go through?
> I feel lust for Jenna, real lust like the kind I used to feel
> alone, and now it's for *her* – her her-ness, her self is

what I want. And this is true for the first time in 29 years. The lust of love – I've never known it before."

Around this time, the shrink decided I'd made enough progress that he proposed hypnotizing me to get at the root of my self-loathing. Since I'm predisposed to trance, I went under within minutes.

After we'd gradually relaxed and traveled a landscape to the inner rooms of my mind, he asked me to imagine coming upon a dial labeled "Louisa Disapproval." There should be a gauge beside it reading somewhere between zero and ten. I saw the dial as something like an oven temperature control, and beside it a gauge like a thermometer, with a reading of about eight. He told me that together we were going to turn that dial down, notch by notch, and the gauge beside it would lower accordingly.

He began to count down, and to voice pro-Louisa feelings that might replace the disapproval. Ten. White light, he said. Nine. You're feeling warmth.

But that's not what happened. As soon as he reached about six, I began feeling a backed up resistance,

> 1/12/1990: "...putting pressure on something with nowhere to go, like pressure on a metal box of water. I could feel how the gauge wouldn't go down and how much disapproval there was, and it – the shame, the I'm-no-good source – was like liquid in a tank. There was so much of it stored up there, all the beatings up of myself, years of accusations. When I recognized that the gauge would not go down, I felt, how sad! What a shame to have been condemned so heavily for so long. And why? I am not bad. I only tried my best."

There was no release valve. I could only stuff. Feelings flooded me: grief for all the years of self-loathing and condemnation, and yet a sense of compassion.

> "The gauge would not go down... Tears beaded out my eyes, almost leaking from pressure, then my breath started catching in sobs and my eyes popcorning around in their sockets."

My eyes were going crazy under the lids! I must have entered some kind of REM short circuit. I was still hypnotized, but violent emotions surged through me. It felt something like getting electrocuted in your sleep. I couldn't breathe for all the mixed up, stifled sobs.

The shrink saw something had gone awry and we needed to abort, but rather than snap me out he brought me back the way we'd come, through the rooms and landscape, though as fast as he could. *Hurry up*! I wanted to shout, but I had no voice. Finally, he told me to open my eyes.

> "I half expected them to keep jumping around so everything would be jumbled, but they stopped. But they looked inside me instead of out, where I saw a black lake of sadness, still and tranquil because it's such a fixture in me, a lake of tears – more than could ever have been imagined, built up over my whole life. Huge and deep and covered over, yet all by mistake, because I really am not so guilty. I am almost innocent."

We never tried that exercise again.

Next on the shrink's to-do list, however, was coming out to my family. I didn't want to; he really had to push me. But I did wish to live without fearing judgment and loss. I had to find the boldness to go ahead.

> 1/14/1990: "Tonight I tell my parents about Jenna and me. I had bad dreams about it all last night. I dreamed I went over all set to tell them but there was some huge family gathering – cousins, uncles, friends, etc. – and they *wouldn't* leave. Someone took several pairs of my underwear, too. As for telling them in real life, how scary to know my place in the family will be changed forever!"

I went over to my parents' house for dinner and, as my mother cleared the dishes, pronounced some extremely difficult words. Funny how vividly I recall standing beside the big white refrigerator as I spoke, but not what I said! My mom, who was ironically enough standing in the very same spot at the sink, turned and responded indignantly, "I *knew* it! I've known for months!" and, to my father, "I told you!" Even as an adult, I could hardly look at her. Those shrink sessions she'd been paying for, she seemed to feel, had blown up in her face.

My father was more accepting. He said something like, "This is sad news for us because it will make your life more difficult." Both seemed deeply saddened to lose their hopes that I'd some day reconcile with Kevin. For years my mom would cry whenever he was mentioned.

So Jenna was welcomed, with reluctance, into the P. family. My siblings were somewhat shocked, but accepting. And I, black sheep of the family, was out of the closet at last! The shrink was quite pleased with my progress.

I entered what should have been the happiest periods of my life to date. So much was going my way. We'd found a zillion friends. Jenna had enrolled in a Women Studies course entitled, *Lesbianism,* where – imagine! – the professor and 95% of the students were lesbian. We befriended the entire class: sixteen lesbians and one question mark. There was a hot motorcycle dyke, a stocky Eskimo dyke, a tall granola curls-and-kerchief dyke, an entrancingly beautiful East Indian dyke and her partner, a super-slim New York fashion dyke. Most were in their twenties and very silly. Dyke potlucks abounded, and dyke outings to various parks and movies. We invited dykes out to the summer cabin and took giggly dyke movies of everyone poking fingers into the centers of squirting beach anemones. Jenna also hooked up with the Asian /Pacific Islander Lesbian Association, which brought in even more friends, more potlucks.

I say "friends," though in reality we had scarcely anything in common other than identifying queer. It was a bit like joining a Freckles Club. You share issues of whether to conceal your freckles or flaunt them, worry about melanoma and sunscreen. But really, *any*body can have freckles. The main difference between us and a Freckle Club was that other people thought we were abnormal and, in some cases, distained us.

Classic baby dykes, that's what we were! We went to marches, to protests, to hear lesbian speakers and concerts. We got into the music – Michelle Shocked, KD Lange, Ferron, Indigo Girls, and the patron saint of lesbians, Patsy Cline. Jenna bought herself a Honda scooter for the commute to school and a leather jacket to go with it – as if dyke cool were possible on a scooter. We tried. We rode it – me on the back in a black bra – in the "Dykes on Bikes" opening of Seattle's Gay Pride Parade. I didn't own any leather yet or a chain for my wallet, but I did think I looked hella hot in men's T-shirts with box Marlboros rolled in the sleeves. I wore no makeup, but I did fuss a lot with my hair. The top part I slicked à la Fonzie, and I'd bought clippers to buzz the sides almost to the skin. One night at Tugs, our second favorite bar after the Wildrose, I'd been up dancing on a table before I took a James Deanish smoke break slung against a windowsill. Two pretty boys dangling from a radiator nearby leaned over to yell the greatest compliment I've ever received:

"When we realized you weren't a boy—" one shouted.

"—We wanted to *kill* ourselves!" called the other. He smiled and added, with a twirl at my face, "Either way, honey, you're to *die* for!"

By my 30th birthday, on Stonewall's twentieth anniversary, my life had reached an apex of wellness. I'd had my first story accepted for publication. I'd been selected from over six-hundred applicants for a full-time English faculty position at Edmonds Community College. We were about to spend two weeks in Hawaii. And I had all the casual friendships I could ask for.

Celebrating at a queer square-dancing lodge downtown, I invited my whole family. My parents sat with me on a balcony and watched with slight concern as Walter whirled around the dance floor with another man. My sister and friend Rosemary, were happy for me in my relationship. Times were good, at least, on the outside.

~

With the shrink I never shared truthfully the extent of my drinking. He gathered that I drank a lot, but any time I was asked how much I drank, I always cut the amount by half... or maybe two-thirds, just as a matter of practice. To an alcoholic, this isn't lying. It makes perfect sense. For the normies reading, our alcoholic thinking runs something like this: "They asked how much I *really* drink, which is not the same as how much I've been drinking *lately,* which admittedly has been a bit over the top and doesn't count. As soon as I have it *under control*, the amount will be true just what I told him."

And, of course, there was that little pill problem he had, himself. Being gravely overweight and inactive, he found it necessary to prescribe himself painkillers for lower back pain. It was around this time I first began to notice his showing up for sessions bleary-eyed or on the verge of nodding out.

His professional advice to me, whenever the topic of my inebriation came up, was: "Drink less."

He knew better than to push AA on me. We both knew what a sorry cult that was, what with the Higher Power bullshit being a ruse for, let's face it, roping you into religion. Those poor people just exchanged dependence on alcohol for delusion – the idea that some Santa Claus God actually gave a shit whether they got bombed or not. AA was for people who couldn't think beyond clichés – the sort who loved Barry Manilow, used Glade air fresheners, and ate at McDonald's with no sense of irony. These simple souls could fall for a story like *God will help you control your drinking*! The good doctor and I, on the other hand, were way too smart to be so easily manipulated.

"Drink less," he told me.

"I will," I assured him.

And I meant it. I would use determination, resolve, self-control. I could stop eating any time even though I loved food, so I should be able to apply the same discipline to alcohol.

Or so I believed. Sadly, it would appear the doctor's education had omitted the fact alcoholism resides in the brainstem, where its primitive impulses remain as impervious to frontal lobe decisions as, say, a real hand is to images from a movie projector. In other words, I could cast a foolproof, thoroughly rational and emotionally sound resolve to drink sensibly on the screen of my mind, and my addiction could deride it effortlessly with a giant set of bunny ears.

So self-loathing continued to weigh me down. The Louisa Disapproval gauge would not go down, affirmations or no.

> 1/29/1990: Tonight I feel so worthless I feel certain nobody would ever stay with me for any reasons but feeling sorry for me. I mean, those are sort of the only reasons I stay. I'm stuck with this me. I try to fix it up and get it all bolstered up and supported and patched, and then it slumps down again, comically, ridiculously – except that it hurts so bad."

> 6/8/1990: "How off balance, how lonely, how *scared* I am. I feel forlorn, friendless, and confused. It's an uphill battle, this whole thing. I wonder if I'll *never* feel complete and as good as other people. *They* aren't really having a high schoolish blast somewhere while I'm excluded. *Why the fuck* do I still believe that fourteen years later? Why does that stuff still hurt so much?"

My solution, or rather, my irresistible reflex, was more alcohol.

10/26/1990: "I can't read whatever I wrote last night. I also don't remember writing it."

12/27/1990: "About drinking, the shrink tells me I am predisposed to it as a self-administered drug, but he doesn't think I'll end up like my dad. I told him how I meditated for an hour and still could find no peace, how I looked at the bottom of everything and saw despair, and how I drink to run from it. Why I drink so much – too much once I start – is that drinking holds out the *promise* of escape from despair. It never delivers until I'm unconscious. Having learned that, I think, is what might save me from becoming an alcoholic, full-fledged."

3/23/1991: "Melancholy. Melancholy. That's what I am. Hungover. Blue outside, a very blue light of twilight. I told such stupid stories last night, believed in something almost here that I was eager, so eager, to get at. In the punchline of this story, at the bottom of the bottle, in the next hour – it was coming! Coming!

"Now I know there's nothing. I was a fool to believe."

Though I wanted more than anything not to, I began to admit in my inmost heart that I was indeed an alcoholic. And though I'd never read a word of the Big Book, I began to sense for myself the rudiments of the First Step – that the physical craving and mental obsession drew me to alcohol with an urge more cunning, baffling, and powerful than any mental defense I could raise.

8/28/1991: "I am a prisoner of drink. Last night it cornered me, and there was nowhere to get away – no way *not* to drink. I did try. I really did *mean* not to drink. But I got pulled to the liquor cupboard and then I crossed over to the bottle's side. The bottle and me, us sneaky renegades, nobody's gonna tell *us* what to do. Bought a pack of cigarettes. Smoked 'em. Bought more of both [booze and smokes]. Who's gonna stop me? And here I am again hungover with a twitch in my eyebrow and I realize, I was tricked.

"But my liquor friend will be back here tonight, knockin' on the door, 'Please! I just wanna be your friend when no one else will!' And I'll want to believe it and chances are I'll open the liquor cabinet or beer bottle and let out the Genie. All wrongs will be forgiven, we'll be glad to see each other. But what's the alternative? To be alone and friendless."

Friendless. Though we had a number of friends, all were actually Jenna's. At the same time I started my new job, she'd begun working toward a Master's Degree at the UW, where she soon headed up the Alliance of People of Color. A long way from the naïve Brookline aerobicizer I fell for, she attracted a myriad of friends gay and straight, mostly of color. We were constantly attending their civilized, intelligent wine and cheese gatherings where, as the others sipped their wines and microbrews, Louisa would get bombed, break stemware, and pass out on the floor of some empty room. This happened more than once. The whole group had to search me out, much to Jenna's embarrassment and shame.

I did understand the attraction of alcohol to be incredibly powerful for me, but I still believed my will could be more powerful. Sure, nine out of ten times I drank after I had sworn not to, but what about those occasional Sunday nights I went without? Didn't they prove I could fight this thing and win if I really set my mind to it?

2/2/1991: "Saturday night and I've got my herb tea and I'm fighting the urge to drink. Not quite sure why I have the urge. Not quite sure why I'm fighting it."

My battle seemed helped, temporarily, when the shrink put me on the anti-depressant, imipramine, a somewhat primitive serotonin reuptake inhibitor. Every bottle bore a bratty yellow warning label against drinking on top of them. So I didn't. For maybe a week.

Now I had to lie to the shrink when he asked how the abstinence was going, because if I told him those fuddy-duddy labels meant nothing to me, he'd guess the extent of my addiction. I was growing uncomfortable with therapy for other reasons, besides. I'd developed a nagging suspicion that the shrink might harbor an attraction to me; especially when he was loopy on pills, he would make little efforts at suave debonairness that freaked me out.

Worse, his indelicacy about what were for me highly uncomfortable sexual issues alarmed me.

> 11/3/1990: "In some dreams, the person I am having sex with becomes a merged, blurred image of Jenna and Zelda. I am so ashamed to write this. I have such an impulse to go on editing out my deepest, scariest feelings. Then I'm terrified: does that mean I want to have sex with my *sister*?
>
> "I asked the shrink, Did I become a lesbian because I got too close to my sister? He said, You got so close to your sister because you were lesbian."
>
> "I didn't like that answer. I didn't like how he said it. There is still so much embarrassment and shame around my sexuality."

To top it off, now that my mother had quit paying for these hundred dollar sessions that had failed to un-gay me, they were a bit too steep for me, even with my new job. In any case, I decided I was cured. I'd come to recognize the correlation between judging others and judging myself. The shrink had helped me find a code of morals and philosophy of living that would empower me to overcome all my problems, including alcoholism. I was finally armed with the facts about myself.

> 12/26/1989: "I watched Dad [hungover] Christmas morning. Being was painful for him. Annoyance at himself, restlessness, pressures, and dissatisfaction. A repressed temper tantrum he doesn't want or understand. I know just how he feels. Trapped! Trapped! You need something! It's all so fucking relentless, this slough of trivia that is existence.
>
> "I want to learn to – what? To stop solving things. To stop fighting. To realize that what percolates through my brain is never *the answer*, because all of it is in constant change, the perceiver and the perceived.
>
> "I'm happy. It's silly to feel on the brink of understanding so much more about myself, and changing the way I live. But I do. I really do. And it excites me."

This era was, in fact, the closest I ever would ever get to wellness without god.

an even more confusing circular revelation—
My in-here MAKES the owl there I am
so afraid of. It's like dreaming up
a monster and running from it in
terror.

I'd like to paint a picture
of that. I'd call it: How I
lived my life for many years. Maybe I
will, if I can ever design a less
cute monster.
                            don't stop this process,

My journal; buncha lesbians at the summer cabin

14: I BECOME A FLANNEL DYKE; 2ND WEIRD THING

In a few days I'd be somewhere out west where it was very pretty and sunny and where nobody'd know me and I'd get a job. I figured I could get a job at a filling station somewhere, putting gas and oil in people's cars. I didn't care what kind of job it was, though. Just so people didn't know me and I didn't know anybody.

-J.D. Salinger
The Catcher in the Rye

Teaching college English was a job I did damn well but didn't like. The reason I taught so well *and* didn't like it was the amount of energy I burned in each class. When I teach, I go into a mode of hyper-connection, tuning into the vibes of the class. What are they thinking? What might I say right now to bring home this point for them? I get very excited, especially about literature, and I stay that way through the entire class, even if the students are working in groups. You'd never guess, if you saw me teach, that I had any issues with self-confidence. I seem a powerhouse of will and knowledge. It's exhausting.

I don't take any shit, either. I learned early on to use the spotlight of class attention to my advantage. While I couldn't confront anyone in my personal life, as a teacher I could name precisely what was going on: "Don't you think that's a little selfish, to be having your own conversation when it makes it harder for everyone else in the class to hear?" Once when two boys in the back row wouldn't shut up, I turned the whole class around because their desks were individual and the chalkboard at the back of the classroom just as good. Another teen who flicked a paper football through my class later told an advisor I changed his life when, seeing said football whiz across the room, I beckoned him out into the hall and advised him to quit school and get a job "pumping gas or something" until he *wanted* college. Word got around, and my classes began to fill up fast. Groups would gather to talk to me after class, and after a while I figured out why their voices shook or they visibly flushed. I'd been idolized.

Which happens to a lot of teachers – but don't think my ego didn't notice! I developed a new, weird symptom of anxiety. Mentally, I started carrying a classroom audience with me wherever I went. I would involuntarily lecture them about slicing potatoes and whether my car was due for an oil change, while certain key students, the ones I'd hoped to impress, were deeply struck by the caliber of my perceptions. I'd resolve not to think that way, banish the audience, and then five seconds later they'd reassemble, listening raptly. They noted. They approved. That's all they'd do – watch and validate. What a fun teacher! What insights on life! God *damn* she's cool!

> 3/23/1991: "Hungover I went for a walk and had much too much feeling. I saw old tree roots with leafy little plants making their way up them, with much moss, and even a dandelion growing in a seam of bark. I bent over a stump looking at spider webs in its holes, which mystified the whole of my Edmonds classroom audience that rides on my back, because I am crazy. What is she looking for? they all wondered. A watch? A lost earring?"

The *most* embarrassing thing with this imagined audience, the game I most cringe to admit, would be the times I'd crank up music and dance in their imagined sight. I'd imagine my coolness, and yes, my hotness blowing away students. Not just the key admirers, but crowds of them watching with a mix of amazement and cloudy desire. It was sort of like those performances at the end of *The Partridge Family*, when the show's former antagonists, bobbing their heads to the beat, see how cool Keith or Laurie or Danny actually are.

I can't be the only one who does this. I guess it started when I was about six and, through the imagined eyes of the Beatles (mostly Paul), watched my dancing reflected in the dark windows of our room. It's a great high for ego and vanity, the way the music lends momentum to the whole fantasy. You know? God, I hope someone knows!

12/28/1990: "I was drinking through all this and imagined their awe and admiration as I danced. Shrink would say I do so to feel good about myself for a little while. I go through life saying, you're nobody, you're shit; then I imagine eyes that radiate, 'you're the ultimate, you're amazingly fabulous!' When I feel okay about myself, how absurd these audiences seem!"

With my new fulltime position, I was onstage all day. I taught three classes per quarter, attended meetings, and served on committees. I was "urged" to attend overnight conferences, and required to advise sixty students quarterly. Every day exhausted me. I could not dial down my wattage. At home I graded mountains of essays and reread assigned texts to be "on it" for tomorrow's classes. And tried to write my own fiction.

The tension got to me. My face felt constantly rigid and developed twitches, while my neck developed a condition I called "rock neck," and my throat constricted so painfully that my doctor sent me for a barium swallow X-ray to find out if I had throat cancer. (I didn't, but watching my skeleton move and swallow was a trip!) I even grew a fibroid tumor in my armpit, although I didn't know it yet. While my tenure committee was pleased as punch, the work was killing me.

4/24/1991: "I hate my students. I don't see them as individuals but as materialistic, consuming, uglifying Americans with values from TV. I forget they've all loved their homes and mothers and know things about their dog, have lost friends in car wrecks, had abortions and births. I lack something that makes me so full of anger and resentment at Edmonds, makes my neck tighten to a rod. I don't know yet what it is."

(Note: it was god, but we aren't there yet.)

This fabulous job I had beat out so many people to win had worked me up to a pitch of restlessness, irritability, and discontent I couldn't stand – not even with the help of anti-depressants. The fact that I was supposed to stay on there until retirement made me feel as good as dead. I also felt incredibly jealous of Zelda, who was off in Europe house-sitting a gorgeous 17th Century Italian palazzo and painting away, fully funded by my parents who claimed to be "investing in a young artist" – one who also just happened to be their youngest child.

So I hatched a plan. An escape. Jenna and I would retreat to the country. As soon as I got tenure – which my father insisted I do first – I'd tell Edmonds to go fuck itself. Then I'd get me a peaceful chunk of land far from the city, and finally be happy.

I pitched the plan to Jenna, who had only about a year left to finish her MA. We both knew living out in the sticks would be harder on Jenna, since she'd likely be the only Asian person for miles. But I also knew she had a romantic streak a mile wide. We'd buy a beautiful cottage on some open land, maybe beside a little brook with a view of the mountains. We'd get all kinds of animals, grow our own food, and create a little lesbian paradise. There, I *promised* her, I would finally be happy.

In the interim, life went on. We moved from Queen Anne into a little house in the Roosevelt district that turned out to be so infested with an entire ecosystem of spiders (remember spiders), its basement ceiling festooned with sweeping hammocks of gauze, that we had to bomb and bomb again, which killed all but the largest. Those giants would appear upstairs, wobbly from poison and too weak to hide. I *hated* spiders and had a special slipper for smooshing them.

We'd set up a finished room in the spider basement as my special writing studio, where I wrote in a constant state of arachnophobia until I'd drunk enough not to give a crap. There I turned out four publishable stories, one of which picked up the Katherine Anne Porter Prize for Fiction, second place. I typed that one nonstop after scribbling its opening line on a margin of a newspaper during a drunken twenty-four hours while Jenna was out of town. It was a romance based on feelings for my friend Allie that I'd never explored. I printed two copies and mailed one to Zelda, who was home visiting from Italy. The next time I looked at the story, it read like a total piece of shit, so I chucked it in the trash.

Zelda called a day later: "Well then, get it *out* of the trash," she said. "It's the best thing you've ever written!"

I sent it out to several small presses and within a month it had been accepted by all of them. The Katherine Anne Porter folks wanted to fly me down to Tulsa to accept the award at a conference where I'd get to give readings, host workshops, and sign autographs. And in October of 1992, off I went.

What a dream come true, to be flown somewhere and hailed as a successful writer! To prepare for my reading in front of a distinguished audience of Tulsa arts patrons, I guzzled as much as possible because I'd selected a passage to read where I had to say "cunnilingus." Fortunately, the first prize winner, a boy from San Francisco, liked to drink as much as I did, so we stuck together as a soused team.

I autographed many copies of the journal. "What I love about your story," a lady I didn't know told me, "is that there isn't a single word of bullshit in it."

For an alcoholic with an ego/inferiority problem, no poison is worse than recognition. When I got home again I found, exactly as I had in Brookline, that I couldn't write anymore. I wanted to be brilliant, but, sadly, all my new stories were written by someone wanting to be brilliant. The problem, I decided, was my damn job and the damn city. In the country, nature would heal me. There I'd drink sensibly, need no friends but our animals, and crank out prize-winning stories as a matter of course. I saved a lot of money for this big escape, which was easy because I'd grown used to living on nothing as a part-timer. I checked my bank balance several times a day over the phone. Yes, it was really going to happen.

~

In January of 1993, I got a call from Mom telling me that Adelyn had been diagnosed with a cancerous breast lump. At the time, I was still nursing a huge resentment against her, following a phone conversation in which I'd said that Jenna and I planned to marry. She had by this time become a committed Catholic who "didn't blame" her gay friends for living against God's ideals.

"You can't possibly imagine, though" she said in a *let's get real* tone that seared my memory, "that any sort of bond you two might have can possibly carry the kind of weight that makes a marriage. I mean, you may have a lot of affection for each other, but a union of man and wife is sacred for obvious reasons – because of procreation."

I don't recall how I answered. What I do recall is pulling at the nap of the carpet where I was sitting when I heard those words, and then repeating them to anyone they would outrage. Until fertility tests became mandatory for marriage licenses, her argument just didn't hold.

1/15/1993: "Adelyn has a malignant breast lump. I am feeling very guilty, this dark cloud of her misfortune and me with so little love for her, unable to reach through my anger. I should. I'll have to call – though I won't know who I'm talking to, or even who she's listening to."

Up until this conversation we'd been making some progress in our relationship. Adelyn's life was in full bloom, and being happy made her much more amiable. With her Ph.D. in Musicology from Princeton, complete with ground-breaking research on the origins of written music (via analysis of the 15th Century Trent Codices), she'd landed a teaching position at Harvard. Dad was pleased. The only trouble was, the position wasn't tenure-track, so she advised Harvard she might have to look elsewhere – i.e. Princeton. So the Harvard Musicology Department scrambled all over themselves to find enough funding to *create* a new tenure track position for her.

Now, I don't know about you, but that happens to me all the time. Every time *I* get hired by one of the world's most prestigious universities, they're always tripping all over themselves to create some new, tenure-track position for me. It gets so old. On the other hand, Adelyn had a difficult time remembering where I taught. Was it Everett Community College? Ellensburg? I had to remind her, it seemed, every time we talked.

Adelyn had also married a graduate student of Political Science with whom she was head over heels in love. All her life she'd been falling head over heels in love – madly, hopelessly, and impractically. And any time she was in love – whether with a high school teacher, college piano master, graduate musicology professor, or later the pastor at her church – she would stalk and talk. That is, she'd insist on telling you in detail the inordinately mundane adventures of her stalking. You heard about drawn curtains of their homes, laurel hedges, parked cars, or sometimes just hallway sightings or inane exchanges that delighted her. In other words, she was just like me, except that she *told* you all about it.

In telling these stories, she was a hostage-taker. Zelda or I compared notes on how we'd literally back our way to the doorway of a room, nodding and making closing remarks like, "Well, I guess you just never know!" or "Sounds pretty crazy, all right!" We'd keep trying to bow out of the conversation until we were literally a few feet down the hall. Adelyn just didn't give a shit. She'd go right on telling you, with the very same captivated, spellbound smile on her face, even as you said you had something to do, until you were physically absent.

So the weirdest thing about *this* romance, at least to Zelda and me in those days, was that even more than the physicist, this guy loved Adelyn back. They were made for each other. He even spoke exactly as she did, using that sort of academese that prefaces everything with "it would seem," "apparently," or "evidently," with the occasional "as it were" tossed in. She had her own habit of referring to individuals as "the poor man" or "the dear woman." In any case, they married and had two children.

Her newly doctoral husband was unable to find a teaching position near Cambridge, and, maybe because he'd been raised in Texas, deemed it more important to pursue his own career than to support his wife's. So he took a teaching position in South Carolina, coming up on weekends, but otherwise leaving her alone to care for their two toddlers while she went for tenure. Stakes were very high on all sides. She loved her kids beyond measure, but she also had to publish, teach, and participate in all the committee and faculty stuff that I found so overwhelming at Edmonds Community College – except that this was Harvard. She cut her sleep to six, five, and then four hours, and had not a close friend or a minute for relaxation – period. No one knows why people get cancer, but stress definitely sets the stage. As she pushed herself constantly, her immune system inevitably declined.

I, meanwhile, was too full of judgment about her husband's interstate commute and their Catholicism (along with anything else I could drum up to resent), and too busy with my own teaching, writing, and drinking to empathize with her. In my hostility, I dismissed the lump as mostly melodrama.

Remember, I was going to ditch the rat race so I could one day be happy. After work, I'd started driving around with a realtor to look at houses outside Olympia, about an hour south of us. Jenna was too busy wrapping up graduate school to come along, so I was on my own when I found *the place* – a two and a half-story log home set on a gently sloping acre and a half of open fields with a few towering Douglas firs. Jenna came down the following weekend and agreed this was it. The floors were tongue-in-groove planks, the open stairway made of split logs, and a loft overlooked the dining room – my future writing space. In mid-March, we moved in.

The only trouble with making dreams reality is, reality is real. To the dream of country living, I brought myself, my alcoholism, and all my problems.

Fear was a big one. I was still commuting to Edmonds, now an hour and a half each way, and still living in constant anxiety. Around this time, I noticed a lump, myself, in my left armpit. I was told, when I consulted a doctor in Olympia, that it was indeed a tumor, most likely benign.

I called Adelyn. We talked. My sister was there for me, ready to support me through my knobby armpit bump, in a way I had never been for her diagnosed malignancy, reaching out and ready to let bygones be bygones. She had left Harvard, left off all her ambitions to heal. I opened my heart just a crack in these conversations, sharing my fears, taking in her advice. But as soon as my tumor was out and biopsied as benign – a product of stress, the doctor theorized – my heart closed back up.

I decided she was making too much of her plight. She'd undergone a mastectomy and, yes, had to have chemo and radiation, but those were just words to me. I squirmed with excruciating embarrassment whenever she spoke of her potential death. In the lifelong competition between us, she had an undeniable leg up. *Everything* in her life now became more significant than mine because *she'd* had cancer. Of course I realized how callous and selfish these feelings were, so I admitted them to no one. But the truth was, I resented her even more.

Our parents flew to Virginia, where she now lived, to help out during her treatments. Walter called her almost daily. With this help and the love of her husband, she pulled through the treatments. Only Zelda and I failed to offer her support. Zelda at least had the excuse of living in Italy. I had none – unless you count late-stage alcoholism.

I felt determined to clench happiness in the country house, which was everything Jenna and I had dreamed of. Our master bedroom opened on a balcony that caught the morning sun. We would sit out there to enjoy our weekend tea and newspapers, hearing the sweet trills of birds and the breeze through the tree boughs. *Our* tree boughs. Now and again we'd see rabbits and deer. We installed a wood stove, for which I built and tiled a platform, and I fenced off the entire property almost single-handedly, sinking eight foot posts every twelve feet. Whenever I labored on the property, I kept a longneck within reach and, remembering those golden days of carpentry with Jim Reilly, pretty much stayed drunk. Stores were further off now, so I'd started buying beer by the case to keep up with my open gullet. In fact once I dug so drunkenly that I thought the blue sparks from our neighbors' power line must be from some mineral I was hitting, sort of like Wint-o-green Lifesavers in the dark, so I kept jabbing at it fascinatedly until a jolt of electricity shot right through the post-hole-diggers, strong enough to nearly yank off my arms. Oops! The neighbors' power was out for days as a result.

In short, I morphed again. The city dyke outfits vanished. Now I wore dirty jeans, flannel work shirts, and muddy work boots. What I longed for was to be both handsome and manly, like Michael Landen in *Bonanza*. I grew my hair out almost to my shoulders and took to tying it back with scrappy kerchiefs. I'd long since quit shaving, so my legs and armpits were full-on hairy, and since turning thirty I'd developed a dark fuzz on my upper lip. If you saw me buying cigarettes at the nearest convenience store, you'd have thought, Is that woman *trying* to look homely?

I tried to let that rustic, country feeling infiltrate everything I did, from the way I'd grab something out of the fridge to the way I'd towel dry after a shower ("I'm out in the country..."), because I believed that was what could heal my pain and fear: the pure goodness of the country.

We got an adorable pair of ducklings, Drew and Frieda, and raised them in the house until they grew up to be – fittingly enough – lesbians. Later on, a hen wandered onto our property and stayed. We also got two half wild dogs: Tashia was half Dingo, half German shepherd, and full on crazy; Kelsey was half coyote, half white shepherd, and quite timid.

5/10/1993: "I can't believe that here is where we've bought land and a house, that we've said, we live here, we are happy here. We walk around to look at our trees, our meadow, and walk the road to where the run over opossum stinks so bad, by the big tree that marks the corner of our lot.

"Today I lay out sunning on the slope of grass with Frieda and Drew. A hawk hung in the air above us and they kept near me, looked up, quacking alarm to each other, went to sleep under the crook of my knees. I'd rolled my pants cuffs up to tan my hairy white calves and I could feel them on my skin, so soft, touches and brushes so warm as they moved about and settled. I wished I'd never have to move, to get up, get dressed, go teach classes seventy miles away, but I did. When I reached my office I found a kind note under my door from Dick M., saying what great things he'd heard about me through students. So nice of him to leave it."

At last the great day came when I responded to my award of tenure by turning in a letter of resignation. Jenna was supporting us now, with her new job at Thurston County Mental Health. Her old MSW friends from Seattle visited us a few times, but I could tell she was lonely. Even in a social service field like hers, Olympia was conservative enough that she didn't feel comfortable being out as a lesbian, so it was back to the closet for both of us. Once again, we became the only lesbians we knew.

I quit taking my anti-depressants, convinced the countryside would cure me of my restless, irritable discontent and depression. But it didn't. The only difference was, now I had no one to blame.

6/25/1993: "I'm finally free and done and it doesn't feel like I thought it would. I should drink less. Much less. Definitely. I think for a while I'll have to pretend I'm someone else to enjoy myself. I'm going to pretend I'm Aunt Bea, who certainly would have enjoyed this place better than I'm able. Handel's *Water Music* is playing. I just don't know how to savor life, is the problem."

~

In the midst of all this came the Second Weird Thing, just as unexpected and inexplicable as the First. I suspect there may have been other weird things between this experience and the Gloucester ghost that I simply missed out of drunkenness or preoccupation. This one, like the ghost, was so overwhelming it could not be explained away.

Sadly, this Second Weird Thing involved a family tragedy. I foresaw it – the tragedy. Yet to write about it is difficult, since by foregrounding my paranormal experience, I seem to undermine the intensity of the tragedy itself. That's not my intention, not for this tragedy or for those still to come that were likewise connected to death. The fact is that many side-effects of Near Death Experiences relate somehow to death – though to a different aspect of death than is framed by an earth-only perspective of life. I'm sure the circumstances surrounding the ghost who walked the beach in Gloucester, so clearly searching for a ship to come in, were tragic as well. In that case, however, I just didn't know them.

My brother Walter had moved to Olympia after divorcing his first wife – an aerie, ultra-feminine, devout Christian who had abandoned her Ph.D. in Literature to become a lawyer – a second time. They had been very unhappy in both marriages, as she was highly nervous and snapped at him critically, impatient with the pace of his speech. So in Olympia, he had married a woman as different from her as he could find: Betsy, a nurturing, mothering daughter of an alcoholic, schooled by life. She was warm where the first wife had been cool, and soft where she'd been brittle. They wanted a child, and she'd gotten happily pregnant. Since she was young and healthy, having already birthed a daughter early in life, all of us felt entirely confident that the pregnancy would go smoothly.

Rationally, I had no reason to think differently. But from the moment I first heard of this pregnancy, I knew something different. I knew the deep and lightless pit of pain and despair that Walter – who was now happy for the first time in his life – was going to plunge into, falling in darkness and soul-saturating grief. And I knew, too, the reason: the baby would die in childbirth. How or why – that I could not say. My feeling centered not on the death itself, but on the grief Walter would suffer afterwards.

Each time the pregnancy was mentioned by my family, a shadow of dread passed over me, as if someone had opened a doorway to despair in my peripheral vision. It was utter bleakness. It tainted all my optimistic thoughts. Over the phone my mother would chat happily about the due date, and each time I would cringe. It wasn't worry or fretting. It was the *feeling* of pain and darkness Walter was doomed to suffer spilling over into my consciousness.

Mom reported: "He says Betsy has announced, 'We're going to have this baby in three months, and we need to be ready for it!'" So they were buying everything – the crib, the stroller, the clothes – all in one fell swoop.

Don't do it! I wanted to warn them. Each thing purchased would only add to their pain. What would they do with the empty crib? Who would take it apart? I saw a banner on a wall – "*It's a boy!*" Who would take it down?

As with the ghost encounter, I had no idea what to do with this experience. I knew no way to classify it. Most of all, I didn't *want* it. Over and over, I told myself I was nothing but a worry-wart. I must just want so much for Walter and his wife to be happy that I was drumming up phantom concerns. The baby would be *fine*.

Wasn't his wife having regular check-ups? Wouldn't doctors foresee any potential complication? Of course they would. I should just knock off whatever doom and gloom trip this was.

A day or two before the baby was to be born, Zelda, who was back from Italy, and I went out for lunch with Walter. Of all places we could go, he chose a local chain restaurant called Happy Teriyaki. '*Happy* Teriyaki?' I thought. God, the irony! He was going to know such agony. I could hardly eat for the sorrow I foresaw, for the guilt of knowing. But I play-acted cheer. Walter was on top of the world. I wanted *that*, not the black doorway, to be true. We left with many hugs, and many a happy "see you soon!" meaning when the baby was born.

I remember sitting in my little Mazda in that parking lot, staring at the wheel and gauges. The baby would die. The baby would die. He would die. What *was* this? Why was it stronger now than ever, almost too strong to stand? What should I *do*?! For months I'd struggled with this question, and here I sensed my last chance. Should I run to Walter's car, bang on the glass and say, "Wait! Something terrible is going to happen!" I had no idea *of what* or *how* or *when* the baby would die. For the past few months I'd thought it would be by miscarriage, now I felt it would be in birth, but it could still be by SIDS or some car accident or sudden illness. I just didn't know anything beyond Walter's pain. How do you say to someone, "Your baby is going to die and you'll be plunged into a darkness of grief so intense it's spilling over to me now" –? It sounds like a curse.

I couldn't do it. Instead I prayed, professed atheist that I was, that the baby would be safe. Let him be safe. Let him be fine. Let me let go of this darkness.

On the morning when the call came, I didn't have to hear Walter's words. I knew as soon as I picked up the phone. What a fraud I felt, pretending to be shocked! What a selfish brute I was, too, for the fact that more than half my attention was distracted by amazement at my own prescience – marveling, whirling in confusion – when all of it should have been on the lost baby.

I'd not foreseen the hospital. The baby himself was wrenchingly beautiful and perfect in every detail. He had bled to death when the mother's water broke. Instead of forming a distinct umbilicus, his blood vessels had been fanned out over the surface of the amniotic sack – a flaw the ultrasounds missed. When her water broke, so did all his blood vessels. In essence, the pregnancy had been booby-trapped from the start.

I held the small bundle of my nephew's body. Zelda held him. We kept him warm while we waited three hours for our mother to arrive from Seattle, which she never did. She'd gone to a museum luncheon, feeling there was nothing she could do to help, especially since Dad was out of town. So she didn't come. Eventually nurses took the tiny body away.

I volunteered to go with some of Betsy's family back to their house. There I cleaned the baby's blood from the carpet beside the bed with a bowl of water and a cleaning rag. I did my best, but the stain was indelible. It was I who took down the "*It's a Boy!*" banner, folded it up, and threw it away. It was I who, with help from others, folded the empty crib and put it out of sight.

I couldn't have saved him, I kept telling myself. I hadn't known what to do. At least no one else could guess my thoughts or my guilt – I looked as innocent as anyone. And most certainly, I would never tell a soul.

Walter's grief, when it struck, washed over him like a tsunami, overwhelming his life for several years. He journeyed with Betsy into that darkness, yet the two of them survived it together, one day at a time. They got fat. They gave up. They just survived. And slowly they healed enough to find the courage to have another child.

I put the experience away. I was ashamed of it. What good was it to foresee a tragedy if you didn't know enough to help? How could anyone else on the planet ever have shared these feelings?

Clockwise from top left: Visiting Portland; Teddy-girl in Copenhagen, 1992; hungover for family portraits, 1992; dyke dream-house, 1993

15: GRUNGE, INFATUATION, AND NEAR INSANITY

...she was getting wet and open
like a flower in the rain.
then she rolled on her stomach
and her most beautiful ass
looked up at me
and I reached under and got the
cunt again.

> *-Charles Bukowski*
> *Like a Flower in the Rain*

Who I am has nothing to do with it.

> *-Soren Kierkegaard*
> *Diary of a Seducer*

9/29/1993: "Jenna's on a plane to Boston and I'm alone. I have a huge slab of turkey ham in my left hand right now. This shows that I am drunk.

"Anyway, why am I so preoccupied with this fear, why do I feel like I hardly *know* her, don't feel love in how she sees me – why not? What if she leaves me, leaves me – kills all of me that's in her, like I did to poor Kevin? I'd deserve it. She is moving up, up, up. We have equal degrees, now. She has a high-esteem job. She doesn't need me. I feel disposable, frightened."

Without my status as a college professor, I had to fall back on my innate self-esteem, which was unfortunately non-existent. No other sources were feeding it. My stories were rejected. I was not sexy anymore. I had no friends. Home alone while Jenna worked in town, I allowed my drinking time to start earlier and earlier in the day. Beer went smashingly well not only with outdoor work, but with vacuuming, dishwashing, cooking and, of course, writing. One day at about noon a neighbor called to discuss issues with our shared well. I recall feeling so damn friendly as I bantered away, laughing, joking, dropping F-bombs as if she and I were ripping it up at a party. Probably overdid that, I realized when I hung up.

The hatchback of my little Mazda began to serve as an alternate recycle bin and beer cellar. From the supply in my car I'd restock the case on the kitchen floor, minus my official number of beers for that day – Jenna and I had agreed on three. Those three empties I'd display in the household recycle bin. The rest of the empties and packaging from spare cases went in the back of my car. Every week or so I'd swing by a recycling station and drop them off: thirty, forty beers that Jenna didn't need to know about.

The more I drank, the more shame and self-loathing I felt.

11/28/1993: "Last night making love to Jenna and feeling totally worthless, undesirable, like scum, so dumb, who would want to make love to me? No one. Jenna felt nothing but trapped, obliged, stuck in an old, decaying relationship. Her contempt was swelling and breaking its restraints, would soon carry her away from me. And it *should*. Because I was nothing, had nothing to offer but a drain. I hated myself, my boring, repetitive love making, my predictable sounds – *hated* them, as Jenna must.

"Then, somewhere in orgasm I broke free like a space walker and saw, drifting from me and momentarily powerless, the *voice* – the condemner, the me-hater, this crippling, destructive voice that feeds me such a constant stream of hate. I was afraid of it, its darkness like a sooty, gummy coating over my every thought and act, almost evil in its despising of me, its will to defeat me. I wanted to look at it, though, to study it, almost, so I could recognize its tricks and not fall for them.

"But I also wanted to feel what it was like to float free of it for a while, to be clean and light and uncoated – how lovely and simple it was! I realized the only times I'm not fighting this clinging parasite are either when I've done something wonderful, or when I surrender to it entirely and take as fundamental fact the hopelessness of my being shit.

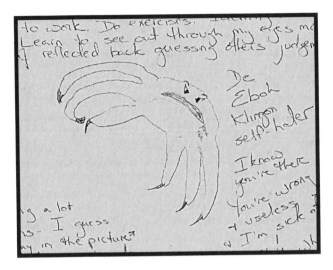

"It thinks it has a job to do and won't die easily. I even saw where its exposed roots were clinging at nothing, because for now it couldn't get at me. So I'll have to work to kill it, disarm it."

Unfortunately, my sole means of disarming the kling-on – getting drunk – was also its main source of strength.

Jenna was supposed to be earning the bulk of our money now, because I'd put about sixty thousand bucks into buying our house, compared to her two. I was supposed to find just a part time job that would complement my writing. So in September of 1993 I got hired on as a barista at a hip coffee shop in downtown Olympia. Dancing Goats, the place was called.

My co-workers were all grungy, retro-artsy kids in their twenties – all of them highly attractive, social, and, with a few exceptions, ready to give out free cookies to friends. Most were 'greeners, meaning they were students or graduates of the counter-cultured Evergreen State College a few miles away. I'd been hired to bring more "maturity" to the place, the bosses said. They also leaked the fact that I'd been a college English professor, which translated in my coworkers' estimations to tight-assed killjoy. At first I responded by classifying them with my naïve Edmonds students. Now that I'd reached the ripe age of thirty-three and was more isolated than ever, their conversations struck me as disarmingly candid. "Okay. I'm gonna go in the back and fart now. You're welcome." "This music makes me want to pull my dress up over my head." "Yeah, that was me trying to be cool, but now I'm saying dumb shit to hide it." I marveled at their freedom to speak aloud whatever they felt like – without booze.

One of my first days there, I'd come in early to hang out at the espresso bar and study the ambience – or something. One of my co-workers, a dark-haired boy, walked in and greeted another boy who was working. For some reason they grabbed each other over the bar and started kissing – a full-on, slow motion face-mash, swapping spit, grappling at hair. Customers cheered and clapped. They pulled away and laughed, both wiping their mouths. The first boy went back to work, and the second barked out, as he strode into the kitchen "That's my shirt, douchebag!"

I thought it very nice that this young couple was so out. But a few hours later when I referred to them as lovers, my coworker Dylan – a wide-eyed multi-racial boy with dreadlocks to his waist – started like I must be crazy.

"Van and Theo, *gay*? That's fuckin' hilarious!"

I described for him what had just happened while he eyed the part of the bar I kept gesturing toward, his smirk spreading into a grin. He laughed.

"Dude, *that* – what you saw – was, like, a pro-wrestling game of chicken."

"What do you mean?"

"Like with head-on cars – you know? Which guy freaks out first. They're just hella competitive, those two, so that was like, who can out-gay the other? Plus they're fuckin' crazy – you have no idea."

I remembered the laughter and applause. So it was all a joke, a parody of gayness. I wanted to feel offended, but instead I felt awed. Imagine having the nerve to plunge into a gay kiss, just for the hell of it. I mean, it had taken me most of a year, and I'd been in love!

Dylan was right: I had no idea. Van and Theo, both twenty-two, played in a local grunge band. As their lead singer, Van might take off his clothes or dump a bucket of paint over his head and smear his way through the audience, climb things, break things, lick things – whatever he felt like. Theo played drums.

Teaching English had turned me wooden by contrast. Was it too late for me to re-learn coolness?

10/26/1993: "Just wish I weren't so socially preoccupied, caring what people think of me at Dancing Goats, for chrissakes, twenty-year-olds, etc. – insecure, cock centered young boys and dreamy romantic girls – what do I care? Why do I fear being serious, dull, older? I wish I could just *be*, and not always see myself through others' eyes and turn into what I think they'd like. It's too much work."

I felt like I was in high school all over again. I started visiting an electrolysis place twice a week to get rid of my mustache, thrift shopping for grunge clothes, and tossing out the occasional "mass" and "hella." I wanted so much to be liked, but I had to leave work as soon as my shift ended to get home to Jenna, so I never saw anyone outside of work. I started to get panicky again, hyperventilating. My self-loathing grew so heavy, I could hardly stand my own company – unless I was fucked up.

2/15/1994: "Am in terrible shape.
"Loathe myself and am a burden to Jenna.
"Loathe myself and drink too much.
"What I want to say is, I suck, am shit, have a dumb, thick head, and wish I could recede to nothing, wish there were an understudy me to take over my life so I could disappear. Worst part is, I don't even believe I *should* stop loathing myself. I can't even see a way."

Later in that same entry comes a minor admission:

"Am a little infatuated with Theo at work, though totally unimpressed by him. He's just a movie star is all, not even that handsome but so sure of his rules of coolness, they form a rock for him, a sort of religion that guides him."

"A little infatuated." It was like a little break in the ice that triggers an avalanche. Those huge walls of glaciers that collapse into the Arctic Sea – even that enormity starts with a tiny break. You know me and infatuation: I could maintain a little crush about as well as I could have one little drink. Into the sea of incomprehensible demoralization would plummet everything I had built up in my life so far. I would lose Jenna, our dream house, my self-respect, and at the very end, nearly every shred of my desire to live. My stage was set. Theo entered as an innocent extra.

Remember how Kevin had been liked by all the girls in English class, and Jenna had been the most popular aerobics instructor at FU? Well, Theo was, in my parasitic eyes, prince of the Dancing Goats baristas. He was also an irresistible slut. His irresistibility brought him ample opportunities for sluttiness, and yet his sluttiness somehow made him more irresistible. He'd been born in Transylvania – really – with compelling dark eyes set in a face slightly too small for them, with an effect like an unwieldy gemstone anchored in a small ring.

Scantily clad girls would wander into the shop asking for him, and if he was there he'd chat a bit with each. Why hadn't he called? He'd take his time responding, leaning on the bakery case with ease, eyes catching on the stream of traffic out front. Why? That was hard to say – he wasn't sure. But he *did* feel really glad she'd stopped by. How 'bout she call him later and they'd do something together? Placated, the girl would depart, and Theo would sigh something like, "That girl is so awesome!" Then maybe an hour or two later, another would stop in, and they'd have virtually the same conversation.

Into the back kitchen where I might be cutting a cake or washing dishes, Theo would sometimes swoop with a harried air. "There's one girl out there I made out with last night, and another one I slept with," he'd say to someone – maybe even me. "It's kinda awkward." He might nervously wash a few dishes or grab some cartons to restock, then amble back out to the front resolved to make everything okay. Though plenty of good-looking guys worked at Goats and a few of them played the field, I'd never known anyone but Theo to fuck so many random chicks with upbeat insouciance.

The girls who worked at Goats fell into two categories: those who rolled their eyes at Theo's affairs and those secretly in love with him. I'd begun in the first category and intended to stay there. "He's not even that handsome!" I'd protest (too much?) after yet another girl came by. "I don't see the big appeal."

Van of the fabled chicken kiss had been best friends with Theo back in South Dakota before the two of them drove out here to seek their fortunes, but he could be coaxed to talk shit about him at times. Yeah, the guy had changed – too much, too fast. He'd fallen in love with himself in the mirror. You might not guess it, what with his sloppy clothes, his hair all whacked out and his posture slumped, but he had. According to Van, a year or so ago when Theo got all into this weight lifting crap was when the trouble began. Before that he'd had one girlfriend at a time.

Later on, when I knew Theo better, I developed a theory of his appeal (because I had to have a theory about anyone popular). His self-worth was unshakeable. Throughout his early years in Transylvania, he'd been an only son with lung problems that put him in the hospital a lot, while his mother fretted constantly. He'd brought her joy by simply surviving. But he also had guidelines for living. One of his grandfathers had been jailed by the Communists for his political views, which taught him the value of free expression, while his grandmother had given him stern lessons in old world etiquette, germinating in him a sense of European culture that somehow survived the American transplant.

According to my theory, somewhere in that mix of cultural currents, Theo had developed a unique sense of identity that wasn't rooted in American standards. Unless you heard him babbling Romanian over the phone, you'd never have believed English to be his second language. He read a lot, digesting classics, philosophy, and history with decided opinions on everything. But he'd mastered Olympia's pop culture just as thoroughly: how to dress, what music to buy, bands to see, hip phrases and gestures. He might show up at work with bed-head and a beard one day, then a buzzed scalp and clean-shaven the next. And *yet* – when he tasted a shot of espresso to judge if the grind was right, you saw the grandmother. You saw old Europe. Couldn't explain it, but you sensed it, even if you were just some teenage girl gazing out from mascara-caked lashes – something strikingly impervious about him.

That maybe the guy was just plain likeable? Well, that would have been too simple.

Imagine Louisa, wracked with her kling-on demon of self-loathing and frantic with insecurity, working side by side with Theo – having him call drink orders to her, slide open the display case so she could lift out a cake, or reach across her for a clean cup – amid the teamwork of handling a rush. Imagine her reaction when those dark eyes slammed into hers, her triumph when she'd make him laugh, her gratitude when he'd scoot a joke her way.

4/8/1994: "I'm an attention/approval seeking mess. This seems to be some kind of fucked up cycle I go through. Audience, audience, I need an audience! Give me someone to show I have a life, a personality, a gem of uniqueness that glints and sparkles! This is the madness I was in when I dreamed of high school boys, danced for imagined audiences, or stalked Kevin or Jenna hoping everywhere to see them.

"I want to think of Jenna's and my life here with our little animal family as a thing in itself – not some bobble to impress others, but private and real. Obviously, there's a problem here: the sense that I'm not enough in myself to witness my own life. I am nobody. I don't count. So I look outside myself, imagine showing or telling someone who will register it, grant it worth. I'm angry about this and yet powerless. I don't have a cure."

Powerless – funny I should use that term.

When Charles Bukowski, the drunken poet, died in March of 1994, a bunch of Evergreen hipsters sat around Goats lamenting the loss. I'd never heard of the guy. Theo was incensed.

"What the fuck? You're an *English* professor and you've never heard of Bukowski? That's ridiculous! He's an icon, a legend – he's Bu*kow*ski, for chrissake! Or he *was*."

The next day Theo brought in a book of Bukowski poetry for me to read. I took it home and poured over it, transfixed. I remember sitting on our split log staircase, drinking in the erotic poems like some delicious sin. These lines exposed a naked ego that sang and bitched and raged and fornicated right there on the page. They cut loose into freedom – irreverent, in your face, fuck-it-all freedom. They aroused me. I imagined that they expressed the credo for Theo's zestful way of life.

Zest! How I hungered for it! Because it seemed I'd let so much of my spirit languish in my forest-green, woolen home of lesbian flannel and muddy work boots. My world risked no open razors. No flashes of sexy brutality. Jenna and I pretended not to shit. I wanted to slam a fist on a table, spraying plosives like a stage actor, and announce that I didn't give a flying fuck about anything! Or maybe not. Maybe apathy was the whole point.

Amid all this inner back and forth with the poems, I narrated all my reactions to an imagined Theo. Next time he came into work, the real Theo had forgotten that he ever loaned me a book. I reminded him, suggesting we talk about it over a beer some night.

We met at the Eastside, a bar with pool tables, and decided to play. Theo had brought along his dark and lash-rimmed eyes, perfect hands, and a muscular back curving over the table. After he'd won a few games, we sat down and talked. If there was one thing I was any good at, it was talking about writing. Years of teaching kicked in, and Theo was captivated. He seemed delighted by the ways I wove phrases together – about the sensuality of Bukowski, at first, but then about my own writing, my life, my thinking. His full attention anchored on me. Oh! Endorphins, dopamine, oxytocin! Such a glorious fix! I was flying. All I knew was that I was rocketed back to heaven at last – higher than I'd felt since I first won over Jenna.

Except for one problem. I needed more. I needed to get even higher, and to clinch my supply. So I talked and talked, trying to reel him in, snare him, somehow force him to elevate me above all those pretty girls. He would see me: I was the one.

But at the same time, the high was tainted. Even as I reveled, I recognized my sickness as sickness. *Can we really play this game again, Louisa? We know where it leads – to emptiness!* Jenna was at home, trusting me. To think of her brought guilt. But just as with drinking, I was zooming down the mountain road with no brakes.

Like Bill Murray in *Ground Hog's Day* rushing maniacally through the special moments of a romantic winter's night, I paraded for Theo all my greatest hits. I whored out my Near Death story, yelling descriptions of god's Light over the juke box blasting Pearl Jam. I blabbered my grandmother's life story, my father's Harvard scholarship, descriptions of lesbian sex – *any*thing to make him *like* me, please *like* me! See how interesting and complex and intriguingly mysterious I am – *please*! Because without your blessing I die. Only you – your interest, your attention, your desire – can raise me up and crown me.

Occasionally Theo would talk, too, about his grandparents or his band or his family in South Dakota. I'd have to sit on my hands and force myself not to interrupt. Because his life was not the point: I'd already thought of more winning things to say.

When I came into work the next morning, hungover, Marie, a co-worker likewise obsessed with Theo, called out across the shop: "By the way! Theo's madly in love with you!" He'd come in for coffee at seven and told everyone that I was one of the coolest people he'd ever met. He wouldn't shut up about how amazing I was, she said. The crew found this amusing for a couple of reasons – among them that I was a lesbian eleven years his senior, so his excitement had to be Platonic.

Even Theo was thrown off by the lesbian part. We were *friends*. He never dreamed that fantasizing about him had become compulsive for me. One morning after getting no sleep because the fantasies had run through my mind all night, I had to work a double shift, and Theo noticed how tired I was. Between shifts I had a couple of hours off. Thoughtfully, he pointed out that he lived only a couple of blocks away. Why didn't I just go take a nap in his bed? He chucked a set of keys my way.

Theo's house. Theo's bed. Can you imagine the thrill? He lived in a trashed out rental with other college kids, including some artsy girl who had decorated the living room with a dozen plaster molds of half her torso, so that the shape of her ribs and one breast repeated all over the walls. How annoying, I thought. In his room Theo-clothes lay strewn about. The bed was unmade. I climbed in, drew up the covers, and breathed his Theo scent. Here he slept, he dreamed, he fucked. For three hours I lay there, my tantalized heart pounding away, and didn't sleep a wink.

And meanwhile, what about Jenna? Like the others, she had transformed into a jailer. She went sensibly to work each day, dressed in sensible business clothes to earn the mortgage for the dream house that was supposed to make me happy. But now I lived to escape it – that whole life. I wanted to be a grunge-hip, urban desperado, like Theo.

When my 34th birthday came around in June, I invited all the Dancing Goats out to our home for a party, though we lived fifteen miles from town and most of them didn't own cars. Earlier that day, Jenna and I took a walk though the Nisqually Flats, where I kept praying desperately to the gods of weather to make the clouds clear off so that sunlight might illuminate my beautiful home when Theo came to witness it. Jenna walked beside me. Her company, I reflected, meant about as much to me as the shredded bark on the paths, just as Kevin had meant as much as the parmesan cheese shaker. I'll never forget the hope and yearning I felt, willing the night to be a success. A handful of Goats did stop by to see my house and have a beer or two. But Theo wasn't among them. Some girl – the others rolled their eyes – was keeping him busy.

My social stock at Dancing Goats had risen considerably since Theo had rated me cool. The Goats comprised a family of sorts, and to join it, you pretty much had to hang out after work and drink. I took on a few night shifts to let me do this. Jenna, my jailer, claimed I stayed out too late and drove home drunk. I explained to her how much I needed friends of my own, well aware that I was completely full of shit. In truth, my every social outing was part of an expansive, highly orchestrated plot to reel in Theo. If I went out and had a wild time with other Goats, word of it might filter back to Theo. To myself, I referred to these social activities as "investments." They provided evidence to Theo that I lived a vibrant, active life of my own.

> 6/28/94 "He's not aware of me, though. I want to dance for him, sing, show and tell stories, be beautiful, be sexual. I want to be wanted by him. Then I'll know I have worth.
>
> "And obviously, dear reader, the writer of this can see there is a problem here. She suspects her entire upbringing of conditional love is responsible. She keeps trying to stop the symptom instead of the cause, to stop herself from thinking about the boy from the moment she gets up (and imagines him impressed) to the moment she falls asleep (and imagines him desiring). But how to stop the whole bullshit ass-backwards core of the problem – this she does not know."

Jenna's and my sex life had dwindled, sliding toward lesbian bed-death. We'd long since quit bothering to take off pajamas for sex, and reached orgasms as a matter of course, without passion. To release this rising flood of lust while resisting the old temptation to tie myself up, I hit upon the alternate outlet of writing lurid sex scenes about Theo in my journal. I told myself this journaling was harmless, even as, time and time again, I wrote my way to orgasm. What difference was there between these and the romance novels in grocery store racks, except that I wrote them myself?

One particularly daring investment I undertook that summer was a trip with Dylan to the old swimming hole on the Chehalis River. This was a play spot almost an hour from Olympia frequented by Goats and their friends on hot days. Since we found the place deserted and I was a lesbian, Dylan and I decided to skinny dip. Then we sunned naked; we drank sodas and ate sandwiches naked. I said not a word about this adventure at work, but as if he'd been handed a script of my diabolical scheme, Theo proposed, the next time I worked with him, that the two of us meet up the following morning and drive out to the swimming hole – just us two. He would call me around nine.

Jenna, I decided, didn't need to hear about this.

But, oh, the pains of withdrawal! Theo didn't call. I waited in a constant state of sexual excitement, trying to write and do chores around the house, all the while stockpiling witty things to say when the phone finally rang. As the hours passed, hope slowly slipped away. I was left with the undeniable truth of how sick I'd become. Here, again, is part of the entry I wrote that day:

> 7/13/1994: "Help me, help me, help me! No one could be more lost! God, I should see the shrink. I don't have the – I don't know what – the wisdom, the discipline, the *something* – to get myself back on track. I know that I am fucked up and have created something to tie my lifeline to. Fucked up! Fucked up! I am not sane. Depression – so make an idol, someone way up in the clouds and dream they'll somehow pull you up to feel worth. It fills my mind against my will.
>
> "Oh, God, Life, whatever – I'm so close to falling apart!"

This is the point at which I felt desperate enough to phone my old shrink's office and set up an emergency appointment for the next day. I soon found myself sitting across from my former advisor for the first time in three years. Except that, as described in the book's opening, by the time I reached him, the addiction had co-opted all my thinking. I wanted to talk incessantly about Theo, to cop that high of telling someone all about him under the guise of bring the shrink up to speed on our "relationship." I mentioned the journal entries only in passing.

As I've described, the shrink, though blitzed himself on pain meds, cut me short to assert that I had a drinking problem and needed help. To my denying addict, this issue seemed about as relevant as whether my neighbor owned a cat. My problem of obsession – if it was a problem – had *nothing* to do with my drinking. Nevertheless, I promised to research Rational Recovery and to meet with him regularly, knowing even at the time that I did so only to placate an unfortunate man whose status and talents were clearly dwindling.

Conveniently, the Olympia phone book carried no listing for Rational Recovery. And as for return visits, anyone who questioned my drinking was cut. I left a message with his secretary canceling my appointment and explaining that the sessions were too expensive.

Instead, I wrote more fantasies! As I had in childhood with the drawings, I pushed their limits, daring myself to write out my darkest, most buried impulses – *fuck me, use me, kill me* – because relief seemed to lie in degradation. "Fucked senseless" was a phrase I borrowed from a Sharon Olds poem. In my normal state of mind, which still returned sometimes, the words made me squirm, but when the addiction was on me, man, they hit the spot! Meanwhile, I met Theo's eyes at work without a flinch.

Then on July 20th, 1994, I drove home from a visit with a Goats friends, high on some imagined Theo conversation. The dogs bounded out to meet me and the house, with its flower baskets hanging bright in the afternoon sun, looked particularly picturesque. But as I got out of the car, I saw something through the French doors, a large book laid open on the dining room table.

It was my journal. She'd come home from work early and read it, every word.

Busted – *again*.

Jenna was both devastated and furious. She knew enough about mental illness to sense I had a problem, but she couldn't help herself. I'd been lying to her for so long, pretending to be a devoted partner. What did I have to say for myself?

I fumbled in that same dumb, helpless paralysis I'd felt with my mother. I tried to tell her I was out of control, that I was nuts and didn't know how to stop – but she was hurt too deeply to hear it. She told me to sleep on the futon couch that night.

I lay there in hell, soaking the pillow with tears. Nothing had changed – nothing! I'd been a pervert child, and now a pervert adult. Theo shriveled down to an ordinary young man, an innocent bystander. Jenna of the smooth almond eyes and punkin' smile – she had tried to love me wholly. She'd left her family in Boston and friends in Seattle and moved to this white, rural outpost where she worked in a small-town bureaucracy – all because she *loved* me! Reilly, Kevin, Jenna – all of them had fallen for a pretty, creative woman whose insides churned with poison and ugliness. *Why* could I not be normal? *Why* did I have this crippling compulsion that drove me to destroy my own happiness?

Jenna spent a few days with friends in Seattle. Then, a week after the journal reading incident, we met with a therapist named Elizabeth in the basement of some deserted public building. The three of us hunched in a cold little room with an orphaned chalk board on casters, where together we reviewed the facts: Louisa drank alcoholically, socialized immaturely, and was vastly underemployed, using her Master's Degree to serve coffee. What's more, she was emotionally unfaithful, intentionally deceptive, and capable of compartmentalization to a pathological degree. That's all we had time for at our first visit! I'm not kidding, either.

With the therapist's support, Jenna exacted a promise that I not work with Theo anymore. If I saw myself scheduled to work with him, I was to arrange for a sub. Obviously, I was not to see him outside of work, either. In short, they were cutting off my supply. I'll never forget the despair I felt on the drive home, or the way the gray, overcast sky seemed to hang over a colorless world. Even the roadside trees seemed to have faded to tones of slate. Without Theo, without that hope of blazing a trail to some ineffable cataclysm of bliss, the world became garbage. Trees and sticks. Asphalt and telephone poles. How do you live for that shit?

Imagine my joy when I showed up at Goats the following Friday night to discover Theo was unexpectedly subbing the closing shift with me and Van. The three of us had worked together long enough to handle a summer night's rush like a trio of acrobats, barking out orders in motion, flipping cups in the air, turning out circus-style antics for people who enjoyed us as part of the night's entertainment. I felt a swooning, joyful love for both boys. We turned the music up way louder than we were supposed to, stuff we weren't even allowed to play. Van had stashed a bottle of Jägermeister in the back freezer, and we all took swigs off it, except Van complained I took too much. The three of us decided to shoot pool at the Eastside after closing. Jenna was out on the town with a friend tonight, seeing a play, so I thought I could squeeze in a game or two and still get home undetected.

Olympia's downtown is not large. Flouncing along the sidewalk between those two fabulous boys, I turned a corner and all but crashed into Jenna and her friend. There were some double takes, some faltered hellos. I met Jenna's eyes with shamefaced cheer. She didn't look a bit upset, which gave me some hope, but the friend looked almost ill, as if she knew what this meant.

"Oh, my god!" I reacted afterwards. I told Van and Theo that Jenna disapproved of my friendships with Goats. In fact she'd tried to make me promise to quit hanging around with them after work altogether, and now she was really pissed.

"*What*?!" cried Van. "That's so fucked up! What is her *problem*?"

"That's some fucked up shit," agreed Theo.

Here I go again, just like a merry-go-round! I thought. One magic partner cast off after another like some slo-mo square dance

– my life just keeps cycling this way! But, hey. As long as I was already in deep shit, we might as well make a night of it.

Groveling isn't pretty. Only twice in my life have I actually gotten down on my knees and sobbed and begged with clasped hands. That night saw the first such scene, with Jenna a motionless idol in the doorway of our bedroom and me in the fluorescent light that spilled from the bathroom door, a quivering lump of remorse.

"Please! I didn't mean to, I don't know how —!" I sputtered in that sliding incline of pitch used by grovelers the world round. Jenna told me in a voice dry of emotion to once again sleep on the couch. She wanted me out of the house by the next day. No, we had nothing to talk about – not while I was drunk. Good night.

I don't think I went so easy. Vaguely I remember continuing to blubber to the closed bedroom door. But later that same night, as I lay dry-eyed on the futon couch, I was visited once again by the Fuck-this-Shit Fairy. She showed up in tattered satin and dirty tulle, as sweet and enchanting as ever. "You always fuck shit up, don't you?" she reminded me. "Well, it's just how we roll, bitch. Now, dear: two simple words – Fuck. It!"

Then she must have touched me with her magic Fukitol wand, because that night I chucked the whole life – the log home, the ducks, the entire happy dykes in the country project. Failed. Fuck it. Game over.

Jenna was gone from my life.

Clockwise from top left: Tashia as a puppy; cleaning the gutters; my 34th birthday with no Theo, a few days before Jenna read my journal; country dyke coziness, all I ever wanted...

16: HITTING BOTTOM; 3RD WEIRD THING

Vague and objectless anxiety in the present, and in the future continual sacrifice leading to nothing – that was all that lay before him. ...What had he to look forward to? Why should he strive? To live in order to exist?

> -Fyodor Dostoevsky
> *Crime and Punishment*

"Incomprehensible demoralization" is a phrase AA's Big Book uses to describe the total loss of control an alcoholic experiences, and where it takes them. Editing this book, I'm tempted to summarize everything in this chapter as: "Then things went from bad to worse, until I didn't want to live anymore." In fact, non-alcoholic readers may be fine with that and want to skip ahead. But the insanity of alcoholism is fascinating to other recovering drunks. We trade stories because the futility, absurdity, and utter recklessness that drive a person to hit bottom all resonate with someone who's been equally crazy. In describing our mutual depravity, we outline the void that is our need for a higher power.

So here I go. This is me, navigating by the prompts of alcoholism, self-loathing, and sexual addiction. Strange as it seems, all my decisions were attempts to seek out happiness.

I was barred from the house while Jenna packed up her things to move back to Seattle, so I stayed in Dylan's studio apartment, first sharing it and then housesitting after he left to visit family in Hawaii. Dylan was an artist, so his place was cluttered with easels, instruments, and frugal thrift shop finds, located only two blocks from Dancing Goats in a building so dilapidated, it was on the verge of being condemned. For instance, a blue tarp covered the roof hatch at the top of the stairs, but every time it rained, water came streaming down the staircase like an urban brook, and the hallway

16: HITTING BOTTOM; 3RD WEIRD THING

lights would fizzle out. I delighted in all of this. It seemed way cooler than my pointless acreage in the country.

All three of the bars I hung out in were now within easy walking distance but largely empty since most of the Evergreeners, including Theo, had gone home for summer break. Seeing as I wasn't missing much action, I swore off alcohol for a month. My reasons were two. First, without Jenna around to police the amount I drank, I feared inadvertently killing myself with alcohol poisoning. And second, albeit somewhat contradictorily, I wanted to prove to myself and the world that I had no problem with alcohol. I could control my drinking *without* help, despite what the shrink said. My only aid was a full-sized calendar tacked to Dylan's kitchen wall where I crossed each of the thirty days with a big X in red felt pen.

Coincidentally, as soon as I quit drinking, a new customer began hanging out at Dancing Goats. Clearly a dyke, she was also quite pretty, with spiky blond hair and alert blue eyes rimmed by mascara. She often showed up with a hefty gay boy, the two of them clowning in the tones people use when they enjoy being overheard. One day, though, she came alone with a U.S. road map which she spread out over more than her share of the counter. She always drank drip coffee with about ten million sugars, her empty packets and spilled granules now making a mess on either side of the map. To a neighbor at the bar she announced that she'd had it with Olympia and was moving to New York City, planning her motorcycle trip there right now!

Wiping up some of the sugar, I said, "Trust me: you don't want to move to New York City."

She started, her stare bright and unflinching as a rabbit's. "I don't? Why not?"

"'Cause!" I said simply. "It's de-humanizing and depressing."

Then I launched into my standard "New York City sucks" spiel, about homeless people with open sores begging at on sidewalks that were pounded by armies of indifferent, spike-heeled office women and arrogant business men; about stepping over dead bodies and getting stuck for unknown durations in packed and airless subway cars without light. She listened. She laughed. She blushed.

Her name was Jesse Perkins and oh, man, was she sick of Olympia! The lesbian community here was so small that everyone had already slept with everyone. Yuck! During my next smoke break she came outside with me, where we lean against the building in the summer sun. When I tossed out a "she" in reference to the partner I'd just broken up with, her attention ratcheted up a few notches. I also called myself a retired community college instructor.

"How old are you?" she asked, surprised.

"Way older than you think."

"Try me." She cocked her head.

"Thirty-four," I said, twirling my cigarette tip on the pavement.

"Whoa!" she said, genuinely taken aback. "That *is*... more than I thought."

I turned the question back at her.

"Twenty-eight," she said. She squinted behind her sunglasses, affecting a James Dean cool. "*And* two years – two and a half, actually – clean and sober. I'm an alcoholic."

Now it was my turn to start. "How can you be an alcoholic?!"

"I'm powerless over alcohol." she said firmly. "When I take even one drink, I can't stop, because that's the way my body reacts to alcohol."

"So you don't have *one* drink?"

"Not for two and a half years! And hopefully," she looked for wood to knock on, "never again!"

That was the first time I'd ever spoken to someone openly sober. Two *years* without a drink sounded horrific enough. But never to drink again? I couldn't wrap my head around it. The weirdest part was, she seemed *happy* about it, like someone singing, "Yippee-skippy, I'm stuck in this subterranean dungeon for the rest of my life!" She must have never loved drinking the way I did.

Come to think of it, that butch, strutty manner of hers irritated me. There was a brash lack of subtlety in her coolness; it was too color-by-number cool, too cocky compared to the morose undertones of blasé cool Theo and his friends projected.

In spite of myself, since she stopped by the shop daily, I'd begun to dress for her a bit. Jenna wasn't even out of our house yet, but with Theo in South Dakota, she would have to do. I wasn't really interested, of course. Who could be interested in someone who didn't drink?! One afternoon she strode in with a helmet under one arm and invited me on a motorcycle ride. No, thanks! I said. The instant she left, the other Goats teased me: the pretty dyke likes Louisa! Even the espresso bar regulars smirked. Everyone had noted our courtship.

I have a theory that the moments when god most directly tweaks my life are the intervals I remember best. God knew I would much rather splatter my brains in the nicks of a roadside telephone pole than even consider the degradation of joining AA. God also knew that only one force in my life was powerful enough to rival my alcoholism: my codependence. Why not use one illness to cure the other?

In any case, there came a beautifully balmy summer morning when I was walking Olympia's 4th Avenue with Marie, the two of us carrying non-Goat coffees and on our way to some quilting supply shop she frequented. The day was gorgeous! The morning air seemed so pure that inhaling was sheer delight, and the sunlight shunted at an angle that struck every detail as if to name it. Abstinent about two weeks now, I felt fabulously free of a hangover as the two of us crossed the street in front of Dancing Goats, where Jesse Perkins was in the process of parking her motorcycle. Chatting away, we tossed out a passing hello, only slightly snubbing.

But ten more steps down the sidewalk, I stopped in my tracks. Some urge of possibility was tickling my thoughts: *do it! do it!*

"One second," I raised a finger to Marie and hurried back.

"Y'know that motorcycle ride?" I called to Jesse. "I'll take you up on it sometime!"

She nodded, her helmet just off. "Sure thing," she said simply.

To Marie's teasing I protested, "So she's crazy about me, so what?"

The next day I clung to the sides of Jesse's leather jacket and watched her gloved hands work the throttle of her bike. We stopped at a light.

"Sometimes, just to feel cool," she told me, "I'll rev it just a little and let my ego swell up a minute. Then I gotta take it down again, though. Or else it'll kill me."

"What will?" I yelled, confused.

"My ego!" she said.

And we were off, zooming out of town, wending our way down scenic woodland roads along a route she didn't have to plan because she'd taken plenty of girls this way. With sun-dappled branches arching past overhead, she yelled something about leaning into the curves with her. Up and down rises and round the bends we swept, parting the air with slender shafts of sunlight flitting over us. I was glad I had come. I had not *felt* the beauty of the world for a long time.

At our turn-around point Jesse touched down and turned her helmeted face to profile. "I can usually tell if a girl's good in bed by how smooth she rides with me," she said as the engine slow-chugged. "And just so you know, you're the best I've had in a long time."

Then we took off again. So much for controlling ego, I thought. Hers or mine.

~

When Dylan came home, I went to stay with Walter and his wife for a while. I'd told them Jenna's and my break-up was a mutual decision – same thing I'd told everyone about Kevin. When I described Jesse to them, repeating some of her better lines from the motorcycle ride, they advised me not to get involved. There'd be risks in dating such an overt Donna Juan. And besides, it was way too soon.

I agreed.

Jenna called one morning. She still loved me, she cried, couldn't we try things again? This time, I was the one refusing; I didn't even have to think about it. The present dangled ripe sexual possibilities with both Theo and Jesse, while Jenna seemed to guarantee a lifetime of guilt and apology. Now came Jenna's turn to sob and beg. I sat in the morning sun on a concrete slab outside Walter's patio door and concerned myself with the details of lighting Marlboros and drinking coffee while she tried to persuade me that during our six years together we'd built something meaningful. I half-listened. Only two cigarettes left – dammit!

By the time Theo came back to town, I'd had sex with Jesse more than once. And very hot sex it was. For one thing I wasn't drunk, so every sensation was keener. What's more, Jesse's energy was completely unlike Jenna's. It was butch dyke energy, almost like a guy's. While Jenna and I had never been with any women but each other, Jesse had loved a string of them dating back to her teens. For her, it wasn't lesbian sex; it was just sex. She couldn't get enough of breasts, she joked, maybe because her mother hadn't breastfed her. She made me feel almost consumable in the pull of her desire.

Clearly, Jesse was smitten. Naturally, she had no way of knowing that my consciousness in bed was mixed. I was channeling to Theo non-stop as a witness to everything we did. Not only did I narrate to him constantly, but I showed him thought-videos. Theo-in-my-mind was highly impressed with Louisa's sensual abandon. It made him desire her as he had in the journal. That the real-life Theo would never actually see or hear any of this seemed a minor technicality – some glitch I'd work out later – because I *felt* like somehow he did. Every encounter with Jesse served, in some psychotic fashion, as a means of seducing Theo.

When I next worked with real-life Theo, he said yep, he'd heard through the grapevine about my fling.

"Yeah," I sighed, one philanderer to another. "It's nothing serious."

"Sure," he agreed, "but just be careful." He looked at me with just the slightest awkwardness. "It only takes two or three times for something to turn 'serious,'" he advised. "You gotta know when to step out."

Was he jealous? Was that what I was picking up? Sweet heaven, could it be so?

~

Since AA was a big part of her life, Jesse invited me to a meeting just to show me what they were like. I got a strange sense of entering the lion's den. Here were people who *abstained*, the shades of defeated drinkers. When the meeting got underway, a guy sitting near me shared that he'd not had a drink for six months, even though his wife was dying of cancer. A lanky, streetwise character somewhere in his forties, he regretted that for so many years he'd not been there for her. But now... he wept. "I can sit next to her bed, and be holdin' her hand, and she know...." he lost it for a bit, "...I'm really *there*." The room silently acknowledged his open heart. I'd never witnessed anything like this.

What really blew my mind, though, was the six months part. I believed him, though it seemed an inconceivable stretch of time. Thank god I had only two days left of not drinking!

The first day I went back to drinking, I explained to Marie over a pint at lunch that I now had clear-cut rules. I could have just one pint at lunch, and only two at night, except at a party, where I might have three. Marie approved the plan as healthy self-care. We talked about how important a commitment to a life plan really was.

"How about we split another pint?" I asked gamely.

"Didn't you just say," Marie looked puzzled, "only *one* pint with lunch?"

What an uptight bitch! I thought. Who'd have thought she'd throw my words back in my face like that!

I ordered one anyway, and Marie came around enough to split it. My two-pint evening limit fared about as well. The first time I shot pool with Dylan, when I'd finished two and complained that I wasn't supposed to have more, his face took on that smirk. He twirled one finger in the air beside his face. "Par-rdy!" he said. So I could have three, which turned into five because that's close to three.

Near the end of August I moved back into my house, alone, and finally resumed writing in my journal with this skeletal list.

8/23/1994
GUILT
"I feel guilty for not wanting to be with Jenna.
"I feel guilty for having fooled her all those years into
    thinking I gave from love and not fear.
"I feel guilty for being so infatuated with Theo.
"I feel guilty for having sex with Jesse and not telling her
    about Theo.
"I feel guilty for not telling Jenna about Jesse.
"I feel guilty for not seeing the shrink.
"I feel guilty for all the people who have loved me."

I'm not sure exactly when, but during this period I relapsed into self-bondage and even tried to draw the old pictures from my childhood – better rendered now – which still worked. Why the hell not? Did I *look* like I gave a shit what was healthy? I was all done with *responsible behavior*, trying to fucking *do what's right* or *live with honor*. I could see now that *goodness* was a child's concept, a fleeting bubble of some storybook world. Same with *truth*. While conformists clung to these moral Teddy Bears, I was bold enough to drop them. It was not only my sharp intellect, but a piercing realism honed by failed hopes that armed me to slice through such bullshit.

8/31/1994:

I
WILL SWALLOW
FIRE TIL IT
SLEEPS IN MY
VEINS

I needed housemates to help me pay my mortgage, so I put the word out. Within a few weeks, Theo moved into my house. That's right. Theo.

I recall feeling a little guilty as he signed the lease. A genuine disclosure of property conditions would have declared that 1) since March the OWNER has spent almost every waking moment obsessing about the TENANT. 2) OWNER has scrawled many pages of masturbatory fantasy about TENANT that has devastated OWNER's six-year relationship, and, finally, 3) OWNER now regularly has sex with a THIRD PARTY while obsessively imagining TENANT is somehow witness to it.

I neglected to give him a copy of that.

So, let's think. Now that I had Theo in my home, should I go ahead and ditch Jesse? Or should I wait until something actually *happened* with Theo? The sex with Jesse was still awfully good, whereas everything with Theo was still just fantasy – a bird in hand versus two in the bush type thing. I couldn't decide. So I called up Kevin one night to ask his advice.

That's right. Kevin.

I had his new phone number – my parents had recently given it to me. And it occurred to me as I sat by the fire drinking wine for hours that as my ex-husband he'd make a fine impartial judge. So I dialed him up in Boston after five years of no contact. And he answered. His voice was the same as ever, that lackadaisical Boston accent I'd once fallen so madly in love with.

How he was doing? – the question didn't even enter my mind. Driven by impatience, I brought him up to speed: Jenna was out of the picture and I couldn't afford my house anymore. This hot lesbian I'd been sleeping with was crazy about me but not educated and just not right. This other boy, Theo, who was eleven years younger and had just moved into my house, was the one I really *wanted* to sleep with – except he was just a friend, at least so far. But to break up with Jesse seemed premature. What should I do?

"I know exactly what you should do," Kevin responded calmly, "but you're not going to like it."

"I'm not? What is it?"

"Stop drinking."

"What? Stop *drinking*?!"

"Yes. You're an alcoholic. You're drunk right now. That's why you thought it was okay to call me."

I protested, trying to get him back on track, but he persisted.

"It doesn't matter what you do with this person and that. None of it matters, unless you quit drinking. You're like your father: an alcoholic."

What the *fuck*? Here I'd only had a few glasses of wine – maybe six. I even told him about the thirty-day thing, but he wouldn't listen. He said he had no more advice to offer. He wished me luck and hung up.

9/11/1994: "I feel guilty for just *doing* what I *feel* like without thinking where it will lead. That's my new approach to life, and it's scary. Is it like alcoholism, spinning out of control? Or is it a higher form of taking control, of doing things I've always wanted, letting experiences make me instead of me making experiences? There's a certain feeling of strength in barging ahead with desires, after so long keeping in check everything that was stirring and needy inside me... Why do I feel like I'm so full of shit?"

10/5/1994 "I'm thinking I need to break up with Jesse. If I'm going to fall into chaos, I should do it as a free agent. Why has talking to Kevin brought all this on?

"How have I misled her? Louisa, how can you *be* with one person in bed but have someone else on your mind the whole time and not say it's bullshit? (I just took a big swig of tequila. I am an alc and know it.)

"But back to the main thing. We were saying something honest. How can you be talking to one person inside your head, seeking approval, while you're having sex with another person actually *getting* approval that's just not worth as much? What we have here for Louisa is stereo approval. Real approval from Jesse, yeah, that's nice. Fantasy approval from Theo and we go '*Oh*! If I could only have *that* I would *know* something and feel so good!' You have to be honest. You have to start, goddamn it, by being honest with *yourself*."

I decided, at last, to take action. First, I broke up with Jesse, feeling nothing but that squirmy discomfort of witnessing others' strong emotions. For a few days after, I would lie in bed listening to Theo in my house. Sound traveled through the wood like a conductor: there went his coins on the bureau. Thunk! Thunk!

Those must be shoes. I willed with all my might for him to burst into my room and say, "I must have you!" But mind control didn't seem to work. So one night when he was driving us home in his Saab, I brought up a casual topic.

"Have you ever thought about maybe... you and me?"

He glanced my way, mildly surprised, then back to the road. "You mean, like, getting together?"

"Yeah." My heart was racing, my face blasé.

There was no sound but Smashing Pumpkins filling the car for a while, and then he said, "I might have, a little. Why?'

Because I've been completely fucking obsessed with you for months and months and I'm insane with it! You are the light, you are beauty, you are god! Only your life force can fill this void! Love me! Cure me! Save me!

Pavement rushed under the wheels.

"I dunno," I shrugged, "just wondered."

That night we put in a movie and made out on the futon couch. I felt extremely anxious and shaky, despite my arousal. Theo was a terrific kisser, but the frantically flashing circuits in my mind decided sex would "mean more" if we held off a night or two. I didn't yet grasp that in those days sex "meant" as much to Theo as cleaning the dryer's lint screen. When he made himself scarce for a few days afterwards, I kicked myself for hesitating and wrote this entry. More than anything else in my journal, it speaks in the unmitigated voice of addiction itself.

> 10/27/1994: "Why not go for it tomorrow night? What you want right now is not dignity. You can salvage that later from the shambles of aftermath. What you want now is reckless desire. So fucking throw yourself at him, fucking do it! Be a whore, be a sex-crazed older woman because that's what you *are*. Make yourself ludicrous enough to get what you want, because you already *are* ludicrous with wanting it. And instead of living with that holed up inside you, you should make it real. That's what telling him was. That's what being a whore will be.
>
> "Do what you need to do, Louisa. Quit cramming me back in your brain which is what I'm so sick to death of. You're smothering me. Let me out. Let me go wild. Pick up the pieces later. It is, I swear, the only way to peace."

The following Saturday, the 29th, I met up with Theo at a Halloween party. That's right. A Halloween party. Only this time I didn't have a costume, other than pretending to be sane. I was hell bent on getting Theo back to the house for sex, but he said he had to stop off and talk a bit with Connie, the girl he'd just broken up with, on his way home. I went to the house, built a fire, poured myself wine, and waited. Hours passed while I grew more and more drunk, yet also more anxious. Finally, near three in the morning, he came home.

We were in my room – my journal *says* so plainly – yet my memory insists we had sex in an empty blue room in a modern style house belonging to some other girl. When I read the journal, my room does not compute. I do remember, though, that from the start, everything went disastrously. I couldn't figure out why I felt shaky, nervous as hell, and bone dry. That this had nothing to do with genuine desire didn't occur to me. You might just as well expect pills to taste delicious.

As he took off the blue satin panties I had purchased special for this occasion, he giggled a bit. "Blue panties. Ha!" he said.

What the fuck did *that* mean?! What was so funny about blue panties that he'd say "ha!"? And why wasn't he consumed with desire too ardent for goofing around?! Wrong, all wrong!

While this encounter was slated to awaken true love in Theo, according to my months of fantasies, I began, to my horror, to sense that in reality mine was just the latest in a long and varied kootchie line-up. He'd done all this sooo many times, it seemed about as forbidden as buttering toast. My role was just to have fun, maybe bounce around with some spontaneous "Oh, Theo!" energy. That's probably what "Blue panties – ha!" was meant to instigate. Instead, I demanded the encounter be "intense," like someone desperately spurring a merry-go-round horse.

As a lover, Theo was skilled. Like someone really good at yo-yoing, he could rock me on top so that just keeping my balance created all the needed movement. But I felt homely, lacking the long, luxurious tresses or tan, flawless skin of a twenty-something. Instead here I was with my thirty-four-year-old hairy dyke calves, displaying all the sexual sophistication of a marching band tuba player. And he did not love me. I was not the one.

In the morning, having coffee, we tried it again with me on the kitchen counter. From the outside this may have resembled hot sex, but I felt accidentally naked and absurdly embarrassed, my stomach all in knots. I wanted to grab my clothes and hide in the duck pen.

Because I was beginning to realize how little what I'd longed for had to with the real world, the real Theo – this person. I understood, in mid-sex, that I was very, very sick. Just one utterance of truth from me, the briefest confession of my thoughts over the past few months, would have scared the shit out of Theo. Everything I said and did was, therefore, a sick lie.

That night Theo had to work. He said he would call, but he didn't. And he never came home to my house again, except to move out. For four days and four nights I sat alone in my house, drinking by the fire and waiting for the phone to ring until I passed out in my clothes. I left Theo two messages, one at work, one at his band-mate's house. All that seemed left was to write furiously in my journal, page after page of analysis.

In spite of myself, I began looking for other supports.

> 10/31/1994: "Truthfully, I miss Jesse. I want Jesse, and yet something bigger in me needs to see this Theo thing through. There are things about her I can't deal with – her intensity of talking about herself, the tackiness of her friends, the education difference, the AA thing. But, fuck – she is so beautiful, and I see that whenever she's there. She is rad. She is my true lover, in a sense."

On the fourth night, I went in the bathroom and chopped off all my hair, buzzing the sides back to urban dyke shortness. I called Jesse and soon ended up in her bed. When Theo finally met me for drinks downtown at the Spar, he wasn't happy about this. Why hadn't I waited? Connie had needed an abortion; he'd had to focus on her and couldn't call me. Now, he proposed a new plan by which we could each live our separate lives and get together every month or so for excellent sex. It could be our secret pact; only we would know we were lovers.

He gave a great pitch, but those hours alone let me see through it. I'd be back-up sex, was what it amounted to. Amazingly, I responded, No thank you.

In the meantime, sleeping with Jesse, I was beginning to hear ideas that intrigued me. Jesse said that being useful to others was more important than serving her ego. She claimed that most of her problems were actually of her own making, that she was often driven by fear, which caused her to step on toes and hurt people. What she needed now was to practice honesty on a daily basis, and to recognize and admit her own character defects. A lot of what she believed ran counter to everything I'd assumed about life. It was as if Jesse, this beautiful, sexy blond who wanted me, had somehow studied all the spiritual teachings of the world and come up with her own unique plan for living.

Isn't god tricky?

My interest was piqued. She had *something*. It wasn't charisma; it was direction.

> 11/16/1994: "How the hell does she get through night after night without a drink? How is it possible to be *that* honest with yourself, *that* unafraid of the night, when you know drinking can blur it all to peace, as it does for me night after night? How can she be that strong and centered on what is true and right?"

> 11/25/1994: "Drunk every night this week – except for the nights I spent with Jesse. Blurring my life away is cowardly and self-deceiving. It leaves me like this morning with my brain struggling to revive. My respect for Jesse is for her courage and discipline not to drink. I want to learn from her – not from AA – how to cope with the world, awake."

But I didn't stop drinking, and I didn't stop chasing Theo. I drank myself falling down drunk at the Dancing Goats Christmas party and chased after Theo right under Jesse's nose, which caused her to say she couldn't see me anymore. Nevertheless, when Jesse's third sober birthday came up at the end of December, she invited me to the meeting to see her pick up her three-year coin – the second AA meeting I'd ever been to. I got on a light buzz beforehand, just a few beers. This one was held in a country cabin miles from Olympia and attended mostly by old folks. They read something aloud: "Those who do not recover are... usually men and women who are constitutionally incapable of being honest with themselves." Wait – was that directed at *me*? Had they all agreed in advance to imply *I* was "constitutionally incapable" of honesty? Well, fuck them.

I couldn't wait to get home and drink at them all. Which I did. But they'd somehow put poop in the punchbowl: I knew they were right.

~

That last blurred month of drinking, I took to not going home at night. What I couldn't stand about my house was the very thing I'd once hope would bring me peace – the simple solitude of the place. The incessant ticking of the clock drove me mad. Since I'd come home so many mornings to find the dogs out of water and Tashia, who couldn't be trusted off a tether, tangled to within inches of her collar, I took to bringing them along on my search for parties. At these I would sit on the floor, passing bongs or trays of brightly colored pills amid blaring music. Or I'd stand in back yards around a keg with high school kids. "I'm too damn old to be going to these things," shouted a red haired girl as we stood smoking and with our red plastic cups. "I mean, fuck, I'm twenty-two!" I opted not to mention being thirty-four, myself.

Increasingly I found myself in places I didn't belong, saying things I didn't believe to people I didn't like – still trying for investments to impress Theo. To keep me from driving drunk, he had offered me a standing invitation to sleep in his room. Sometimes he came in and slept on the floor. Others he got in bed beside me, uninterested as if I were his sister. I remember hovering over him in the morning light, watching him sleep. He wore a bone necklace that pulsed in a dip of his throat, the beads rippling with an unerring rhythm like waves curling over a beach. But he was not mine, and I was nothing without him.

I spent the morning of New Year's Day, 1995, toying with whether or not to kill myself. I'd gone to a party where Theo was wrestling on the bathroom floor with a giggly, dark-haired girl and kicked the bathroom door shut just before midnight, much to the consternation of other guests. I'd had to unleash my kiss on Dylan, who laughed with surprise. Suicide felt like a form of New Year's resolution. What a relief it would be to just throw in the towel! Ever since I was little, I'd been trying, trying. I wanted to be done with that. Getting all the way dead would work best.

I wrote a list in my journal of reasons not to. *Picnics. Being on a boat. Scrambled eggs. Cozy bed.* These words are penned at all angles like floating confetti. Amid them appear the words "wine" and "beer" – because they made life bearable. As I was so occupied, Theo called, upset.

"I got home late and you weren't here. What the fuck? Did you drive wasted?" I told him his front door had been locked; he said it was open. I told him I'd sat out front in my car until I got too cold to wait any longer. He asked a bunch more questions, then practically ordered me to come over. He could sense I was going down.

> 1/1/95: "I believe I wasn't ridiculous today. It's not ridiculous to go hang out with a friend on New Year's Day and do nothing while they mat a picture. No, it isn't. It's not ridiculous to bring your dogs over when you feel you've been neglecting them. That doesn't make you ridiculous. It's not ridiculous to play poker and lose five bucks and then sit and watch the others play.
>
> "Not ridiculous to sit with a boy you're attracted to, even if he's eleven years younger, and tell him your pains and confusions, that you want to stay, and then go. He will not tell the others about me in a mean way. He will not call me a burden or a psycho or fucked up.
>
> "No one can help someone who is lost and falling."

Jesse couldn't help me, either.

> 1/6/94: "Oh, Jesse, I am drinking! Drinking and dwelling on Theo. These things I do to fill up the hole, this wine, this obsessing. The bottle is almost empty, Jesse. Then what will come between me and the world? Oh – my dogs know how to live and I do not! Damn me for every drink I have."

My favorite story of incomprehensible demoralization, which I've shared at several meetings, comes ten days before my last drink. Theo came over to my house one evening and I drank myself sloppy and tried yet again to seduce him, blathering about the childhood drawings I could get off on, wallowing on top of him as he napped on the couch until he asked me to please get off. He drove my car back to town to do his laundry, then to Thekla, a downtown dance bar, where I continued to drink and kept forgetting who his girlfriend, who had joined us, could possibly be. The two of them made me leave my car at Thekla and drove me to Theo's house. On the way I insisted we stop at a convenience store where I bought a big bag of Cheetos. The moment we got to his house, I staggered straight to his bed before that bitch could get to it, hoping he'd finally have sex with me. But I passed out. And when I woke up in the night, I was alone. I decided to brush my teeth with Theo's toothbrush.

When the two of them came to get me the next morning, I saw with my bleary vision that I'd gotten Cheetos stains everywhere. Orange smeared the surface of Theo's pillow and sheets. "Go wash your face, Lou," he said sadly. Seeped into Theo's toothbrush and spattered all over the sink and mirror were orange Cheetos bits. Orange stained my fingers, my shirt. But most of all, it had spread around my mouth like a big, wide clown mouth.

Isn't Cheetos-face a funny reason to howl and rail at god – later, of course, when you're alone in your house – for the nerve to kill yourself? For Cheetos-face you scream your throat raw and double over in sobs and kick furniture askew so that your poor dogs cower and hide. What is it you're screaming? *I hate you, I hate you!* —?

A night or two later I got so drunk at a party that I couldn't walk. Jägermeister and vodka, mostly on some mildewed couch in a raunchy basement. I kept falling down, which concerned others. Right when I thought I had walking down, there was the floor again under my face, dammit. Nothing hurt, but it got old. Some Goats put me in the back seat of my car and drove me to somebody's house, where they tucked me into somebody's bed and said goodnight. I was too tricky to fall asleep, though. I lay around til I was sure they were gone, then flopped out to the kitchen. I clomped my keys from the table. There was some kind of note I couldn't read.

My car was parked right out front, but something was all fucked up with the ignition, like where the fucker was at. Took for fuckin' ever to find it. But I did, and took off for home. Fast. Maybe tonight it would happen. I was seeing worse than double. Quadruple? Lots of picture-echoes, anyhow. I drove fast in the dark. My car was awesome, the way it hugged the curves. Coming up at about 80 mph on a narrow bridge over railroad tracks, big old striped reflective signs marked each concrete wall. Fuckin' A – so many signs! So many stripes! Which was real? Maybe I'd slam into one full speed, and maybe I wouldn't, but we'd definitely find out!

I flew across the bridge, slamming into nothing.

…*Not* real! Aced that! On I sped, half a ton of Mazda GLC practically unmanned, a yellow painted line between me and death for whoever.

I'd pulled into my driveway. Hell, yeah. I got out and stood up triumphant in the chill night air, one elbow propped on the open car door for balance. God damn, was I bad-ass! Could I drive good drunk, or what? If only Theo could see how I—

But here came Weird Thing number three, out of nowhere.

Something shot through me – a force, a thunderbolt. It shot from the night sky, through my bones, and into the soil I stood on. It was a force of knowledge, deep like a sub-sonic bass, from something powerful:

This is the last time I can help you.

It felt like getting thought-Tasered. My train of thought flash-faded like an overexposed photograph and in its place stood the plain truth, revealed. I understood that I'd toyed with murdering innocent people. I knew my recklessness was infantile, my thoughts of suicide self-pitying. I acknowledged that I, Louisa, could indeed tell the difference between right and wrong but had let my life fall to ruin through sloppy dishonesty. Most of all, though, I knew that voice. I knew it because I'd heard it twelve years before:

You cannot stay. You're not done yet.

I remember looking up at the starry night sky – that glittery blackness far above the foggy puffs of my breath. "Is it *you*?" I knew exactly who it was. I felt humbled. I felt ashamed.

The next morning, a disgusting mess greeted me in the kitchen. Some moron had slopped oatmeal all over the stove and left the milk standing out overnight. I was the only one living here now, so it had to be me. But I couldn't remember anything after that moment I'd looked into the stars and grasped the truth. So clearly I recalled clearing those twin reflectors on the bridge. So vividly could I recall the bolt of knowing, the starry night, that moment of honesty. But from that moment on, sheer blackout. Nothing recorded. How could that be?

All my life, I'd driven drunk enough to kill people. The night I turned twenty-one, I bombed down Broadway at 80 mph, blowing off at least four red lights and not noticing the flashing lights behind me for blocks. Radio off, smoke out, I turned the young cop my biggest eyes and said with Marilyn Monroe dumbness: "It's my birthday, and I was supposed to have the car back by midnight! But it's so late, my parents will *kill* me!" Twice more, I got off in similar ways. And for every time I'd been pulled over drunk, there were perhaps 100 when I should have been. Just last week, I'd caused a minor head-on collision, going too fast to control a right turn, swinging wide, slamming brakes, and bumping face to face with the car waiting at the intersection, but only softly. The other driver got spooked because she had no insurance and let it go – without realizing I was too plastered to stand.

What if something *had* helped me, some power that sharpened my consciousness, then, its work done, left it limp? What if the voice meant business?

That morning I called up a friend of Jesse's who was in AA – but also educated. Some sort of counselor, Jill was a slip of a woman just under five feet tall. She lived alone with a horse-sized Great Dane in a remote country cottage and had struck me as subtly courageous. I asked if I could come by for a visit.

I showed up at Jill's so putridly hungover my eyes should have been swimming with puss. She served coffee. "Help me! I can't stop drinking and it's going to kill me!" I didn't say. Instead, we chatted for hours about everything but. Slung beneath my brain was some black, rotten banana holding it up like a hammock. A vice tightened on my temples. But still I talked on, pretending everything was marvelous.

Finally, I said I'd be on my way. "I'm kind of tired," I confessed. "I had a bit too much to drink last night."

I saw Jill's mind pounce on the real reason for my visit, which until now had eluded her.

"Really?" she said. "Do you think you might be a *drunk*?"

The word shocked me. "No! Not at all!" I laughed. "It was just, last night was, a little overboard!"

But Jill had already dashed into her kitchen where she was rifling through drawers way too busily.

"Where is my meeting schedule?" she said. "I know I have one!"

She kept telling me to wait. When no meeting schedule materialized, she grabbed a phone book and copied down the number of AA's local hotline for me. I stuck the note in my pocket and later put it on the pile of clutter under the kitchen wall phone. There was no reason to get all drastic.

I kept on drinking and obsessing.

A few nights later, Theo's new band was to perform at a dilapidated house full of squatters, known as Glass House because of its now shattered sun deck. A rotted portion of its living room floor was held up by props from below, marked off with warning paint. I'd partied at Glass House maybe five times, but now it seemed to have moved. Circling blocks in search of it, I felt sure that everyone there was having THE great time, while I was missing out. *You're left out again*, my self-loathing pointed out. *Nothing has changed since high school.*

Desperate for a drink, I drove to Van's house. Van was glad to get a ride to the party but refused to give me the strawberry beer in his fridge, just because it had been a birthday gift. He had no other booze. "Can't you hurry?" I yelled toward his room while he hopped into his pants. He'd be upset if I drank that beer while he was busy. Mustn't do it. By the time we got to the grocery store, I was shaking so badly I wanted to pop open a beer before the cashier had rung them up, the way you can with snacks sometimes, but I waited until I'd paid, then chugged right there at the checkout. To show Van I wasn't a drunk, I'd only gotten a six pack. They seemed to vanish down my throat, each shrinking to the size of an airplane bottle. At the party, I never left the keg line. With my full cup, I'd just go to the back of the line.

Midnight passed. When the keg ran out, I gave three dollars – all I had – to a kid who said he'd bring back more. We screamed about it in the kitchen. Theo's band was warming up in the living room, absolutely deafening, the guitarist and bass player standing as serious artists with downcast eyes.

On the mantelpiece were red cups of flat, warm beer so I drank them. The band started playing so I watched. This stupid, fucking moron Louisa stood there like a figure carved from hardened shit and watched the boy she'd dreamed about hit the drums, super cool. Super cool! Hit the drums! Girls would watch him. They'd fuck. We'd fucked. But that was over now.

The beer boy hadn't come back, so I took another mantelpiece cup. Here I stood and could not get drunk. I could still speak. I could still move. I could still wish for a way to dash my shit brains out. And most of all I could still hate myself with this boundless, soul-consuming hate.

I realized something: No matter how much I drank, the self-hate would not diminish. Hate had learned to pick its way around the flood of booze and never be washed to sleep. It had grown too powerful, and even alcohol could not fix me anymore.

Nothing could fix me.

Another young boy was trying to get my attention. I could read his gestures: You're standing in the middle of the rotten floor! It's gonna collapse! Truer words were never signaled. And look: here was someone's fatted cigarette butt in my beer, waterlogged below the surface.

With a parting look at Theo I walked out of Glass House. On the grass strip beside my car I stepped in a fresh pie of dog shit, and the stink overwhelmed me once I got in. It's true, I thought. My whole life is dog shit.

Late the next morning, on January 29, 1995, I went down to let the poor ducks and chicken out of their pen, where they'd been cooped up for days. Free at last, they ran their little waggle-butts up the hill, but I had no strength to follow. I had no reason to do anything. I was done. Life – the whole gamut – was not for me.

Back in the house, my eye caught on that phone number Jill had scrawled. The AA hotline. Now a plan came to me with great clarity. I would call that fucking number, and if the person who picked up was an asshole, I would go buy a gallon of vodka, and drink it all at one go. I could *do* that. I didn't fear it. And if I drank fast enough, that would be it. So I grabbed Jill's note, and I picked up the phone.

"Alcoholics Anonymous." A little old lady's voice came on the line, somebody's grandma, sweet as pie. She listened. "Okay, honey," she said, "a meeting far from town, we can do that. You just hang on there while I find one for ya. You just hang on, honey."

Such kindness. I wanted to cry, but my eyes were broken.

That was January 29, 1995. I've not had a drink since that voice reached my heart – for seventeen years as I write this. And I myself have been as kind and loving as that grandma, many, many times, to those who are lost.

A week or so before I hit bottom, Jesse took me out to shoot artsy photos. I showed up certain I could hide my hangover and self-disgust. But when Jesse said, "Look hopeless," it might've come a bit too easy.

17: BRAND NEW SOBRIETY; WEIRD THINGS 4 & 5

It's down to this.
I've got to make this life make sense.
Can anyone tell what I've done?
I miss the life,
I miss the colors of the world.
Can anyone tell where I am?

-3 Doors Down
Away from the Sun

What I recall most vividly about my first meeting, which I went to that very night, driving along dark, rural roads in the rain, is the gravel of the parking lot. I'd sighted the little house set off the roadside, but when I pulled in and heard my tires crunch on the gravel, that's when I realized this was actually happening. I was really here, outside an AA meeting the grandma had recommended. I was about to walk in among those self-proclaimed alcoholics. Seriously? Had it come to this?

Inside a large room were oblong tables arranged in a rectangle and a small number of people, as I'd arrived early, chatting with each other. I got coffee, my hands shaking crazily as they always did now, alarming to others but same old shit to me. I saw ashtrays and lit up gratefully. On each table were little baskets of penny candy, and I took all the best stuff from the two nearest my corner seat, unwrapping each with those damn trembling fingers.

The meeting began. One man there did his part to change my life. This guy, who looked enough like Danny Glover that, to me, he was, stretched a cord across the room from his experience into my lonely, barren awareness in a way I'd never have imagined possible. He described driving his eighteen-wheeler on the Interstate, thirty tons or so swaying behind him at seventy miles per hour, all the while swigging whiskey. He'd jump awake in terror, thinking, "You *can't* pass out!" But as soon as he felt okay again, he'd take another swig. "Thoughts ain't got no hands to grab that bottle away from me. Thoughts can't stop my hand from tipping it, because I needed every drink I took."

I reacted first with shock – good *gawd*, man, you're even worse than *me*! – then empathy. I knew exactly what he meant since I'd done pretty much the same thing countless times, just minus the thirty tons.

His tone held that same slant of emotion actors play up in every "share" on TV or in movies – that mix of regret and trust in the group. And yet – there was something alive in the room no actor could fake: the energy of his intention. He infused the whole room with a desire to help someone else, namely that dying woman in the corner whom he recognized as a newcomer. Every eye in the room spotted me as a "wet one," though I had no idea. They remembered that kind of pain and longed to help me learn the way out. I couldn't grasp that yet, because kindness, in my mind, was still something you doled out to *get* something. The power of kind intentions, the energy of love itself – those were mystery signals on my radar; I could pick them up but not identify. And they drew me back to meetings without my knowing why.

I went home that night without stopping to buy beer. Somehow, I went to bed stark raving sober, after writing this.

> 1/29/1995: "I went to an AA meeting tonight. Was so uncomfortable and out of place, and felt I will never, *ever* stop drinking, so why even *want* to? I know drinking so intimately. I know me with a drink, a glass of wine or a beer, better than I know anyone in this world. I love to drink. I love it like freedom and happiness. I want never to stop. I wish I could drink every hour of the day, and until the night is gone."

I went to another meeting the next night, and another the next. With my short dyke haircut, dudded up in my army jacket and black leather boots, I strode into meetings feeling way cooler than anyone else. I could scarcely believe I was hanging out with people who talked of God without sarcasm. At a meeting called Capital City, I thought, "What the hell am I *doing* here with a bunch of pantywaist, religious old farts? Fuck this!" I resolved to walk out. Except nothing happened. I didn't get up. I heard yet another anthropomorphized *He* and thought, "This AA crap is stupid. I'm outta here!" But I continued to sit there. It wasn't paralysis, exactly, though I do recall a weird, tickly sensation in my thighs, which lasted through the end of the meeting, when I joined hands with those pantywaists but did not say the Lord's Prayer with them. I still don't say that prayer. And yet, I was included among them.

Slowly I began to recognize the words "God as we understood Him" meant that others' belief in a *He* God didn't have to affect mine. Just think "Good Orderly Direction," I heard at another meeting.

Not wanting to run into Jesse, I avoided meetings at the Olympia Alano Club. But when the AA schedule listed a meeting there as "Beginners," I figured her three years sober made her way too expert. She came in anyway, ten minutes into it, and sat down. That meeting, at about ten days sober, was the first at which I ever spoke the words, "I'm an alcoholic." Hearing me, Jesse teared up. When we went out for coffee after, she was ecstatic, but promised to stay out of my recovery. I think we both suspected already that she *was* most of my recovery. We slept together within days.

~

Paranormal after-effects of Near Death Experiences tend, for most people, to occur most frequently in the months and years immediately following their NDE. I did not follow this pattern. Perhaps because I'd been so intent on denying god and anything paranormal, in the ten years following my NDE I experienced a grand total of two Weird Things. Whatever spiritual entity conveyed the message of the Third Weird Thing to me – "This is the last time I can help you" – must have had to use a fricking bullhorn to get through. But after that, they came relatively thick and fast.

At about two weeks sober, I was invited by Zelda and her crazy Italian husband to a "vodka slamming party" at the summer cabin. Zelda had gotten to know many of my Goats friends (who liked her better than me, actually), so that Theo, among others, was also invited.

What a *Great Time* that sounded like! The word "slamming" implied so much more revelry than, say, "swallowing." I pictured all of us sitting around the campfire, everyone slamming away while I drank O'Douls, laughing along. Theo would be struck by my fortitude: what a complex woman she is! Then he'd forget about his girlfriend and fall in love with me.

My new sponsor, Jill, advised me not to go. I insisted I'd be fine. My plan was to load up with a ton of candy, near-beer, and sodas so I could just hang out without drinking. Jill disagreed. "You're free to go," she said, "but if you choose to, I can't sponsor you anymore."

Aha! I thought. Here's that cultish AA pressure!

"Well, okay," I said, "I'm just gonna go, so you don't have to be my sponsor. But thanks!"

I took a special shopping trip, fantasizing away about Theo, and filled my cart with don't-drink junk food. On the way home I pulled over at a nature reserve where I routinely walked Tashia and Kelsey, of whom I had custody. At the top of a grassy ridge I paused and, looking up at the pale winter clouds, attempted to pray for the first time in my life.

"Dear goddess," I whispered. "I don't know what you are or what I'm doing, but I ask that you please help me with this new life. I don't know how I can live sober, but I promise to try if you'll show me the way. Thanks. Amen."

About twenty minutes later I pulled into the driveway and, as always, left the gate open while I carried in groceries. Through the glass doors I saw Kelsey, the timid half-coyote, tear up the driveway and down the road, barking like some crazed attack dog. I ran out yelling after her, baffled to see her in all-out pursuit of a big, double-trailer dirt truck.

That's when I turned and saw Tashia lying across the yellow centerline.

Blood trickled from her mouth and from somewhere under her body. I realized she was paralyzed, the faint dust of tire treads crossing her ribs. I knelt with her in the middle of Mullen Road, sobbing for long minutes, oblivious to all else. She was still conscious. She shifted her clear brown eyes and swallowed. When I bent to kiss her face I saw, at very close range, her blood trickling among the embedded pebbles of asphalt; up close it took on a sudden intensity of detail, a aerial view of a landscape with multiple rivers trickling down its canyons.

At that moment, the same voice spoke again:
Look!

That's all it said this time, my own thoughts banished not quite as electrifyingly, but just as unmistakably.

Look! was a command, and I knew instantly what it spoke of. Tashia's living blood was mingling with the physical realities of asphalt. The voice forced me to see that death was real. The blood flowing inside me would mesh just as mundanely with similar pavement if I kept on as I was. "Get it!" the voice was commanding.

Then Tashia died, right before my eyes.

I know if I were you, reading this, I'd be thinking, "She describes it as a 'voice,' but clearly it was just her psyche. Probably her guilt had grown strong enough to somehow break through her denial so it *seemed* to come from outside." In case you're thinking something similar, I'd just like to interject that I'm not a moron. I was thirty-four years old. I knew what a strong thought felt like. I even knew what a powerful revelation felt like. If this 'voice' had been one of these, I would *say* so! I don't lie to you! I am telling you that I had an experience not characteristic of normal living. I cannot be any more clear on that point.

I felt both stunned and intensely awake. I also became aware Kelsey and I were hanging out in the middle of a normally busy road. I picked up Tashia's body and lugged it to the shoulder. The truck driver came by again. He looked out and saw my tear stained face, but he didn't stop.

Vodka slamming party? What ludicrous bullshit! Louisa was still up to her old tricks, chasing a Theo-fix. And those tricks, quite simply, would kill her. I could keep choosing delusion or I could *Look!* at truth: I had a fatal disease that dominated my mind. For a moment I grasped that all my hunger for popularity, for validation from idolized heartthrobs, for admiration, glamour, social gold stars – all were like some Harlequin Pied Piper beckoning to me always from a distance. His flute promised always the *best* time, the *most* fun, not here but just over there! I'd been chasing that figure all my life. Now I recognized him as a demon who would lure me to the precipice of death.

My religion was coolness. All my life, I'd been a blind follower.

At the time, I believed I beheld this truth too profoundly to ever forget. I didn't yet understand that the mind of an alcoholic is like an Etch-a-Sketch: just shake it up a little, and the picture is gone. But the clarity of that moment proved just enough for me to leave the coolness church.

I grabbed Kelsey and brought her in the house. Groceries everywhere, vodka not-slamming supplies, seemed to mock me. What should I do? Should I call Jenna and say, "Now I've killed our dog, too" –? Not yet. I could call Theo, or I could call Jesse. The phone sat on the table.

If I called Theo right now, I could be super emotional without faking, get some drama mileage out of Tashia's death. I could tell him I needed him here. Calling Jesse, on the other hand, would mean a surrender to her continuous pull. I'd end up in a relationship with her – I just knew it. But I also sensed that choosing Jesse was the path of sobriety and Theo the trail of the Pied Piper.

I called Jesse.

Less than half an hour later a motorcycle came roaring up driven by Wild Scotty, a newly sober boy with New Orleans energy so hyper, you quaked to imagine him drinking. Jesse sat behind him because her bike was in the shop. "Sorry for your loss, man," said Scotty, "but I can't stay. God bless, y'all." He pulled a U-ie and was gone, leaving Jesse with me.

She stayed for the next eight years.

We shut Tashia's body in the basement, where Kelsey whined and scratched at the door until I let her in to smell death. She understood, stepping backward from the body. The next day Jenna drove out and we put our dead dog into the back of her pickup truck. She'd bought it for all the country living we were supposed to enjoy together, but most recently it had transported our ducks and chicken to a friend's farm. A few hours later, having tearfully buried Tashia in the woods by the summer cabin, Jenna and I stood on that same deck where six years before we'd adventured inside the sunny warm sleeping bags. Now the planks were slick with winter rain, and the bond between us was as dead as Tashia.

As soon as the house sold, I moved in with Jesse to a tiny apartment in the Martin, another decaying building of downtown Olympia. She'd pretty much been living with me since her back went out a few weeks before when she was lifting Kelsey for a bath. At first the spasms were so bad, I had to spoon feed her. The consequences of moving in with someone were not something I weighed much. I'd always lived with someone. I couldn't imagine *not* doing so. Most of my stuff went into storage. Our kitchen was tiny with ancient appliances, and the entire building infested with sugar ants who formed a highway to our Mr. Honey bear no matter where we stashed him. There was a dusty old derelict dumbwaiter.

Our neighbors were mainly hipsters, but with a few strange old characters who had haunted the place for decades.

Poor Kelsey found herself transplanted from open acreage to two small rooms, with occasional quick walks to downtown's tiny Sylvester Park. If it rained too hard, I'd just toss the ball down the building's stairwell and she'd go bustling after it, tail helicoptering with excitement. Watching her, I reflected that living here would have driven Tashia insane. There was no space for her, and she'd been far too wild for most families to adopt. Was it possible she'd somehow given her life to save mine?

My own life changed even more drastically than Kelsey's as the days passed without drinking: thirty, sixty, ninety. I went to a meeting almost every night. With my conscious personality, I still felt superior to every person in every meeting. I still marveled to think that I, Louisa, of Vassar Phi Beta Kappa and the Milliman writing award, was mixing with these common people – uneducated, uncultured average Joes who talked about God and knew next to nothing about Existentialism. A homeless man I'd once stepped over as he lay drunk and warbling outside Dancing Goats became my friend when he got sober – perhaps the most cultured associate I'd found thus far in sobriety. In spite of the scarring that made a patchwork of his face, he'd read much of the English canon, possessed remarkable wit, and told very real stories of rubbing elbows in Hollywood. Ben, I think his name was. He went mad again, though, after three months sober – some demon rode on his shoulder – and I'm pretty sure he died. They all said sobriety was a matter of life and death. Let's not get carried away, I'd smirk to myself! Criticisms and caveats occupied my thoughts throughout meetings, and yet deeper down, I knew, or felt, or simply experienced the fact that I was learning more from these people than I had in all my schooling or upbringing put together.

"I can't fix my broken brain with my broken brain," I heard one man say – and the truth of it, the dead end fact of it, bowled me over. "That's why I need God, or I'll keep doing the same thing and expecting different results." "All my best thinking led me here – to wanting to die." Tidbits like these kept hitting home despite all my cynicism. They kept resounding with truth.

Telling my family I was sober in AA proved even more uncomfortable than coming out as a lesbian. My identifying as an alcoholic cast a heretical light on the official P. family stance that Dad was *not* an alcoholic. I could hardly believe it myself.

So much of my relationship to alcohol was subconscious that the tensions of breaking from it erupted in eerie dreams over the next two years. At about 50 days sober came this one:

2/18/1995: "I dreamed there was an alien monster in my home. It was reptilian, very old, and I'd shut it in some kind of basement at the summer cabin. It got out and would Vulcan-touch people's brains to steal their power. The first one it touched was Dad, and he was a total gonner. Also Megan from Goats, who I used to drink with. With other people – my mom, Walter – I couldn't be sure. When I tried to kill it, it shattered into a multitude of little tadpoles that slithered off, but I caught one and bit off its head. To cure people, I had to kiss them on the mouth and spit in a tiny bit of its brains. The monster was insidious and cunning and strong – not afraid of me even when I scattered it. And if I swallowed any of the brains myself, I'd be taken."

Jesse became the stable center of my sober life. Outside sex and sobriety, we were an unlikely match. Yet she spoke emphatically and colorfully during AA meetings and had earned herself quite a reputation in "the rooms." Since she was so adamantly butch, I shifted toward femme to complement her. Not every day but often enough I wore flowing, second-hand dresses and went for a willowy look, with painted nails, jewelry the whole bit.

How strange it felt to be partnered with someone I hadn't chased down through obsession! To just *let* someone love me was something I had never done. Jesse's story was a swashbuckling tale of high adventure, though I could never be sure how much of it was true. Her mother had died quite young of leukemia, having grown up in the plume of the Hanford nuclear plant. Her father, a Mormon, purportedly skipped town with the funeral money to woo himself a new bride. He returned two weeks later with a real life Mrs. Brady who brought three sons to match his four daughters. Except that Jesse's two older sisters were spirited away in the night by their biological father, and this hefty Mrs. Brady beat her two remaining stepdaughters ruthlessly. She threw them against walls, punched them in the face, whammed a toy baseball bat down on the spine of Jesse's sister, who later brought a lawsuit against her.

Finally, when she was thirteen, Jesse punched her step mom back. Her father interceded, shouting that he'd been married five times and was damned if he'd divorce again. So they sent Jesse into the Mormon foster home system. She started drinking, running away, and dropping out of high school.

Before long she had a rap sheet: street fights, wrecking cars for insurance, corrupting a minor, trespassing, and finally assault with a deadly weapon. The last came from beating up one of her dyke rivals and threatening her with a knife while her accomplice fired a gun in the air – for which Jesse spent six months in jail. Some time afterwards, she got sober because of a beautiful girl who helped her move out of her cocaine house just days before the cops raided it. During her first months sober, she worked undercover to bust drug dealers by setting up purchases with her old friends while wired by the police.

Jesse could be creative with the truth, as it turned out, so I still don't know how much of that story to believe. A scar on her ribs, for example, was supposedly the product of a knife fight. When she described blow by blow a fight where she rescued a girl being drowned in a high school lavatory, mistook the stabbing for a punch and went right on fighting, then, as she recovered in the hospital, received a visit from the rescued girl, I couldn't help saying, "Man! That sounds like an after school movie!" We'd been together a few years when she came out of the shower one day and confessed the scar came from having a mole removed, and that an after school movie might indeed have inspired the story.

Early on, though, I fell in love with Jesse's story and wrote a long poem immortalizing it, which she cherished. If I couldn't drink or use drugs anymore, I could at least have lots of exciting sex with a beautiful and daring lesbian. She didn't exactly fit the P. family mold, however.

> 3/5/1995: "Am a little messed up today. Saw Momma yesterday and introduced her to Jesse. Harsh, harsh disapproval! Show of disappointment in me – negative reinforcement, punishment through looks and voice. I feel guilty today, like I've let my parents down.'

In the restaurant where I introduced them, Jesse showed up in her leather jacket and motorcycle boots, complete with key chain. When she stepped away to use the bathroom, Mom gave an unequivocal thumbs-down. "Yes, she's very, very pretty. I'll give you that. But all that strut and swagger! And she had no idea who Caravaggio was!"

We had yelling fights from the outset, Jesse and I, about Jesus and overpopulation, or who did more dishes. And yet, I needed her. Without a sobriety cohort, I didn't feel I could make it. After all, there was *nothing* I knew how to do without booze. Ever since Vassar, I had lived every single day in one of two states: drinking or, equally important, waiting to drink. Now each time my mind reached for that anticipated relief and found it missing, a flutter of panic resulted. I felt exhausted, stuck on a fluorescent-bright, never-ending treadmill of life's demands.

> 4/4/1995: "I fear every coming minute, every hour of consciousness that I have to get through on my own – just me and the world. But the good side is, I know I *can* do it if I just hold on and keep going. And that is courage. I have courage now, I am rough-riding the world, life, being. Every moment I do so is a triumph. Hard to describe. At the end of every day or even incident there is a sense of exhilaration – I am being in the world, naked, and I am managing. I might not do everything perfect, but I'm trying. Me, Louisa, in this bright, happening world."

To help stamp out my obsession with Theo, I composed a little poem entitled, *Fourteen Reasons Theo is a Butthead,* that I made myself recite any time I felt the old obsession revving up. "One is when he kissed you, then went up straight to bed. Two is when he met you, then left with Heather instead." Atrocious rhymes, but they did the trick! I could derail the fantasy now, when nothing I had tried before had worked. It allowed me to keep a friendship with the real Theo, letting him be human.

He and I had often talked of taking a trip to Greece together. Ancient ruins, beaches, the quaint island towns – how glorious that would be! So when $30,000 from my house sale landed in my bank account, I set aside five of it for just such a trip – for just *me*, alone.

This plan upset Jesse to no end. She wanted me to either take her along or not go, but for what was practically the last time in our relationship, I said no and bought my solo ticket. Even my new sponsor, Jeannie, advised me that traveling alone with less than three months sober would be risky. But this was something I had to do. Theo presented me a mixed tape – Smashing Pumpkins, Screaming Trees, Soundgarden – and wished me well.

Here came the Fifth Weird Thing, which opened a period I refer to as my "Season of Miracles" in Greece. After my plane tickets arrived, I kept thinking for no particular reason of my college friend Allie, the one I'd written the prize-winning story about. I'd dropped our friendship in my frantic chase for Kevin thirteen years before, and now I kept wishing over and over that I could make things right with her. I'd heard she met a blond South African boy in the Peace Corps, married, and started a family with him in Luxembourg. Was Luxembourg, by chance, anywhere near Greece? I checked a map. A thousand miles separated the two. But for some reason, I decided to call Allie anyway, after thirteen years' silence, and let her know her I'd be only a thousand miles from her, and thinking of her.

I got in touch with Elizabeth and asked for Allie's number. A few nights later I dialed her up trans-Atlantic. Her voice was so indescribably Allie, my heart leapt to hear it.

How odd! she said. She and her family were leaving in the morning on a Greek vacation, *too*! What a shame that our dates didn't overlap. The same day I arrived in Athens, May 10th, they were departing from Crete. But wait a second: it didn't take us long to discover an incredible coincidence: we'd both be in the Athens airport from 1:30 when my plane got there, until 4:30 when hers left.

The intercontinental lag made a mishmash of our excitement. We set up a lunch date. "Come find me!" she said. "It's been so many years! I love you!"

After we'd hung up, I sat in silence. Why had I just called someone I hadn't spoken to in over a decade, to tell her I'd be a thousand miles from her? If I'd called just a few hours later, we'd have missed each other in distant wings of that huge airport.

How does one explain such a synchronicity – a two-hour lunch arranged in lives half a globe apart? Could it be called, just maybe, a miracle? Nah... what a bunch of hooey!

Top: Rough riding life wide awake, 1995; Jesse dressing up in my girlie stuff in our first apartment, 1995; even Kelsey falls for Theo, at the island cabin

18: A SEASON OF MIRACLES

*Though I cannot tell why it was exactly that those
stage managers, the Fates, put me down for this
shabby part in a whaling voyage...; yet, now that I
recall all the circumstances, I think I can see a little
into the springs and motives which being cunningly
presented to me under various disguises, induced me
to set about performing the part I did, besides
cajoling me into the delusion that it was a choice
resulting from my own unbiased freewill and
discriminating judgment.*

> -Herman Melville
> *Moby Dick*

At ninety days sober, I was still of a divided mind: I had a
faith mind, and I had a practical, anti-faith mind. But in Greece, the
miracles kept coming so thick and fast, I had no choice but to live in
conscious connection with god.

Because flying terrified me, it had always been a cue to drink.
I'd always gripped my armrests in anticipation of beverage service.
But now beverage service brought no relief. I was stuck with my
terror. To stave off panic on the long flight from New York I
practiced deep breathing and paid close attention to my stewardess
– a kind woman who spoke Greek – as a way to stay in the moment.
It helped.

At the Athens airport I found Allie and met her little family.
Her long black hair was streaked with gray at thirty-one, and she
had more laugh lines, but other than that, she was the same girl I'd
half fallen in love with at Vassar. The two of us sat down with
Greek salads to do thirteen years' worth of catching up. I gave her a
copy of the story. She joked that she half wished she *were* a lesbian,
but now she loved her family, even though they sucked up all her
energy.

We talked about her mother's alcoholism and I shared the small degree of insight I had – that the desire to get sober can only come from deep within the alcoholic. My father, like her mother, would most likely drink himself to wet brain and premature death. She cried a little and took my hand across the table. "I'm so glad," she said, "that you've found what you've found."

I understood that I could lose it all with just one tilt of a glass. Traveling cheap can be stressful, taking shuttles and busses in unknown cities among signs you can't read. So when I finally made it to my hotel, where the palms and orchids of the bar beckoned exotically, I consulted my international AA directory and set off on foot for a meeting, walking several miles across Athens. I waited almost an hour outside a vine-covered, stone building before someone came to unlock. Yes, there was an AA meeting soon. How strange to see the same Twelve Steps on the wall, along with hokey black and white photos of Bill and Bob! A range of unlikely characters shuffled in, English speakers from various parts of the world fidgeting and whisper-chatting through readings that opened the meeting. I'd already resolved not to speak; I was too jetlagged and shy to make the effort.

As soon as the meeting opened, a woman shared, already upset and crying. There was something familiar about her. She wore boxy khakis, and her hair hung messy and loose around her tear stained face, so it took me a while to recognize my stewardess from the New York flight. She shared how she'd screwed up her cross-check at the airport jetway and accidentally inflated an emergency slide. "I'm such an idiot!" she wept. She'd delayed the plane for *hours*. All those people inconvenienced, all because she was a brainless fuck-up! This would ruin her record. She might lose her job, but more than anything else, she didn't want to drink over this.

While she was speaking, a weird bolus of compassion took form in my chest. I had no choice but to release it, cross-talk or no.

"I'm Louisa, and I'm an alcoholic. You were my flight attendant on the trip from New York, and I watched you work. And I can say without doubt, no way are you a fuck-up. Who was the *only* flight attendant who spoke Greek? Who comforted the little Greek boy and brought him a coloring book? Who never lost patience with that old Greek lady who kept hitting her call button a million times?" By now she was staring in amazement. The whole meeting was. "Who ran around the plane translating for coworkers, but never missed a beat with us? You take for granted all the stuff you did right and see only your fuck-up. Maybe there's even a reason that plane needs to be delayed – who knows? But I do know one thing: if that airline fires you, they'll lose one kick-ass flight attendant."

I stopped. The room glowed.

"You're an angel," she whispered. "God sent you." Half the room was tearing up along with her.

Now I could begin to understand what that truck driver at my first meting had felt for me. With all my heart, I wanted good things for this woman – a stranger I'd never see again. She, like me, was keeping sober one day at a time. She, like me, was both vulnerable and courageous.

The whole meeting picked up our energy. Most of that motley group spoke with heavy accents – the gay Irishman, Shamus, with his leg-humping dog, the African man who said, after his name, "...and I am alcohol." Afterwards, the lot of us went out for dessert at a garden café overlooking the city where everyone wrote all over my tourist map telling me where to go and not go. I felt elated, connected to these souls. We talked until the street lights came on, when Louisa from Seattle wondered aloud if she ought to blow the money for a cab ride home.

"Don't be a fool!" said Shamus, in his brogue accent. "This isn't America! We're *civilized* here!" He was right. Walking the darkening streets, there were times I'd half jump out of my skin only to see children chasing a ball through the shadows, their parents calling them in languidly from alley doorways.

Traveling while raw with new sobriety is risky, no doubt. But the same vulnerability that throws one out of self-reliance can be a wonderful tool in god's hands. Again and again I sat down alone at restaurants in front of a complimentary cordial of ouzo and asked politely that it be taken away, even when I couldn't remember why I was doing so. Every time I'd traveled with Kevin or Jenna, I'd gotten drunk by evening or earlier every day. In exchange for doing things differently this time, I was awake to the gifts of fortuity that came along every time I prayed for help.

Delphi holds the ruins around the Oracle of Apollo. There's not much left of the Oracle itself, no steam rising from what was once a geyser, but since it was the original seat of Gaia, and since Gaia was pretty much my goddess, I took the time to pray to her there. I asked that she help me stay sober and keep me safe. I also thanked her for the amazing beauty of this world.

In the Greek town of Olympia, where I went next to see the ruins of the first Olympic games, my first little adventure taught me the hazards of wearing lipstick in public while trying to walk alone. My first evening there, I got asked out by every young shopkeeper or vender, until I ended up pursued down the street by a gaggle of six young men all asking me out for the night. I am not exaggerating. One had said, "Tonight, when you lie in bed alone, you will long for me. I will be waiting at the bar with many vines on the door!" Another even jogged backward in front of me while frantically spitting out every pick-up line his English would allow. They wouldn't take no for an answer. I was rescued by my waiter from lunch, and older man named Taxis, who had just left work for the evening. He recognized me at the hub of this commotion and came over, waving the boys away in scolding Greek. He offered to buy me a drink. When I said no, he settled for ice cream. He explained to me that the boys would have a lively summer as soon as the busloads of Scandinavian college girls arrived, but that this early in the season, I was it for pretty much the whole town. What else did I expect, he scoffed, parading around in lipstick and shorts without my father, my brother, or a husband? From this experience I should have learned to be on my guard. But I didn't. I decided that outside a small town like Olympia, I'd be fine.

So along came the greatest test of my sobriety to this day. I'd bought tickets in advance for a boat to the island of Crete, but my taxi dropped me off at the wrong cruise ship. By the time I figured out my ticket was worthless, we'd already set sail. With a long line of passengers behind me waiting to check in, I was told to come back in two hours, when they'd see what berths were left. So I lugged my suitcase and two shoulder bags to an out of the way spot on deck and sat on them, waiting. Obviously, I was upset.

A curly haired, balding man asked me in French to take a picture of him. He asked why I sat like that, on a pile of luggage, and I tried to explain, though my French is not as good as my German. He turned out to be Belgian and fluent in both, so we switched to German. I was missing all the beautiful sights, he said, stuck back in a corner like that! But leaving my stuff unguarded would not be safe, he agreed. Two hours? Why not just stow my bags in his room so I wouldn't have to worry about them?

For some reason that sounded practical. Certainly it was no trouble, he assured me politely. His room was close by and he was happy to help out.

"Verschwunden!" (disappeared!) he said, as he locked them in.

Baggage free I sat out in a deck chair, enjoying the sun-dappled Aegean and drinking coffee from a china cup as the gentleman downed cocktails. There was only one problem. As we chatted away, I began to notice he was addressing me with the familiar "du," instead of the formal "Sie." My inner grammar book identified an error: "dutzing" was appropriate for children and loved ones – neither applicable to me. But what if there was another category – slutty whores for whom one has no respect? For a while I continued to chat, addressing him pointedly as "Sie." But the feeling got worse. When simple communication takes a lot of effort, you tend to miss the undertones or vibes slipped into the conversation. Nonetheless, my slime-o-meter was beginning to spike.

"Vielleicht nehme ich jetz mein Gepäck," I suggested. He looked at his watch. No, no, he said, there was still lots of time left! I could see it now: he thought he was shepherding me toward a rendezvous. "Ich glaube, ich möchte lieber..." I persisted, and stood up.

In his cabin, everything happened very fast. I'd shouldered my bags and hefted my suitcase just in time to see him shutting the door. I somehow managed to swing my camera bag into the breach. He grabbed at my shoulder and was trying to kiss me, his florid face mooning closer with despicable air kisses, one of which sponged my cheek as I veered aside. I managed to get a foot, then my elbow, into the opening and shove the door back. "Das geht *nicht!*" I spat furiously.

I bungled my way down the narrow passageway, off-balance and weaving. "Komm zurück!" he kept calling in mock-love tones. I yelled back what I knew best: "Fuck you, asshole!"

Half palsied with panic, I staggered to the concierge window where there was still a line. I sat on my suitcase and shook all over. I didn't cry, I just trembled violently and breathlessly, inside and out. The coffees I'd had earlier didn't help.

About twenty minutes later, the Belgian asshole passed by with a male acquaintance. He pointed me out with a smirking phrase of French, while his friend blatantly sized me up. They laughed, exchanging more words, and headed toward the restaurant.

No space was left but a berth sandwiched among five other women in a closet-sized room where I couldn't abide while conscious. Once my bags were safely stowed there, I ate dinner in the cheap cafeteria with a bead-selling Swiss hippie chick and her toddler love child, speaking German again. She agreed that men were pigs. But, having a small child, she turned in early. I was still wide awake with my nerves jangled, my fear off the charts, and my outrage mounting by the minute.

The ship featured a deluxe bar running down the center of its main deck, open to one side and lit with amber radiance. It was hosted by a friendly bartender who was currently serving a few idle tourists. I circled it lap after lap: along the bar, around the corner, and back again on the non-bar side. The moon had come out. Classy bottles lined the glass shelves, each doubled by the mirror behind it. My eye snagged on my good buddy Jack Daniels, looking just like home. There were my classy pals, Wild Turkey and Beefeaters. Absolut. Bacardi. Everybody was here. They sang to me like sirens – don't fight us! Any one of them would burn a path down my throat and flare away this fear, make me powerful. The bartender smiled, anticipating an order. But I took just one more lap.

Fuck that fucking fuck-face with his kissy-mouthed, pink face! I could feel his fat hand on my shoulder, recall the stink of his cologne. And then that laugh with his buddy, as though I were a stupid whore! Belgian waffle fuck-face! I should've punched in his florid nose. What I ought to do now, I'd belt a few shots, find the bastard somewhere, say, "Du bist ass-wipe!!" and then knee him right in the balls. My teeth grit with the thought. All I needed was a little fortification.

Do that, came a thought, *and you'll have thrown away your new life for him.*

No – not for *him*! I protested. For *me*, to show him he can't—

Bullshit, came the thought. *You'd be shooting yourself in the soul.*

But fuck! What else could I *do*? I was a wreck, brimming with rage, fit to explode! And humiliated! The only way out of those feelings was to flood them. That's all I knew! I couldn't stand this frazzled torture a minute longer.

My eyes lighted once again on a young man I'd seen every time I'd circled around, a boy in his early twenties dressed all in black except for silver earrings. He was reading a paperback. In 1995, those jet-black dreadlocks on a white boy as good as stamped him, Made in USA.

He's a good person, my thoughts said. *Go and ask him for help. Just go to him now, and I'll help you know what to say.*

But, wait – wasn't that exactly what got me into trouble? Trusting men?

This one has goodness. Trust him.

I remembered Taxis, his kindness. Some men *were* good, even here. So I walked up to the dreadlock boy's table. Under the elbow of his tattooed arm lay a large sketchbook.

"Do you speak English?" I asked.

Irritation splashed his face. "Yeah."

"Can you do me a favor?" It was hard to begin, but soon, as if I'd pried open a stubborn faucet, the rest spouted out, my voice shaking so uncontrollably I sounded like someone imitating a sheep: "I'm super upset because... a really bad thing just happened to me... a little while ago so I'm... all messed up inside and... I... need to calm down. I really need to calm down."

He said nothing.

I sat down uninvited and gestured at his sketchbook. Now I knew *exactly* what to ask for. "Could you maybe, like, show me each one of your drawings and stuff? Like, could you turn the pages for me and tell me a little story about each one? That would help a lot!"

He scoffed in disbelief, as if to say, 'what the hell, lady?' I could see he was wary of my urgency, which, from his perspective, smacked of mental illness. Or I might be a con woman. I was dry-eyed; even the sheep voice could be an act. He checked around as if to see if I had cohorts. Decidedly, he shook his head. Nope. He wasn't going for it.

Then I added the lone word, "Please." I sat there, dry eyed and trembling. I folded my hands like a child. The drinks, the bottles were howling at my back. I'd worried that explaining this might make me seem even weirder, but now I had nothing to lose. "I'm an alcoholic and I have ninety-some days sober. And I don't want to drink. I'm very upset, and I don't know what else to do."

His face changed a little. "So... you're asking if you can look over my sketches? See, I don't..."

"No, not *me* look. I need *you* to show them to me, each of them, and tell me stuff. You know, little stories, little memories, where you were, stuff that happened." I nodded as if to say, you know the drill.

"Wow..." he looked away, his mouth suspended in a kind of shocked lassitude. "That's a pretty weird thing to just walk up and *ask* somebody."

I waited. He looked at me.

Then a miracle happened. The angel in that human being opened his heart. All he did was, he changed the angle of the sketchbook, which he'd been guarding protectively, a little toward the center of the table. I don't think I've ever known such trust and kindness from a person who knew me not at all. With my wildly shaking hands I skidded the book all the way sideways between us and opened it to the first page. It showed some kind of fountain or statue he'd sketched.

"Where was this?" I asked. "When were you there? What was it like, the weather?"

He answered monosyllabically and with shrugs at first, about drawing after drawing, until I recognized his sketch of Sienna. "That's the town square, isn't it?" Then I volunteered a story of my own, of how Jenna and I once saw a big black spider there trying to dance across a busy street, evading an unbelievable number of cars and mopeds before, tragically, he was flattened by a truck. We could see him clear as day on a cobblestone, flattened.

The boy liked my spider story, and he smiled. Slowly he loosened up, turning pages himself. At a sketch of the Mausoleum in Paris, I tapped the paper and rattled out a prompt – "Little story, little story!" – with toneless urgency. After some baffled ah's and uhh's, he began: "Yeah, so there were, like, a million pigeons here, okay? And so, there was one of those pigeon ladies, you know, like in Mary Poppins?"

I kept my eyes glued to the page and listened, not so much to the story itself as to the way he produced his words, edges of consonants, the plosives, the palatal phonation. When you really, really listened, they became almost tactile. I examined not just the drawings but the rag of the sketch paper, the indentations, ways graphite reacted to the surface. I listened to the rustle of heavy paper bending, whispering, as he smoothed it down. These sensations began to blur for me – the thingness of the thing. Without even consciously planning it, I put myself into a trance just deep enough to insulate me a layer from the clamoring world. Slowly, the curly haired devil began to fade from my thoughts. Slowly, the screams of the liquor bottles dwindled, and my pulse returned to normal.

Travis, the boy, asked me after a while what had happened. I told him. He could see how that would really piss someone off, he said. He didn't know much about alcoholics, but he could go to the bar for me and get me an Orangina if I had the money. He brought me back some free pretzels, too. It's always the act of kindness that releases tears, and when I saw him approaching with these gifts, they broke through. Travis didn't like crying; he grabbed a few napkins from a neighboring table.

He'd grown up in the Midwest somewhere, but now was in art school, traveling for the summer in Europe. I told him about me: lesbian, alcoholic, break up, house sale, trip. We talked til the boat appeared nearly empty, in part because his berth was just as crappy a sardine can as mine.

In the morning around six, the boat docked. I cut in line with Travis, waiting to disembark. He looked dough-faced with lots of eye crusties and didn't care to talk; he only wanted the line to move, which it didn't for at least twenty minutes. I kept scanning for the waffle-Satan, wanting to point him out, but he never showed – not that Travis gave a shit. Eventually, they put us all on a bus to Chania.

"What I really need," I said as we jostled on the bus, "is to find someplace with coffee and a bathroom."

"Word," said Travis.

The only place open on a Sunday at that hour was a super fancy restaurant right on the water, bedecked with flowering trellises, where neither of us could afford breakfast. So we pretended to look at the menus, ordered coffees, and then milked them for all we could – many refills, more cream and sugar – and took turns enjoying extended trips to the bathroom with our toilet kits.

Travis brightened up a lot after that. We both needed currency, but the banks were closed and we couldn't find a cash machine. We pooled our maps; both were out of date. "It's Mother's Day and I gotta call my mom," Travis said. "I always call her. If I don't call her, she'll have a cow." He kept repeating those phrases as we walked, for over an hour. His kind heart began to make sense to me; someone had taught him well. After we'd managed to find first a cash machine then the international phone station, we had to wait on its steps, which were broad and impressive, smoking, until at last it opened. Travis hurried in to call his mom, but I dawdled a while before deciding to phone Jesse. It cost a lot of drachma. My own mom I didn't think of calling – our family dismissed Mother's Day as a commercial device.

When Jesse picked up and I began to describe what had happened, my rage surged again. "I had so much stuff I couldn't *do* anything, I couldn't push him away! Fucker! I fucking hate him!"

"You need to get to a meeting," Jesse urged.

"I don't think so." I was irate. AA was dumb.

"Call the Chania AA number," she said. "Call them right now – promise you will."

Oh, well! I promised. I got more change from the attendant, fished out my listing, and dialed. The phone was red, I recall, with worn and marked up corkboard beside it. An answering machine tape started up initially, but then someone picked up. A human voice spoke two words: "Alcoholics Anonymous."

"I'm Louisa," I said, "and I'm an alcoho-ho-ho-" I burst into tears I hadn't even felt coming. I cried so hard I couldn't speak. The red phone became a life ring I clung to for all I was worth.

The hotline guy had an Aussie accent intense as Crocodile Dundee's. He asked if I were at the downtown phone station. "Listen, dahling, you're okai. You're going to be foin. You stye royght wheh you ah – you heah me? I'm going to throw on some clothes and hawp on a bus, and I'll be theh in fifteen minutes. Okai?"

"Okay," I sobbed. I hadn't even told the guy what was wrong.

I couldn't stop crying for a while, which made Travis uncomfortable. Waiting on the steps out front with me, he wasn't sure what to do. He was right to refrain from touch, but he sat right next to me, smoking and watching for the AA guy. Pretty soon he had a bus to catch, so I told him to go.

"You gonna be okay?"

You're an angel! I wanted to tell him.

"Yeah, I'm fine." I asked if we should trade phone numbers and "shit like that."

"Nah," he smiled. "Let's just promise to remember each other." He gave me a quick B.O.-scented hug and jumbled off down the steps.

That's one promise I've kept. Thank you, Travis. Thank you, always. And your drawings really were good, too – I wasn't just saying.

~

Here is what can happen when an alcoholic reaches out to AA for help. Bruce, the Australian, took me all around old, charming Chania, introducing me to other drunks in recovery – artsy expatriate alcoholics here, there, and everywhere that I'd never have guessed could be in AA. With each of them he discussed what to do with me. They agreed I should stay with people in the fellowship, but it took a while for Bruce to decide whom.

The house Bruce took me to looked a lot like the Flintstones' – built from stone slabs and almost as old. Its small courtyard was rampant with flowers and so bright a white that it dazzled my eyes right through my sunglasses. There was an old, claw-foot bathtub shielded by a low stone wall, flowers all around it. John, the American artist who lived here with his young French Canadian wife, came outside with blue and green paint smudged all over his arms and grumpiness writ on his face. He had two years sober, coming back from a relapse. His grumpiness vanished as soon as Bruce recapped my story; he invited us both in for lunch.

There was really only one main room, with a wooden addition tacked on in back where they slept. By the wooden table a large window opened on a pedestrian avenue that crossed immediately outside it, so that passing neighbors could pause and talk to us over the flower box. John cooked on a camp stove that was perched atop a mini-fridge.

> 5/26/1995: "I want to remember that little room with so many paintings on every wall, the Walkman speakers playing first The Sound of Music then Bach's two violins, the two tiny mewing kittens. One big pot for all the cooking. The bookshelf with Homer and German and Russian titles, the blue elephant mask John made from a gourd. The toilet outside in a little booth where you had to fill a bucket from the bright, bright sink round the corner to flush it."

Lunch was goat stew and tzatziki and bread, plus an old lady neighbor passed in through the window a hot, delicious zucchini dish; she had so many in her garden already! As we ate John explained that he couldn't offer me a room because two of his wife's friends from Quebec were visiting, but he later talked to the hotel matron down the block who gave me a nice room for a whopping five dollars a night. The place was just past the wood fire bakery that served as a community oven. You could drop stuff off – a roast or plucked hen or whatever – and pick it up a few hours later, no charge. Into my room delicious scents wafted like acts in an ongoing variety show.

I stayed for two nights, spending my days with alcoholics and their friends. The visiting friends of Gillian – the Canadian wife – were a gay couple who spoke English and brought me with them to the beach. That night two other artists came over for dinner. One was Russian, but only John could also speak that, so he'd translate to French for Gillian and the others. Bruce and I missed out on a lot.

On the night of my 100th day sober, John took me to an AA meeting. I clambered on the back of his beat up scooter and off we zoomed, whirring down narrow passageways of that ancient Venetian town and even through the farmers' market – just like in frickin' movies, with our tires buffeting over cobblestones as we threaded our way among stands with stacked fruits and crockery – where stall keepers closing up and hosing down called greetings to John. The warm night air was full of scents, shouts of Greek, barks of distant dogs. I held on tight to John's jacket and truly understood for the first time how tremendous life could be without alcohol. I couldn't remember the last time I felt so vividly alive. "Thank you, goddess, thank you goddess!" was my prayer.

At that meeting an older Finnish couple shared in rudimentary English. He had twenty years; she'd relapsed a month before trying to "make suicide" with pills and lots of vodka. I remembered a similar plan someone else had entertained a hundred and one nights ago. And now, life couldn't be sweeter. What a sweet fuss they all made over me and my hundred days! I hugged everyone; I loved everyone. On that night, the full significance of AA family struck me deeply. Back in Olympia, Washington, AA had seemed primarily Jesse's turf. Now I understood that, "Alcohol being no respector of persons" around the world, my disease was global. And so was my solution.

I said goodbye to John, Bruce, and the others the next morning, and traveled on with a degree happiness I'd never known in my whole life. I stayed sober through an almost-romance with a German boy, a masonry restorer, in the beach village of Matala, where I also hung out with a sun-baked Frenchman named Grayson who lived in a cave near the nude beach, my favorite hangout. The latter offered to show me how he could "make sperm," which he thought, being a lesbian, I must be curious about. I wasn't scared, though. I just said, "Non, merci," and dove off the rock we'd pulled up on.

I also had a peak experience on the island of Thira, in that beautiful jewel of a city, Santorini, where I finagled the highest hotel room in town, though doing so entailed letting the owner pinch my ass. Perhaps the happiest moment of my life I spent on the rooftop terrace of the highest restaurant in town before it actually opened, waited on by a boy who brought me my own decanter of coffee and poured his heart out to me about the troubles his new baby was causing his marriage. This boy was the spitting image of Theo. I don't know why he spilled all his troubles to me. But after I'd done my best to help him understand his wife's perspective, and after he'd thanked me and left me completely alone to enjoy the morning sun on distant islands and the pristine ocean air washing in from the horizon, I experienced a total freedom from self-loathing – a love of being exactly who I was in that moment.

> 5/26/1995: "I was a beautiful woman. You'll just have to believe me – I was a Queen. Not vain – I just knew it, no need for a mirror or make-up. I felt like thirty-four and eleven months was the sexiest age in the world. I felt perfect."

Simple narcissism? Maybe. Or was it also recognition that such moments are a gift? Up there I knew joy and serenity with no partner and no drink or drug – alone, sober, and filled with immeasurable bliss. From that day on, I knew it was possible.

~

One more AA miracle materialized on this trip. My last day on the island of Paros was gray. I was PMSing, and in spite of the beautiful scenery began to feel lonesome and discontent. I'd rented a moped to ride around the island, which seemed something better done with a lover. I knew what I needed was a meeting.

My AA directory listed only a resident phone number for this island – someone named Jessica. At every payphone I'd pull over and call her, but she never picked up. My last meeting had been over a week ago. Worse still, the night before I had accepted a drink the barmaid promised was 100% virgin. As I took the first sip, I tasted alcohol and felt its vapors explode in my brain.

Sweet Jesus! It swirled through my consciousness like liquid lightning. "Louisa! Sweetheart! Darling! It's *me*! We *love* each other!"

Yet there went my hand, extending the glass toward the barmaid. Her Greek coworker read the bottle labels until he found one with a small amount of alcohol. "But it won't make you drunk!" he promised me. "I give this to alcoholics all the time!" agreed the barmaid. "Just slit your throat a *little* and you won't bleed to death!" they may as well have said. I asked her to please pour it out and give me a Sprite.

Today, though, I needed desperately to speak the word "alcoholic" to someone who would understand – i.e. another alcoholic. But the phone responded only with endless ring tones.

Next, my hydro-boat to the island of Mykonos got delayed because of high winds, so I decided to wait out the four hours beside the dock – at a bar. I sat alone and watched people laughing with friends as they handed about and enjoyed frosty beers and pretty cocktails. My overpriced Sprite was long since gone. The simplicity of ordering a beer came to mind.

"Goddess, please help me get up and leave this bar," I prayed.

But I didn't move.

Instead I became aware of two men at a table directly behind me trading playful, brassy intonations and laughing freely. I peered around just in time to see one of them, a portly bald guy with glasses, tip back his beer. The other guy, tan and blond, seemed faintly familiar. For reasons still unknown to me, I turned and asked: "Excuse me, but are you two friends of Dorothy?"

They looked at each other in startled silence. Then the blond one, pushing forty but quite handsome, clarified, "Do you mean... Dorothy and Toto?"

"Yes."

They consulted each other and laughed again.

"Indeed we are! Great friends of Dorothy!" said the blond, meaning they were gay. "And you?"

He invited me to join them. I turned my chair to their table and, within three minutes and for reasons equally unknown to me, volunteered the fact that I was an alcoholic.

"Hey! John, alcoholic!" exclaimed the blond one, extending his hand. "Sober eleven years in AA."

We shook hands. I was safe. Home. I'd found family.

"So, Jessica's slacking on the hotline!" John clicked his tongue when I told about getting no answer. "I'll give her some grief for that!" Alcoholic Anonymous on Paros, he said, consisted mainly of five sober drunks who met in each other's houses.

Like Chania John, this John was also an artist. The bald fellow sucking down beers was the friend of a friend, awaiting for the same boat to Mykonos. John invited me to come along as he showed off the town. We walked first to his charming, artsy little apartment to grab some money, then to the centuries-old convent where he taught painting. Later, as departure time approached, we drank iced teas in a garden mostly shaded by graceful old eucalyptus trees while the bald guy sucked another beer. John and I had so much to talk about! When I told about last night's "virgin" drink, he identified all over the place. Fuck! Oh, man. No wonder I'd been squirrelly today! Who wouldn't be?

"And it's just so lucky," I said, "that I ran into you!"

"Lucky?!" John smiled faintly and shook his head. "Louisa, that's not luck. There are ten thousand other people on this island every summer. Ten *thousand*. Five of us hold down AA on Paros. And, besides, I never go near that tourist trap place by the boat. I only went today 'cause of this guy!"

The bald guy shrugged

"You're feeling shaky, and then you turn around and ask the guy with eleven years in AA if he's... a friend of Dorothy's? How many times have you done *that*?"

"Um, never."

"A miracle is nothing less than miraculous," John underscored as the three of us headed back to the boat. The wind had died down, and our visit was over. "Don't be afraid to recognize and thank God for it!"

~

5/22/95: "What have I learned on this journey, this time alone in strange places? I'm learning my ordinariness, that I'm just a person, that there's no urgent focus or hysteria concerning my needs and questions. What I'm starting to learn and to want most – is how to let go and find a comfortable spot inside where, in essence, I have everything I need.

"There is no need for fear in the unknown.

"There is no need for sadness in boredom.

"There is no need for shame in loneliness."

Clockwise from bottom left: Saviors on Crete, Bruce above me, John and Gillian to the right; Oracle of Delphi with bus friends; on Mykonos before heading home; I could say this was Greece but it was actually an ocean trip with Jesse later that summer

19: CODEPENDENT COCOON

*The primary fact that we fail to recognize is our
total inability to form a true partnership with
another human being. Our egomania digs two
disastrous pitfalls. Either we insist on dominating
people we know, or we depend on them far too
much.*

*-Twelve Steps and Traditions
Step Four*

I could write a whole book about my first three years of
sobriety. Maybe I will. I'll call it, *The Tortures of Early Sobriety.*
What to tell you and what to leave out – that's the tricky part. How
do you summarize the psychic struggle of learning to live all over
again?

My early sobriety was particularly tortuous for two main
reasons. First was my disdain for the Twelve Steps. They seemed to
me a bunch of simplistic one-liners, so I rushed through a mere
gesture of "working" them to placate Jeanie, my sponsor. For one
thing, I believed I had no need of this so-called "psychic change." I
was sure that just going to meetings and not drinking between
would fix everything, because alcohol had been my sole problem.

In fact, it had been my sole solution. It had allowed me to
function by muting my self-loathing and inflating my ego to the
point where I could barge through difficulties. Without it, I had to
realize that my entire approach to living was ass-backward and that
the Steps were my only route to a new life.

The second reason was my codependence. Rather than looking
at ways I held myself back, I enlisted a decoy person whose
character defects I could focus on and pick apart. So, even though I
knew in my core that Jesse and I were not suited to each other, in
September of 1995, I moved with her to Seattle.

I understand now that Jesse was still in early sobriety herself.
The fact is, both of us should have had "UNDER CONSTRUC-

TION" duct taped on our foreheads. As I've said, her three years seemed to me at the time an eternity. Today, if I meet someone with that amount of time, I feel sympathy for them. Like Kevin and me both crying out in our sleep, she and I were both trying to figure out how to navigate this new, harsh world without the option of numbing out.

It's amazing how when you first become attracted to someone, you can easily dismiss the very faults that will later drive you insane. If her room is strewn with clothes, she's just carefree! If her housemates complain that she never does her chores, they're just bitchy! You can even find out she's pursued by horrid, rapacious creditors. Then you move in with her and suddenly all these problems land in your lap. Her shit is everywhere, she does no chores, she owes you money – and you're shocked.

> 4/17/1995: "What is so *wrong* with me?! Why am I so pissed that she forgot to return the videos again??? I am so pissed I could scream. I WON'T PAY FOR AN EXTRA DAY OF THEM! I AM SICK OF PAYING FOR *EVERYTHING!*"

> 6/11/1995: "Jesse has an ability to put aside the things she ought to do and enjoy the moment. If she can't deal, she just doesn't do it. I could write down right here a list of all the things she needs to do and hasn't, all the bills she needs to pay and hasn't.
> "Okay – I just paid off all our 'shared' bills. $450. Hard to do."

I thought paying shared bills would alleviate my tension rather than establish a pattern. Not the greatest logic.

Our little apartment was on a side street of hip and groovy Capital Hill, with a fourth floor window that framed the Space Needle like a post card. Broadway in those days offered a colorful pageant of gay life and still had many quaint, old storefront buildings that have since been demolished for condos. Just two blocks from us was the Gay & Lesbian Alano Club, where we went for all our meetings. The atmosphere sort of merged the humility and service work of the program with a fashion/dating show of queer coolness and flirtation. Jesse and I both worked in the old Broadway Market, Jesse as a juicer at a health bar and me selling housewares as badly as ever – while commuting to Olympia two days a week to teach at The Evergreen State College.

When we moved to Seattle, I had about $25,000 in savings from the sale of my house, plus an array of stocks. Jesse had a trail of overwhelming debt and a knack for tapping any resource available. She already owed me $700, but that didn't seem a big deal. I didn't understand that she was a "debtor" – that spending was her primary means of bolstering self-esteem and that she was just as addicted to those little jolts of purchases as she'd been to cocaine, booze, or attention from girls. No amount of nagging or even raging on my part could help. She had to hit bottom with debt which was exactly what I kept her from doing, first with my savings and later, when that was all gone, with my parents' bailouts.

Collection agencies tracked Jesse to Seattle and garnished her paychecks, but there were still other debts. She owed many thousands, a lot of it for medical bills. Her method of addressing this mess was to pretend it didn't exist. We didn't answer the phone and we threw away the notices. So what did I do? I volunteered to pay for a lawyer and all the fees involved in filing for bankruptcy – well over fifteen hundred dollars – out of my savings. In my mind, I was "teaching" Jesse how responsible people dealt with debt. It seemed an incredibly magnanimous and noble act from a loving partner. Jesse, I felt sure, would be forever indebted to me.

Jesse also longed to go to college. I could "teach" her the way there, too. I physically walked her to the community college assessment office and waited for her to test. My savings likewise covered both her tuition and books – until she could get scholarships and loans. What I thought of as support and generosity, I would later recognize as attempts to "fix" Jesse, since I couldn't fix myself.

What I got out of the deal would take a number of future Fourth Steps, pain, and prayers to recognize: self-worth in the twisted form of feeling superior. A sense of power in benefaction. Being *owed*. I had no obsessive infatuation to keep me afloat, so I constructed myself as a virtuous martyr.

I tried "teaching" Jesse to track daily expenses on a little note pad, just so she could *see* in black and white how the little things added up, but she would have none of it. To Jesse, frugality meant shame. If we were shopping and I said aloud, "We can't afford that!" she'd shush me with a horrified wince. She threw away her tips by eating out, ordering six-dollar smoothies, and buying ever more jeans and T-shirts. When the time came to pay rent, she had nothing left – month after month. My savings dwindled accordingly.

> 11/29/1995: "What frustrates me is not the money she takes from me but that she is BLIND to the ways she does! She is BLIND to the toll of her double-tall lattes. Meals at the Gravity Bar, scones, etc. add up and she doesn't see it! Buying pricey bags of coffee when they're *giving away* the day-old for free?! It's money taken out of *my* pocket. She doesn't see that she's saying over and over, Here's another five dollars I'll tell Louisa I simply don't have!"

Jesse wouldn't wash dishes, either. We tried an arrangement of alternating weeks, but during her week the dishes simply piled up to the same towering heights her former housemates had bitched about. She wouldn't shop for groceries. And every night I cooked for both of us, because otherwise, she'd just order take-out. I recognized some of what was going on, the same way I'd recognized the madness of my drinking. But I knew no other way to live.

> 12/4/1995: "I have surrendered my life again. The main thing about Jesse is, I can never give her enough. So I stop giving to myself and give it to her. The primary things I have ever asked for from her are help keeping the house in order and help with the groceries. She doesn't give me either."

Lastly, Jesse wanted my constant attention. Even more than with Kevin and Jenna, my journal entries complain about not getting the solitude I needed to write. Like Jenna wanting constant romance, Jesse seemed to insist she be the most important thing in my life.

> 12/4/1995: "*Pay attention to me*! she may as well shout. Her parents never did, so I have to. But why do I take on the job if I don't want it?"

That I could have simply walked away seemed as realistic as stepping off a skyscraper. At some level I didn't believe I could survive without Jesse. Since I first recruited Zelda to be my cohort,

I had leapfrogged from relationship to relationship with never a spell of time on my own. What living for myself would look like, I had not the faintest idea. And I did love her. When we weren't fighting, there were periods of intense loving when all difficulties were forgotten.

> 11/23/1995: "House-sitting at my parents' last night, we had sex and came at the same time, and seconds later I heard huge BOOM- BOOM-BOOM!s pounding like bombs falling in the street. I jumped up with Jess and ran after her, down the stairs, still not sure if it was the washing machine or bombs, into the basement where it was *so* loud! The washer seemed to be saying, 'BOOM! BOOM! I'm gonna walk, I'm gonna blow up!' Jess dove across the room and hit the dial to silence it, and we opened it up – the green blanket! Then we laughed, me in my panties, Jess in boxers, still woozy with orgasm, two topless girls side by side peering into a washer. We laughed and hugged and kissed before we fixed it."
>
> "Other than loving Jess, I am scared to death of living…"

And I was. I was pretty much a dry drunk – stark-raving sober without a spiritual solution. Meetings at the Gay Alano Club were more like self-help sessions than an avenue to the spiritual experience outlined in the Big Book. It seemed to me most people shared by complaining about stuff, then congratulating themselves for not having drunk over it. That's how I thought meetings worked: vent and claim. I had no idea I was missing a little detail called Recovery. Without it, my impulse to drink kept resurfacing, and anxiety ruled my days.

> 9/8/1995: "Sitting in a women's meeting, I started feeling like it was too much to say I'd never drink again, planning my relapse, thinking of how the escape was still there. 'Just drink! Drink like before!' I do admit I couldn't control it for long, though. I drink to get drunk. There's always further to go, and I'll always chase it."
>
> 11/23/1995: "I worry relentlessly about things I have to get done! Then, when I stop even for a bit, all my emotions rush in to fill the space – and they're *sadness*.

Whenever I'm genuine, I'm scared. No – sad. Well, sad because I'm scared."

11/27/95: "I'm a mess. A nervous, tense, depressed, unhappy mess. Maybe it's my new espresso job, but I can hardly function. My face is tense again, twitchy, feel like I have a brain tumor."

12/6/95: "How I envy our two friends in the psyche ward! I wish I could just check in, too. What a relief it would be!"

1/1/96: "Happy Fucking New Year! I wish I would just snap. Sometimes I want to destroy things, cut myself, jump out of a moving car – because I just can't stand it another second: and *it* is life."

I've never had such weird dreams in my life as I had in those months of new sobriety. My journal overflows with them, night after night, weirdness more acute than at any other time in my life. I can choose only a few here as samples.

1/2/1996: "Last night I dreamed I was having sex with another me who was cold and sort of dead. My dead face looked up and resented me for having sex with her body. Horny-me wanted to think the cold, dead me underneath was a stick-in-the-mud, but really she/I just wanted to hump and was willing to deal with the guilt and shame later on: I *was* sick and I *was* bad and sexually greedy – so tough luck."

2/21/1996: "Someone knocked on the door and I opened it. She had a deep blue face painted on like a tribal mask. 'Who are you?' I asked, fearing a devil. 'Who are YOU...?!' she countered. Woke with my heart pounding, scared."

3/9/1996: "I'd secretly killed two people by some computer command. No one knew except the daughter of the woman I'd killed. She sent me a letter, and in reading it out loud to my family, pretending warm emotions, I had to keep skipping over the murder passages. I knew all my life would be haunted by guilt, even if I could get away with it. I'd done it – killed someone. They were dead now. There was no way to undo it."

3/28/96: "I found two babies under my parents' bed, which I'd forgotten there maybe a week. One was bigger, about a year old and I wasn't as worried about her. The other was smaller and a little me. I wanted to nurse her but my breasts were shut down, the nipples like dried up nozzles of Elmer's glue. But I got her to suck and finally she got a little milk. I was so thrilled my breasts worked and I could feed her like a real mother! She smiled and I knew she loved me.

"I brought her up to my old room to nurse, then I milked myself into a glass and got excited – both happily and sexually. A teenage Zelda burst in and I had to hide what I was doing. She had a carload of popular friends waiting outside, got out all this food for them – bread, cheese, lettuce, etc. – and laid it all over my bed to make sandwiches. I was furious. I yelled at her for using Mom and Dad, and for her cliquish friends. She yelled back that Mom and Dad liked her friends and it was none of my business.

"I got so mad I threw my milk right in her face. I knew it would revolt her and that she would taste it against her will, but I would *not* be ashamed – I would be defiant and proud. Oh, the RAGE I felt!"

You don't have to be a dream expert to see there's a lot going on here. I imagine the doubles had to do with reconciling my old and new selves. There's also guilt, and some kind of creative/ nurturing/ sexual power reclaimed in the flow of breast milk.

Too much furniture was getting moved around in my psyche too fast. It strained me emotionally, and I developed depression. Jesse could write you a chapter about how difficult I was to live with, not wanting to go out, living in my sweatpants. We started seeing a couples therapist, Donna, who promptly put me on Zoloft. It helped, though it also took away my orgasms. This, for me, was a huge deal. The doctor I saw terrified me with the assurance that they "usually" come back. *Usually?!!* It seemed to me the best way to keep mine was to stay in practice, so I bought a stack of girlie magazines and would wank for ages, sometimes an hour at a time, for one wimpy little climax. This was nothing like my old compulsion, though. Though I did close the door to concentrate, these "workouts" were far from secret. I joked about them with Jesse and even some of our sober lesbian friends – who all commended my smart idea.

Donna, our therapist with sixteen years sober herself, also diagnosed me as codependent. She told me codependence was a disease and every bit as dangerous as alcoholism. There was an aspect of me she called "the accommodator" who automatically adjusted to fill whatever I imagined to be Jesse's needs. The only one who could stop this pattern, she maintained gravely, was me.

But then, at a session only a few weeks later, when Jesse broke down sobbing that she simply *could not* continue working part-time while going to school, this same therapist tacitly approved as, right there in her office, my accommodator pledged to financially support Jesse for as many years as it took her to finish her degree. She would earn money only during school breaks – summer and Christmas. The deal was *supposed* to be that, after she finished her BA, we'd switch roles, and then she'd support me for just as many years.

Ha. We'll see how *that* worked out!

Still, Jesse's stock always rated high at lesbian Alano Club meetings because she was beautiful and spoke movingly, which made her a much sought-after prize. At the time, these peers made up my whole world, so it seemed that *everybody* wanted to get with Jesse. Our sex life still had frequent bright spots. In bed she'd taken to tossing out the phrase, "Marry me!" Each time she did, I felt distinctly uncomfortable saying nothing, like I was hurting her feelings. What could be worse than not making the other person happy? So, in February of 1996, when I had a year sober, I fixed that.

"Okay," I said.

Jesse was pretty taken aback. I think she was saying it more to sound sexy than as an actual proposal. Now she was kind of stuck. How could she say, "I didn't really mean it!"—?

2/5/1996: "Me and Jesse will marry 6/22. I think I might really have a baby."

Odd that I would write of a baby, because I don't remember wanting one that far back. In hindsight, I can't think of anything more foolish than deciding, at one year insane – I mean, sober – to get married. I was a mess. Self will run riot was the driving force behind such a lifelong decision. Since I couldn't sort out all my feelings and difficulties with Jesse, I would plow over them by getting married. Then it would be a done deal. Everything would be set. Donna jumped up and clapped when we told her, so there was another person I'd made happy.

> 2/18/1996: "The thing about my alcoholism nowadays – now that I'm feeling better and have more energy – is that mornings terrify me. I don't know how I'll pass the day, and unless I get to be alone through the whole thing with no obligations atoll – like, not even meet Zelda or Jesse at such-and-such a time – I am terrorized. The idea of spending the day with Jesse makes me anxious and tired. There will be another person to respond and explain things to. I'll have to constantly make sense or account for myself. In fact, I need to talk to Donna about the way Jesse bullies me whenever I withdraw and assumes I'm gonna leave her and demands attention and confirmation that I'm not. When I least want to deliver. And me being co-dependent, I always take responsibility for her feelings. I shift to my good self to be loveable."

> 2/19/1996: "Too much energy, anxiety, fear – not knowing how to live. Glad to have energy, but don't know how to live."

In any case we married – not legally, but with a certificate real enough to us – ten years almost to the day after Kevin's and my wedding, in an old stone Methodist church before a lesbian minister. First down the aisle was a procession of Jesse's best men, then my bridesmaids. Jesse and I came down the aisle together, arm in arm, Jesse in a white sailor top and jeans, me in a vintage floral dress with a tiny waist I dieted for weeks to fit. My family (minus Adelyn, whom I didn't even invite) as well as friends from Dancing Goats and AA filled the pews, and this time the trio played Handel instead of Bach. At the reception, a tall wedding cake with two little brides perched atop it occupied the very same spot on the same picnic table where Kevin's and mine had stood a decade earlier.

It's so easy to get married, to go through the motions, to orchestrate the large dance of the ceremony. So easy to say vows, and even to mean them. I truly believed that was all I had to do – to *will* us a future happiness.

A friend from the photo lab where Jesse now worked took all the wedding pictures, several rolls of film Jesse insisted she develop herself – so none exist.

~

We couldn't afford a fancy honeymoon on my little teaching income, supplemented now by part time work at Espresso Vivace, which was supposed to be my new Dancing Goats. So we took a budget one, visiting my real Dancing Goats friend, Meghan, in New Mexico, where we tagged along on a series of excellent house-sitting gigs she'd lined up. We took videos of all of us lip-synching in our underwear, fed llamas who actually spit when pissed off, and tried to avoid drips in a leaky, spherical hexagon hippie house. Not your classic honeymoon, but we weren't your classic couple.

Upon our return, Jesse and I drew on my savings again to move into a big old rental house on Beacon Hill. We had a real yard now and wanted a companion for Kelsey, so more savings, several hundred dollars, got us a little purebred whippet. Whippets are a trip! Never before had I met a dog with the self-centered assurance of a cat. Sydney didn't even like us at first. Instead he ignored Kelsey's ferocious snarls and snuggled confidently up to her belly within minutes of meeting her. Kelsey basically raised him. He became the only whippet I know who could walk off leash and loved to fetch. He wore toddler clothing from Goodwill around the house, mostly sweaters and hoodies, and I zipped him into red onesie pajamas every night of his life.

Two rooms we rented out to twenty-something boys from the program – Jonny, a surfer dude, and Ryan, a film editor who slept beside a spare Volvo engine. These boys not only got to witness the explosive fights between Jesse and me, like the time we physically grappled over the car keys for who got to leave whom, but also to live with the flaring resentments and mood swings that characterized my second year sober without having worked the steps. Anger was a new emotion for me. A cereal bowl left in the living room, some of our food missing, a toilet paper roll unchanged – these things could trigger a sudden flash of vehemence in me.

In this house, I would finally hit bottom in sobriety. In many ways, hitting bottom sober is more painful than hitting it drunk, because we have so much more awareness, so much more consciousness to hurt. I had no recovery to speak of. I'd gone through the motions of working the Twelve Steps only to satisfy my first sponsor, and now I had a new sponsor who didn't believe in reading the Big Book together or even writing fourth steps. All I did was go to meetings and not drink between. The cynicism with which I'd once judged AA people still applied to the program – to the steps and the literature. I liked meetings. I liked getting glimpses into the struggles of others and learning from them what aspects of my inner experience were classic alcoholic, but I didn't see how some book written in 1939 by no one in particular was going to help me, let alone revolutionize my life.

At least now, being sober, my neuroses were so apparent that I began to develop a sense of humor about them. Humor is grace. Even without step work, God was entering my life as little gap or insulation inserted between my emotions and the conviction that they were true.

11/22/1996: "Help! Help! Help! Help! I am terrified inside! Terrified! I hate winter. I hate Christmas. I hate illusions of cheer and coziness when the fact is it's DARK and dreary out and all the flowers DIE and ROT and trees turn BARREN and absent so you can't talk to them. Whenever my mind starts all that glowing amber cozy Christmas cheer bullshit, which for me is so linked to wine and rum and gin & tonics, I am going to JUST SAY NO to the whole kit and caboodle and pretend I'm situated in Siberia for a six month stint, where all is bleak and harsh and I just have to cope."

1/31/1997: "I had two years sober on the 29th! Yay! Who's sick? *Me!* Who sucks? *Me!* Look in the barnyard. Peek under your pillow. Yay! Lardburger. All that's nonsense but I have such a surplus of *feeling*. Been seeing a pattern lately – reactions toward Jesse exactly the same as Jenna: 'Reclaim your life! Don't let her steal it!' Which makes me realize it's *me*, something *I* do. I place my lover's interests ahead of my own and become her caretaker. Because heaven forbid I make my own choices! Heaven forbid I be free!

"If it's *my* life, *my* choices – why don't I get that? Instead I just bob around cork-like among others (or my projections of them) steering by reaction rather than any course of my own. And isn't that so dumb – like sticking your hands into puppets and then being afraid of them?

"Of course we know:
1. I'm afraid of everything
2. I'm not good enough
3. I won't ever be loved
"So I fake everything in hopes I'll look better than I believe I am, with fear of being found out as a fraud. I need instead to give, do, *create* in the name of the goddess."

Praying with a cigarette one day, I asked my goddess to direct what she would have me be, and it seemed to me, quite vividly, that she responded: "Quit killing the cells I give you, for starters!" So I quit smoking. But rarely did I seek direction in other areas of life. My spirituality was still characterized by sudden "deep" epiphanies, while my primary faith remained anchored in my own intelligence, in achieving what I wanted through self-propulsion.

Non-legal newlyweds, 1996

20: MY SISTER'S DEATH; 6TH WEIRD THING

"Mr. Rochester is not likely to return soon, I suppose?"

"Indeed he is – in three days he says: that will be next Thursday; and not alone either."

-*Charlotte Brontë*
Last page of Jane Eyre Adelyn read

Familial love is the strangest kind. It doesn't always look the way we think it should. Maybe it's hidden under a hoary exterior of hurt and resentment. Or maybe it's one element in the intricate, circulating mobile of a relationship – a counterweight to many rival emotions. The stronger those rival emotions, the weightier the love.

Adelyn suffered a cancer relapse in 1995, about a month after I got sober. One thing about self-centeredness: the myopia it generates is genuine. Hashing through my own crisis, I heard the *story* of Adelyn's illness, but to me it was only that – a drama I could critique from the safe terra firma of health. Talking with her on the phone felt incredibly awkward. I could sense the blockage of my denial, but the solution – to drop my fear in favor of honesty, empathy, and unconditional love – seemed beyond reach. There are, in fact, some emotional shifts toward candor and authenticity that we know much as we know the moves of an Olympic gymnast. We know what they're supposed to look like, but we're nowhere near that coordinated, and we fear the humiliation of catastrophic backfires. So I spoke with her stiffly, keeping my guard up.

She'd found a lump in her armpit after healing from the mastectomy and called the hospital; over the phone an intern advised her that it was a swollen lymph gland and would resolve itself. Trusting that intern cost her life. Medicine is like that sometimes. A year later, she'd developed a spur on her spine that turned out to be malignant, and around the same time discovered she was over a month pregnant. Oncologists advised her to abort the pregnancy, not only to allow radiation treatments but because cancer thrives on the estrogen and growth hormones of pregnancy. But she refused. She chose instead to forego treatment until she'd delivered the baby.

I decided I could spot a gesture of martyred self-sacrifice when I saw one. Adelyn's problem was that she'd been too influenced not only by the church, but by the scores of Victorian novels she read in her teens. Getting filled in over the phone by Mom, I rolled my eyes. Catholics! What a dumb choice! Of course, I'd never been pregnant myself. I had no inkling of the feelings she was contending with.

I kept my opinions to myself, but did the same with my support. I didn't visit – Virginia was just too far away. I hardly phoned. When I did, I kept my list of wounds intact. There was to be no undoing of that long string of insult and counter-insult that defined our childhood, no unsaying of her slighting my gay relationships, or of her more recent observation, based in all earnestness on the size of my head, that her five-year-old's brain size had already exceeded mine. I'd never relaxed around her. I couldn't. I was always too braced for her to come out with one of those withering witticisms, quips or implications my smallish brain would struggle to decipher even while realizing the struggle itself validated her contempt.

What I did mostly was post notes all over the house reminding myself to call her. These were on the fridge, by my bed, and on countless to-do lists, often underscored – CALL ADELYN! For years after her death they'd haunt me from random drawers and notebooks – CALL ADELYN! – flaring with irony. At the time, though, our chats were tense and superficial, dominated by an uneasiness I camouflaged with a slew of jokes and clichés. They exhausted me.

In December of '95 when I had just under a year sober, she flew out to visit my parents with her baby. What a shock to see the changes that cancer, chemo, and motherhood had wrought on her – her eyes had aged drastically. Would they go back to normal, I wondered, when she recovered? What baffled me completely, though – her attack fangs were missing. They seemed not just concealed, but gone. My sister was reaching out for my friendship, entirely ready to put the past behind us, and I was knocked for a loop. We had a private conversation while she changed her baby's diaper. She wished we could spend more time together, she said.

She used the old dumb-talk voice, or her version of it: our being sisters meant "there's always a lot to... tok-o-bout!"

Where was Adelyn, the arch, intellectually caustic sister I had known? This one wasn't intent on winning. She insisted, against Mom's advice, on coming out for Thai food with me and Jesse, who seemed to compel her attention. When Jesse stepped away to the bathroom, Adelyn gave the opposite of Mom's "didn't know Caravaggio" speech. Jesse was a good person, she said, with a good heart. Imagine! Jesse – who dropped malapropisms right and left and botched half her popular allusions to history and science! Adelyn admired her?! Listening to Jesse talk about her lost mother, she teared up right there at the table. Who *was* this woman?

I didn't welcome this change. It threw me. I was all ready to meet with biting sarcasm, aimed preferably at *me,* though any target would do – the ineptness of our waiter, maybe, or the tackiness of the restaurant. Even AA! Instead she spoke of Jesus and the people at her church with kindness in their hearts. My mind jammed up, trying to recalculate every response I knew to my mean big sister. She came in peace. She brought love. I couldn't grasp the fact that I was still trying to play in our old playground of resentments, which she'd spiritually outgrown long ago.

That would be the last time I saw Adelyn fully conscious. Five months later a scan picked up metastases all over her bones. Sometimes it seemed like the staff at Georgetown University Hospital was out to kill her. They dismissed the pain in her hip – at the age of forty – as arthritis. Again she trusted them implicitly, limping with a cane throughout her pilgrimage to Lourds, until the cancer-rotted femur actually broke off in the socket, spewing malignancy into her bloodstream. The response? Hip replacement. That was the final blow.

Now she was loopy on morphine whenever we talked on the phone – her thoughts zig-zagging all over the place. This small, wavering voice that would stray from topic to topic, wandering among the cubicles of her mind – I couldn't recognize it! To me some fundamental law seemed broken, the great and powerful Oz made vulnerable to fizzles and sags. I *wanted* to feel cowed by her, *wanted* to duel witticisms. The deal with morphine, she explained me, is that you can still hear every word of people's conversations even though you can't react. "People talk like I'm not even there, just because I can't *show* that I'm listening. It's crazy!"

She wanted me to notify our parents that the cancer had spread to her liver. Since the news was fatal, she couldn't deliver it herself, yet we made feeble jokes about Mom and Dad's mental limitations. "Just plant the liver concept in their little brains," she said. She also told me she hoped to die of a hemorrhage, a quick and relatively painless death common with liver cancer, rather than lingering on.

The world spun when I hung up. Could it be true? It had to be. Yet my mind was still jamming, stuttering.

> 4/23/1997: "Phone call yesterday from Adelyn, cancer's spread to her liver which means she has four to six months left to live. Guilt is my ever-present static. I'm powerless; I can't make Adelyn better, I can't make her safe, can't lessen my parents' grief. I can be loving – and that's all I can do. I can open that channel."

I was in the midst of teaching a Modernism course at Evergreen, so I set up my flight to follow its last day, in late May. My parents, as confused as I, left for an Australian vacation at Adelyn's insistence. But I didn't fly out in May. I went the next day. And my parents had to turn around as soon as they reached Sydney and repeat the twelve hour flight because Adelyn was dying. Her hip replacement incision had split from infection, and she was in intensive care. She now had, doctors told us, about two weeks left.

We gathered at her Fairfax house where the niece and nephew I'd met only as babies, now seven and five, recited an endless stream of jokes, exuberant in our company, while her two-year-old, Darius, toddled about fixated on his toy ambulance. Their cuteness and trust in the world broke your heart. Feeling like a stealthy intruder in this "study area" of my big sister's house, I found nothing fit my preconceptions. Would grumpy Beethoven have filled a home with stuffed animals, colorful potty seats, and Zwieback? With squeals of children's laughter? *I don't know her; I know only my childhood fright.* I kept realizing it with every children's book and baby toy I'd pick up.

Her losing battle to maintain order was written all over the house. Stacks of newspapers listed ponderously in the kitchen, because she'd believed in recycling while her Texan husband did not. Piles of dirty dishes filled the sinks and covered countertops, while garbage overflowed from multiple bags around the bin. Mama to three and dying of cancer. I wished I'd come. I wished I'd helped.

At the hospital, all of us encircled her cot at the ICU – the Happy Little P. Family reunited for one last time. Her eyes skittered delightedly around the circle of faces. "Oh, you came all this way!" she quavered, almost protesting with apologetic gratitude. Her phenomenal brain resided in a skull now alarmingly evident. Love radiated from her – blind, sorrowful, unconditional – in the intervals between fading consciousness.

Transferred to a regular room, she commenced dying. She would crane her bird-like neck for sips of ice water through a straw, weak as a feeble hatchling. That's how most of us appear, I think, toward the end. The family took shifts throughout the day. During mine I took her hand and tried to find words to apologize for all of it – never having been a good sister, never a proper aunt to her children. She interrupted me: "Don't…" That one word was all she could manage, her eyes still closed under the morphine. But she squeezed my hand: don't beat yourself up, don't take the blame for a mistake we both fed and maintained. No one had told her she had only two weeks to live, but she seemed to sense it. During Zelda's shift, she moaned with sudden volume, "Oh! I want my life back!"

After dinner at the house, Walter and I returned to the hospital to sit with her overnight. Over and over she would remember her children, crying out frantically: "I've got to go *home*, I need to *see* them!" She'd try to clamber out of bed, yanking her tubes and monitors, oblivious to her weeping hip incision. Over and over Walter and I had to press her back down, assuring her they'd come in the morning, and with an influx of weakness and pain, she'd comply. She'd raise her arms, bloated with saline, over her head and drop them in heavy frustration.

Late at night she called out for a priest; there was none, and he would not be on shift until morning. We told her to wait. There was plenty of time. Wait for the priest, wait for the children. But death came early – before the priest, before the children, before the morning had fully dawned. For me, it brought a powerful re-experience of the Light, which I call The Sixth Weird Thing.

Walter and I both slept in chairs in her darkened room. But around 5:00 in the morning, something nudged me awake. The first thing I noticed was that next to nothing had accumulated in the urine bag on her cot. She's dying, I thought quite factually; her body's shutting down. At the same time but with a different part of my consciousness, I glanced around the dim room trying to identify a kind of knowing, a kind of excitement stirring inside me and in the room itself. Something was gearing up. What was it? What was happening?

Then I knew: the Light. The same Light I'd known fifteen years ago, with all its tremendous bliss and Love, it was— what? Where? Seeping into the room *through the window* like slow mist or fog. There was nothing I could see with my eyes, yet I could sense it passing over the sill, skimming across the floor and gathering, pooling – a little more, a little more – around Adelyn.

The Light brought joy. For my sister, it had come! I could sense something like a cloud of it now, made up of countless tiny points of Light. Thousands. Maybe millions. They were not photons, nor did they reflect any. I saw them with my spirit, because each one was a spirit itself. Each was a Life. Angels of love, countless energies humming and swirling around her – a gathering of spirits. They already knew her better than I did, better than anyone on earth, and they were preparing to bring her back, amping up for the transfer. I knew this. I knew it sharply, with a clarity more certain and direct than earthly knowledge. My heart pounded with it – with the honor of perceiving their work.

Earlier that day I'd spoken from a hospital payphone with my AA sponsor. "Tell her everything," she'd urged, "hold nothing back." I'd tried and failed with my blanket apology. But now those words seemed to dilate with new meaning. Because there had been something else Adelyn said to Zelda: "Dying of cancer at forty-one is the ultimate put-down!" Put down by whom? Something was wrong; something needed to be shifted. Pain weighed on her heart. And unspeakable fear. *Help her to cross,* a voice told me. *Help her! You know the way; you can show her. Do it* now.

Still I sat in my vinyl chair in that indifferent, practical hospital room. She was not conscious, after all. But she'd *told* me on the phone: "I can't show it, but I hear every word..." The voice grew more urgent. *She needs you now!* But what would I say? What was there to say? *You'll know. Only begin. Now. Right now.*

I stood up, obeying. I crossed to her bed and knelt beside her.

I began to speak close by her ear, holding her hand, and as soon as I began, the words flowed: "You've had a wonderful life," I told her. Everything she had done, she'd done beautifully. She'd brought beauty into the world through her piano – her love of music had brought it to life. And her amazing mind, she had used it so well. She'd made a beautiful home with her husband, created three beautiful children and given them love. All of it was good and – here I knew to say – "Jesus sees all you've done and he's proud of you."

"But now," I said, "your body doesn't work anymore. It's broken, and there's nothing on earth that can fix it, so Jesus will bring you home. His love will be all around you, warm like the sun but all through you, just love." I could almost feel it now, radiating around us both. Joy lit my voice. "You'll be in light that's so bright and warm – light that *is* love like you've never dreamed you could feel! Oh, and you'll be so safe and loved, Adelyn! *Everything* you ever wanted, *everything* turning to love! Jesus loves you so much. Because you're his child, God's child, and God loves you more than you can imagine. I love you. Walter loves you. We all love you."

With that, I was done. I lingered a bit, wondering if more words would come, but I sensed that something had awakened in her, some spark I should let kindle on its own. I returned to the vinyl chair. Walter had woken at some point, though I don't know how much he overheard. He glanced, owl-like, from me to his clearly unconscious sister. We sat in silence.

Twenty minutes later, Adelyn let out a faint cry and sat up abruptly. Blood came spouting from her nose as from a spigot. The force of her pulse drove it, surge after surge spraying into her lap.

Walter and I panicked. I forgot all about the Light. I knew only terror and tragedy and disaster. "Help! Please help! Help us!" we cried out, dashing into the hallway and back, down to the empty nurses' station and back, terrified by both the spectacle of what had happened and our powerlessness to help. By the time a nurse ambled into the room, the blood spews had stopped and Adelyn's body lay limp as a dropped marionette.

"Mrs. Trevor!" the nurse all but brayed into her face. "Mrs. Trevor!" She slapped insistently at Adelyn's hand. I wanted to club the bitch. While she went to get a doctor, Walter tried frantically to call Adelyn's husband, accidentally mixing up numbers. Neither of us could figure out why he couldn't get through. We yelled at each other. We yelled at the phone.

Finally, into the room came a pretty and pristine Asian doctor who applied her stethoscope. "She's hemorrhaged," she informed us curtly. "Her heart is still beating, but it'll stop once it runs out of oxygen." Folding her stethoscope, she stepped away,

We all stood there. No one did anything. No one spoke. I felt a howling outrage that no one was trying to resuscitate her, no one doing *anything* to save her life while there was still a chance! I understood there was no hope and yet I wanted to grab that doctor's skinny little neck and throttle her for the curt way she'd said, "it'll stop." You mean, she'll *die*!

But the next moment, something – quite abruptly and unmistakably – supplanted my feelings with a sense wholly different: "All is well." I became aware – or I should say fully aware, because the sensation had been competing with my panic for some time – of Adelyn's essence hovering overhead, looking down on the room's activities. What I mean is, throughout the entire fiasco of Walter and me screaming for help, running around and trying to phone, I'd had stereo perception, a bit like looking through a spyglass without closing the other eye. In my peripheral awareness I'd sensed Adelyn's spirit viewing all our frantic efforts, our running about. She'd been trying to tell us not to be afraid, that she was fine, she was wonderful! To her we'd appeared like frantic baby chicks scrabbling about in a tilting cardboard box.

Perhaps you'll know what I mean if I say that Adelyn's love had a specific quality, a specific pitch or flavor I'd know anywhere. I'd felt it in childhood whenever she was around something she loved, or as a teen when she talked about her crushes, or during those awkward moments of Christmas or birthdays when we momentarily dropped our defenses and actually hugged. Most recently, I had felt it in her love for her children, that specific essence of Adelyn-love charging the space around her. Now I felt it, potent, distinctive, and clear but coming from… from…. just *above* me – that's all I knew. Adelyn-love for both Walter and me, and her intense desire to sooth us. Yet it was also bigger than that now, bigger than a select target; it glowed beyond us and shone on everything. Adelyn-love loved. Adelyn *was* love. Love loved.

Her joy spread to me. All my fear and loss evaporated in its brightness and left me with happiness so profound it was all I could do to conceal it – which I *had* to, because nothing could be less appropriate. Joy. Elation. It resonated in my every cell. Or maybe not cells themselves, but in their shared energy – I don't know. All I know is that I felt as if I'd just come back, myself, from the other side. I knew perfect peace, sitting not ten feet from the empty shell my sister had discarded. I remembered the tantrum with which I'd fought god's decision that I return to my body. But Adelyn didn't have to fight. She was free and more joyous than life inside a body allows. I *knew* it. I wanted never, never to forget that feeling.

But as I sat there at the foot of her bed trying my best to conceal this joy, I picked up a strong and urgent thought: "Explain to Darius. Do not leave him out."

As soon as we got back to the house, though I was exhausted, I went straight to Adelyn's two-year-old son who was sitting alone on the dining room floor, a strain on his face as he ignored all the keening around him and played with some small toys. I knelt beside him and spoke the words I was guided to say. "Darius, your Mama loves you *so* much with all her heart. She wishes she could stay here and be your Mama; that's all she wanted to do. But she couldn't. Her body stopped working, and she can't be in the world anymore. She had to leave it." Darius was to my left, and I felt Adelyn to my right. "But she loves you *so* much, Darius, so very, very much. And she'll love you, always, wherever you are."

He listened with a grave scowl, his eyes on the small white storm trooper he kept bending back and forth.

I asked, "Can I hug you, Darius?" He shook his head, eyes down. He was angry, but I knew he'd understood. My own feeling of completion, of a mission accomplished, was like nothing I can describe. I'd done right. It felt like I had a new keel, a new stability and direction, whose source was goodness.

Adelyn was buried a few miles from their rental house, under a cherry tree in bloom. Despite her tremendous intellectual and scholarly accomplishments, all she'd wanted on her tombstone, beneath her name and dates, was the single word, *Mama.*

~

There was no one I could tell what I'd experienced that morning in the hospital. Even the prospect of speaking it seemed crazy, contrived, exaggerated to make me seem special. What a heartless, selfish bitch to be off on her own woo-woo trip even as her sister lay dying! After all, I hadn't physically *seen* anything. Maybe it all came from the unfilled urine bag; maybe that was my one real clue and the rest nothing but fantasy.

That I could set aside an experience so genuine and vivid still amazes me. Compartmentalization, practiced for decades around my sexual compulsion and obsessions, came easily to me. On one level I did know I'd re-experienced the Light, that it was celestial, and that Adelyn had conveyed both feelings and messages to me after she left her body. But on another level, none of that could actually happen. So I sealed my non-possible knowledge inside my Weird Things vault along with the other instances and, turning away, conformed my thoughts to the standard model.

Unfortunately, once we returned home, I found it difficult to care about anything. I felt no connection with my Evergreen students, and no investment in whether the class went well. At the quarter's end, I resigned from my teaching position. A few weeks earlier I'd been fired from my Vivace job as well, for being recklessly insulting during a manager's review, so now I was unemployed. I didn't really care. Depression washed over me. Now I had no income, no savings, and no inclination to find work. And I began to doubt my experience in the hospital room, to judge the universe as tragically unfair.

> 5/29/1997: "Up pretty early today – seems like for no reason. What do I have to say? Not much. Every day I live now is one she doesn't. I made cupcakes yesterday. She can never bake again, or freeze stuff [Adelyn used to freeze cupcakes for our grade school lunches], or decide what's a good idea. Maybe she liked deciding what was a good idea.
>
> "It was more than she could stand, this being swept away toward death no matter what she might do. She would resolve to take action, get out, all this catastrophe shoved aside. But toward the end all that would happen was some twisting of her feeble neck, arms flopping up onto the sheets beside her head, where her skin dipped into concave temples and her eyes, far too big, too blue, two enormous pale globes exposed, didn't see much, led her inward instead, released the prop of externality, and floated away, so that she was quiet again, journeying somewhere. Then Walter and I, who had leapt up to stop her – conspirators with death – would look at each other and wordlessly sit back down."

> 6/2/1997: "I had a dream she and I talked about her death. She told me she would come to me in music. We were good in that dream. There was a let-down of fears and a love-trust that felt freeing. I miss her. I miss her, and her dying and being buried was such a horrible— Well, I don't know how it was for her. I only know she didn't want it. She wanted to be *here*."

Meanwhile, life dragged on. Jesse and I had already purchased plane tickets for France that summer, because Jesse had been studying French with a pretty, young teacher on whom she had a crush, and wanted to experience the culture firsthand. With that despicably selfish practicality we're all horrified to sense in ourselves, some part of me was relieved, as I'd been with my grand-mother, that Adelyn's dying schedule hadn't impinged on our trip. Yet we had no business going in the first place – I knew that. Neither Jesse nor I had any income, so we were traveling on Louisa's credit cards alone. Jesse was adamant: she *must* experience France. And I had no boundaries other than conflict avoidance: I *must* placate Jesse.

It was not a good trip in any way. For Jesse, the frugality of my Greece trip was out of the question. She couldn't possibly walk another step with all this baggage, so we'd take this expensive hotel right here. She was hungry *now* so instead of getting groceries we'd sit down at this pricey restaurant. We hailed cabs instead of taking busses or walking. In fact, we fought so frequently that we had to set up a system whereby we alternated being boss for a day. At times we were allies and I still loved her, but at others she spent my money so carelessly that we started yelling matches right out in public.

By the time we came home, I'd added over twelve thousand dollars to my already substantial VISA bill. And I still had no job. In the weeks that followed, getting out of bed became increasingly difficult. I hung around the house in my sweats, reading the newspaper. Donna had doubled my Zoloft already, but it seemed to do nothing. She doubled it again. Still nothing.

Through a temp agency, I at last landed a data entry job. Each day, I was given a computer print-out. From that list, I would enter a doctor's name. Then a patient's name. Date of visit. Sixteen digit code. I'd then press control-enter, which merged a new transcript into the patient's database records. Then I'd repeat.

I did that for a year. An entire year spent in a cubicle.

I just wanted to be left alone and not think. A major sector of my soul went to sleep. I did not create, exert hope, or trust the world. Our supervisor permitted use of headphones at work, so I developed close relationships with the hosts of many National Public Radio shows. I had no other friends. Jesse worked a few hours a week at the same place, and together we earned just enough to make rent. That I'd formerly stood before sixty college students and, fully conversant with every line of *Hamlet* or *Oedipus,* cracked spontaneously jokes, seemed impossible to me. After work I did nothing but watch TV and grow a fat ass. And I really didn't give a shit.

Adelyn's death had been the last of several unexpected jolts in my life, and after losing my sanity, Jenna's love, the country living dream, and, finally the mainstay of my life – alcohol and its attendant god of coolness – I had lost my bearings. I thought of death constantly. Journal entries for that year are riddled with cross-outs and insertions, as if I'd lost confidence even in my ability to express myself. In mid-entry I'd sometimes switch to a narrator's voice – writing some aspect of Adelyn's life. Gradually, my entire journal shifted to a series of jumbled, half-sense letters to her.

> 8/5/1997: "I don't know what was you, always telling me your news but bored with mine – why? I guess it just depends on the level of trust in the conversation, because when we had our tête à tête in the restaurant when you told me to get my own tusk and build my own ivory tower, I think you listened hard and tried to understand me. You were at Princeton and excited with excelling, and I was stalled out, and you wanted me to get some of what you had. I'm sorry I judged. I was a big judger when I was a drunk, and still am now but just try not to be."

There are approximately twenty such letters over the course of a year. Some read almost as though my sister had become my god – or maybe a guardian angel.

> 3/5/1998: "Dear Adelyn –
> "I'm having trouble again knowing what's what. None of it's a huge deal, I know, except that I'm not happy. Something in me's very lonely, some core not connected to my doings or my God. You say it's up to me to figure out why and do what I need to do. Yes, my life is precious. Yes, I want to embrace it. In your opinion, I'm needing to have a baby – and maybe you're right. Your birthday's coming. You'd have been 42. So weird, this life, wasn't it?"

Survivor's guilt, they call it. Not only had I failed to love my sister while she was here, I was also developing a terrible suspicion that the wrong one of us had been allowed to live. Let's compare the two, shall we? Over here we have Adelyn. With her three MAs and Princeton Ph.D., she'd stood poised at the brink of international acclaim in Musicology, delivering papers at Oxford and teaching in a tenure track position created *for* her by Harvard's Musicology

Department. With her husband, likewise doctorally brilliant, she'd been raising three beautiful children. Next, let's take Louisa. Having drunk and smoked most of her life away, she couldn't produce a major work of writing, possessed great expertise on nothing, and was caught up in a dysfunctional lesbian relationship while putzing around a messy rental house. Despite gulping triple doses of anti-depressants and complaining in AA meetings, her crowning achievement of a given day was often dragging her lame ass out of bed.

Which life was worth more?

I'd hit bottom in sobriety. There was no lower to go. In the past, this would have been my cue to hook up with the Fuck This Shit Fairy, dump the relationship, and reinvent myself. But by this time, I'd finally progressed enough to sense that I needed to change not my external life, but who I was *inside*.

I'd arrived at a junction of only two alternatives: tip the bottle, or seek god. What was my choice to be?

Adelyn engaged, and on a visit home, bathing her firstborn

21: TRANSFORMATIVE MIRACLE OF THE 12 STEPS; WEIRD THINGS 7 & 8

God screens us evermore from premature ideas. Our
eyes are holden that we cannot see things that stare us in
the face, until the hour arrives when the mind has
ripened; then we behold them, and the time when we saw
them not is like a dream.

                    -Ralph Waldo Emerson
                    Spiritual Laws

The two clean and sober boys who rented rooms in our house were changing. They appeared somehow impervious to my bitching. They laughed freely. One day Jon, the surfer dude, said something extremely annoying. I'd been wallowing in some kind of discontent – I don't remember what. He smiled, gestured circularly around my sternum and asked, "Wha'sa matter? Got a god-shaped hole?"

The two of them had been regularly attending a solution-based meeting, one grounded in the Big Book of Alcoholics Anonymous. According to Jon, it was changing his life. "If you're not happy," he said simply, "why don'cha try it?"

Aha! I thought. Here again comes that AA cultish pressure to conform! But Jesse was equally miserable. She pointed out that we had nothing to lose.

This is a boring and pedantic chapter because it describes the outer events that brought about an inner transformation of my life. Inner change cannot be translated into words. If it could, no one would still be fucked up. The fact remains, though, that I'm a different person today than I was at the time of Adelyn's death. The Twelve Steps work differently for every person; here is how they worked on me.

In its golden era, Drunks R Us, now spoken of fondly by many who remember, drew a hundred or more sober hipsters to the Fremont Baptist Church basement every Monday night. The median age of attendees was perhaps 24; the average number of tattoos per person perhaps seven. Piercings – I can't guess. Leather, denim, ratty T-shirts. The number of *fuck*s per sentence, in various syntactical forms, was astronomical, followed closely by *shit*. "I'm like, fuck this shit, dude, you know what I mean? My shit is so fucked up!"

And yet the meeting's format was enforced as strictly as that of a Catholic Mass. The chairperson read and reflected upon a passage from the Big Book while more people than not followed along in their own Big Books, busily annotating. If the chairperson called on you, you stood with your book, contemplated the passage, and spoke your experience on that particular topic – and nothing else. If the meeting was on Step Nine and you'd not yet reached Step Nine, you passed thusly: "Well, fuck. I'm still on my fuckin' Fourth Step, man, so I'll just shut up and listen, thanks."

Jesse and I had never seen anything like it. Bible study – that's what it smacked of. A full hour on the nature of humility featured in Step Seven, which led to dozens of people pointing out their own vanity, egotism, and fear. A full hour on the insanity referenced in Step Two, which led to scads of anecdotal evidence that no human power can overcome addiction. The leading figures of the meeting – a tattoo artist with a big afro, a bleached dreadlock white boy, an intense artist woman, and a hilarious lesbian – could all quote the text from memory. Was this whole thing just some clique where coolness was defined by how slavishly you worshipped the Big Book?

In spite of myself, I was drawn back enough times to pick up the gist. Without god, we were absolutely fucked. We suffered from a three-fold disease: physically, mentally, and spiritually. Physically, we had an allergy that caused us to break out in a virtually irresistible craving any time we took a drink. That part I'd known already. But I'd never before fully grasped the full import of the Curious Mental Blank Spot. No matter how fervently we resolved not to drink, some part of our minds kept reintroducing the idea in a favorable light. Over and over and over. No matter how determined, we would eventually hit upon a moment when we simply could not remember why we'd decided not to drink. Indeed, it would seem a fine idea, something quite easy to control! The alcoholic's life was a continuous game of Russian roulette. Whenever the Curious Mental Blank Spot chamber spun into place, we would drink – unless.

One resource could keep us immune where our own minds could not: a spiritual connection to a Higher Power. Once we sobered up, this same Higher Power could alleviate the array of selfish character defects we'd come to rely on to mismanage our tangled lives. On our own, we could do neither.

I'd never heard God spoken of as these kids spoke. The tattoo artist was a tremendously gifted orator. From his mouth came words I still carry with me these fifteen years later. "A relationship with God is like any other: the more you hang out, the tighter you get. All I ever said to God my whole life was, 'Fuck off, asshole!' From the get-go, lying, cheating, breaking into homes – I did not give a fuck. I was *owed*. And yet this same God that I fuckin' *hated*... saved my ass. Fuckin' *loved* me enough.... to save my worthless ass. That's grace, man. That's fuckin' grace."

Even God swore His Ass off when these kids paraphrased, yet all of them spoke with reverence. They were grateful. Some made terrible fun Christians, evoking roars of laughter, but they usually apologized and got back on track. What they revered was their *own conception of God* – no one else's. But they wanted, through the Twelve Steps, to let this power infiltrate and guide every aspect of their lives.

Jesse was sold. She asked the hilarious lesbian to sponsor her and began reading *Doctor Bob and the Good Old Timers* as a mandatory pre-requisite. At first I asked the intense artist woman to sponsor me, but we were not a good fit. There was another, less prominent woman about three years younger than I who seemed to have roots reaching into the soil of life and a solidity I longed for. She – Karen D. – agreed to sponsor me. Karen was a fabric artist (meaning she designed and sewed weird clothes) who lived in an old carriage house of a rich estate. Its cozy rooms were crammed with fabrics, paintings, extreme knick-knacks, the perimeters rimmed with shelves of home canning.

At our first meeting on a rainy winter's evening, I somehow talked her into believing I'd completed Steps One and Two, so we started out by reading "We Agnostics." When we reached the question, "Do I now believe, or am I even willing to believe, that there is a Power greater than myself?" – she paused and asked for my answer. I told her I did believe in a goddess, but not one who loved me or heard my prayers. Pain welled up in my heart and overflowed in tears at Karen's kitchen table. "God doesn't love me!" I sniffled.

But, to my astonishment, she pulled me up short.

"That's self-pity," she said. "You're having a pity-fest for yourself, here. And that's not from God. It's not what we do here, okay? Why should *you* be so unique that God wouldn't love you? 'Yeah, I'm love itself and I want good things for all – *except* Louisa!'" She looked me in the eye. "You need to get over it. Pronto."

She had me wear a rubber band bracelet, and whenever a thought of self-pity or self-loathing came to mind, I had to snap it and say: "Not from God!" I worked with Karen for three years. Under her guidance, the Twelve Steps recast my entire understanding of life. I developed new beliefs and a new capacity for loving life, my fellows, and a god of my own understanding.

How did she do it? Though she could also be kind and gentle, Karen was the type of sponsor who calls bullshit. When we did my Third Step, that *decision* to turn my will and my life over to the care of God, she said the first evidence of having taken it would appear in how soon and how thoroughly I wrote out my Fourth Step. Delaying meant I'd been full of shit.

A Big Book Fourth Step begins with writing a list of every person you resent and every incident or trait that fuels your hurt or anger. You then identify the ways these people's actions seemed to threaten or diss you. Finally, you look at your own part in constructing each flawed relationship: How were your expectations selfish? How did you lie to yourself or others? In what ways did fear motivate you? You read all this to your sponsor during a Fifth Step. In the end, you see clearly and without exception that you, yourself, are responsible for all your feelings and relationships.

My current condition, Karen explained, was like having a nervous tic that caused me to repeatedly punch myself in the face, whether with my own hand or someone else's, then bawl and point at them. Until I could identify my self-destructive reflexes, I couldn't ask god to remove them, so I'd stay in the same rut.

So I worked hard. That first Fourth Step featured 236 resentments. On it was my entire family, of course, including relatives. There were 20 resentments from grade school, 42 from high school, and 21 from college, all with specific names and deeds. There were people from Manhattan, Boston, grad school, Kevin's family, Fitness Universal, Jenna's family, the lesbian gang, Dancing Goats, Jesse's family, and my current life in AA. I resented entire classes of people ranging from Broadway street kids to right wing Republicans. Everyone had harmed me, snubbed me, thought they were better. In other words, it was an entirely typical Fourth Step.

For my Fifth Step, we took nine hours to review them all.

Karen let me get about as far as high school before she brought out her big guns. I remember even the name she chose to call me out on, the two of us sitting with tea at my dining room table. Tashia Bell. Tashia's offense? "Ignored me. Popular though dull. Cutsie. Liked and accepted and dated effortlessly."

"Okay, okay, so this Tashia girl. She's pretty? She had friends?"

"Right. And she didn't even talk very much."

"So she did nothing to *deserve* her popularity, and worse still, she refused to share it with Louisa..."

"Right."

"...who was starving for it miserably. So let me ask you this: what good things did *you* wish for Tashia? What did you offer her, in your heart?"

"What do you mean? I wanted to be her friend."

"Because you wanted to share goodwill to brighten her life, or so you could feed off her parasitically?"

"No! See – she had it made, and I was shit. She was up there and I—"

"—didn't give a shit whether she was unhappy inside, whether she was as confused as you, whether she had trouble at home. Louisa's not interested. Louisa's like, 'give me the goods, bitch!' You saw her like a vending machine whose sole purpose was to make your life easier. And, dammit, the vending machine ate your coins! You put in your token of friendly chit-chat and she failed to deliver. Fuck that bitch!"

"But compared to me..."

"Comparing her outsides to your insides..."

"Yes, but—"

"The fact is, you knew *nothing* of her insides, what was behind that shyness, and you didn't care enough to find out. You didn't have a kind, helpful, considerate, loving thought for *any* of these people – not one. It was all about poor, sad, unpopular Louisa, so you dehumanized them. Other people can sense that, you know. It's not attractive."

"Selfish, self-centered, dishonest." I wrote the words, and slowly began to see their truth.

During the next eight hours, I began to see a pattern enacted over and over again throughout my whole freaking life. Being broken and insecure, I approached people expecting them to simply *not have* any brokenness of their own, to have it together so they could make me comfortable, and – most importantly – validate me as worthy of attention, respect, desire, etc. I wanted approval from you, solely to fix me. When you failed to perform as I wished, I resented you.

That was the only model of human relations I'd ever known.

Karen said I had a step-ladder concept of human relations. She made a little drawing of one in my notebook. People were either above me, so I clawed at their ankles, or below me, so I stepped on their fingers. The whole step ladder had to go, she said. We brainstormed a new model, a view of life like constellations of stars. Some people grouped together in galaxies, but none were higher than another. I could travel among them without judgment.

I also shared with her all my fears, and how they might look if I let faith replace them. I shared a sex inventory of all the ways I'd been selfish in sexuality, including the story of Zodiac ("Oh, Louisa!" she laughed, "my god, you *are* a piece of work!"), and what it might look like if I behaved in matters of sex as my goddess would have me be. I shared all my secrets. Telling her about my childhood drawings and self-bondage ritual, I blushed, got majorly pitted out, and felt sweat beading on my upper lip. She listened, the only human besides the shrink to hear everything. Big deal! She'd heard far weirder stuff, she guaranteed me, and pointed out that I'd harmed only myself.

Then she wrote me a list I still have, of all my major character defects. Louisa was judgmental, controlling, and vindictive, a dependent or domineering people-pleaser who wrote scripts for everyone and tried to play God by willing others to follow them and fill her selfish needs. Why? Because she was fearful for her security, scared she'd miss out. Conversely, if my security and worth came from God, she said, I could quit the whole "dog n' pony show" and learn to love others from a place of abundance.

Which seemed impossible, I said.

Of course it was! Karen agreed – without God's help. My new responsibility was to "pay attention!" Karen stressed this over and over. If I just drifted along, I would stay in my old patterns. What Steps Six and Seven should amount to, she said, was my willingness to *recognize* when I wanted to employ a defect, and *try like hell* not to. Only then would God step in and give me just enough help to act differently.

In the months that followed, I experienced a sort of paralyzing void whenever I tried to practice this. If I wanted to plunge into self-pity but instead identified and arrested it, I seemed to hover in a stalled out emptiness. If I wanted to snap back at Jesse, to judge friends, exaggerate stories, or gossip just a tad, the prospect of doing *nothing* instead felt like that sensation when you've misjudged how many steps in a staircase: all wrong. And yet again and again, I held back and asked my goddess to fill the emptiness.

Slowly, growth began – a true evolution. I learned to let down some of my defenses among friends, and to let god be whatever it wanted; I didn't have to know.

> 3/28/1998: "Jesse and I are at the cabin with friends. What fun we've had! I'm old and fat but cast all that to the winds and played and power-skipped and climbed things and lay down in the sunshine. We ate cookies and played Monopoly and I was myself. I sang out loud my 'Cutest Little Mousketeer' song about Sydney and told them all I could hardly believe I'd done it. Then later when I heard Jon actually *singing* it to himself while he washed dishes, it was so weird! Weird, too, is learning to trust people, but I am learning it's possible.
>
> "I truly have no idea what life is or to what purpose anything exists – anything at all since we all die sooner or later, whether admired, despised, or obscure. I have no idea what I'm part of or why I'm doing anything – I just live it, this hand I've been dealt, like a cell or an ant functioning within the whole. I talk and look and eat and feel emotions, and these trivialities are huge to me – they comprise the known universe."

In May, a year after Adelyn's death, Jesse and I flew out to spend a week with her widow and children in Virginia. I became an aunt. I loved and played with my niece and nephews as I should have years before. Tragic as it was, I began to accept my sister's death. The degree of pain I would tolerate before turning to prayer grew increasingly less, and the answers I got began to make sense.

> 6/14/1998: "Dear Higher Power: I woke this morning in a huge amount of fear. My whole face aches with it. My

neck and shoulders are tight with it. Fear tells me I am not enough, have no right to be here, suck in general. I'll also 'miss' the 'right' way to spend the next few hours, will be in the wrong place at the key time. I am screwing up *right now*, and the world will punish me by _____ing my ____.

"Okay, I prayed a while and an answer came to me. 'Selfishness – self-centeredness! That, we think, is the root of our troubles…' So, no wonder I'm scared. When I put the spotlight on *me* on a dark stage, I'm isolated and terrified. When I am one of the strands in Goddess' lush moss, I'm okay."

As I found stronger spiritual footing, the gears of my outer life began slowly to recommence turning. Still inputting data day after day, I sent out job applications. When I got rejected for a tutoring job at UW Bothell's Writing Center, I called the director and asked why. Overqualified, she said. But after our conversation she passed along my resume to the Director of Computing and Software Systems, who hired me as a technical writing instructor. I was soon up in front of students again, earning twice what I had at Evergreen.

But Jesse, meanwhile, grew increasingly unhappy. As I tapered off my anti-depressants, she was gaining need of them. She suffered a series of illnesses, which frequently caused her to dump her class load, overwhelmed. Once her tonsils swelled up. Since we had no medical insurance, she went to a low income clinic, where a doctor remarked carelessly, "I don't know what's causing it – could be cancer!"

Jesse wanted a biopsy and we had a huge fight. "How can you put *money* ahead of *my life*?!" she screamed when I proposed waiting a bit. I caved. The next day she had biopsy taken under anesthetic at a cost of four thousand dollars – to me. Two days later, the swelling vanished. But not the medical bills, which added to our hopeless debt.

Though we continued to fight often, I never questioned my commitment to the relationship. I was done with dropping the tray and walking away. Sobriety, for me, meant standing by my wedding vows, showing up for weekly couples counseling, and trying my best to love Jesse as she was.

8/4/1998: "We're in crisis, me and Jess, and I'm scared every day, what if we don't make it. If we didn't, that would be despair for me. All we've built. All we've been through. I want us. That's not codependence, it's a lot of good things, a lot of meaning."

Except it *was* codependence – as rife and denied as my drinking had been in years past. I wanted Jesse's profound gratitude for all I gave her, but wasn't getting it. So I gave more, and expected more, and resented more. Because we shared a bank account, Jesse's inability to live on a budget became my inability, as I had no boundaries, no limits, and would not even consider the solution of separating my finances to cut her off. Instead, broke as we were, my parents became our shared horn of plenty. They paid off our largest VISA bill at $15,000. Then Jesse wanted a house, and for my parents to come up with the down payment. I went to them to ask for it, feeling like the fisherman in *The Magic Fish* whose wife keeps demanding more and more wishes. They practically laughed at my audacity at first, and turned me down. Zelda called later to scold me for letting Jesse push me to make such a ridiculous request.

But in the end, my mom's generosity won out. With money left to her by her mother, she put up the $30,000 down payment, and I took on the mortgage. Jesse was on the mortgage to improve her credit rating, and because in theory she would one day contribute. Yet within months of moving in, she found the house too "tacky." Our bedroom was in the '80s style basement, where she began ripping out doors, bathroom fixtures, and flooring when we had no money to replace them. Our fights escalated. At least three times, Jesse pulled off her wedding ring and flung it on the floor. Once it rolled under the fridge, and we later had a terrible time getting it out.

> 11/18/1999: "Jess and I had a huge fight this morning while I drove her to school about our Christmas card photo. She wanted a downtown scene somewhere Xmasy, I wanted to keep it simple so we could maybe actually *do* one this year. Instead of yelling back I'd honk the horn whenever Jess yelled at me to make her shut up. Boy, did that piss her off!"

> 12/5/1999: "I am tired in general of feeling the gravitational pull of Jess's self-centeredness! Ack! Today it just seems *overwhelming*! While I'm at it, I'm sick of her not

wanting to work or support herself. Of *course* she doesn't want to work – who does?!"

One day I called Karen at the tail end of a huge fight. Since my Fourth Step, I'd given up yelling back, but I still didn't know how to disengage. Jesse had flung her ring again, shouting that she was done. She'd pursued me into our basement bedroom, which didn't lock, pried the pillow off my head to scream more, and when I hid in the closet, she came in there, too, and screamed down at me where I huddled. My hands and voice shook as I reported all this to Karen.

"Louisa, did you do Six and Seven or not? You are *half* of whatever is going on there. Seek God. Make choices. And don't call me up with this kind of drama any more. You might enjoy it, but I don't have the time." And she hung up.

I was shocked. What *was* my part? Signing up for all this? Yet the implied solution – that I ought to get out of the relationship – seemed far too drastic and scary to contemplate. Who would I be without having Jesse to blame for everything?

~

Meanwhile, Karen and I had reached Step Nine – making amends to those I had harmed. I'd come up with a categorized list in Step Eight, and Karen guided me through the process of tackling it. In every case, I met with her beforehand to decide what I should and should not say. Karen coached me: "You do not grovel. Swoop in and take up the turd you left. Say, 'Y'know what? That's mine, and I want to clean it up.' You don't apologize because you're beyond sorry; you're *done* being that person. Now you act out of integrity and accountability to God – not as a selfish, needy person who wants to be excused."

There was a Vassar housemate I'd accused, going along with my four other housemates, of chewing and spitting out other people's food from the fridge, an innocent girl we kicked out of the house. A year after we graduated, one of those housemates had visited me in New York where she repeated the same behaviors in her sleep. I wrote a letter to the accused girl owning that I'd made her a scapegoat to save my own hide, then withheld the truth when I learned it. She wrote back to say that, though she had a happy life now, that incident had marred her entire Vassar experience. She requested that I write letters of exoneration to every girl who had lived in that house. I could only track down two of the four, but I did as she asked.

I went back to Edmonds Community College and made amends for quitting, bringing replacements for all the office supplies I'd stolen. I wrote to Zodiac, now a pediatric emergency specialist, to admit the wrongs I'd done without disclosing twisted details that might harm him further. Same with Reilly. I met with Jenna and her new girlfriend, clearly a far happier match. I drove to Olympia to confess to the former owners of Dancing Goats that I'd stolen about three hundred dollars by stuffing the tip jar, and together we devised a re-payment plan. With the Vivace manager I'd mouthed off to, I owned my jealous immaturity. I met with my parents, with Walter, with Zelda. Over a three-year period, I followed through as honestly and honorably as I could with all forty of my amends.

The Ninth Step, done right, offers perhaps the most powerful experience of all twelve for the alcoholic who has lived her entire life seeking what her ego can *get* out of others. The last thing your ego wants is to approach a person you've wronged and acknowledge that your actions were sick and misguided, and then to listen as they describe *their* experience of your selfishness. Yet when you gather your faith and walk through this process again and again, with person after person, two spiritual truths become manifest. First, you learn the importance of doing what is right rather than what is easiest, and to respect others, respect the truth. The Hippocratic Oath, *First, do no harm,* takes on a non-medical meaning. Secondly, you learn to trust god that, even with your worst faults exposed to the light of day, you are worthy of love and compassion. In this way, you begin to build a self whose source runs deeper than ego.

As those years elapsed, I also read many popular books on spirituality – by Carl Jung, Thomas Moore, Ernest Kurtz, Thich Nhat Hanh, Jon Kabat-Zinn, Jack Kornfield, Pema Chödrön, the Dali Lama, and many others. I remember how shocked I was to discover that Chögyam Trungpa had died of liver failure due to chronic alcoholism despite all his Buddhist wisdom and attempts at self-discipline. He'd believed he could fend off his condition without admitting powerlessness and tapping into a power beyond himself. So he died at 48.

Karen, meanwhile, had given me a new model for navigating daily relationships. I was to think of every social gathering, or even casual conversations, as a potluck party. My responsibility was to show up with whatever offering I could bring: my best homemade guacamole. Maybe other people would like my guacamole, and maybe they wouldn't even try it. I could only offer. Some people might show up to the party with old bean salad from the back of their fridge – sick, and not knowing they were sick. I was to politely decline their beans of gossiping, complaining, or negativity without judging or blaming. It was the best they could muster, and a simple 'No, thank you' was good enough.

For my amends to Kevin, Karen directed me to seek out the rabbi who had married us. I was to follow his advice on how to proceed. So, fifteen years after he'd heard our vows as a young, sincere rabbi with disarming blue eyes, the rabbi answered that same front door that Kevin and I had knocked on weekly for our "Jewish lessons." His jet-black hair had gone snow white. The children he'd so patiently hushed were long since grown and gone. He and I sat outside.

He asked what I knew of Kevin's life, and I answered that, according to my parents, he'd recently remarried. Yes, Kevin knew how to contact me.

"But he's made no attempt." The rabbi considered. "So you last talked to him while you were drunk. And now your life has turned around, and you're happy." He thought some more.

"It's not just that I'm *happy*, it's that I can *see* all the harm I caused."

"Mmm." All of sudden he looked incredibly sleepy. He said nothing for some time, and I felt a twinge of concern that he might, like my old shrink, be on drugs. But then his eyes shot open. "I think," he pronounced, suddenly alert, "this amends would actually be more for you than for Kevin. You would raise memories by showing up, and maybe pain. You've changed very little in appearance since those days. Sometimes absence is a greater gift – the gift of letting him focus on his present life." Those blue eyes, when they looked right at you, were still pretty intense.

I protested. "Couldn't I just—?"

He interrupted. "You asked for my advice and here it is: pray for Kevin. Pray for joy and thriving for his wife. Pray that she be to him all you never could. And leave him alone."

So I did.

Even so, a few years later, god arranged a special bonus opportunity for me to make amends. At our twentieth Vassar reunion, I saw Kevin and his beautiful young wife – who, ironically enough, also went by "Jenna." At the picnic dinner I had just started trying to talk with Kevin, my heart all a-flutter, to make my direct amends, when his Jenna intervened. She wheeled up an enormous, frilly carriage with their baby in it and asked for his help, somewhat glaringly, right *now*. She struck me as reflexively jealous regardless of her looks and my lesbianism. I remembered the rabbi's words – was I causing trouble? – and resolved to let be.

But god wasn't finished here. Packing for this visit, I'd somehow missed the memo about bringing a sleeping bag if you were staying in the dorms, so I had none. That night, trying to sleep on my dorm cot with no blankets (the organizers could find me an extra sheet, no more), I got colder and colder. Shivering, I did the only thing I could think of: I put on every bit of clothing I had – pants and shirts layered over one another until I looked like an over-stuffed scarecrow in a ballooning outer layer of sweats. On my head, from which lots of body heat supposedly escapes, I wrapped a long-sleeved T-shirt, tucked like a turban. Around midnight I woke, still freezing and needing to pee.

I peered out my door. The halls were dim and deserted. Rather than take off my stuff, I waddled stealthily to the bathroom just as I was. But when I came out, right there, standing unavoidably between me and my door stood Kevin and his Jenna, dressed in formal evening attire and giggling about something together. Friends had told me they were staying at the finest hotel in town, where a fulltime nanny was watching their daughter. We exchanged surprised hellos.

"We just wanted to see how the freshman lived," Kevin explained.

"Oh! This one forgot to pack any blankets," I laughed. "That's how come right now I have on all the clothes I brought!"

You can't imagine how absolutely ridiculous I looked. Think Michelin Tire Man.

"Nice hat," said Kevin, puzzled, but not meanly. His wife, beautiful in her evening dress, couldn't help staring with apparent shock.

"Yeah, thanks!" I said, adjusting it a bit. I blushed deeply, but I also smiled warmly at the two of them with the echo of all those prayers. "Well, have fun!" I said. "Good to see you! Have a wonderful night, you guys!"

Lying flustered under my worthless bed sheet, I talked to god in an out loud whisper. At least my heart's pounding with embarrassment had warmed me up a bit. "Okay, okay, I get it!" I prayed. "Humility, humility, humility! Kindness from a clown, I see, is genuine. I see what you're saying. Can that please count as my amends?"

Something goddish seemed to answer, *You done good, little one. You're learning.*

~

Early on I'd told Karen I didn't plan to sponsor other alcoholics because I wasn't a "people person." She responded, "Let's worry about that when you get there."

She was right, again. Once I'd made a few amends I started raising my hand at meetings as someone available to sponsor. Because I was a good talker, both newcomers and women with time approached me – though I felt like a fraud. All I actually had to do, though, was read the Big Book with them, including all the notes Karen had had me write in my margins. When the book asked us something, we answered it; when it told us to do something, we did it. Some sponsees didn't stick around, but others did.

Working with these women, I began to see my same character defects, my same twisted thinking and all the pain it caused me, played out in their minds and hearts. I knew how they suffered, and my heart longed to help them.

Let's just stop right there and look at that line again: "I knew how they suffered, and my heart longed to help them." Had such *ever* been the case with the Louisa we've been following? That Louisa sobbing on the track in high school, or boozing with the A-7 gang at Vassar – did she hope to ease *anybody's* pain but her own? Louisa high on vanity at the Peppermint Lounge, dumping Kevin for Jenna, or Jenna for Theo – do we see any compassion or effort to help others?

None. So this empathy and love, along with enough humility to acknowledge that it was the wisdom in this 1939 book, not I, that had changed my life – all this was entirely new stuff that didn't come from me. When I heard Fifth steps and helped my sponsees perceive, as Karen had helped me, the thread of selfish fear and manipulation tangling their relationships, I loved them twice as much for their struggles and vulnerability. I helped them accept that they were only human, yet loved by god, and that god-reliance would move them away from their fear-driven, self-sabotaging habits.

At the same time, I grew to see how plain and ordinary all my sickness had been, even if some of its symptoms had manifested in eccentric forms. I began to understand that I was no perverted monstrosity – just a garden-variety alcoholic. Everything I had suffered now helped me to help others. Whenever a sponsee, in tears, confessed to me about cutting herself, or staying in kinky, abusive relationships, or carrying the shame of remembered incest, I'd tell her about my self-bondage compulsion; I knew self-hate, and I knew shame. If she'd harmed others by callous detachment, I'd share about my ex-partners or my dying sister. That's what we do, I'd say, in our sickness. My sponsee's pain was my pain; I'd often cry along with her. But god had brought me to my feet, and so it would her, through the simple steps in this book.

"So let's go back to reading, okay?" I'd wind up. We'd wipe our tears and turn back to the life-altering words of Bill, Bob, and those first hundred drunks. I was, in other words, a garden-variety sponsor.

~

These next two weird things, I can't say exactly when they happened, but sometime during 1999. Both occurred while I was driving. For the Seventh Weird thing, I had taken the Mercer Street exit off I-5 and was waiting at the light to cross Fairview. I was on my way home late on a Sunday night; there was practically no traffic. But when the light turned green, a soundless voice spoke clearly in my head:

"*Don't go.*"

My first thought was simply, "Okay." I checked my rearview and saw no one behind me, so I was free to wait. The voice seemed almost to originate from inside the car with me. But my next thought was objection, not unlike the way you'd respond to a backseat driver: "How long '*don't go*'?" I couldn't help it. After all, green means go, and I wasn't. I was just sitting there obeying an invisible voice.

Silently, out of nowhere, a car speeding at 100 mph or more shot through the intersection just in front of me. It flew through the red light at a velocity beyond any driver's control, faster than any car I'd ever seen. Zoom! It was gone.

Imagine how I felt, sitting there, intact. I understood my life had been saved – yet again.

"Thank you!" I said, out loud. "Thank you for saving me."

Nothing came back, so I now drove through the intersection. Before long I heard the wails of several sirens. Somehow I had a suspicion it was Adelyn behind this – her spirit, her echo. I'd been writing letters to her frequently during this time. In any case, it was someone who knew I could hear them.

A similar message came as I was driving home from West Seattle several months later on a night of heavy rain. To get into the northbound 99 exit lane, you have to cross a bus-only lane. But the old VW Bug I was driving at the time had no rear defrost, and its side mirrors were rusted out, so I could see nothing behind me in the dark. I signaled to cross the bus lane, delayed momentarily, and was just about to go for it when that same voice came again: "*Don't go!*"

Now, keep in mind that the part of me acknowledging spiritual forces and the part that wants to get somewhere in traffic are about as disparate as two parts of a mind can be. The result: I felt intensely annoyed. The awe I'd experienced only months before when the hundred-mile-an-hour car shot in front of me, that seemed a faint memory, whereas the need to reach Highway 99 was, well, imminent! I complained, "Not now! You'll make me miss my exit!" Somehow, in just that little lag of half a second, the memory of last time grew stronger. This *was* the same voice. Fine: I switched off the turn signal. I'd miss my damn exit.

At almost the same instant, a two-section bus roared past on my right, throwing up a flood of road water that completely overwhelmed the little bug's wipers, to the point that I was totally blind for a moment. "Holy shit! Holy shit!" was all I could chant in a toneless panic. While the wipers caught up, I understood what would have happened without the voice. "OUT OF SERVICE" blazed in the darkness, the sign on the rear of the bus seeming as dismissive as a flip of the bird.

"Okay, I get it! I get it!" I apologized. "You're real! I'll never doubt you again! And for whatever reason, you want me to live. Thank you."

Though it may seem more "normal" to decide against a blind lane change than to sit waiting at a green light, this second experience shook me more deeply than the first, because my illusion of safety had been so complete before the voice intruded. That terror I felt when the bus bombed past and blinded me – it humbled me enough that I edged a little closer to accepting the fact that some spirit voice did in fact speak to me, and that the messages it offered exceeded my own human knowledge.

Morphing through depression at the summer cabin;
our first kids, Kelsey and Sydney

22: BUMBLING MOTHERHOOD; HUGE 9TH WEIRD THING (PART A)

I was haunted by the stereotype of...motherhood as a single-minded identity. If I knew parts of myself that would never cohere to those images, weren't those parts then abnormal, monstrous?

-Adrienne Rich
Of Woman Born

Shortly after my 39th birthday, when I'd been sober five years, my mother offered to pay for artificial inseminations so that I could have a baby with Jesse. In spite of the turbulence of our relationship, we'd been talking about it for several years. I knew nothing about being a mother, but I did want a child. I even fell into the classic trap of believing a child would help to heal the troubles between Jesse and me. She promised there would be no more fighting.

I first got inseminated on the last day of August, 1999. It didn't take. Over the next ten months we went through ten failed attempts, ten cycles of hoping and losing. In the clinic's waiting room, I read bad news about hardening eggs – that a woman 40 years old who has sex at the ideal point in ovulation has only a 5% chance of getting pregnant. I'd previously read an article saying that frozen sperm lost 50% of their mobility and longevity. A gong of doom sounded in my gut. Didn't that make my chances about 2.5%? Here went a major chunk of my inheritance, squandered on an unrealistic dream.

For almost a year, I'd been charting my morning temperature. On the day it rose for ovulation, we'd call the hospital for a sperm pick-up time, drive to First Hill, and from the tenth floor sperm bank receive a tiny vial containing at most a half teaspoon of pure sperm with a headcount penned on the side: 16 - 20 million. "Keep those guys warm!" the nurse would say. I'd always tuck them down my bra. Then we'd zoom across town to the University District clinic, where nurses transferred the spermies to a syringe while I got in the stirrups. The uterine catheter always caused a lot of cramping. It was an experience far from sensual.

Ten times we'd done this. Ten times I'd been three to four days or even a week late before an enormous period. When I lost the tenth, taking Clomid by then, I finally gave up. I told god I was okay with whatever she decided. I would finish out the year with two more attempts, and if no child resulted, I would trust it was for the best.

At the time of my eleventh attempt, I was sponsoring five women, all with pains and problems similar to mine. Together, they knew my whole story. To celebrate my fortieth birthday, all five gathered at my house and presented me with an ice cream cake. Someone started "Happy Birthday" on a note a bit too high, so that their soprano voices filled the air with an almost eerie purity. All five knew what I would wish for; I had to fight back tears. Pathetic as I was with my hard eggs and barren womb, why not hope one more time as a birthday wish? I felt all five, plus Jesse, wishing along as I blew out the candles.

A few days later, I got inseminated at 8:00 AM. Jesse and I went directly from the clinic to pick up Adelyn's kids, who were visiting from Virginia, and bring them to the summer cabin. In answer to much begging, we swung by McDonalds, the kids being too young to properly despise the place. I figure it was while I was handing out those McMuffins and hash browns, ruling on disagreements, helping with ketchup cups – actually being an aunt – that the egg and sperm did their thing.

The day came when I emerged from the bathroom with yet another pregnancy test. Jesse was sitting in an armchair looking defeated in advance. I showed her the indicator.

"You're pregnant," she said quickly and tonelessly. "You're fuckin' pregnant!" And we danced around the room.

There are virtually no journal entries for this period. I simply didn't have the time. To make our mortgage payments, I'd started teaching two sections of technical writing, one of them 45 miles away in Tacoma, plus a hybrid online/weekend section of freshman composition in Edmonds. I was constantly buried under mountains of essays, stressed about prepping, and wiped out from pouring energy into classes. Now, on top of all that, I began feeling the effects of pregnancy.

This also meant I had less attention to devote to Jesse. For several years, she'd been struggling emotionally and spiritually. She went for walks and had deep talks with her sponsor, the hilarious lesbian. After one such talk, shortly before I got pregnant, she told me with flat out honesty that she didn't know how much she was still in love with me, and how much she was staying with me just so she could finish school. In other words, she dared to speak the truth.

I remember being panic stricken near the washing machine when she said this and utterly refusing to take it in. We *had* to make it work, because I wanted the little lesbian family of my dreams. Never mind that Jesse's affections had already wandered more than once. There had been two young women artists in AA, the French teacher, and a bicycling friend with whom she developed sudden closeness. In 1999 I'd encouraged a month-long trip to Africa with the French teacher because I knew their traveling together would snuff out any infatuation between them – which it did. They came back a week early and quarrelling. As for the bicycling friend, she straight up asked Jesse if the two of us were in an open relationship. If not, she asked, what were the two of them *doing* together?

"Are we?" asked Jesse, after telling the story.

"God, no!" I said briskly.

"Well, yeah. That's what I told her."

Only faintly did it occur to me that each of these explorations had been cut off by the other woman, not by Jesse. I didn't let myself wonder about what might have happened if the other woman were good to go.

For some time, our romantic life had been in decline. The few journal entries I wrote during this period vent frustration at what I considered Jessie's sexual selfishness. They might also indicate an unconscious waning of my lesbian orientation.

> 1/24/1999: "But the worst of it was [that sex seemed] all about *her* body and *her* arousal and her *orgasms*. When I had to ask for mine plain out, she said I'd wrecked everything and would just have to go wank. So this, along with her saying how her working out at the gym is all for me, going over her every muscle as if it's some luscious meal for me when really I don't care, don't even notice – all of this I've taken together as Jesse's self-centered sexual vanity casting me in some lusty lady role that I can't relate to. How I felt last night was mainly pissed and resentful and sorry for myself. I wanted to

announce no sex for a month or something – that would show her, I thought.

"But that's my old way of doing things and rampant with character defects I want to outgrow –lack of communication. I expect Jesse to know what I want and don't want, without telling her."

I'd hit the nail on the head. My problem was not, and never had been, Jesse. It was my inability to perceive, accept, and speak my own truths. But even seeing a character defect isn't the same as letting it go, especially when we live in an unacknowledged degree of fear. I feared being alone, so I couldn't speak things that might bring it about. Codependents always latch onto what the *other* person needs to realize: Aha! I was so wrong! If Jesse would only change herself in all the ways I thought she should, our sex life would revive, and our lives would be great.

To bring this change about, I had a two-part plan:

A) Think it at her

B) Have a baby

~

Pregnancy is, I think, the ultimate spiritual experience because it highlights so astoundingly that we are passengers of bodies overseen by a life force we know nothing about. When, after forty years of living in the same body, I experienced the vast changes it underwent brought about by a microscopic particle originating from a tiny vial, I became aware of the administrative genius constantly orchestrating our cells. An incredibly complex unfolding of brain and bone and eyesight and individuality was going on inside me, all according to its own wisdom and utterly inscrutable to me.

1/23/2001: "The first time we heard the heartbeat with Doctor Brandon was like a first time hearing the baby's voice. It sounded so determined: 'I *live*!.. I *live*!' That's when I first realized not everything depended on my own will and prayers – that the baby itself had a will to live."

Since my health insurance depended on my working, and with Jesse *still* in school, I got zero maternity leave. That is, I taught two sections of Technical Writing straight through my pregnancy, childbirth, and into infant care. Right to the end I kept waddling in front of my class to expend a ton of energy teaching and devoted the rest of my time correcting stacks of student papers. During the two-week absence I targeted for the birth itself, students worked from an online version of my course, emailing completed assignments to me and meeting briefly with a kind woman from the writing center who handed out what I emailed to her. Jesse was consumed with her own work at school and had little tolerance for my complaining.

> 3/8/2001 (*eight months pregnant*): "I get a bit emotional from sleep deprivation, I guess. Last night I didn't think I was adjusting myself too often, but Jesse asked/told me to go upstairs and sleep on the couch. At first I was only a little hurt and took my pillow and went, but when I got there and it was so cold, my heart pounding from climbing the stairs and nothing but the polyester afghan and doggie blanket to stay warm, I cried and cried. I just felt hurt and rejected, like I do so much for her. Yesterday she scraped up the car on a gas station pole and all I did was try to make her feel better. I kept thinking about that and crying. We have no money and I am *so* tired!"

Can you hear those violins? What would have happened if I'd had the self-worth to say, "No way! If you don't like it here, take your own ass upstairs and sleep on the damn couch!" We'll never know. What I do know is, this cry-time of savored martyrdom seemed a much easier option.

I had no love for myself in the sense that grants a person the self-esteem to stand up for herself. But a different love was growing inside me – for the baby. That fierce, protective love of motherhood was taking root, which for many women like me becomes the first strand of a confidence based on nobody else's approval. You love the baby more than yourself. You'd take on a dragon to defend that little life, no matter what anyone else thought. Now, at last, I began to understand Adelyn's choice to take on a delayed battle with cancer rather than abort her youngest.

> 4/6/2001 (*six days before birth*): "When I thought you were coming the other night, I kept saying, 'Don't be scared, little boy!' Because it does seem a scary thing to get pushed down and through such a narrow portal into

an alien world where you have to work to survive – breathing your own air, using your own guts. You're so safe now, little boy, surrounded by my life, my breathings and heartbeat, and you're not alone – neither of us is.

"I'll miss you so much, my silent little roommate! I've felt your little wiggles and shifts and decisions about where your arms and legs will go. You have something to say about almost any position, and I know what you don't like. And hot tea in the morning makes you peddle away at every gulp! 'I'm alive! Goddess tells me to move!' I feel your funny little hiccups, never quite in tempo. And my emotions, you sense. When I was scared by the earthquake, how still you held for hours!

"My secret little other, my guest, my friend – we love each other from inside the same body. And when you are out and gone into the world, I'll never feel these feelings again. The only thing that consoles me is thinking of love like a pool we'll both be immersed in. Your little soul will be protected by my loving, and by Jesse, too, who wants to love you. So I'll wait for your signal, little one, and I won't wish to rush you."

One night around midnight, I got up to pee for about the third time. I saw a hobo spider (remember spiders) dashing across the bathroom floor, grabbed some toilet paper and thought to it: "I'm sorry for this, hobo spider, but you're venomous and I'm going to have a baby. Bless you." Then I squatted to squish the spider, and at the same instant found myself spurting water onto the bathroom floor.

I didn't go into labor, though, because the cord was wrapped twice round his neck, which kept him from dropping. Twenty-four hours later, I was given Pitocin. Induced labor only yo-yoed him, his heartbeat plunging as each contraction nearly strangled him. The doctor made a decision to pull him out with suction, though it would strangle and temporarily "stun" him – a fairly common procedure. He consulted with Jesse on this but not with me, as I couldn't stay conscious between pushes.

The big push came, and the crowning. "Oh, Louisa!" my sister-in-law Betsy exclaimed, "he's *cute*!" The phrase boggled my mind. I'd forgotten that this huge mass I was passing, which I pictured quite literally as the giant turd-like object once encountered in space by the crew of the USS Enterprise, was actually my child.

For over a minute, there was no sound of crying. The nurse tried to distract me with the placenta, but eventually, through my confused thoughts, I felt panic present itself. What if the black despair I'd sensed years ago for another's unborn baby was also to be mine? I seemed to be falling slowly, like Alice in the rabbit hole, about to plummet into that same bottomless void – but, no: *He will live!* I either prayed it from the place of fierce mother's love or was told by a voice outside me – I can't say which. But in the next instant, Keno's first tiny bleats filled the room.

I'd never seen a newborn in my life, let alone held one, let alone breastfed. How could anyone expect me to know how to do this stuff? Jesse was far more confident a mom than I. Raised Mormon with dozens of nieces and nephews, she was practiced at changing diapers, cleaning his umbilical stub, and holding him – a natural mom. She'd have pretty much taken over everything if I hadn't been the one lactating.

That was another amazement two nights later, that sensation like hundreds of tiny salmon eggs bursting inside my breasts when the milk "came in." No one had ever told me about this! In this culture, where breasts are relegated to sex toys, women talk very little about lactation, but mine seemed to take charge as working organs. They "knew" what to do – never mind the bimbo to whom they were attached. In fact they struck me as a tad annoyed at the forty-year wait and now all the more serious about their work, which was just as specialized as that of lungs or kidneys. Over the year that followed, they developed differing personalities: the left was irresponsible – lazy and constantly plying excuses for why she got backed up and engorged or produced less milk. The right, despite being slightly smaller, was all efficiency and flow, and seemed more directly concerned about the baby's health.

I'm sure I'm not the only one to know her boobs this way.

My career of martyrdom continued into motherhood, though. Less than two weeks after the birth, before I could even pee straight, I found myself back in front of a white board, lecturing and taking questions. How I survived all that on next to no sleep, racing to my office during mid-class breaks, where Zelda or Jesse waited with the baby so I could nurse him a few minutes, I don't know. I enjoyed life very little. My sense of aesthetics left me completely and I found my thoughts lacking any sharpness or clarity. I developed post-partum depression, hyperthyroidism, and chronic exhaustion. And I felt guilty for all of it. Wasn't life as a new mom supposed to be enthralling and invigorating? And wasn't Keno an incredibly easy, happy baby? There must be something wrong with me to make me such a Grinch of maternity. I looked forward constantly to the day Jesse would finish school and start work, so that I could stay home, rest, and enjoy being a "normal mom." Love for Keno was the only sure anchor in this life awash in chaos.

> 7/24/2001 (*three months*) "At the bank the other day, I had him up over one shoulder and he pushed and twisted the other way so he could see the tellers and line of people instead of the back corner – a preference, an action, a little will. I love *his voice*, so miniature and round like a jack ball, and his almond eyes of awareness and passing scruples, bursts of mischief he can't really mean, and his little movements that happen so fast because he's compact. He loves and trusts us."

But, astounding as it may seem, Jesse did not *want* to finish school and take over wage-earning to support the family. She'd found in one of her history teachers a mentor who specialized in medieval witchcraft, and now she became determined to continue on in graduate school (with me continuing to support her) and earn her Ph.D. in Medieval Studies. With papers I edited and partially rewrote for her, she'd been getting A's and could envision herself becoming a respected scholar teaching at some university out in the Midwest.

My codependence had oriented every poor choice I'd made in relationships throughout my life. But loving Keno finally changed that. I could martyr myself, but not my child. Here was a person who really *needed* my care, someone for whom whatever sacrifices I made actually aligned with god's will for me in a way that sacrifices for Jesse did not. Inside, I resolved I would not go on exhausting myself to make her dreams reality. I said no. I told her she was free to go to night school if she paid for it herself, but our deal had been, she would get her BA and then work. This was pretty much my first boundary I'd ever laid down since traveling to Greece without her, and she felt wronged. She moped visibly through her departmental graduation ceremony, glaring at me resentfully as I sat in the audience. But I was impervious. I knew I was done. There was one last ploy to get money from my parents –

some online degree for which she needed just $25,000 – but they refused as well.

My inmost intuition foresaw that this boundary would render me obsolete in Jesse's world – baby or no baby. But I didn't face it. Instead I wrote her a cover letter and revamped her resume to help her apply to a law firm downtown. She interviewed well and landed a full time paralegal position. But she hated working, hated the place itself, and the firm was too often on the side of the bad guys. For instance, they defended a fuel pipeline company after the rupture of one of their pipes flooded a river with fuel that subsequently caught fire. Two boys fishing in the river had burned to death – one in a hospital after telling his harrowing story.

Whether in response to this case or other factors, Jesse's mental and emotional health went off a ski-jump. Dead people hanging in the trees, she claimed to see, flashes of swaying corpses. Voices spoke in her head, she said. PTSD – posttraumatic stress disorder – was the diagnosis from our couples' counselor (yes, we were still seeing her). She sent Jesse to a psychiatrist who prescribed anti-psychotic medications. Jesse's life, our therapist maintained, had reached a level of stability that allowed childhood wounds to surface. Keno's babyhood was bringing up the death of her mother. All these things were causing her psychic turmoil and pain.

But all Jesse *really* wanted, I felt sure, was for me to pay her way through graduate school.

The baby had taken her place.

I was a mom, now. My friends in the program seemed far more adept at it than I. They perused books on parenting and blended homemade, organic baby foods, whereas I practiced the Flailing Panic Method of Parenting. Daily demands I just barely scraped through, exhausted and constantly harried, the most incompetent, bumbling, unqualified mother ever. Of one thing, though, I was certain. I'd scored the most precious, perfect, beautiful boy any parent could ask for. Even before he could talk, Keno's sweetness, moving his teddy bear's paw to its chin to sign "thank-you" in addition to signing me thanks himself, assured me that his was an unusually bright spirit. I still can't help wondering if he's the reason I was brought back from death.

> 1/29/03: "It's my eight years sober birthday tonight! Happy birthday, me! Today I was lying in Keno's crib with him trying to get him to sleep. My head ached and I

was exhausted and vaguely anxious about I know not what. Despite all this, I was thinking, in some ways this is as good as it gets: snuggling next to a little one whose face smells of cookies and fruit, and whose stuffed bear that he keeps mooshing into your face likewise smells of sweet things past, letting him bang on your shoulder because he wants to play 'Hey, you woke me up!' and keeping your eyes closed even though his little 'hey!'s are so hard to resist – these are memories I shall cherish all my life.

"God, do I love my son! His bedroom's in a basement because we're poor, but I'm blessed with a loving family. Goodness I wish to him, goodness from him and around him, like a glow that wards off harm! But I myself must learn to live with less fear if I'm to teach him to step broadly and use his gifts."

The fact that I didn't go to an AA meeting even for my 8th birthday shows the degree to which I'd drifted away from the program. Karen had left AA to focus on Catholicism, and I'd found no one to replace her. Without a sponsor myself, I was sponsoring no alcoholics. I seemed all done with spiritual progress. That god was amping up the lesson of a lifetime for me, I had no inkling. A tremendous breach was about to open in my life – change that would drop the earth from under me and force me to find all my bearings anew.

The time had come for me to wake up. So god sent a messenger to warn me – manifesting in my weirdest Weird Thing this side of death: the life-changing Ninth Weird Thing.

~

It started with an ordinary dream – a dream perhaps more vivid than most but well within the bounds of normal. In the dream, I was visiting Walter and Betsy back in Olympia, in the house where I'd stayed after Jenna kicked me out. Sitting on their sofa, I noticed something dark inside a houseplant with juniper-type needles. There, half camouflaged amid the branches, lurked an enormous SPIDER.

I'd always been terrified of spiders, so I was in the dream, too. "Look!" I cried, pointing. Ack! Arachnophobia! We were all disconcerted, but no one else seemed prepared to do anything about it.

I thought: *This spider is so huge, squishing it would leave a mess even worse than the spider. But if I don't deal with it now, it could hide anywhere...*

Someone handed me a glass and, steeling myself, I somehow knocked the spider into it. It landed on its back. But instead of righting itself, it just lay there long enough to give me a good look at its belly. There I perceived a remarkably intricate pattern: interlocking triangles of brown, dark gray, and light gray. My revulsion dissipated, replaced by fascination – such a perfect geometric design! To think that even something as lowly as a spider's belly should carry an emblem of artistry and intention – diamonds of orderly precision – it boggled the mind.

Then I woke up. I told the dream to Jesse while she dressed for work, but as with most of what I said lately, it went largely ignored. I even described the pattern, the way the spider had held still to show it.

Around 10:00 that morning, I was running late to deliver an activities binder to another mom in Keno's toddler co-op. I'd already shouldered the diaper bag, hoisted Keno onto my hip, and scraped my keys off the counter when I noticed – what the hell was *that*?

In the computer room, directly over my swivel chair, a strange black ping-pong ball adhered to the ceiling. I took a few steps closer, squinting with my forty-three-year-old eyes. Could it be? Shit, it was! A humongous frickin' spider, legs drawn in.

Oh my god! I'd never seen one so big, except for the one at Walter's... No, wait – that was a dream. Last night's dream. "This is crazy!" I thought. "To dream of something at night and see it come up the very next morning?!"

But I had no time to reflect. Sleep deprived and habitually on the verge of tears, juggling toddler accouterments and already twenty minutes late, I did *not* need a creepy problem like this! It was just too damn big to squish. If only I could pretend I hadn't seen it. But no. Unless I dealt with it right now, it could hide anywhere, and then—

Wait a second. Even those *thoughts* were from the dream! Curiouser and curiouser! I stared at the spider-ball, questioning it. Why on earth had it picked such an exposed spot, almost like it *wanted* to be seen, directly above the chair where I so often sat? At some level I asked the spider:

Why are you here?

The spider, somehow insistent in the fact of its existence, sent me a response:

I'm here for you. You know why.

My heart pounded – fight or flight. Did I know? I seemed to experience the moment in two layers. There was my frazzled, overtaxed mom self on the outside, about to lose it, but underneath, a deeper, calmer self – the dreamer – whom the spider had addressed. My inner self heard the challenge and, for all appearances, absorbed it without response. I believe today that apparent passivity is our natural reaction to the deeply meta-physical, because the inner self doesn't chit-chat. My soul simply swallowed the message whole.

Don't freak out, I coached myself. *In the dream you were brave. So you can be brave now.*

To Keno I said, "We can't go just yet, honey. There's a great big spider Mama has to deal with."

"Big pydoo?" he echoed.

I pointed, allowing time for his mystified gaze to follow my finger. With toddler gusto he affirmed: "Big pydoo up high!"

I set him down on the kitchen floor. I got out a glass. I clambered up on my wobbly swivel chair and, squinting reflexively, raised the glass over my head. The spider didn't budge for so long I wondered if it might be dead. But at the last second it expanded like an umbrella. Too late. It landed – plink! – inside the glass. I slid a postcard over the top.

I stepped down and peered through the glass just to confirm its mammoth proportions. Oh, jeezus! Teeming with heebie-jeebies, I jammed out the front door and scampered down the front walk all the way to the sidewalk. This thing was so freakishly huge I wouldn't drop it anywhere in our yard. No, sir! I went as far as the neighbors' rockery before I finally shook out the glass onto one of their bushes.

The spider fell on the shrubbery – a juniper, as it happened. It landed on its back. But instead of flipping over, it just lay there belly up. And, yes: on its belly I saw a pattern. There were inter-locking triangles of brown, dark gray, and light gray, displaying a perfect geometric design. Diamonds of orderly precision.

No. No way—

I took a step back, my heart racing. What the *hell*? Jesus! Was I nuts?! Was this some kind of skipping phonograph needle inside my brain that kept making me *think* something had already happened? Some kind of déjà vu, jà-vu? But it wasn't. I knew that pattern. I had seen it last night. I had described it to Jesse hours ago.

I tell you, I felt so desperate for a regular-world explanation that I actually scanned up and down the street for any kind of far-fetched scenario, maybe camera crews, TV hosts of some kind of in-your-brain gag show. I checked the telephone poles for possible hidden cameras.

Scientists, maybe? Some kind of experiment?

Hell, aliens?

But I saw no one, nothing. Just the ordinary world.

So I bent in as close as I dared to really, really look, just in case my eyes had invented something. The pattern was the same. At that moment, as if my certainty were its cue, the cumbersome spider righted itself and began a crab-like retraction into the shadows. Then it was gone.

Again I searched the sidewalk, the trees, the length of the quiet street. I felt trapped in the Twilight Zone, sole inhabitant of some warped dimension. Because I didn't *know* any world like this, where people could dream something so specific one night and then physically *see* it the next day. How could that work? My brain whirred at full effort without finding an answer. It felt a bit like clawing at straw with thick mittens on your hands: I could not snag a single idea. The only thought to take shape was this: Keno was alone in the house. With a parting glance up and down the street, I ran back in.

Still sitting on the kitchen floor, he looked up cheerfully. "Big pydoo, new home?" he asked, using our phrase for such matters.

"Yes," I said. "Mama gave the spider a new home outside."

I picked him up and held him tight. I knew another one of those Weird Things had just happened to me. Like the others, it made no sense. So, there was nothing to be done but to stash it away out of mind. Another of those freaky, paranormal things had really happened. I'd known the future visually this time, even if only on the belly of an ordinary spider. Why couldn't I foreknow some-thing useful, or at will, or that I could at least show off to amaze my friends? What could a spider above the computer have to do with anything?

Clockwise from top left: Oops! 185 pounds of preggo mom; two moms, one cutie-pie; Keno loves making brownies; Professor Keno at almost 2 – all his idea

23: GOD REMOVES THE TRAINING WHEELS

No outrageous circumstance in which he found himself,
no new mad thing brought to his notice could add a jot to
the all-encompassing chaos that shrieked about his ears.

> -Evelyn Waugh
> A Handful of Dust

Before you read this chapter, I need to emphasize that it's not the truth. It's *my* truth. In break ups, more than in any other aspect of life, reality is subjective. If Jesse were to write an account of the following months, hers would be entirely different and equally valid, if not more so. So keep in mind that I can only write what I remember going through, however influenced by character defects that experience may have been. I've done my utmost to be rigorously accurate, and yet this account is grossly unfair to Jesse. Both statements are true.

I'd also like to toss in a reference to Karma. I know next to nothing about the Hindu concept, except that there are three kinds, and one of them – *tamas* – is the province of the Fuck-this-shit Fairy. It's reckless, unheeding selfishness. When I was in the grip of sexual obsession, whether with Kevin, Jenna, or Theo, I didn't *plan* to hurt others. But there was always that place where I decided "fuck it," and on that tray of things I let crash to the floor were the hearts and trust of others. Karma, as we all know, is a law of cause and effect.

So anyway. At the time of the Ninth Weird Thing, Jesse had just found herself a new mentor – an upstanding woman we'd known in AA for years, Barbara Richardson. Barbara was in her early fifties and married to Stanley, whom we'd also known for years. Their history was somewhat racy: Stanley's first wife had once been Barbara's best friend, so for years the couples did everything together – while Stanley and Barbara concealed a torrid affair. But that was long past. They'd since made their amends and married twice – once civilly and once religiously. They were a shining example of the spiritual rehabilitation AA could bring about.

Barbara alerted Jesse to an opening for a paralegal at the law firm where she worked. The job offered better pay and more positive, good-guy work, so I revamped Jesse's resume and cover letter, and she got an interview. Barbara bowed out of the interview process because the two of them had become such fast friends, but Jesse still landed the job.

My first clue that something was awry came when Jesse brought home two big grocery bags full of Tupperware – all the lunches I'd packed her for a month. The food was still in them, untouched and moldy. She set the bags down with defiance; she didn't like being told what to eat, she said.

The second clue was the twenty-two checks she bounced that month, all to downtown restaurants and gift boutiques. Because I was ashamed to tell my parents, I borrowed from our friends to cover them. Again, she was defiant rather than remorseful. Our couples therapist devised a plan for Jesse: she could keep $500 pocket money per month while the rest was to go toward the household. But Jesse couldn't stick to it and bounced still more checks.

The third clue was a membership Jesse purchased at Barbara's gym. Suddenly Jesse, who had always bemoaned getting up early, was bouncing out of bed at 5:00 every morning to go exercise with Barbara before work.

What was I not looking at? The Barbara Richardson I knew from AA meetings was a rather prim lady, a Catholic Republican who wore coordinated "outfits" – sometimes even with a jaunty silk scarf. Seventeen years Jesse's senior, she said "Lord!" and "darn!" and yet Jesse claimed they had mind-blowing conversations about God and spiritual matters. In counseling, our couples therapist applauded Jesse's newfound "God-friend." Having developed a support of her own, she maintained, was a major step for Jesse toward curing her PTSD. When I admitted to feeling jealous, the therapist set me straight.

"Jesse," she said, "Louisa's obviously upset, so I'm just going to put this question to you directly: *Is* there any romantic aspect to your relationship with Barbara?"

"Nope. None."

"Louisa, do you *hear* this?"

"…Yeah."

"And Jesse, do you promise that if the friendship ever *does* develop romantic overtones, you'll let us know?"

"Of course – but it won't."

"Louisa: Jesse has just provided us two solid assurances. She's trying to heal. So I'm going to ask *you* to work on your issues of jealousy and possessiveness – as a partner. Can you do that?"

One Saturday morning in May of 2003, the two of them left for breakfast and an AA meeting on Vashon Island – a scenic getaway spot away from the city. At 1:00 Jesse was supposed to rejoin me and Keno at my friend Rosemary's place to brainstorm about an espresso shop she wanted the three of us to open. Except she didn't show up. I left her maybe four different voicemails – "Where *are* you?" Rosemary waited with me until 3:00, listening to my irate tales of the Barbara fetish, then offered to baby-sit Keno for the evening so the two of us could talk it out.

I went home. Five and six o'clock came and went. Out of sheer craziness I tried going to a neighborhood movie alone, but found myself too hysterical to follow the storyline. Panic forced me to walk out.

When I pulled into our driveway at 7:00 PM, I saw Jesse sitting on our front steps. She met my gaze through the windshield with that same steely defiance. There was no concern, no remorse. In the car, I screamed. I grabbed a bag of trail mix and flung it all over the interior in a conniption of frustration. There's still trail mix under the seats. But Jesse didn't flinch. She was fixed on her right to something, just as firmly as I'd been fixed on my refusal to put her through graduate school.

What had really happened was that she'd finally kissed Barbara. At a restaurant they'd gone to after the meeting, instead of coming home, Barbara had remarked that she simply couldn't begin to imagine what it would feel like to be kissed by a woman. Jesse had obliged by moving beside her and planting the best slow-churning Frenchie she could muster. I learned all this months later through an email mix-up. Barbara wrote to her step-daughter, a lesbian wanna-be, that the kiss "set off fireworks," and Stanley, her husband, saw it left up on a screen.

Some marriages end swiftly. Others break-ups drag on like a slow motion show-down in a spaghetti western –the kind where the shooters get hit again and again, their blood spurting, their bodies reeling from each bullet and yet refusing to die. Ours took eight months because we both feared it. To me, at that point in my codependence, and perhaps to Jesse in hers, the prospect of ending our relationship felt as safe as sawing a rowboat in half in the open sea. Neither of us was complete in herself. Thus Jesse felt compelled to lie to me, and I clung to the hope in her lies. So, it seemed, did everyone else. Stanley, as Jesse often pointed out, had no problem with her closeness to his wife. She spent hours at their house with *both* of them and took special fishing trips with Stan, just the two of them.

The therapist decided we were too enmeshed. She advised we take time apart to each develop our independence, so we arranged for me to spend one night a week at Zelda's empty house. The plan worked ideally from one perspective: now Jesse had time for passionate sex in Barbara Richardson's car.

I was determined to fix everything, as though Jesse's feelings for Barbara were nothing but some dust and clutter obscuring the reality of her deep commitment to me. It seemed to me impossible that Jesse could choose a Catholic, Republican married lady ten years my senior with – yes – slight Martha Stewart nuances, over *me*. Vanity teamed up with fear to create a story I could brandish in the face of an uncooperative reality. The boundless longing and craving Jesse had shown me in Olympia – that was for me *only*, because of my irresistible womanly ways. The fact that sexual obsession is like a spotlight, that it can be shone on anyone with astounding sameness was something I, of all people, should have known. That former targets are last year's headlines, I also should have known. But knowing, for a codependent, is a matter of choice.

I'd win her back, dammit. In June, for my 43rd birthday, I dressed up as glamorously as I could in a willowy halter dress and sandals. We hired a sitter and indulged in a rare – at least for me – date at our favorite restaurant, Café Flora. Our waitress happened to be a lesbian who clearly considered us a cute couple.

Candlelight. Freshening my lipstick in the bathroom. Hoping I sparkled as I tried on my birthday gifts of earrings and a pendant. Yet I could feel Jesse's interest aimed elsewhere, away from my smile, away from my company. I was as worthless as the parmesan shaker, or the shredded bark path at the Nisqually Reserve. I had no worth. My antics were completely devoid of the magic which shimmered around Barbara. And that, despite all my self-deception, I could sense.

> 7/7/2003: "Well, I don't think I've felt this lost since my drinking days. Tell me, future me, how it all turns out – Jess and her PTSD and her infatuation with Barbara

Richardson. It's like some badly written novel where the heroine gets exactly what she doled out to others. Who'd have dreamed it possible a few years ago for *my* Jess to be enamored of *Barbara Richardson* from Book Thumpers?! What a wild, wild plot twist! But it's real and it hurts – hurts like anything.

"Why don't I just leave? Keno. He is why. Also, what the program's taught me about how we don't shoot the wounded – ironically something that Stanley once shared. I know Jesse is ill, and that Barbara's support is helping her. What I *want* is my little family – and Barbara gone from the picture entirely."

How could I protect that little family? One night, when Jesse told me she felt too ill to go to the gym in the morning, I hatched an ingenious plan. I got up quietly before 5:00 AM, having lain awake almost all night, and took her cell phone. I waited until 5:45 to dial Barbara's number, planning to catch her just before her workout.

Instead I woke Barbara up. She answered with a luxurious kitten-stretch voice that should have told me everything, then quickly stiffened when she realized I wasn't Jesse. No, she wasn't going to the gym today, either, as it happened. I asked if she could meet me for coffee at 8:00, across the street from their law firm. She agreed.

I caught a bus downtown and arrived well over an hour early. I waited, trying to pray. Barbara was in AA; she believed in Jesus; she must just not be aware this friendship was harming my marriage. At 8:03, in walked Barbara, trim as always, wearing a beige business suit. Pale concealer blanched a reverse raccoon mask around her crinkled eyes while blusher shimmered on her cheeks, temples, even chin. Her hairstyle had morphed to match Jesse's: closely clipped and spiked in a faux-messy tousle. That Jesse had been having sex with both of us for weeks – albeit, more with Barbara than with me – was nowhere near my radar.

I'd been rehearsing all night what I would say:

"I know that you're only trying to support Jesse through her PTSD illness, and I do appreciate that. But something's gone wrong. She's just not *there* for our family anymore. All her play, all her excitement, her love – it goes to *you* now."

My tears spilled hot and plentiful. Barbara nodded sympathetically. Years later she'd tell me it was all she could do not to whoop with relief. ("I thought, *YES! * She still doesn't know!")

"I need Jesse. Keno needs his mommy. So I'm asking you to *please* do whatever you can to send her back. She *listens* to you. Help us, please."

Mock-pain rumpled Barbara's pink face. With earnest intensity, she assured me she would do just that. I described catching myself slowed to thirty miles per hour on the freeway because I was too busy crying.

"Oh, believe me," said Barbara, "I know jealousy!"

I mustn't worry, she said. Jesse was almost... almost (and here she smiled fondly, her head inclined in an upward gaze reminiscent of 1950s acting) well – like a *daughter* to her! Perhaps Jesse was leaning too heavily on Barbara's... spiritual support. But she would do all she could to get Jesse back on track. That I could take to the bank!

I hugged her goodbye and left confident I'd fixed everything.

I later learned that Barbara did make a verbal effort that night to rein back the affair. I think she did have compassion for me, as I'd had for victims of my obsessions, but sexual addiction, like others, doesn't come with brakes. Her words only further inflamed their passion: *Ah, no! We can't! We mustn't!* It's the favorite refrain of all cheaters.

> 9/16/2003: "The night of September 10 is when shit hit the fan. Jesse went to By the Book. I went out to pick up her meds from Safeway, then put Keno to bed, and went to bed myself around 10:00. At 11:40 I got mad, decided I didn't want to sleep with her that night, got out the sleeping bag for the couch. 12:25 and I'm lying there sobbing and praying, sure she's out with Barbara having macchiatos, high on that infatuation buzz. Car pulls up. Jess comes in.
>
> "'Where have you been?'
>
> "'Aww – I was afraid of this!' she responds with sickened disappointment. 'I thought maybe, *maybe* she'll have just gone to sleep, but *no!* You have no right to interrogate me. When you go to Zelda's, do I call and check up on you? You could be out all night for all I know!'"
>
> "'But I *don't* go out. I read a book and go to bed.'
>
> "'That's not my fault! It's *your* night and this is *my* night. Donna told us to spend these nights apart and I'm doing *exactly* what she said!'

"'Where were you?' Stony silence. 'Where *were* you?!'

"'You have no right to ask!'

"She went downstairs and kissed Keno, then came back and told me she could understand that maybe I'd forgotten the 11:00 call-in rule was no longer in effect, that if I could just *own* my faults and apologize, she'd forgive me. She went to give me a hug but I shrank away.

"'Don't touch me!'

"She threw her hands up: 'That's it! This is fuckin' ridiculous! You're crazy! I'm getting my own place, dammit!' And she stormed downstairs in disgust. So I waited til I thought she was asleep, got dressed, and went to my parents."

I rang my parents' doorbell at 2:00 AM. After many rings my mom toddled to the door in her robe. She hugged me, comforted me, and put me to bed in my old room.

What amazed me most as I lay there crying was the intensity of Jesse's rage. It was that sort of boundless, smiting fury you'd aim at a gadget that refuses to work right just before you smash it. If she'd had a button to instantly annihilate me, I sensed, she'd have pressed it. She moved out within days into a Capital Hill apartment building owned by Stanley's brother, who gave her a major break on the rent.

My little family had ruptured. One evening soon after, Keno, who was two and a half, ran to the bathroom and pointed to my towel. "Here's Mama's towel!" he declared happily. I saw what was coming. "...and here's Mommy's – !" He looked at the bare spot where Jesse's towel had hung, bewildered. Turning to me, he asked, "Where's Mommy's towel?" I told him Mommy didn't live here anymore, but instead she had a super cool new home he was going to see in a few days. His gaze slid from mine to the carpet. "That makes me very sad," he said, with more heartfelt loss than a two-year-old should know. Later, he lay face down on the rug at my parents' house and mourned in a flat voice: "My family is dead."

For months – yes, months – I still hoped to fix everything and bring Jesse home. Dressed up I went to her apartment for a family dinner, bringing her flowers and a Matchbox 20 CD. Keno was elated to have us together. But our meal was interrupted by a phone call Jesse answered in a voice I didn't recognize, smirky like a teenager. She assured me the call had been from a sponsee, but while she was in the bathroom, I picked up her phone and saw BARBARA. She'd lied. My frantic tears frightened Keno. Jesse threw together a preposterous tale about the order in which calls showed up on her phone log.

"Stay for dessert," she said. "Please stay!" So I did. I even tried to believe the phone log bullshit.

Other nights, she came home again and slept with me. From her old spot in the bed she would assure me my fears were groundless: Barbara was a friend who provided her the faith and courage to heal her PTSD, no more. All she wanted was to get well again for the sake of our family; *I* was the one causing harm with my jealousy.

> 10/1/2003: "I went to talk with Jesse's ex-sponsor, Bradley, today. He's sure the infatuation is just a phase that will run its course. My sponsor says the same. And my cousin keeps telling me to just send her healing thoughts of love. But how long will it take? Tonight I wanted to escape so bad, to get drunk, go to a psyche ward, or just disappear."

> 10/7/03: "And now I'm waiting for Jesse to get here to spend the night with me. So I can only conclude that I am… clinging to something that isn't there? Maybe still in love? To be honest, just before the phone rang, I was trying to force myself to accept that she was probably with Barbara tonight. But then I was so happy to hear her crying to *me*, saying she can't carry her emotional burdens another minute. And I just couldn't offer her *nothing* and have her turn to Barbara, so I told her to come here. And now, I hear her at the door."

The problem, I was convinced, was all Barbara. Since I had her cell number, I'd call and leave her scathing, murderously rage-filled voicemails. I sent her emails brimming with hatred and curses. From this experience, I learned a lot about rage: venting it does not ease it. It feeds it. It pours gasoline on the flames and whips them up with the gusts of your voice. Writing in my journal, I'd feel the rage build in me to such a crescendo, tingling in all my limbs, that it seemed I could have torn Barbara limb from limb.

11/2/03: "Barbara: You took advantage of a young woman's mental illness to soak up the worship you crave. You tell yourself that simply because there is no sex involved you are within your rights to take up all her time and companionship. You ignored my pleas when I came to see you. And I HATE YOU FOR IT! I *HATE* YOU!!! I wish you *all* the suffering of *all* the families you've destroyed. Bitch, I could bash your wrinkly old face to a pulp on the sidewalk, I could keep bashing until your teeth and nose and brows were pulverized, until no amount of plastic surgery could make you even vaguely recognizable, and it would feel GOOD, every damn second of it, because you *deserve* it, you horrible, home-wrecking old cunt!"

In November, Jesse arranged to come over after Keno was asleep to tell me "the truth." She sat me down. She got very grave. And she explained to me, *not* that she and Barbara had been boffing their brains out since summer, but that lately they had, in fact, developed some degree of attraction. Wait, wait! she said. They'd both agreed, for my sake, not to act on it.

11/23/2003: "How long I must have been chopped liver in Jesse's eyes! Oh, goddess that hurts! It hurts to the deepest core of my being because that's where I love from."

Kevin had twisted and crumpled the little metal sculpture – and now I knew why. I knew what had moved Jenna to read my journal, and the shock she must have felt rounding that corner in Olympia to run into me and Theo. To love sincerely and be betrayed – nothing else cuts so deep. I couldn't stop crying. I grocery shopped while bawling, wiping the splashes from my glasses to squint at prices. I remember coming to a full stop in the Fred Meyer juice aisle, feeling as though the pain had risen to such a pitch that I simply couldn't take another step.

In a few weeks I found a receptionist job in Bellevue, although the boss often told me I could not appear at the front desk looking so tear-stained and puffy-eyed, so I'd have to switch places with the accountant. At home I gave Keno horsie back rides around the house, tears plopping onto the backs of my hands while I whinnied and crawled, hearing his happy giggles and squeals of "Giddy up, horsie!" Alone I'd sometimes kneel in classic poses of prayer, or I might make it halfway downstairs carrying the laundry basket and suddenly seize up, praying in panicked whispers. "Please, god! Send Jesse home to us! Send her home, please!" I groveled to Jesse over the phone, falling to my knees in my kitchen and saying over and over, "Please, please come home!"

There was no way I could be happy, I believed, without Jesse.

"But it is clear," says the Big Book candidly, "that we made our own misery." While in the thick of the affair, I blamed Barbara. Later, I would blame Jesse. It's taken years to recognize that I actually caused all this pain myself. What resonated inside me was the fear – or the self-loathing conviction – that I wasn't loveable. Losing Jesse to Barbara confirmed the worst accusations of my inner critics. What I lacked was the self-worth to detach, to set Jesse free to live her own life, and turn to god for guidance and strength in living mine. I chose, to an extent, to sink in that warm bath mourning and misery because I knew how to find it, and I preferred the utter self-pity it offered to the terror of admitting I had no idea how to live life for myself – with or without a partner.

I was, however, finding my way as best I could. And I didn't drink. I understood that a single drink would pull me back into the ocean of using, where I would drown. Keno needed a sober Mama.

Terrible fights broke out between me and Jesse, but so did continued overtures of reconciliation. For Thanksgiving, Jesse proposed the three of us rent a cabin at a mountain resort near Leavenworth that served a full-scale dinner so we could share the holiday as a family. Keno was overjoyed, of course. We played in the snow as a family. There was much laughter. That night Keno lay in bed between us, little hands clasping at both of us while I sang all his night-night songs. Afterwards, I crawled into a separate bed, but hoped Jesse wished otherwise.

I'd found a way to spy on Jesse's phone calls through our shared account. There I discovered that the minute she'd left my house after returning from Leavenworth, she'd phoned Barbara. My hopes that our little family was reuniting were dashed yet again. Still, I wouldn't give up. That little family seemed all I had.

But it wasn't. In truth, Keno and I had a much, much bigger family. I'd just turned my back on them, is all.

~

I'd long since quit going to AA meetings where I had friends. Most were in the hipster hoods of Capital Hill, about half an hour's drive from my house. As a Flailing Panic mom, it was quicker for me to just pop into an AA meeting up the street and sit with kindly older folks who never said fuck. But one friend from the hipster meetings had refused to let me drop. Brent called me regularly and urged me to come try out a large, podium-format meeting on the hill – one that provided childcare for Keno.

I was reluctant. I'd become such a hermit in the past three years that I didn't remember how to socialize, especially with scenesters. I didn't see how struggling to make conversation and remember names was going to make anything better, but Brent insisted. He told me this meeting drew a lot of hot lesbians. He even picked Keno and me up so I wouldn't have to find the place myself.

Walking into the meeting was like entering a "This Is Your Life" game. Again and again, people approached me with open arms. "Where the fuck have you *been*?" or "Holy shit! Last time I saw you, this lil' dude was in your stomach!" or just "Lou-eeeee-zahh!!!" Struggling to remember names but sure of all these faces, I couldn't believe I'd somehow convinced myself none of them cared. They hadn't chased after me, no. I needed to reach out. But now that they could see the grief written all over my face – some even knew the story – they were ready to support me.

By the time the meeting started, about 150 alcoholics sat in rows of folding chairs facing the podium. Each speaker tagged the next. About mid-way through, a woman from the old golden-era Drunks R Us tagged me. Brent signed encouragement, and I walked down the aisle to the podium.

After eight and half years in AA, I knew only one thing to do: speak my truth. In front of that group, I shared what I felt – that my partner of nine years had dumped me for someone new. My deepest love had been chucked. I virtually sprayed the front rows with tears and mucus. In fact, many didn't know what to make of me. Some perhaps felt my share was inappropriate, that I should keep my focus on alcohol and not force the meeting to play therapist. But those who knew me opened their hearts to me, as did many strangers. I saw it in their eyes.

When the meeting ended, many people came up to hug me. Among them was a guy I'd never seen before, a six-foot, muscular young man with a shaved head and earrings who reminded me of Mr. Clean. He introduced himself simply as John – John Church, I learned later. He looked at me squarely and said, "You're going to be all right. It took a lot of courage to share what you did, but that's how we heal." He asked politely if he could give me a hug, and I assented. He was very large, and his hug made me feel very small.

But Brent had been right about the hot lesbians. There was a British punk girl who caught my eye, so I returned the following week dressed up for her. Nothing came of it, except that I became a regular at that meeting and soon began attending others.

One night, walking in with Keno on my hip, I saw Stanley sitting alone amid the rows of chairs. Jesse had always claimed he was on her side, so I'd dreaded seeing him, but as he rose to greet me with tears in his eyes I saw that he'd suffered every bit as much as I. Even more, perhaps: he'd dropped a lot of weight and his face looked strained and gaunt. We hugged each other without a word. Once we started talking, though, we couldn't stop. When the meeting began, we sequestered ourselves in the church kitchen and carried on in whispers. Stanley's eyes seemed unnaturally wide, and I'd never seen him so hyper.

He'd been researching sexual obsession, he explained. They were high as kites, the both of them, on forbidden sex. When I corrected him with Jesse's sworn assurance that they'd *not* acted on their attraction, Stanley laughed out loud.

"And I thought *I* was crazy!" he had trouble keeping his voice low. "Oh my god! You don't know Barbara like I do!"

Talking the next day over the phone, Stanley convinced me they'd been having sex for months. He told how he'd stumbled on his daughter's email, forwarding Barbara's account of the fireworks kiss in May. He told of a night Barbara came in at 3:00 AM "singing like she was on cloud nine" and fresh from a shower. He *knew* Barbara high on sex, he claimed, and that was her.

I stood in my living room absorbing this – the denial that held my world together falling to rubble around me. Orange speckles shrouded my eyesight while the rug's patterns seemed to rear up at me. I didn't actually faint, but came close enough to have to squat and drop my head. I was forced to see: my little dream family – Mama, Mommy, and baby – was gone. I shook and my voice shook. I had to get off the phone.

Could Jesse be an outright liar? The rock of my early sobriety around whom I'd built my life, that woman of honesty and honor – did she exist only in my mind? Was it possible the real Jesse had been cheating for months now, having sex with both *me* and *Barbara*? Had I kissed lips and tongue that were recently…?

Jesus. I had.

But I was still in the mode of grieving. All this will perhaps seem quite maudlin and self-indulgent if you've never had the experience of being dumped for another by someone you loved for many years and trusted implicitly. But if you've experienced losing your world in that way, you'll know exactly the pain I'm describing. I didn't know how to let go and move on. I'd get up in the middle of the night as if our bed were one of nails and, with nowhere to go, stumble around the house holding my guts in. If Keno was at Jesse's, I'd straight up howl as loudly as I could, again and again. I didn't care what the neighbors heard. "Kevin, Jenna, I'm so sorry! I'm so sorry!" I wailed more than once. Kelsey, my coyote mix, would follow me silently. If I sat down to bawl, she'd lie down such that we were touching, her back against my calf or her paw placed on top of my foot.

Of course Jesse denied everything: Stanley was a damn liar. Okay, maybe she *had* kissed Barbara *after* she moved out in September – but certainly never in May.

My first step out of victimhood wasn't very pretty. The alternative, I thought then, was to claim the right to judge and punish others. I'd make Barbara writhe! Writing was something I did well, so I composed a lengthy letter to their law firm accusing Barbara of recruiting Jesse out of sexual interest. It opened: "Dear Mr. Cressman: I do not believe Horton, Franks, & Smith condones the recruitment of young, attractive paralegals for the sake of sexual pursuit, but I must tell you that this is tragically the case with your manager, Barbara Richardson, and my former life partner of nine years, Jesse Parker." I wove in plenty of sarcastic references to Barbara's age and horniness and snail mailed copies to everyone in her department and the firm's director. The plan worked fabulously! Though a loyal coworker gathered up all the copies in the department, the one to the director got through. Barbara called Stanley from a sidewalk payphone, screaming that her career was *ruined*!

When he described her rage and pain, I gloated with delight. My AA sponsor, on the other hand, was aghast: nothing could flout the principles of AA worse than what I'd done. She would have fired me if her own sponsor hadn't forbidden it: this Louisa woman was so clearly out of her mind, the grandsponsor said, she needed help now more than ever.

But as wrong as the direction of that step had been, after the bang of vindictiveness wore off, I began, slowly, to take steps in the opposite and right direction – the direction of healing. As ardently as I'd prayed my instructions to god to send Jesse back, now I prayed to be healed. "Please, please," I'd cry-whisper in my bed or car or the shower, "take my pain, goddess! I can't do this. I can't live." God, unfortunately, didn't do jack shit, so my eyes started drifting to the top of my bureau, which was by now littered with a dozen crumpled phone numbers people in meetings had scrawled for me. I looked at them. And the night finally came when my pain grew unbearable enough to start me dialing.

It wasn't easy. When your sinuses seem packed with concrete and you have absolutely nothing to say – except "I hurt! I'm alone! Help me!" – reaching out to people you hardly know isn't exactly glamorous. No, it's the ultimate vulnerability, and it requires a magic spiritual ingredient: humility. You *invite* compassion. You acknowledge that you need it, that others have it to give, that you are connected in your humanness by this give-and-take of love. All my life, my one and only friend, the only person I had ever called just to talk, had been Rosemary. Now, slowly, the acquaintances I called began to become friends. They began to invite me out, to include me in get-togethers. At meetings, my shares held back nothing. People who'd never even met me knew my struggle. I remember my start of surprise when a heavily tattooed construction worker pointed me out in a crowded meeting. "And this lady here," he said, "is the most honest fucking human being I've ever heard in my life! I need that kind of courage to share what's goin' on in *me*."

Courage? What courage? I was a wreck.

By the time I turned nine years sober that January, my fellow drunks had handed me two major chunks of wisdom. Bradley, Jesse's former sponsor, told me: "Some day, all this pain you're in now will help you help others." The second insight I didn't like so much. Cardboard Box Tony, an old-timer who'd lived insane on the streets for years, told me squarely: "There's nothing Jesse's done to you that you haven't done to her in equal measure."

How could *that* be true?! I'd harmed *others* in the same ways Jesse harmed me, yes, that I knew. But how had I lied to her, betrayed her, manipulated her as selfishly as she had me? I simply couldn't see it. Yet.

A lawyer advised me that, since Jesse was a good parent, on Keno's birth certificate, and earned more money than I did, any battle for full custody would cost at least a hundred thousand dollars with little chance of change from our current 50/50 agreement. So I found myself a half-time mom, single and alone for the first time in twenty-six years. Gradually, in little spurts, I began to accept that my house was *mine* – not *ours* – as was my car, my clothes, the food in my cupboards. You can't imagine how revolutionary a concept that felt to me – unless you, too have lived as a serial monogamist and had to quit cold turkey. I hadn't been single for more than two months since I walked into Clayton's dorm room more than twenty-five years before. I had no idea who I was outside a *we*.

What could I possibly do with all this empty time when Jesse had Keno? What had I ever done? Tentatively at first, I took my seat beneath the spider's ceiling spot and began to write again. Poems at first, then little stories and essays. For so many years I'd longed for the solitude to write, but now I felt terrified of actually having all the solitude I could want.

> 3/28/04: "I dreamed of looking out at the view from my parents' house, hearing the scream of jets airplanes and seeing bombs falling and blasting up the shallows of Portage Bay – more and more bombs decimating the whole landscape. I knew nothing could ever bring back life as it had once been, as I had known it.
>
> "But then last night, after the meeting, I went to a party at Stanley's for March AA birthdays, where I met lots of newcomers and medium-comers, and Stanley himself was overjoyed to see me. I prayed with Faye before we went up to see the bed where Barbara used to sleep while she and Jesse were falling in lust. Where Barbara picks up her mail, Stanley keeps a framed photo of Jesse, Keno, and me. He says it's just by coincidence.
>
> "It felt so healing to be there, among some who knew me and some just coming to know me. A gathering full of life and attempts toward Goodness. I pray god to let the love in AA carry me toward new hope and purpose as Louisa in the world, seeking the light and path of Good."

That prayer, like all the others, god answered in ways I never expected.

In Leavenworth for a hopeful Thanksgiving;
Keno a few weeks after the break-up

24: I TURN STRAIGHT (AGAIN); HUGE 9TH WEIRD THING (PART B)

God is to be found in the darkness, not away from it...

> -Sandra Cronk
> *Dark Night Journey*

Practicing the Flailing Panic Method of parenting day after day had drained away all my sexy. Fellow FPM moms know how utterly exhausting is that ceaseless obstacle course of diaper bags, changings, car seats, bagged snacks, fatal disaster prevention, and nap schedules, that has to be run while you're constantly sleep deprived, anxiety-ridden, and hormonally out of sorts. Desire simply left me. In terms of priority, sex was right up there with perfecting my handstands. In the months when Jesse's attraction first strayed to Barbara, I'd been carrying about fifteen spare pounds, and, trust me, I didn't wear them well.

If anyone could harness the power of jealousy in a weight loss program, they'd make a fortune. To Barbara I owe many things, but among them is the family gym membership Jesse purchased, which included free childcare. I worked out several days a week, tearfully at first but eventually, after we'd separated, with increasing confidence. My abdominal muscles had split apart into a pair of suspenders during late pregnancy; my doctor cautioned that I'd risk a hernia if I worked them too hard. In fact, the first time I tried an abdominal machine, a lengthwise bulge of guts poked out of my stomach from sternum to crotch like a backwards dinosaur ridge. I did three reps before I called it good, and I'll tell you, those muscles sang like dying opera queens for about three days. But I was patient. The more I worked them, the narrower the bulge got – though it still shows up in certain exercises.

Gradually, I got my groove back. Identity and energy returned. One day I gathered up a bunch of Jesse's stuff and, cranking the

Beatles' "Get Back," set it in front of the house. Rain started. I responded to her upset voicemail, "If ya don't like it, come n' get it!" Also during this time, I made up a rule similar to Theo's "Fourteen Things" poem, that *any* time I caught myself romanticizing Jesse's memory, going into that minor key trance of loss and longing, I *had* to sing Gloria Gaynor's "I Will Survive" aloud from beginning to end. Walking the dogs in parks she and I used to frequent always brought back happy memories. Remember how Jesse used to— Aw, dammit! Here we go again: *At first I was afraid, I was petrified...* I can't tell you how sick of that song I got! But the dread of singing it worked like operant conditioning, and my thoughts began to avoid the track.

Having worn nothing but Jesse hand-me-downs for years to compensate for her compulsive buying, now I hit up Goodwill for all kinds of form-fitting sweaters and jeans. My neighbor, a former Playboy model who'd narrowly survived a plane crash and transformed into a wholesome lesbian mom, came over to give me blonde highlights and a cute haircut for free. She threw in an hour-long pep talk about how cute and sexy I was – which was much needed. For about a month I'd had a profile up on a queer internet dating site, but hadn't responded to any messages. Now, at forty-three, I began to date.

During the first four months of 2004 I met for coffee or food with half a dozen lesbians, some more attractive than others. The first was a local pianist who'd lied about her age (Google tagged her at fifty), had two lovers already (who knew about each other), and reminded me of Kevin's wrinkled aunt. Note to self: no first date dinners, because you're stuck for at least an hour. Next was a pretty young thing so passionate about dogs that just the *thought* of them made her sob in the midst of our coffee. Another was a pixie-cut, foundation-masked businesswoman who reminded me of my mother's museum friends. Obviously, the suburban cop had munched *many* a donut since her profile pics were taken. None of these women raised the faintest spark of attraction. Then along came a beautiful woman of my exact age, slim and graceful, with luxurious auburn hair, clear dark eyes, and a killer smile. She also had oodles of money and had adopted a pigtailed little girl of color just a few years older than Keno. After two dates, she seemed very interested.

Yet even for this babe, I could muster no spark. What could be *wrong* with me? I remember checking out her ass as we walked Green Lake with our kids. It was a perfectly nice ass, yet the prospect of seeing it without sweatpants spiked alarm in me. When she came over to my house and sat it on my couch beside mine, that unease escalated. I found myself jumping up to do things again and again – to the point where kissing became out of the question. She sighed with that insight and eventually I had to confirm her intuition; I *wanted* to be interested, but for some reason I wasn't!

Maybe what I needed was just a take-charge butch. I contacted a small, wiry dyke who worked construction machinery for the city. She was also in AA and messaged that she'd noticed me years before at meetings. We met for coffee, and she was kind of cute. When we parted, sure enough she grabbed me, kissed me, and was gone. Wow. Disturbing, but flattering. I liked being wanted. The only problem was, I was taller than she. I didn't like that.

A day or two later, I was trying to re-finish the bathroom that Jesse had torn up because it was tacky. Cranking the radio with my handsaw miter box out on the sunny deck, I was cutting one-by-fours for molding, feeling butchly capable and musing about my upcoming second date with the little construction dyke.

Halfway through a board, I took a break to check email. There was something from Jesse – a response to my earlier assertion that I was too sick of her lying to even look at her:

4/28/2004: FROM: Jesse Perkins, TO: Louisa P.:
"It seems you need to hear about two things before you can start your healing process. I'm going to tell you everything. It is true I kissed Barbara before she left for Hawaii."

Before Hawaii meant May. Scanning further down, I read that they'd "messed around" all summer. Without any emotion I could identify, something snapped inside me. In spite of everything Stanley had told me, I'd chosen to believe Jesse that there had been no sex until after she moved out in September. I don't know if you've ever been lied to about something that really mattered to you, but something major happens when you find out you've been duped. The new truth pulls your old, trusted truth out from under you not like a rug, but like a world. Like the earth. What you thought life held, it did not. What you had steered by was never there. Disillusionment is a violent process. The hundred little scenes I carried from that summer, all the things we'd done trying to "heal," the little stories I'd shared about my day, the meals I cooked, the jokes I made, my bleaching my hair to avoid triggering

PTDS memories of her brunette step mom – all these scenes came back interspersed with imagined ones of the two liars grappling and cumming together. *Snap!* goes your faith in life itself.

At the computer, I stayed dry-eyed and outwardly calm, except that my heart began to pound. I found I could not read text. I got up and returned to the sunny deck. I knelt and resumed sawing the board I hadn't finished. And by the time that board clattered to the deck, I had fallen in love with a man.

That big, strong, shaved head man who had hugged me at the podium meeting – I wanted him. John Church. I wanted him to wrap his kind arms around me and hold me, where I'd feel small, and safe, and protected forever. If I didn't get him, I would die.

Somewhere in sawing that board, I turned straight. Personally, I think the world's categorizations of gay and straight and bi (and for that matter most of male and female) are contrived. For fourteen years, I'd had reasons for loving women. I don't know if that made me "gay." But the feeling of surrender I wanted now, to the safe harbor of a loving man – the very notion of it had repulsed and infuriated me throughout all my days of dykedom. Even with Theo, I'd wanted nothing to do with that. But John Church would save me. He was strong and good.

I gave up sawing and paced about the house with my heart still pounding – a condition that would continue for almost a month. John Church! John Church! How could I get him? I called the butch dyke and canceled our next date, not even caring that she was pissed. John Church. How could I get him?

About one month prior to this, at the party Stanley threw for March AA Birthdays, one of those people "just coming to know me" had been John Church. I'd shown up in some tight clothes that got me noticed by a number of men, and he had asked if I might give him a ride home.

When we were alone in my car, he said, "You know, Louisa, a lot of my closest friendships with women start off with a bout of attraction. And I get the feeling you and I are gonna be good friends, because— What I'm saying is, you have a nice shape, and I'm not the only one who noticed it tonight."

Embarrassment flooded me. How dare this guy talk about my "shape"! Especially enclosed in my car, a place where people make out. I snapped at him with unmistakable castigation: "Yeah, well I'm a lesbian, and I've been one for fourteen years!"

He laughed, completely at ease. "I *know* you're a lesbian! If you *weren't* a lesbian, I'd probably have tried something subtler – I hope! I'm just saying, that's all. How 'bout you try just taking the compliment?"

Again, I was flattered but flustered. He was wrecking my spiritual, fellowshippy groove and I couldn't wait to get him the hell out of my car. He asked me to pull over by a fancy building, the very place Kevin had wanted us to live, that old, converted hotel I'd kept saying was "lovely." When he waved goodbye, I thought, phew!

What a fool I'd been! I thought now. I should have pounced on him right that minute! Now, at least, I knew where to find him. So what I did was, I composed a note. It took several versions to strike the right balance of flirting and friendliness. I asked him to call me so we could meet for coffee, maybe after the podium meeting. Then I jumped in my car, drove across town to his place, and had to wait outside at least twenty minutes until someone came out of the building and let me in. In the lobby, one of the many dozen mailboxes was so overstuffed it had bits of mail poking out. I pulled something out, tearing it, and sure enough found John's roommate's name. Now came the slow process of feeding my note into the crack at the top of the mailbox.

Done! The trap was laid! Now, we just wait.

I drove home mad with elation. But wait – what if he'd found himself a girlfriend since last week?! I prayed and prayed, "Don't let him have found a girlfriend – pulleeeeze, god! I need him! I need him!"

The following entry tells of later that same day.

4/29/2004: "Yesterday I picked up Keno from daycare and it was a glorious day. I carried him on my back to the green field high above the water at Carkeek, where we sat on a bench facing the sun, which was glowing bright off the water, and threw the stick for the doggies. I told him to look for a dandelion to blow, and he ran off to the far extreme of the field and into someone's yard. I had to chase him down, but I couldn't get mad. I offered to blow up his yellow balloon so it would zizz over the grass for Sydney to chase. This we did for some time, Keno laughing with delight, running to try and grab it first. It was beautiful. I was aware how lucky I am.

"But I longed so much for John Church to be there. I hungered for him. Why? What has happened to me? Suddenly I am just as obsessed with him as I ever was with Theo! It's as though all this time my obsession has been hovering, waiting, until suddenly a target appeared: John Church. I want desperately to sleep with him. I [put a note in his mailbox], and when I came home and found no message I couldn't believe it and plunged from a high of sex and love and future camping trips and sharing the island cabin, down to tortured, lonesome ruin.

"How can I have a life as rich as the one I've been given and feel it's not enough without the selected someone? If John had been there, I could not have been with Keno and the dogs in the same way. Why don't I love myself enough to give *me* the kind of glowing love I feel from obsession?

"I have to trust Goddess. Goddess, I want love.

"Oh, now it is 10:00 and my chosen one has not called! Maybe they didn't check the mail."

As it turned out, they didn't check it for almost a week, and then finally, on the afternoon of the podium meeting, John called. I'd been unable to sleep for fantasizing nonstop, even though I couldn't quite remember what he looked like. All I remembered clearly was that hug. What I really hungered for, I can tell you today, was god's love – the energy of god's love that had passed through John's hug as he wished me healing from a place of love. My little brain had decided it had came from *him*, whoever the hell he was, and I was on a mission to find more.

Once again, god used my codependence to lead me toward the next step of wellness. As Jesse had led me to sobriety, John would teach me how to love my fellow human beings. From him I discovered how it feels to channel god energy to others without thought of return – which answered all my prayers and changed my life forever.

He invited me to the apartment for fish tacos before the meeting. I accepted, dressing hot and planning to proposition him as soon as I could get him alone. There seemed no point in slogging through all that "fall in love" bullshit of getting to know each other gradually, growing closer and more attracted, then finally kissing like it was a big deal. Whatever. I knew now that all that romance stuff was nothing but some fucking movie bullshit. Why was it bullshit? I never slowed down enough to articulate it to myself, but my reasoning ran thus: If even the most loyal love can be exposed as a worthless delusion, then intimacy itself must be worthless. Why not just cut to the chase?

> 5/5/2004: "When I first saw John, I worried I'd made a mistake and would have to backpedal. He was cooking and shy and hardly looked at me, and he looked different than I remembered. He had on a big baggy shirt and for a while I worried he might be fat. But I told myself to calm down and see if he didn't grow on me, which did happen.
>
> "After the meeting we went out to the B&O. I kind of knew if I spoke up we'd be in bed soon, but I didn't know *how* soon. All I know is, he seemed kind and aware of my pain, and I thought I could trust him enough to have sex. I felt lonely, I told him, for physical companionship, which he responded was only natural. After I verified that he was old enough [thirty-six on his driver's license], I asked if he'd like to come over to my house, and we went. Things did go quite a bit faster than I'd have liked. I mean, we made out on the couch for about fifteen seconds, literally, before he jumped up and said, 'Let's go upstairs!' which was emblematic of how little we knew each other [there *being* no upstairs]. He didn't even know my last name. But I'd bought condoms; I made it happen.
>
> "In the morning I despaired, thinking I'd misjudged and that he had no affection for me. But then I remembered how, when we were sleeping together in my bed, several times he gave me little tiny kisses on my shoulder. They seemed to echo in that empty cavern where my heart used to be. They seemed to come from sweetness."

That same day I left with Keno on a trip to visit my friends from Vassar: Elizabeth, who lived in Boston, and Allie, who was in the country for a short stint. I'd recently quit my receptionist job because my boss was a coke fiend and megalomaniac who read private emails and had the entire office bugged. So before I started looking for a new job, I decided to blow all my frequent flyer miles to see my old friends.

The stable, mellowed, married lives of Elizabeth and Allie mirrored what mine might have looked like if I'd settled down with Kevin. By contrast, I was living some wacky *Alice in the Lava*

Lamp tale, filled with nonsense scenes of near madness. Elizabeth and Allie could only vaguely relate to my hysterical infatuation with a man I knew virtually nothing about, while my naïve questions about men in general must have struck them as child-like. I typed John heavy, heartfelt emails from Elizabeth's computer, which he answered with hesitant, regretful ones.

> 5/2/2004: FROM: John Church, TO: Louisa P.
> "I do question whether it was the right thing for us to do. We're both vulnerable, scared, lonely, and – oh, yeah – horny. It made perfect sense to me last night that we should have sex, but I can't help sending mixed signals because I don't know what the fuck I'm doing. I'm trying to walk this 'Spiritual Path' but totally prone to temptations of the flesh. I don't know what to make of this. I am confused. Yet I don't feel terribly bad about it. Honestly, it feels like progress. What a mind-fuck. I hope this doesn't freak you out. I am really trying to be straight with you."

I responded with many voluminous emails about every single thing I did and thought while in Boston.

When I got back, I dressed in my sexiest Goodwill outfit – a low-cut yellow sweater, floral mini-skirt, and spike heels – drove to his building, and climbed that grand staircase Kevin had liked so much. At the top stood John with his arms folded. The closer I got, the more I could see his expression was all wrong. He looked... fatherly. He gave me a pat-pat hug nothing like the engulfing squeeze he'd offered when we first met, and we left for lunch. At an outdoor place, over iced tea, he gave me the axe.

"I talked to my sponsor. And then I talked to another guy who's not actually my sponsor, but whose program I respect. And they agreed it would not be right for me to..." he paused for the right word, "*capitalize* on this situation. Because the fact is, Louisa, you're not well."

He looked at me squarely. He just sat there with those words on the table between us and waited for my response. What I'd heard was something different. More like, "The fact is, you're nuts, and I'm not getting saddled with some crazy-ass bitch acting out on me just because I screwed her."

I tried to appear the acme of sanity. I explained that I was not asking him for anything but companionship (sex). I didn't want any gifts (payment) or commitments (marriage.) All I was asking was for him to please – and here I started to cry – not shut me out.

My crying upset him instantly. "Y'see," he said, slightly aggravated, "all this is my fault. I fucked up; I already fucked up. I saw a chance and I jumped on it, because that's what guys do. What I'm trying to do now is minimize the damage. Certainly you're a desirable woman, Louisa. There is no doubt of that. But you're also a woman in a shitload of pain right now, and you're trying to find a shortcut out of it – just like booze or drugs. And I..." he hesitated again. He could sense I was still upset by the unwell stuff. "I don't believe it's God's will for me to participate in that."

I was devastated. My only relief from emptiness came in motion and progress, and his words had placed roadblocks in front and on all sides of me. There was nowhere to go. There was no way to live. I could only insist.

"You don't know God's will for you."

"In this case, I'm thinking I might. I'd like to be your friend."

I kept arguing, but I tried to do it by sex appeal rather than harangue, so as not to seem too much the crazy-ass bitch. I leaned forward in a hello-cleavage pose and gave him my most fetching, big eyed look. "Can I just ask you this? To keep an open mind about... us?"

"Mmnnn... No. I don't think so."

"Wouldn't that be 'contempt prior to investigation'?"

"No. More like, 'we let God discipline us.'"

"Well, I'm asking you, anyway," I said, sitting back. "Let's just see what happens."

That, he did agree to – meaning he was not going to change his mind. And I agreed as well – meaning I'd pursue him relentlessly until I bagged him.

~

I continued to throw myself at John all summer and well into the next year. Here was sexual addiction every bit as consuming as with Theo. Except that *this* time around, I was sober. Crazy, sure – but sober crazy. At first I scared him. For one thing, I knew nothing of heterosexual protocol. Lesbians call each other whenever they feel like it – it's a two-way street. So when John would say, "I'll call you tomorrow," I'd remind him of Keno's nap schedule and suggest optimal windows. Then, if he failed to call or if Keno went down at a different time, I'd call to let him know. He often didn't pick up, so I'd try again later and leave another message. Why not?

One of the sober girls I'd befriended, Jaki, tried to teach me heterosexual etiquette. "I *won't* call a guy, period. It's a matter of honor." I couldn't believe straight people still played all those stupid, gender-based courtship games! It seemed like something out of a Patty Duke show or Rapunzel hanging out in her tower. Jaki also informed me that all guys preferred long hair, whether they knew it or not. Period. End of discussion. As of that day I started growing mine out, pathetically thin as it was, and have worn it that way ever since.

I borrowed *Mars vs. Venus* from another friend to study up on male patterns of thinking. I took notes. I really did, 'cause I was gonna crack this case. Men like to solve problems. They like to lead and be followed. They feel successful when they make a woman "happy," but any direction from the woman implies their way is wrong. Weirdly enough, John fit every stereotype in the book.

Still other women explained to me the practice of bikini waxing, which had somehow caught on while I was busy being gay. I'd never heard of it. My underarms hadn't been shaved in over a decade, so they felt itchy now. In all aspects of being a hetero girlie-girl, I was a beginner all over again.

So it was that, to snag me a John Church, I morphed yet again. My new guise: Slightly Slutty AA Cougar. I bought tight mini-skirts, more tight jeans and sweaters, along with my first push-up bra. Now I wore make-up daily and sometimes did my nails badly and rarely left the house in flat shoes.

Unfortunately, I'd also started therapy with a new counselor, Richard, who strongly discouraged my infatuation.

> 7/1/2004: "Richard spanked me so soundly for trying to 'overturn' John's stand on being my friend. He seemed to say I was exerting self-will and trying to run the show and manipulate things into what I want, which he has articulated as wanting John to want me more than I want John himself. He sees me causing harm for the sake of my ego, salving my pains and insecurities with a quick fix at the expense of another, rather than living my own life with integrity and independence."

Live my own life?! Ha! As easily said as "drink less."

Gradually, I refined my approach. Sure enough, if I waited long enough, John would call and propose we do something. Even if he didn't, he seemed more receptive to my calls if I spaced them out. Over the next year I filled an entire *volume* of a journal with John Church obsession. But these entries are far from being re-runs of Theo entries. The game had grown far too old, too apparent. Just as with my self-bondage obsession and then with drinking, I'd long since passed the point of contempt for this compulsion, such an obvious mechanism for escaping pain.

5/29/2004: "Do you know what a huge waste of time it is being infatuated? All the minutes spent staring into space, all the narrating internally various captivating anecdotes from my life? All the hoping and build-up around opportunities to see him at meetings (dressed right, looking fabulous) that don't come to pass because he's not even there, all for nothing?

"I keep on with the illusion because letting go seems to mean falling backwards into the dark churning sea of my own worthlessness. There's nothing to grab, not even a flimsy reed. Only me with no 'other' to focus on pleasing, no direction in which to point my energies, no grade, no hope, no promising nirvana of success.

"That, I realize, is Life as I have no clue how to live it."

7/5/2004: "This has nothing to do with love. I'm more like a desperate salesman giving out self-samples and trying to woo and persuade the customer to want the whole package – me. Read my new published story! Listen to this amazing music I'm cultured enough to know about! And when you have a sense of how deep and artsy and sensitive I am, elevate me, admire me, so I can feel okay in your eyes!"

Even bigger differences this time, besides my being sober, distinguished John from Theo. John genuinely enjoyed my company; he was happy to sit with me at meetings and even came to admire what I articulated in shares, leaving work early to attend when I was chairing. He came over to my house and helped cook for my birthday party barbeque. He came to a gathering at the island cabin, and we often went out with others for fellowship after meetings. Another major difference from Theo: John was celibate. He refused me, not because he had better women to pork, but because he was trying to do what was right. This may sound like wishful caca, but it's not: parallel to my reflexive, compulsive infatuation with him, I learned to love him genuinely as a friend and fellow alcoholic, the same way he loved me:

> 7/1/2004: "I guess in a weird way we *are* in a relationship. It's just not a sexual one. We do have intimate encounters, but they're just about talking and sharing thoughts, or my giving him a silly birthday present, or him fixing something for me. He said, 'I wish you could see yourself the way I see you.' And I said the same to him. We have a kind of love. We do.

> 7/15/2004: "On the phone Tuesday, I had called him upset and asked, 'Do I call you too much? Am I a pest?' He said, 'You don't call me too much; I like to have someone call me. I don't call you back because I'm an irresponsible crackhead.' At the end of the phone call, he told me he loved me. He said we had our own weird, unique fucked-upness. And I said, 'I love you, too, John, in our own weird, unique, fucked up way.'"

This was the summer I entered what the Big Book calls the fourth dimension of existence. I exerted myself in all the right directions – taking action that would heal and transform me – for all the wrong reasons. I had during this period two states of being: times when the infatuation killed the pain of loss, and times when it did not. During those windows of remembering, the pain was excruciating. My little family of three, that I'd so deeply loved and believed in, was no more. The loss revealed an emptiness so vast, I simply *had* to do something to fill it – but what?! In AA I'd heard again and again that service to others works when all else fails. I saw it was my only option for getting out of myself.

One night, feeling rejected by John because he'd shown interest in some other girl, I "cried over the cruelty of it." But I also prayed desperately, reading and rereading the Saint Francis prayer, asking god to show me where I might bring light. The Fix-It-Guy from the summer cabin island, Tom Weiss, who had worked on our place since I was a teen and been recently diagnosed with incurable cancer – a whimsical, kind man who'd accepted and supported me with kind interest throughout all the stages of my life – popped into my mind.

> 5/16/2004: "Then I thought of Tom Weiss with cancer – he's been given 'til September to live. I thought I would go out to the island in the morning and see if I could be helpful to him. So I packed up, and Keno and I came down here to the cabin.
>
> "Called Tom Weiss. Went over. Ended up spending time alone with his wife and having an extremely honest and heartfelt conversation with her. I felt so familiar with grief, so immune to awkwardness. She told me everyone else pretended Tom would get well; no one else had let her be honest, speak her fears of being alone."

I remember that afternoon, the way an emaciated but warmly joking Tom led Keno out to meet their baby chicks, leaving me and his wife alone. I remember the silence in that small room cluttered with found shells and yellowing photos, how long I let it extend, on and on. Silence: so much more than people ordinarily let happen – in the calmness of knowing idle chit-chat was the last thing this woman needed. Let her choose, I thought. And when at last she spoke, it was of what was actually inside her. "I can't imagine," she said simply, "his not being here anymore." The honor of that trust – it felt like a zenith of human privilege. In moments like that, time slows down. In place of social awkwardness comes the smooth simplicity of knowing there is nothing either human has to hide or fake. We listened. We spoke. We sat in the same room with love and death and acknowledged both unflinchingly. I'd never felt so close to god or life's purpose.

But what about my sick half? As soon as I was on the ferry home, or heck, in the car driving back to the cabin, I began to imagine how I'd describe the experience to John, showing him what a deep and spiritual person I was. The torture, the humiliation of planning to whore out for infatuation chips what had been a pure and genuine experience – it's beyond description.

> 5/17/2004: "I'd felt so happy to be alive, to kiss a baby chicken. But now all I think of is sharing it in an AA meeting, using it to woo John as I wooed the chain of others before him. It cheapens experience, this letting my obsession use things of real value for some ego-driven

plan to impress others, to feel valued by my designated demi-god – who is now John."

It was like having a nervous tic. I hated it, but I couldn't stop it. Sure, a good man was losing his life, but look how spiritual Louisa got talking to his wife! (What's that Merton quote at the opening of this book? "Teach me to bear a humility that shows me, without ceasing, that I am a liar and a fraud…")

But at other times, I dove into the relief of infatuation without a fight. Even in these times, though, god lured me toward healing in ways I knew nothing of, the way chasing a fake bunny leads a greyhound to exert itself in speed and grace. John was thoroughly committed to the program of AA because, as a former crackhead, his life depended on it. Infatuation told me the best way to win John's admiration was to work as outstanding an AA program I could, becoming known in our community. It was worth a shot. If I could grow to become a profound enough spiritual giant, maybe he'd fuck me.

So I went to countless AA meetings in search of him, almost every night of the week. Half the time he wasn't there, but I'd end up connecting with a number of hurting drunks anyway. My shares attracted sponsees crippled with all sorts of emotional pain and difficulties. One or two damn near terrified me with their craziness, but even so I met with them weekly to read the book, and so learned to love them quirks and all. To further impress John, I took on all kinds of service work, making coffee, setting up chairs, answering phones at the Intergroup office or routed to my home in the middle of the night. I went out for fellowship, showed up at parties, hosted movie nights, played board games, went swimming, tossed Frisbees, and ventured Truth or Dare with sober drunks I'd not known even a week before. Strippers, hookers, drug dealers, and meth chefs, plus embezzlers, burglars, and armed robbers, all of them striving to change their lives, working at blue collar or retail jobs and going to meetings to learn how to live – these people became my closest friends.

Gradually, I shed the last vestiges of my ingrained P. family snobbery, coming to grasp not just with my mind but with my heart that academia is *not* what educates people. Living life, loving deeply, losing painfully, and struggling to get back on our feet – these are our true teachers, and many people of great wisdom – as John was then – have no high school diploma. Staying removed from the smells of humanity, taking refuge in a private sanctuary or ivory tower – those were conditions that sharply raised one's risk of head-up-ass disease. I'd had a whopping case for many years.

It never occurred to me that by shifting my values, by unlearning what I had been overtly or tacitly taught while growing up, I was breaking loyalty to my old clan – the clan of the P. family – in a way that would eventually blow up in my face. Of course, the P.s knew nothing about camaraderie from steerage to captain's table, nothing about a way out, or working all sides of the triangle. So when they saw my behavior changing, they tried to interpret my motives based on the old criteria. Signals of disapproval came back to me only faintly at first: *Louisa must think befriending all these nobodies makes her a somebody. She's really scraping the bottom of the barrel, just so she can fancy herself popular; why else would she surround herself with such scummy people?*

Convicts, whores, and drug dealers – these were bad people with or without addiction, not the kind you invited into your life. We were supposed to distinguish ourselves from the masses, not join them!

> 5/26/2004: "I try to believe God smashed my old life because it was limiting. I need to change my whole approach to living, which has been to cocoon with my partner. God is forcing me to reach out for companionship. I fear rejection and failure and embarrassment, but I need to trust God and offer what I have. I've always felt love for people as they share in AA. I'm able to see their innate Goodness. But then, when I get up to talk with them, my old fear and self-consciousness kick in and I close up, hiding inside. So often I've shared to newcomers that all you can do is offer your good intentions, give what you have in the spirit of packing into the stream of life – and God smiles upon it."

There came a pivotal Saturday night that summer, a rite of passage in learning to love others, when John's non-deliberate teachings altered my perspective forever. It was an epiphany I've shared many times in meetings, but it remains my truth.

I asked John to grab a late dinner with me after the podium meeting, hoping to lure him into bed so he'd fall in love with me – just for a change. He said sure, but that he wanted us to go to the post-meeting fellowship restaurant to see who else showed up. On our way there, I kept trying to tell him some fascinating story about me, which he kept interrupting as we passed various people from the meeting. Each time John would put out his hand, ask sincerely how they were doing, then invite them to join us. The first of these I thought was too cool a hipster for us, but he responded kindly, chatting a bit. The second I thought was too crazy, but she did the same. The third I thought a dull loser, but his warm gratitude made me ashamed. I was touched to see how easily John broke through each person's protective bubble and stirred their unique spirit into play, as if he saw their soul and not the slew of labels I attached to them. Yeah, that was great and everything, except I wanted John's attention all to myself. Tonight was the night I'd finally land him in the sack.

At the restaurant we sat down at a booth where, hoping no one else would show up, I resumed my efforts at captivation. In hobbled a hick boy on crutches with a bandaged foot and his splay-toothed, overweight girlfriend, both newcomers to the meeting. To my horror, John waved them over. The boy explained that his foot was infected, not with flesh-eating disease *exactly*, but something close to it he'd acquired as a junkie. John offered him our chips and salsa, and he dipped in. The girl's teeth were painful to look at. I mean, my teeth are crooked, too, but this was the kind of crooked that reminded you of braided piano keys. As John talked with them, each began to open up. The hick boy told of getting the shit kicked out of him weekly by his drunken dad, and the day he punched back, then ran away to a life of fist-fighting. He said that part of his sobriety was the gift of knowing he never had to fight again, "'cause we've ceased, man." The splay-toothed girl talked as well with an appealing shyness, covering her teeth with her hand. She knew exactly how they looked, and her every utterance took courage. Both were in their first month of living sober. Both, in John's kindness, gained a sense that they belonged.

More people from the meeting wandered in, including almost everyone John had invited on the way over; he waved them to our booth and joked with them. Soon our crowd spilled over into the neighboring booth and a long table adjoining it, and the chatter got so loud you had to shout. I was so busy talking and laughing amid all the playful energy, I didn't even notice when or how John moved to the next booth.

But at some point I looked over at him, and I realized I had not realized. What I mean is, I understood that for a few minutes, something more powerful than obsession had cured me. John smiled through the hubbub as if to say, "toldja so!" The visual that came to me was of the cord of love I'd meant to string to him alone having unraveled, fanning out into dozens of threads that touched every person there tonight and, in my affection for them, awoke a joy I couldn't generate myself. It was the joy of god. And it felt wonderful. Love itself, not John Church's love, was my missing piece.

I'll never forget walking back to my car alone that night, so aware that I could not let this discovery fade. It would, I knew, unless I did something drastic. I whisper-talked with god as I walked, and struck a deal with it. I asked god to help me remember this night, and to overcome from this time forth whatever prejudices fear flung between me and strangers. My obsessive love shot at single targets like a fire hose, but I wanted god to teach me how to make it a fountain of countless outlets, showering on everyone. I accepted that I was still slightly crazy around John, and for whatever reason god wasn't ready to fix that just yet. But I asked if, at the same time, god could teach me more of what I had glimpsed tonight.

By the time I reached my car I had sworn a pact with god. I promised that *every time* someone in a meeting annoyed me – whether they were too damn cutesy, or self-important, or self-pitying, or *any*thing – I would undertake a mission. My mission would be to make a beeline for that person as soon as the Serenity Prayer circle broke, shake their hand, and learn three things about them. I would break through their protective bubble just as I'd seen John do tonight over and over. I asked god, in return, to remove my lingering shyness.

I've kept that promise. Today, as a result, I have hundreds of friends – more than I know what to do with – simply because I've had no choice. This does not mean Facebook friends; it means people with whom I've connected face to face, having made a connection, even a passing one, that lets us see each other's vulnerable goodness. It turns out that if someone annoys me, it's usually because we share overlapping faults. That's why my judgment rears up – whether as jealousy or disapproval or both. But those faults are there to mask a struggle that is just as much mine: we share humanness, and a disease of addiction. Befriending such strangers can teach me the humility to accept, along with theirs, my own character defects.

And there we go again, steerage to the captain's table! Camaraderie in not just our vulnerability to alcohol – but to ego and insecurity, to self-loathing and grandiosity, to hiding our truth, to fearing others' judgments and living inauthentically to please them. I do it. You do it. We all fuck up. But god loves us for trying. We can only do our best and fail again. Progress, not perfection.

It's astounding how many of these "beeline friends" have remained in my life even after they've moved far away. That's where Facebook comes in. Earlier today, as I write this, I got a call from a girl who, years ago, was the new hottie all the boys in meetings liked too damn much, what with her blue stubble of hair and smoky voice. She made me feel jealous, shriveled-up, and old because I thought if I could have all that attention, my life would be perfect. I caught myself in mid-annoyance and, without so much as a sigh, fulfilled my mission, crossing the room, sticking out my hand, and learning three things. Weeks later, this girl asked me to sponsor her. And now she called from Florida where she's all grown up in grad school, wanting my advice, my willingness to listen. At the end, we said, 'I love you,' and my heart filled with the hope of good things for her.

One problem with my annoyance vow, however, was its built-in obsolescence. The more comfortable I became with my own flaws, the less I felt triggered by seeing them in others. "Oh, I know *that* way!" I'll think now, instead of getting pissed. "That's a car-share – one you've said in your head already to an imaginary meeting while you drove, so now it comes out a bit canned. I've so done that!" At a meeting of a hundred idiosyncratic, self-centered, showy drunks, I'll often not resent a single one. So now I have to pick out my beelines manually. Who's hurting? Who looks scared? Who might need a gift of good wishes? I stick out my hand and, before you know it, we're meeting for coffee, or I run into them at the pet food store, or they call me out of the blue in tears.

John is the one who opened this door for me. I honestly believe god gave me the fixation on him that day as I sawed through the 1 x 4 molding so that he could teach me the thing I was still missing – open-ended love.

Mind you, John was no saint. On two occasions during August and September of 2005, what with my flinging myself at him non-stop and "snuggling" on various sofas, he fell off his Platonic wagon and slept with me. Each time I was euphoric, believing I'd clinched him at last. Granted, our chemistry fell short of cataclysmic, but who cared? I'd bagged John Church!

> 8/15/2004: "He'd had a terrible day at work, and I picked
> him up afterwards to go to the bonfire meeting. But it

was cold and windy there, and the quality of shares low. I asked, did he want to talk, and after some misunderstanding we got in my car. Then I asked if I could kiss him. He said yes, which completely surprised me. But he was still sort of holding back. I asked what he was thinking, and he answered in this weird kind of monotone, "I'm thinking... that you're hot—?" I asked, "What else?" but he could only repeat it. So I kissed him again and whisper-asked if we could go to his place. First he managed to say that what he wanted most was never to hurt me – but then he agreed. Boys are so strange! All of a sudden it was like, "Who wants fresh pizza?!" At his place he rushed around to get candles, big hurry, exactly like in May at my house."

Afterwards he jumped up uneasily and put on "Drops of Jupiter," by Train, while he busied himself gathering laundry from around the room. To this day I can't hear that song without remembering the dreaminess of lying there, feelings swirling through me as I watched him pick up various shirts and tentatively sniff the armpits. Obsession is a powerful drug. In that memory I'm not even with John himself. I'm with the Other, the Chosen One: sniffing shirts is an ideal being almost without identity, a Reilly-Kevin-Jenna-Theo-John, indistinct but radiating brilliant power. In its glow I was again the delightful child who charmed strangers around the world. I had seized my worth from the demon of self-loathing.

God willing, that was the last obsession of my lifetime. As John had stood by me in my painful time of madness, I've since stood by him through a series of painful losses. There have been times when he's lost faith in AA and in humanity itself, when I've reminded him what he taught me that night at fellowship, to reach out and love without conditions. For years I nagged him to go back to school, until he did, with flying colors. I kept telling him he'd someday fall in love, and he has. Somewhere in John's transition from personal Messiah to best friend, I came to internalize the distinction between what one human being can be to another and what can only come from god. And so of one more addiction, I was cured. Don't worry, though! There were still plenty left.

~

But what about the Huge Ninth Weird Thing with the spider? What did that have to do with anything? Soon after striking my annoyance pact with god, I got to find out.

A friend from my old gay and lesbian Alano club days invited me to her birthday party. Though we'd fallen out of touch, Jassy was, without a doubt, the most woo-woo person I'd ever known. While many people profess a faith in a spiritual practice, she'd staked her life on hers – and survived. About seven years prior, diagnosed with stage three breast cancer, she'd declined chemotherapy, radiation, and all medical treatments prescribed to follow up her double mastectomy, leaving instead for a three-month retreat in Puerto Rico, where she ate wheat grass and meditated. It worked. She'd been living cancer-free ever since, exploring a wide range of woo-woo healings: aroma therapy, light therapy, Reiki, and others.

What drove me to actually get out of the house with a small child and drive across town to see a friend I hadn't visited in years, I can't tell you. I experienced a sense of mission that would turn up in other spiritually pivotal visits down life's road: just *go*. I knew no one else at the party. Jassy found some toys for Keno, so I was able to socialize. The conversation turned to dreams and clairvoyance, and for some reason, I chimed in.

"I had a clairvoyant dream once, but it was about the dumbest thing. A huge spider. I'm like, what?"

While everyone listened, I told the story of the dream spider, the real spider, and their matching tummy patterns. No one interrupted. "It was the weirdest thing I've ever experienced," I finished, "but about something completely pointless."

Jassy spoke up. "Spiders aren't pointless," she said deliberately. "I'm pretty sure that was a spirit messenger; it must've shown up to tell you something. Hang on – I've got books."

From her woo-woo library she pulled out a few volumes on animal totems and read aloud to me. Several cultures, she read, drew a mythical connection between the spider and threads of the mythic Fates. Phases of our lives are spun out, measured, and cut. Spider might visit as a harbinger of great change in one's life.

She looked. "So last spring – wasn't that right around the time you and Jesse broke up?"

I considered. "No," I said. "At that point everything was still okay."

"Or so you *thought*," smiled Jassy.

In a flash I realized her instincts were right: the spider had come at the turning point when was actually losing Jessie, when she and Barbara were just starting out. It had come as a harbinger, telling me a phase of my life had ended and a new one begun. That's why the dream had been set at my brother's house – at the point when Jesse entered my life.

As soon as I made it home and got Keno down for his nap, I took a seat at my computer underneath the spider's perch and Googled spider spirit messengers. Images of the Fates spinning and cutting life threads came up, along with Arachne cursed by Athena to spin as a spider forever. Some were drawn on ancient vases, others in frescos. I considered that these myths actually pre-dated the Greeks, and had been part of the human culture for many millennia. Then I clicked on a passage from Ted Andrews' *Animal-speak*, and the words seemed to address me directly:

"If spider has come into your life, ask yourself some important questions. Are you not weaving your dreams and imaginings into reality? ...Do you need to pay attention to your balance and where you are walking in life? Are others out of balance around you? Do you need to write? ...Remember that spider is the keeper of knowledge of the primordial alphabet..."

A maelstrom of realization blasted from my mind the stubborn, rational skepticism I had chosen over god. I remembered what the spider had conveyed to me:

I'm here for you. You know why.

I remembered the courage it had summoned in me: "In the dream you were courageous. So you can be courageous now..."

Jesse had brought me to AA, which saved my life. But at the point when the spider visited, all my dreams and imaginings had served *her* happiness instead of mine. We were due to part. The spiders, dream and real, marked the beginning and end of that thread. I'd gone forward blindly, not knowing god's path for me but equipped with enough courage to stumble along it. As a result, I'd shed a layer of fear and learned to love my fellows.

You know why. I raised my eyes to the spot on the ceiling where the spider had been and saw through it into the depths of a universe stretching far beyond my comprehension. In the diamonds of orderly precision I understood the intricate energy network interweaving all living things – that is god. I offered, from my deepest heart, this long overdue response:

I know... that you are.

We tend to think of faith as an exertion of will, of the resolve to believe. Wrong! Now I found out how it felt to be flooded by it. The last walls of my intellectual dam collapsed; god consciousness rushed in a torrent through my mind and body, and it said:

We are life's love. We are you; you are we. And, yes, we can do real stuff!

I cried and sputtered all kinds of half-formed prayers. In spite of all the miracles, all the Weird Things – my journey to the light, the ghost in Gloucester, foreknowledge of a death, the serendipities and soundless voices – in spite of everything god had shown me, I'd held back. Because while we always understand, at some buried level, the interconnectedness of life on earth – of every cell in every creature and plant – those moments when we actually really *feel* our place in that divine network are few and far between. They come perhaps once in a lifetime, and for most of us, that moment arrives only as we die.

But I also sensed that the portal would close again, and that I would forget nearly everything I grasped so clearly at this moment. That did, in fact, happen. We can't live in divine transport and still run around as critters who eat, poop, and sleep. Two things about me, though, were permanently changed. First, I know now with unshakeable faith that god's energy infuses this earth. Never again will I question its influence and guidance for anyone who seeks it earnestly. God cannot override physics, forestall tragedies, or answer Santa-prayers, but it *does* infuse with courage, strength, and guidance those who ask for help. It's done so for millions of alcoholics who, provided they give up their notion of self-control, have found their mania for alcohol and drugs entirely removed.

There's been a second lasting change in me since that afternoon, and this one has to do with spiders. I *like* them now. If they build a web in my yard or house, I name them. I take care to help them out whenever I can, because a real, commonplace spider helped *me* out by delivering god's message. Though I'm not entirely immune to heebegeebies, and I do reluctantly execute some poisonous hobo spiders, I can often pick up daddy-longlegs or web-spinning spiders with my bare hands. I talk to them reassuringly as I carry them to the door. To be honest, I often call them "girlfriend."

Clockwise from top left: Soused by my friend Lloyd at a lawn party; with John Church and high on obsession; symbolically true, Keno holding me up; Elizabeth and Allie 20 years post-Vassar

25: ON FORGIVENESS

Imagine! Every person
that you see
is someone   different
*   from every*
other person
*   in the world.*

-Mister Rogers

Adelyn was my first big forgiveness.

The dead offer us an easy, bunny-slope course in forgiveness because we're not afraid of them anymore. They're not around to compete, to impose views that threaten our 'rightness' about anything, or throw down a gauntlet of even the tiniest challenge – it's better to use butter than olive oil! or you built the fire wrong! or no, that's not how it went! – disagreements we take up as affronts. If we're not right, we're not worthy, or so we fear. And fear is, of course, the biggest blocker of love's flow. Perhaps the only one.

In living with any individual while safeguarding our drive to exist as an independent, self-propelled entity, we bump up against them and react with self-defense. It's part of the assignment of being human, living in an enclosed body, driving a brain: *Defend yourself!* In most instances, the fear we experience is subtle. We don't even recognize it as "fear," but as a slight unrest or discomfort – "eh!!" – that we categorize under the label, Annoyance.

No, the dead are not around to "annoy" us with bumpings up in the present day. Had my sister lived, I am quite sure we'd have major conflicts today, much like those I have with my surviving siblings. Her brain was so very powerful and she viewed so many things from angles radically different from mine. Right now I'd be telling you about her many faults, maybe her conservative political views and Catholic religiosity and all the things that make her so difficult.

But she died. She left only memories. And memories are things we can approach without raising our shield, without (though it took a while) anticipating the barbs or slights or contradictions that necessitate one. I could begin to see Adelyn's essence, her spirit, her fundamental desire to love the world. That's what we miss out on from behind our shield. We see only the shields of others. Once we know someone presents no threat, we can lay ours aside and begin to see with compassion.

AA has taught me to do this. Because when we come into the rooms of AA, as Ernest Kurtz so clearly articulates in *The Spirituality of Imperfection,* we learn how it feels to take off our armor, united by our shared weakness rather than strengths. We focus upon embracing that weakness rather than camouflaging it. To a full room we admit, "I can't take a drink, guys, without turning into a guzzling maniac. I've tried and I fail. I can't manage my life, guys, without bungling everything. I've tried and I fuck it all up. And I want so much to impress you all, because I don't believe that as my regular self, I have a shred of worth. But really, I am just like you."

Clatter-clatter! The armor falls to the floor. In normie society, you'd get a bunch of disturbed, uncomfortable reactions like, "Pull it together, man! Hoist yourself by your bootstraps!" as people essentially say, "Don't show me your wounds! Ugh! You must want something from me, and I've got my own shit to deal with!" AA is not a pity-pot, though. It's a dropping of pretense. When we stop claiming to be "fine," we encounter the loving support of a room filled with equally flawed and vulnerable human beings. In AA, it's okay to be human. It's even okay to be broken. We all acknowledge that without the guiding influence of our Higher Power, all our efforts to thrive sorely miss their marks.

But we also see that *with* god's direction, living by love, we can be lifted above our circumstances and limitations. We can live inspiring lives of both outer accomplishment and inner contentment. To the outside world we can look like we finally have our shit together, when the truth is, *god* has our shit together.

When I look at my memories of Adelyn without our mutually protective barriers, I see my sister. Her overeating was like my masturbation. Her endless talk of crushes was like my secret sexual obsession. Her intellectual vanity was like my physical vanity. The parallels go on and on. She once even compared her cancer to my alcoholism, which works better if you compare the root conditions that put her at risk. She took the marching orders we were given as children – be better than everyone! – quite literally, and came very close to pulling it off. What got lost in the dust of that chase, though, was self-care. I felt worthless and drank because it fixed me. She felt worthless and ate, but also out-performed everyone in her circle. The idea that we were loveable as we were – well, it came to her in her last weeks of life. In a letter to our cousin written shortly before her death, she wrote that if Jesus were to let her live, she would give up musicology and devote her life to "Him and His needs in other people." Choosing the needy over acclaim – that's not in the P. family lexicon. When I read this letter, written from a place so close to god at a time when I wasn't, I miss the heart of my sister, which, beneath all the armor, rivalries, and barbs, had always been powerfully beautiful.

That's forgiveness.

Since her death, I've lost many, many friends to addiction. We're a high-risk group, and those who fall off the beam often plummet to their death. But depression, illness, and accident also take their toll. With each of the people I describe below I had, at some point, some vestige of conflict. With each death, I learned a little better what is essentially human in each of us. That shift of perspective, from competing against the living to communion with the dead, repeated over and over, has gradually taught me to adjust my eyesight. Now you don't have to die for me to glimpse your intrinsic, over-arching, absolute innocence – the goodness of spirit in you.

See if you can get to know these spirits a bit.

Lorian

Lorian was one of those young women who, hearing my pain-filled, gut-spewing shares at the time of my break-up, promptly asked me to sponsor her. She was an artist living off a trust fund – a willowy, almost-beautiful blonde currently at work on a photography show of people's scars. Her self-esteem was prone to swan dives. She obsessed over boys. She cowered in fear of put-downs and meanness from people she perceived as better off – i.e. everyone. Yet she trusted me with her most reluctant confessions.

Lorian annoyed the heck outta me. One time when I met her at a coffee shop, she arrived ensconced beneath a hat, sunglasses, and a silk scarf partially concealing her mouth and chin. Why? Because she'd made out for two hours the night before with a mutual friend of ours and acquired an epic case of beard-burn. It made her weep at the absurdity of her romantic attempts. I kept telling her it wasn't a big deal, but she wouldn't hear it. "It's not *normal*!" she countered. "Why *me*?" Another time she'd skinned a largish patch from her shin while shaving for a date and had been forced to wear tights. She wept outright at the absurdity of her beauty-care attempts. The world was making a mockery of her. "It's only a shaving scrape," I said. "No!" she wept. "It symbolizes everything I try to make happen! Everything backfires! Everything I do becomes pathetic!"

To be gainfully employed beyond her trust fund, she enrolled in a Vietnamese barbering school. The only Caucasian, native English-speaker in the entire class, she would call me nightly weeping from the slights of her fellow students. "They all ignore me! No one wants to talk to me!" I suggested the fact that everyone else's first language was Vietnamese might be related. No, no, she wept of the particular girl in question today, "She *does* speak English! She *could* talk to me! She just doesn't think I'm hip enough!" Every few days I heard more tales of cruel shafting from this community of too-cool barber wanna-be's. And who knew what they were all saying about her in their own language? She'd caught them more than once looking her way and then pretending they hadn't.

I visited her at her apartment building where she whispered to me about the maintenance man who stalked her. "He smiles in this creepy, predatory way! Once I came out my door and he was *right there*." Inside her apartment, I discovered she was a hoarder – the most extreme case I've ever seen. Her floor plan consisted of narrow aisles among big plastic bins, stacked and labeled. "Ticket stubs, programs, and reviews: 1992-1997" I read on one. She loved everything too much to part with it. The walls were lined with racks and racks of shoes.

She continued to make art about depression, her own afflict-ion. I recall a video for which she did voice-over. Her voice repeats in toneless deadpan: "I could be joyous, like the fleas in my carpet." No, I admitted to her frankly, I didn't like it. I told her I believed everyone had some degree of choice about how they experienced the world. I quoted Abraham Lincoln on happiness. She was hurt, of course. And inside, I became determined to fix her.

Lorian believed herself an alcoholic because every time she drank, she vomited, yet she insisted on repeating the experiment every few months. This sounded nothing like alcoholism as I knew it whereby alcohol was to the drinker as spinach is to Popeye. But when I described her to my sponsor, the response was, "What's the worst you could do by taking her through the steps? Give her some tools?"

So for several months we met and read the book together, usually at Capital Hill coffee shops since she had no car. As is my usual practice, we read by alternating pages, changing the sexist pronouns to "he or she" and avoiding "He" for god. All went well until we reached Step Four. Lorian outright refused to take a "fearless and thorough moral inventory" of herself. She got her therapist to write me a letter saying that attempting the step would be too traumatic, which she held out in some spirit resembling triumph. I tried for a while to persuade her, but she would crumple at my lack of compassion.

"If you kept shooting yourself in the foot," I told her, "wouldn't you want to unload the bullets? The fourth step lets us see how we harm *ourselves*, how we set ourselves up."

Nope, said Lorian. Not true. *Other* people harmed Lorian ruthlessly and that was a fact. Instead of pressuring her to write a Fourth Step, I should be commiserating with her on the latest installment of wrongs suffered. So eventually, unable to move forward with the only cure I knew, I resigned as her sponsor.

After that, frustration and judgment reared up in me whenever I heard from her. She seemed to cherish her misery, to group me with the fleas in her carpet for believing happiness was possible. I saw in her refusal to write a Fourth Step an overriding cowardice, a rejection of truth. Part of me wanted to slap her: "If you won't get honest, god can't help you!"

I must have hurt her during some exchange, because she vanished. Two years later, acting on an intuition that should perhaps qualify as Weird, I Googled her unusual name plus suicide. As I'd feared, up came her obituary. She'd moved to Los Angeles, it turned out, where she had photographed a show of mentally ill people. Despite the show's relative success, she'd swallowed a bottle of Celexa along with a number of other prescription drugs, pulled a plastic bag over her head, and lain down on her bed to die.

Life. Lorian just couldn't do it. This effort of being a vulnerable child in a difficult world – that relentless gamut of demands that you and I well know – overwhelmed her.

I remember her delicate soul in the days we spent at the summer cabin – which she loved. She took beautiful photographs of objects both animate and inert, on the beach and in the woods. She cooked at the old gas stove in a flighty, panicky way. Something about her seemed almost antique, like a waif from the 1940s, some staidness of old photographs in her dress, the waves of her hair, her way of saying, "Oh!" with a slim hand to her cheek.

No one else can be Lorian. She was the most delicate flower I've ever known. What annoyed me was recognizing myself in her, more transparent and pronounced: all the same demons I battle rattled her about like a helpless doll, and she simply lacked the pluck to fight back.

I miss you, Lorian! I wish I'd loved you enough to embrace us both.

Lloyd

Lloyd was a junkie I first met at Drunks R Us in the golden era, a tattooed Irish boy in his early twenties with long blonde hair, a boxy jaw, and huge blue eyes. He was bubbly and sarcastic, profanity pouring from his mouth in comic audacities. But he relapsed and vanished. About seven years later, around the time I began stalking John, he'd started showing up around AA meetings again while still high. Having done time in prison and lost a front tooth but acquired a lot more tattoos, he often slumped on an electrical box outside the podium meeting, too high and ashamed to go inside. Week after week there he was, eyes bleary and bloodshot, his face and hair filthy. Each week I greeted him with a curt, guarded hello, afraid of his rampaging disease. "Keep a safe distance," fear coached me. "Don't get snared by his sordid neediness!"

But good men took him under their wings. Eventually, Lloyd began showing up *inside* the meetings again, his eyes clear, looking like a young Viking and cracking the room up with his sassy, profane shares. He'd found a sponsor and was working the steps. He kept a beautiful Siberian husky with him and one night, after making my pact with god, I went up to him, stuck out my hand, and learned three things about – not Lloyd but his dog. Thus began our friendship. He adored this dog, who had some Eskimo name and whom we took for a walk one time when both of us arrived early for the meeting. Why a week or two later Lloyd chose me, a tattooless mom eighteen years his senior, to holler at, wave over across the street, and trade phone numbers with, I'll never know.

After that he'd call and I'd sometimes drive him places with the dog, the two of us fighting over radio stations. "Your shit is so fuckin' retarded, man!" He'd change it to something awful – heavy metal. I'd snap back at him, "Douchebag! Excuse *me* for liking music with *notes*!" I'd change it back and swat away his hand if he tried to mess with it.

There was a lot of prison still left in him. He once called me aside upset because someone in his clean and sober housing had broken a major rule, and he'd witnessed it. He feared the impending house meeting. "Man, in the big house, you *never* rat out a bro to the man. It's like, the *law*." I told him he could keep quiet unless he was asked a direct question, in which case he'd have to answer truthfully. "I *know*, man! If I lie, I lose God, and if I lose God, I'm fucked!" He ended up repeating what he'd seen and surviving the repercussions. And he stayed clean.

Another time he asked me to chair a fairly hard-core NA meeting. Watching the tough guys file in – motorcycle and street gang types – while I sat at the front of the room with him, I got cold feet: "Lloyd, I'm just a plain old alcoholic. I never shot up in my neck or used my intestines for a tourniquet, I don't have any incredible tales…"

He turned those clear blue eyes on me. "Y'know what? I've listened to your shares for years. You've fuckin' helped me like you'll never know, and you can help these assholes. Now shut up and chair the fuckin' meeting."

Flirting, but playfully and with finesse, wasn't out of bounds, either. One night after a meeting he rescued me from a wasted, belligerent drunk who, having heard my share, got in my face about whether I was gay or straight.

"Yo, dude," Lloyd cut in, prison hackles bristling, "she's a dyke, okay? She don't like dudes! Deal with it and move on!" He pointed down the sidewalk, glaring. But as soon as the coast was clear and someone else pointed out that I was, in fact, straight now, he broke into a boyish grin and slung an arm over my shoulder. "'Course she is! But the fewer guys know it, the better my chances!"

At a friend's summer party where the two of us got in a super-soaker fight, he pulled no punches. He soused me ruthlessly and insisted he'd mutilated me. "Rematch any day, bitch! *Any* day!" he yelled across the lawn with gang-banger gestures. It was all a game, all part of being one's able to hack it. Because the belligerence vanished the instant I asked him to do something for me – carry mom stuff, get some paper towels for a Keno mess, bring us a plate of food because I couldn't manage. When my boy ventured too close to the fire, Lloyd scooped him up without missing a beat.

By late 2005, this junkie had blossomed to his full self – tan, robust, and handsome. He'd become a carpenter and was moving to Tacoma with Louise, a butch contractor friend also from the golden era DRU. For many months, I heard nothing from him.

One morning, a call at 6:00 AM surprised me. Lloyd had been crying. He told me a long, involved story about his new puppy pooping all over Louise's kitchen floor, his having overslept the chance to clean it up, and Louise's accusation that he'd been using. He was so damn pissed by that shit, he said, he didn't know what to fuckin' do with himself! Fuck, man! He was at a park now with the puppy, and he cried all over again. I tried to comfort him, assuring him Louise was just worried, and told him to get his ass to a meeting. In the back of my mind, though, I was thinking that Louise knew junkies and would accuse no one lightly – so chances were he was already lost.

I made him promise again that he'd go straight to a meeting. I called him sweetheart. I remember exactly where I was standing in my kitchen when love made me say it. He thanked me for being there, and we said goodbye.

The next time I saw Lloyd, he was in a coffin, masked with bad make-up and a high collar concealing his tattoos. His Catholic parents, weeping in the viewing room, had him dressed in a suit. Half his face was concave, with temples, eye socket, and jaw scooped out. The other side, that had lain downward, sagged in deflated pouches. Where his Viking earrings had been were only holes. He'd shot up heroin while on methadone, overdosed, and lain dead at the top of a building staircase three days before he was found.

In his last few months he'd caused a lot of wreckage, exploiting friendships and cursing out his brother, but never phoned me. I sometimes wonder if he was too ashamed. He'd fallen for the illusion of independence, as so many do. In the bustle of his great new life, he'd let his god-connection slip. Addiction had regrouped and caught him unawares.

From Lloyd I learned that no one, not even a strung out prison junkie, is all that different from me. I'm grateful for every annoying phone call, every far-flung story, every curse uttered with irreverent zest. I loved that sweet boy.

Vanessa

One day I was sitting in a squalid and depressing public health facility waiting to take an HIV test when my phone rang with an unknown number. Bored of magazines, I answered – then instantly regretted it. On the line was an unstoppable chatterbox already talking a mile a minute: Vanessa. I'd stuck my hand out to her weeks before in acute annoyance, because this girl *insisted* on being a center of attention. She had a voice that sounded like Joan Jett on helium and she was now telling me truckloads of troubles. I could only look helplessly for a nurse, hoping the call of a needle would rescue me.

"…And since my class starts at eight and I have to take the bus across town I told her, no freakin' way! cause I get up at six as it is and I need that class, there's no freakin' way I'm not taking that class, but she's all like, you have to be willing and evenings don't work for me and my weekends are blah, blah, and shit like that, you know what I mean?"

Gradually I began putting together an ominous inference, based on the deluge of information funneling through my phone. Vanessa was not happy with her current sponsor. "And we've done like One through Three plus I have a service position at A Way Out; I'm the coffee maker, and that's my service position so that's good, and I go to the business meetings even though there's like people there I really don't get along with, but she's like, that's not enough service, and I'm like, hello! I'm a full time student *and* I work, so it's like…"

"Dear god," I said, not to Vanessa but as she chattered on, "please don't ask me to do this. I can't handle it. I have three sponsees already – isn't that enough?"

"…but if I'm gonna read my Fourth Step to *someone*, I don't want it to be some hoity bitch who chaps my ass, cause there's some pretty serious shit on that thing and I don't want some uptight biddy with a stick up her ass lookin' at me like…"

She's a sweet girl… came to me.

"Yes, but listen to her! I'll lose my mind!"

She needs help, just as you've needed help…

"…so like when I heard you sharing on Step 7, and plus all your other shares, too, I was like, 'Damn! This woman is righteous!' You know? I mean you crack me up but you're always right on, too, so I was wondering, maybe, if you know, you could… be my new sponsor?"

"Sure. Sure I'll do it. I'm kind of busy right now, but how about you call me tomorrow and we'll set up a time to meet?

"Oh, sweet! Oh, fuckin' awesome! Yes, yes I will!"

I closed my phone and knew I'd been changed as I could not change myself. What I did not know was that this girl, this fireball, would become one of the dearest friends of my life.

Vanessa had run away at sixteen and taken up with the street kids who loiter on University Way as a sort of modern day band of gypsies – the self-named "Ave Rats." In that "family" she lived for several years, using and dealing every kind of drug, panhandling, stealing, having unprotected sex right and left, getting in fist fights, and once pulling a knife. The gang raised her. She was nineteen when she resolved to quit drinking with no program. She'd tell a favorite story of sitting in front of the University Book Store stark-raving sober, wearing a red wig and revving a chainsaw, not cooperating when police had a problem with it. She was twenty when she started AA, and twenty-one at the time she called me. She said her only worry was that, being bisexual, she might harbor something of a crush on me.

"Which would you rather?" I asked. "Play games or get well? It's one or the other: knock it off."

And she did. Looking at Vanessa, you'd see a somewhat chunky girl in coveralls with fair skin and dark pigtails. It took a while for you to realize she was stunningly beautiful. Her eyes had a pixie flair to them as elvin as her helium-voice, and something about her lips brought to mind the word "ruby" – some perfection of contour, set in her heart-shaped face.

But her priorities lay elsewhere. Vanessa was training to be a welder, dammit, and to climb the ladder in a man's world. She'd already started on this plan long before I met her, but holy shit, did I hear about it a lot. The sexist jokes, the slurs and put-downs, "accidental" ass smacking, pranks or omissions – every few days it was something else. She'd call up absolutely livid, talking a mile a minute. It was with Vanessa that I devised my current sponsorly boundary: I was willing to listen for ten minutes, timed. After that, I'd give her my best shot at insight, and we'd hang up.

One thing about Vanessa from the outset: she was the most obedient sponsee I'd ever had. If I told her to do something – call my answering machine daily with three things she was powerless over – she'd follow through to the letter. She'd later share at meetings of the day that exercise bore fruit: "I started listing my three things and then I said, 'Fuck! I'm powerless over *everything!*'" Here I stepped in with sponsorly timing: all things *except* herself, in her reactions and choices.

She still talked a mile a minute.

"I'd so clearly claimed that station, but he just shoved my shit to the side and took it. It's *bullshit*! They wouldn't do that if I weren't –"

"But they *do* do it, and they're not going to change. The only one who can change is you."

"But those fuckers—"

"Shush! You called for my take on it; here is my take. Focus on doing Vanessa's best work, and when you have the skills, and the knowledge, and the confidence to become *impervious* to every injustice thrown at you, you'll earn their respect and even the *assholes* will have no choice but to show it. Okay?"

Her voice shrank. "Okay."

> 8/17/2005: "On the way home I got an annoying call from Vanessa, my sponsee, who is always in fear. I told her, 'You've got to recognize this state as a *state*, even though you spend most of your time in it. You need to imagine the alternative, living in love and faith."

Vanessa's was the longest Fourth Step I've ever heard. Her Fifth Step took thirteen reading hours, which we covered over three consecutive days. The trouble was, her memory was so accurate that she recalled every name and every action of every Ave Rat on every night of those four years she lived among them. Three cross-referenced notebooks. Hundreds of names, each with multiple resentments. Honesty so frank it cut to the heart of human weakness. We eventually made up names for the imagined disses that came up most often. "Stealing all the sexy" referred to a rival girl admired by all the guys. "Assumes I'm a gullible cluck" stood for anyone who lied to or cheated her. There were times we laughed ourselves into soundless convulsions, and times we cried for irrevocable pain and loss of innocence.

By the end of that fifth step, I loved Vanessa intensely. In her spare time, when she wasn't working or in school, she played obstreperous guitar and spat flaming lighter fluid in various dive bars around Seattle, still honing her sword swallowing skills in private lessons. Her current service position was as Chip Chick for A Way Out, meaning she handed out coins to those marking months or years of sobriety. Up in front of an audience she made a huge production of it, miming drum rolls and guitar bashings, jumping around yelling "Hell, *yeah*, motherfuckers!!!" In fact, practically everyone at the meeting absolutely dreaded chip night because it made them captive observers of The Vanessa Show.

Now that she was done with her Fifth Step, more than a year after she'd first annoyed the hell out of me, I approached her as she stood ready with the tray of coins.

"So honey," I said, "I'm gonna ask you a question: Who's birthday night *for*?"

"Um. The birthday people."

"Right. So… who should get the most attention?"

Her clear eyes strayed momentarily while her mind parsed through all her Fifth Step had revealed.

"Got it," she said simply.

I believe the entire meeting was floored when Vanessa stepped calmly up to the podium and said, sweetly as a church girl, "Hi, I'm Vanessa, alcoholic, and tonight I'd like to honor the birthday people." It was all I could do to sit still in the back row without jumping up to cheer, "Hell, *yeah*, motherfuckers!!!"

About a year later, she called me hysterical because a Metro bus had hit her car, but the driver, once she chased the bus down, denied it. I told her to get off the phone with me and get all the info she could immediately – the driver, the route, the time, and any witnesses.

"But why? She claims it never happened, and I'll never—"

"Get on it, *now*!"

Later, when she'd won several thousand dollars and laid plans to travel Europe, she wanted to give me $100. Instead I let her take me out for dinner at my favorite restaurant, Café Flora. By that time, she'd restarted the steps with a new sponsor and would soon start earning her journeyman's license in heavy diesel equipment repair. Already she earned several times what I did as a teacher.

By the time she turned twenty-five, her welding and repair skills had helped to build the new Tacoma Narrows Bridge. Her schedule made it hard to see her, but I always felt joy when I did. I'm not just saying that to be Hallmark; ask anyone who knew Vanessa. The girl was so positive, so upbeat, and so free in letting loose with 100% Vanessa no matter what anyone thought, she freed *you* to do the same – which is joy.

Two years ago, a mutual friend told me Vanessa was pissed at me. I'd missed the housewarming for her newly purchased home outside Seattle, after she always came to my parties, which meant I wasn't a good friend. I realized Vanessa's annoyance could mean only one thing: I wasn't being a good friend. Within a few days I was driving thirty miles to have dinner at her house and meet her new boyfriend. I remember that sense of fulfilling an important mission, same as when I went to Jassy's party. The sense of significance lingered throughout dinner, which she'd picked up from some fancy vegan take-out place special for me her way home from work. Thirty days from becoming a journeyman, she worked so much overtime there was no leisure to spend all the money she earned. In a basement room she showed me all her welding stuff. She put on her welder's mask and held up the biggest adjustable wrench I'd ever seen in my life.

I felt some kind of ominous dark shadow, a foreboding of sadness and loss, come over the room when she put on her mask. I thought maybe it was bad ju-ju left by the burglars who'd recently broken in through the window behind her; they were coming back, I thought I knew, and this time they'd take much more. I said nothing, though. Later we hugged goodbye and each said, "I love you."

That was Friday. The following Thursday I got a call telling me Vanessa had been killed on the job. As she squatted to weld something on a barge at the Seattle waterfront, someone began operating a nearby crane without the required spotter. Wearing her welder's mask, the same one she'd shown me, she had no peripheral vision when she stood up to warn her of the approaching steel that dashed her brains out.

Hundreds of people overflowed from every doorway at her memorial service. Counter-culture Ave Rats and tavern musicians stood side by side with construction workers, trade instructors, and AA people like me. Many of us spoke in her honor. God, do I miss that girl! To this day I still talk to her during my runs. I can't say how grateful I am that I answered my phone that first day and opened my heart in good faith.

Gary

A lot of men and women in AA have been in prison, so I'm not sure why I felt so afraid of Gary Longboard when I first saw him around. The word "thug" came to mind. A big man always wearing a hoodie, he carried a sizeable skateboard and habitually stroked the beard along his jaw's edge. My son was about four years old when I heard Gary share in his deep, heavy bass voice about the morning he woke to find his own son dead from SIDS.

"I'd been the last to change him that night. I put him on his stomach, maybe I should've put him on his back. I don't know – he'd seemed like he was, you know... just his regular self." A long silence followed, until the big man sniffed back tears. His relationship hadn't survived, either, he said. He'd gone from having a little family to having a TV.

I made a beeline to Gary after the serenity prayer and hugged him. I'd had a terrible fear of SIDS, I told him. I couldn't imagine living through it. I'd lost only my partner, but that had nearly killed me. We traded numbers and from then on I saw him as a gentle giant. I'll never forget the time I called him, feeling lonely, and told him I felt like a boring loser and didn't know what to do with myself.

"I hate Sunday afternoons," I said, "especially since I'm single. I get depressed and lonely."

"Yeah, I know," said Gary. "Then it's always hard to call someone cause you don't have jack shit to say."

Pause.

"Are you saying I don't have jack shit to say?"

There was a long pause.

"It's cool with me," he said.

I remember the relief of laughing. It was okay to feel lost, okay to be human and come up empty-handed.

"So I can be as boring as I want?"

His tone was like a soft, rumpled blanket. "Well, I mean it's definitely *less* boring for me. I'm watching TV either way. Holding up the phone, there's always a chance you might say something slightly interesting. I seriously doubt you can top my solo boringness."

But Gary was coming out of his shell, experiencing a psychic change. His eyes were bigger, brighter. I remember a time when he, two fellow Meth-heads, and I dawdled outside a church waiting for rides from people stuck inside at a business meeting. Gary was two weeks shy of two years clean. He said he'd read in some treatment literature that the brain required two years to recalibrate after prolonged use of methamphetamines.

Big as he was, he did a little dance on the sidewalk and half-sang. "I'm gonna have a normal brain! Brain! Brain! Normal brain!" He reminded me of the Cowardly Lion, wagging his loose clothes as he danced. "I'm gonna sell insurance!" he cried joyfully.

"I'm gonna have a two-car garage!" All four of us joined in his song: "Normal brain! Normal brain!"

Armed with that fine normal brain, Gary eventually landed a better job (not selling insurance), a new girlfriend, and moved with her to the Midwest to start a new family. Since he was in his mid thirties, we were all stunned to learn he'd gone to the hospital with chest pains, where he died from a heart attack, fully conscious of what was happening to him. "Am I going to die?" he'd asked his girlfriend. And an hour later, he had.

Like Lloyd, Gary taught me that even the toughest looking thug can conceal a heart of child-like innocence. Because of him, I reach out to newly sober convicts confident that 90% of their life experience is identical to mine. Instead of sticking to "safe" chit-chat, I try out quirky humor, candid thoughts, and confessions of social awkwardness. And more often than not, they respond in kind, because people are just people, whether they've fucked up or not.

Dave

In 2006 I joined a clean and sober mountaineering group called OSAT (One Step At a Time) that I've yet to tell you about, and took a course which culminated in an ascent of Mount Rainier. No leader had been designated for our party until the last minute, when Dave was called out of OSAT 'retirement.' John Church, who was my tent partner, and I really thought they'd scraped the bottom of the barrel with this guy. I thought of him as an old fella because of his bent neck, stooped posture, and the translucent band of white hair encircling his head, but it turns out he was only two years older than me. What had aged him prematurely was a lifelong battle with depression. By the time we met, he'd reached a rare mindset of fighting his depression with mountaineering adventures pretty much not caring much whether he lived or died. He took on terrific challenges like leading our group to the summit of Rainier, yet with an appalling lack of machismo. He wore bright orange plastic boots and lime green helmet, both from the '80s. When, at base camp on Rainier, he cheerily brought around freeze-dried cheesecake to each tent, he had smudges of black soot from his Whisperlite all over his face. What kind of leader was that? He accidentally left two rope teams behind, not watching to see whether they could keep up, but eventually we all reached the summit crater.

A house-painter by trade, Dave led climbs up some of the most hazardous peaks in the Cascades, carried multiple packs for people over raging cataracts, and led the way across treacherous terrain, all with the nickname, "Don't Follow Me Dave." He had humility – a surrendering self-acceptance. Deep in the wilderness, he'd rotate the map doubtfully, saying, "Which way does it go?" or one time, "…baste well and place in 350 degree oven… Dammit! I brought the wrong directions again!" One time near the summit of Mount Shuksan, another OSAT instructor emphasizing safe descent of a steep slope above a drop-off found his lesson undermined as Dave hurled himself down the incline in somersaults. "If I can't have fun," Dave said, popping up covered with snow, "then what's the point?"

When a group of us kayaked and canoed to a campsite deep in the North Cascades wilderness, Dave somehow smuggled along a full sized helium tank, so that in the morning we woke to a huge bundle of bright balloons – dozens of them – floating magically among the trees above camp. Keno was enchanted. "I thought they'd look pretty," Dave confessed when we cornered him on it. And when Keno begged for a canoe ride on the red waters of sunset, everyone was too busy to take him out – except Dave.

The next morning Dave sprinted the length of the dock, ballyhooed absurdly, and dove naked into the freezing lake, his white, clenched butt not an altogether welcome sight to those of us enjoying the morning sunshine. On a trail run where he, our friend Anna, and I encountered a black bear, Dave walked up to it waving his arms: "Shoo! Shoo! Get outta here!" And the bear, rather shocked itself, lumbered off. I did follow him on two ascents of the Olympic Brothers that both, unfortunately, cliffed out short of the summit because we'd lost the route. He was sorely disappointed and thanked us all, his green helmet askew, for putting up with him.

A bullet to the head took Dave one dark winter. A few days before I'd made a comment that I, too, suffered from depression at times, and his response was downright withering: "You have no idea," he hissed bitterly, "what I go through!" I didn't know what to make of the change in him, so I judged him as self-pitying. None of us knew he kept a gun in his home left over from his service in Grenada. When the pain became too great on that December night, he used it.

Dave died sober. He left a loving note, and laid out clear evidence that he'd been faithfully taking all of his depression medications. Only on the last day he went without, perhaps to meet with his maker as naked as he'd dived that morning into Ross Lake. I still keep his obituary taped on my refrigerator. Every time I read it, I remember the strange, sincere mix of playful humility and outrageous daring that was Davey. Without the suicide part, it's a great way to live life.

Laurie

Laurie showed up as a pretty dyke in a wheelchair at the Suns of Madison meetings when I'd first moved to in Seattle, having broken both feet as she jumped from a third story window to leave an argument. I was newly sober and looking to impress Jesse with my service work, so when Laurie announced she needed help with daily chores, I volunteered to take her grocery shopping. After our second trip I also vacuumed her apartment. When I'd finished she read me her poetry about a daughter she'd lost to the foster care system. They were horrible rhyming poems, embarrassingly cliché but deeply heartfelt.

Laurie was a sick one. She had enormous blue eyes and knew it. She got quite physically close to me as she read the poems, which she clearly heard differently than I did, and her manner changed to suavely pained. Awkward as a teen in my new sobriety, I was unsure how to head off her advances without hurting her feelings. I faltered for responses and backed away, joking nervously while alternating reactions inside: "This isn't so bad!" and "This is horrible!" Finally I scrammed, traumatized by the whole scene. From then on I tried to avoid her.

Several years later I heard she'd gotten pregnant again in an effort (because for a lesbian, it *is* an effort) to birth a child she could keep and love, but that once again, relapse had forced her to give the child up. She eventually did the same with a third baby.

What Laurie inspired in me went beyond annoyance. I didn't much like her and, to be honest, was never all that glad to see her back in the rooms trying one more time to get clean. I viewed her with cynicism no matter how movingly she shared, because I still harbored that shame of feeling compromised in her apartment. A decade of using constricted her big eyes to dark sinkholes of need, she'd lost teeth, put on weight, and even limped a little from her messed up feet. One night, late for a meeting where I hoped to bag John Church, I saw her alone outside smoking a cigarette. She greeted me by name and offered a weak smile. I only grunted hello and didn't slow my high-heeled pace. About Laurie I already knew plenty, way more than three things! I, for one, wasn't taken in by her bullshit, and I wanted to be sure she knew it.

She hung herself the following night.

We just never know.

Her partner had left her because of repeated relapses. She'd gotten high one last time, written a note, and lynched herself from a basement ceiling beam. Not until I attended her funeral did I grasp the full tragedy of her life. The photo display showed her childhood – Laurie as a cute blond toddler with bows in her hair and lace on her little skirt. The big, clear eyes were already striking, and her gap-toothed smiles in grade school broke my heart. By high school, along with Farah Fawcett hair and heavy makeup, began the signs of trading on her looks. By eighteen, I could see, she was well into chasing that elusive harlequin of coolness. She'd become a full-blown addict.

The manipulative hag I shunned outside that meeting – she'd been deformed by prolonged illness. Now, looking at the pure little girl in the pictures, I asked myself, did that child *want* to grow up to smoke crack? Did she *want* her life swallowed up by addiction? No more than I'd wanted all the twisted compulsions that plagued my life. Think of how determined she must have been to become a good mother, carrying two more babies to term, giving birth, loving the infant, feeling all the joy of believing *this time* she'd get to have her dream! But addiction, as my friend Gwendolyn put it at a treatment program for pregnant addicts, is stronger than a mother's love. Without rock bottom, I-give-up honesty and a sincere opening to god, Laurie never had a chance.

No matter how long I live and how much good I do, I'll never get to speak a final kind word to her. I can never take back that moment of cruel and unnecessary judgment. But I do have a chance to withhold condemnation and offer kindness to those still here.

Rest in peace also, my AA friends Blake K., Michael W., Julian, Jonathon, and little Marah, slip of a girl with the long golden mane – all taken in youth. You, too, Derek S., Erik H. and now Rico, lost to cancer without health insurance. In your memory I remind myself that every one of us is doing the best we can with the faulty, jerry-rigged wisdom we've pieced together. We have flaws. We fuck up. I certainly do. But every time I come back to what matters, every time I choose love and compassion over being right and knowing better-than, I honor your memories.

Clockwise from top left: Sweet Vanessa at one of my parties; sweet Lorian at the summer cabin; sweet Gary on someone's front steps; sweet Lloyd, always a bit out there; sweet Dave taking Keno for a beautiful canoe ride. I miss you all and remember your unique spirits!

26: MORE ON FORGIVENESS...
AND FREEDOM

Therein lay the flaw, and the flaw of life itself. Life is a long failure of understanding, Mrs. Palmer thought, a long, mistaken shutting of the heart.

> -Patricia Highsmith
> *"The Trouble with Mrs. Blyyn, the*
> *Trouble with the World."*

By the start of 2005, as my addiction to John petered out, I still had a long way to go toward forgiving Jesse and Barbara. But serendipity, god's favorite tool, set up a series of stepping stones to get me there.

Driving home from the podium meeting one summer night with Keno fussing in the back seat, I felt frustrated because I couldn't go out for fellowship. Another Saturday night and here I was going home early and suffering FOMO (Fear Of Missing Out) again. I stopped at a light, turned to the back seat to hand Keno a baggie of snacks, and turned back.

Into the crosswalk stepped two blonde women dressed so much alike it seemed silly: both wore short, spiky blond hair, short jackets, and jeans, except that one wore them tucked into boots. Funny how best friends do that, was my first thought. Then I recognized them, Jesse and Barbara, the two of them heading out for a night on the town. My guts imploded. They had everything I was denied. They looked happy, in love, and excited about the evening ahead. Jesse was half skipping sideways next to Barbara, telling some kind of story or insisting on some point with a huge smile on her face. Barbara's smile was more subdued, her arms folded and chin tucked as she walked.

Fear gripped me, that they might see me in all my lonely patheticness. Really I had no need to worry; they were in a world of their own as they passed just in front of my car's hood. Distractedly I answered some question from Keno as I stared at them heading down Denny Way.

What had I just witnessed? What did it mean? I hadn't seen Jesse in such a playful state for years. I'd forgotten she could look like that. Her face, that face I'd known so well for so long, was lit up with a zest for living that our relationship had squelched – at least after the first few months. What if she really *was* better off now? What if this entire catastrophe had been, not some huge flub-up on god's part, but *supposed* to happen? What if things were unfolding exactly as they should?

Sometimes forgiveness takes a decision every bit as deliberate as jumping off a high dive. You can hang back wishing you had it in you, or you can just go for it, ready or not. I wished them both happiness. I was crying, trying to keep it silent for Keno's sake, but I sent them my blessings. "Love each other," I thought, "and be happy." I still had plenty of pity for myself, all alone and unloved, but my wish was genuine nonetheless.

The next stepping stone came from inspirational author, Marianne Williamson, in person. Stanley and his high school girlfriend had given me her book, *A Return to Love,* at one of those AA birthday parties. John was also a Marianne devotee, though I studied up not only to be able to talk with him about her, but also because her words truly did encourage me. So when she came to speak in Seattle in January 2005, it was a big deal to me. I tried to get John to come along (then have sex and fall in love with me), but since his work schedule conflicted, I went alone with Keno.

By the time I reached the church where Marianne was to speak, I was late and horribly frazzled. The night was rainy. The only free parking I could find was many blocks away, and Keno had needed to get out of his stroller and pee on a tree in the thick of pedestrian traffic on University Way. Another woman reached the church doors at the same moment as I, and because of a recent incident of being the first person excluded from a full-to-capacity event, I imagined she might get the *last* seat in this house, and decided I had to beat her.

> 1/10/2005: "She held the door open for Keno's stroller and me, but I looked her over and judged her harshly. I begrudged her smallness, heavy make-up, high heels, even her bangs. Then, as we sped down the hallway, neck-and-neck, I thought, 'Have some compassion,

Louisa; this poor, overdressed lady is probably just as desperate as you are to hear Marianne Williamson!' Only when she stood up on the stage did I realize she *was* Marianne Williamson."

Maybe because of having raced her down the hallway, I felt connected to Marianne as she spoke. As a result, I found the courage to raise my hand when she asked for questions. Once I was handed the mic and began to speak, I was amazed to feel tears welling up and my throat constricting. Somewhat shocked by the intensity of these feelings, since Jesse's truthful email had hit me almost a year before, I asked, "How do you tell the difference between real love and codependent love?"

Behind me, kind people were distracting my wriggly, energetic three-year-old with prayer books and pamphlets. "I'm sensing that you've been betrayed," Marianne said. "And you're wondering how it came about."

I nodded, accepting Kleenex from the kind people.

1/10/2005: "At some point, she said, ego gets ahold of the *idea* of love, and begins to trick you with it: 'Look how *I* sacrifice!' She said also that some of codependence is laziness/fear not to look closely at what's really going on."

Home from that event, I got out my Fourth Step listing many pages of resentments for Jesse's harms. The fourth column – *my* part in those issues – was still blank. With Marianne's words in my ears – that we make ourselves martyrs and even set ourselves up for pain so we can be the noble one – I tackled that column. I stayed up late, after Keno was asleep, and wrote out the whole thing.

I saw how ego had convinced me that control and judgment were love. From the start I'd imagined myself the better partner, played the benefactor, and known what was best for Jesse. All through the relationship I'd viewed myself as superior – not only more "cultured," but more spiritual and giving. If only Jesse would behave as Louisa thought she should, everything would be fine. Every sacrifice I made, every time I covered her overspending or hunkered down during fights or waited up for her while she was out with Barbara, I was keeping score. God saw it, I'd thought. My martyred victimhood would grant me worth and value and maybe someday self-esteem. Mom hadn't seen my silent suffering, but dammit, Jesse would! I wanted that chit from her, and I wasn't going to give up til I got it.

I'd been free the entire time to say, "Go forth, Jesse, and do your thing!" But I clung to the relationship year after year because I feared a) there would be nothing left of me without it, and yet, contradictorily, b) I'd have no excuse not to flourish. All my energy and attention was poured into managing Jesse. As Marianne puts it, "There are payoffs for holding on to small, weak patterns. We have an excuse not to shine."

Cardboard Box Tony's words came back to me: "One day you'll understand there's nothing Jesse's done to you that you haven't done to her in equal measure." I'd used Jesse for security while I lied to both of us. My campaigns to 'improve her' had attacked her basic worth, rejecting her as she was, implying she wasn't good enough. Sexual addiction had come to her rescue as a quick fix. Who should know better than I how completely it consumes us?

The next morning I called Susan, my sponsor, and told her I was ready to read my Fifth Step. Susan heard it. She added to the list of character defects by which I'd set myself up. Fear, in short, had made me a liar to myself and my partner. I didn't trust god, which translates to trusting reality enough to scrutinize my motives. I saw now the degree to which I'd turned my back on god to chase the false idol of "everything's fine."

I was ready to own all this now. The result? Healing happened. My disease shrank and my god-love grew.

> 3/3/2005: "Last night I ended up thinking of Jesse, how we did love each other for much of those nine years, despite our incompatibility. I cried at the passing of all things. I cried and hugged my Kelsey, who's been with me the longest of anyone. I cried thinking of how I'll lose her, too, some day, and Keno will grow up and I'll become an old lady. Life is change – and love of its fleeting beauty.
>
> "God is curing me, slowly but surely."

Barbara and Jesse made it for perhaps two years, both of them relapsing along the way. Afterwards Jesse dated for a while, hit some new bottoms, sought out some new sponsors, and became a Buddhist for a while. She grew, too, pursuing her path. She's no longer the codependent girl I met in Olympia or the compulsive spender I lived with for so long, because she's worked rigorously in both AA and in Debtors Anonymous. In her new relationship with a woman who has no difficulty holding clear boundaries (financial ones, especially), she's an excellent mom to both our son and a new daughter. In fact, now that I see her from a respectable distance instead of as a codependent partner, she's among the most honorable and trustworthy people I know. I may still get annoyed with her now and then, but beneath that, I know I can rely on her implicitly to do the right thing. Jesse is a good woman.

Meanwhile Barbara went back to Stanley and the two of them restored their relationship. For five years, next to Barbara's name on my Eighth Step list there remained notation, "Fuckin' NEVER!" When I chaired 9th step meetings, I would actually hold the notebook up and show the group: "Fuckin' NEVER!" – not because I was proud of it, but because we all feel like that about some amends, and that's okay...for a while. If we let god work on us, though, even the greatest reluctance fades.

An excellent trick for gauging Step Eight, to determine whether you owe a Ninth Step amends to someone, is to ask yourself whether you'd want your behavior inscribed on your tombstone. So, for example, in the case of my behavior toward Barbara, it would read: *Here lies Louisa P. Expressed hope rival would develop uterine cancer and die a slow, tortuous death; composed painstakingly crafted correspondence intended to destroy rival's career reputation, cc'ing six different coworkers.*

Not exactly my best moments.

Five years from when Jesse moved out, I went to my sponsor's house and drafted a list of harms done to Barbara.

I got Barbara's number from Stanley and sat for some moments in a Starbucks armchair, praying for courage, my heart flopping all over the place. Courage doesn't negate fear; it just lets you act in spite of it. I hit dial. The call went to voicemail, thank god, where I controlled my breathing just enough to ask if I could meet her to set right my wrongs. My own voicemail picked up Barbara's response. How remarkable! she said. She and her sponsor had just decided it was time for *her* to approach *me* for amends. Via texting, we set up a meeting at my favorite café, Louisa's.

Forgiveness takes guts. As I parked in the lot behind the café, my heart was racing and adrenaline tingled through my body. My arch-nemesis of so long was in there. What would I say? "Leave that to god," I told myself. "Let's just walk into the café."

Alone by a window sat a small, harmless woman with a latte. This all-powerful Godzilla who had ravaged my city had shrunk down to a nondescript, ordinary customer perhaps five-foot-three almost frailly thin. Yet I had to push myself to take every step toward her table. Close up, I could see she was just as nervous. She stood, and we hugged.

Back when I drank, there was always this moment after I'd sworn I wouldn't drink today of relinquishing control, of saying fuck it. It's funny, but when we're all queued up to do the right thing, especially in scary amends, the moment we surrender to it feels oddly similar. Here I go, come what may! But *this* time, we let go to god instead of to addiction.

We decided I'd go first. Sure, why not? I had the note card my sponsor had helped me write, but I didn't really need it. I explained that I'd blamed her for the demise of an unhealthy relationship that actually *needed* to end. I'd believed that I could lessen my own pain by inflicting pain on her. As a result I'd intruded hatefully upon her privacy and attempted to discredit her professionally – I named all the specifics. Then I asked if I'd left anything out, and what I could do to set things right.

"This!" she said, gesturing at where we were. "This is plenty. I don't feel like you owe me anything. I'm the one who caused the real harm."

Next she read aloud her amends letter to me, which was sincere and sweeping in owning all her wrongs. I don't think I could have written a better one. The only thing holding me back from a full sense of absolution was a problem I have with overacting. I'm talking about real life acting, even though for the person speaking, it's not acting. Like, my mom uses the dramatic tones of a 1940s movie actress every time she expresses sorrow or compassion. To her, that's how you show you mean it. So what I'm saying is, Mom would have really loved Barbara's amends. Myself, I had to try to ignore her pained facial expressions and the minor strains of her voice to believe her feeling was genuine – which it was.

When Barbara finished reading, she sat back and relaxed visibly while we continued to chat, now without a script. The only trouble was, Barbara fell into precisely the trap the Big Book warns against, of disclosing information of which the harmed person has been happily ignorant. Namely, I'd assumed all my raging voicemails and emails carried some kind of hurtful impact; that's why I was making amends for them. Never had I questioned that.

10/29/2008: "She said my hate messages fell like a child's stick arrows – that she'd felt no guilt or compassion. She'd been so smug in her victory that I had no power to hurt or insult her. I was classified as a 'sore loser,' and all my screamed outbursts met with eye-rolling."

The picture she painted was just a little too vivid. At one point, she described me as a worm on the sidewalk hurling threats at her. That put me over the top. Time skipped back and deep in my guts something detonated: anger. I was back in 2003, the gullible chump whose self-worth hinged on the actions of others. My life was sinking, sinking... It felt awful. In that moment I felt enough strength surge into my arms to stand and flip the café table in one move. I felt enough breath fill my lungs to roar, "Fuck you, bitch!" But that wasn't what I'd come here to do – put new phrases on my tombstone. And Barbara was describing a past she assumed we could both laugh at. So I prayed through my pounding heart: "Help me, god. Help me, love." In answer I was reminded of something Richard, my old therapist, used to say: We think anger makes us powerful, but in truth, only love does.

Who had lied to Reilly during the year she carried on with Kevin? Then who ignored Kevin's pain to drink with the parakeet and woo Jenna? Then who ran into Jenna walking shoulder to shoulder with Theo? Hadn't I always felt, if I were honest about it, *exactly* as Barbara had described? In other words, wasn't her sole crime being just like me?

The wave of anger passed, and we laughed and talked some more. I've seen her since at meetings where we get along just fine, and I always wish her happiness.

~

Before I started attending Al-Anon, I used to think the idea of making amends to oneself was pretty hokey. I made none. I didn't understand that a lot of the harms I did myself – ongoing condemnations, criticisms, and comparisons – fueled the self-loathing that caused me to act out and harm others. Close to my heart I still carried guilt for those years of self-bondage. I still blamed myself as the only person who could have warped their youth with something so creepy. But god changed that. Who'd have thought my practice of greeting and learning three things about anyone who annoyed me would lead to healing around this particular wound?

Cya annoyed me so much, I had to keep greeting her again and again. She showed up at my homegroup in 2004, carrying with her so much rage and self-pity that they formed an almost visible storm cloud above her head. "If you had my life," she seemed to broadcast, "you'd be pissed off, too!" My efforts to befriend her were rebuffed; she did *not* want to talk to some cheerful AA bitch. She scowled as she told me her troubles were more numerous and serious than she cared to explain to a stranger.

So I decided to kill her with kindness. Every time I saw her, I made a point of greeting her – whether she fucking liked it or not. One night she brought along an adolescent son; he looked as grim as she did, so from then on I reminded myself that any service to Cya was also a service to that boy. How was he, I would ask? Trouble! she'd respond. Gone were the days, she told me, when he'd been as cute and easy as my little boy – but of course, *Louisa* was so lucky in everything! She faked a smile and dropped it. Really, she did.

"Wow!" I remember thinking. "This woman ain't afraid to hate my guts!"

This continued for several months. Sometimes I couldn't help suppressing a smile at the blatancy of Cya's bitterness. I loved her for it, in fact, for all her human foibles that I recognized from my own experience. I knew there had to be more to Cya than that hoary hide, or she'd long since have quit coming to meetings. I can't say I noticed immediately when she quit showing up. I guess I assumed she'd relapsed.

So I was completely surprised when, perhaps six months later, I received a call from a cheerful, gracious woman claiming to be Cya.

"You were always so nice to me," she said, "even when I was really negative. Now I choose the monthly speakers for my new home group, so I thought of you. Would you be willing?"

I'd handed my number to her on countless slips of paper, but I always figured she used them to wipe her ass. I never dreamed she'd *call* me. The meeting was in Redmond, a long drive away. Of course, I agreed to speak.

"The Doctor's Opinion" describes my experience when Cya ran up to hug me in the church auditorium: "I knew the man by name, and partly recognized his features, but there all resemblance ended." This Cya would laugh full-out at practically *nothing*! She knew everyone at the meeting and scrambled to hug them, talking all over herself. She was as over-the-top happy, joyous, and free as she had been dour before.

When I marveled at the change in her, she blushed: "Yeah, I was pretty messed up back then," she said, "and you were one of the few people who kept reaching out to me, even when I hated you for it. 'Cause I *did*..."

At this particular speaker's meeting, I was given a full fifty minutes to tell my story, as opposed to the usual twenty-five. Because of that length of time and the fact that I'd probably never see most of these Redmond people again, I decided to share more of my story than I'd ever shared before. I touched on the bondage disorder. Standing at a raised podium and speaking into a microphone, I described for the first time the drawings I'd created as a child, the unspeakable shame and guilt of being caught with them, and the fact that these pressures had erupted in an obsessive compulsive disorder that plagued me until I was almost thirty. I didn't describe my self-bondage ritual specifically; it seemed a bit risqué to explain to a large room of alcoholic men, some well and some not. Even so, my voice shook and my armpits ran with sweat as I recounted what had been in my drawings, how I'd felt when my mother shamed me, and the years I'd struggled with a related compulsion. From there, I went into my "normal" years of drinking, what happened, and what it was like now.

I finished speaking and took my seat while the meeting wrapped up with announcements and such. Sitting there, I backlashed into mortification: "God help me, what have I *done*? Perversion isn't alcoholism! That was so inappropriate! Cya must be dying with embarrassment!" I rose for the Serenity Prayer wishing I could bolt, although even then I could see in the eyes of my fellow alcoholics a loving inclusion.

Serendipity struck just in time! Amid the shuffling to form a big circle, a woman I'd never seen before trotted a beeline down the main aisle of the room. She arrived somewhat breathless at my side, about ten years younger than I with sandy brown bangs, and grabbed my hand. Just before the prayer, she whispered in my ear: "I drew those exact same pictures as a kid!"

If I'd seen angel wings on her back, I could not have been more amazed and grateful. We spoke the prayer together, the two of us squeezing hands. *The courage to change the things I can...*

When the circle broke, we met each other's eyes. She thanked me for having the courage to share so honestly. She'd never dreamed someone else would tell *that* part of her story! Like me, she'd experienced a trance, and the drawings had been her darkest, most shameful secret. Though she wasn't ever caught, she'd spent much of her adolescence fearing she must be a pervert.

"I always thought I was the only one!" she exclaimed.

"Me, too!" I said.

Around the two of us a sizeable group of people was gathering, waiting to thank me, so with another quick hug, she was gone. She told me her name, but I forgot it, which is perhaps fitting. To me she's simply a fellow sober alcoholic out there somewhere – a woman almost as weird as me. In fact, I saw something similar in the eyes of all the people waiting to shake my hand, a look of awe as if I'd just walked through fire. Vaguely I could sense that the majority of those men and women carried some form of shame for sexual behaviors of their past. To each of them I'd given a ray of light. In fact, it was that experience, along with my experience sponsoring women with sexual shame, that emboldened me to tell my whole story in this book.

By the way, I saw Cya again just a month or two ago at my homegroup after five years, sitting kitty-corner to me and knitting busily. She sent me a smile, but I couldn't place her at first. Grey-haired and radiating a sort of matronly contentment, she looked like someone who'd always been happy. Holy crap! Cya?!

We hugged after the meeting and I apologized for the puzzled look I'd sent her.

"That's okay," she shrugged, laughing. "I mean, you're so *popular,* and I'm not."

So it truly *was* Cya! I saw that over the years she'd settled down somewhere between her crabby self and the boundlessly exuberant woman of the Redmond meeting. I was glad. No one can maintain that pink cloud forever, and it's the landing, the application of faith to one's daily grind, that poses the true test of sobriety. Though she still lived in a distant suburb, she'd brought a friend to this meeting because it was near the friend's home. This woman, glancing about impatiently, hardly responded to my greeting, as if she were anything but pleased to be here. Grumpy, that's what she was. Pissed off about life and eager to leave. Yet I could see Cya was upbeat and loving toward her regardless of the response, offering kindness and hope with patient persistence.

It doesn't get any better than that. It really doesn't.

Clockwise from top left: Annoying people partying at my house stone cold sober; some of my favorite annoyances, Courtney, Matt, and John C., girlfriends who made me jealous; Ack! Droves of annoying sober drunks invade the summer cabin!

27: 10TH WEIRD THING; VANITY, SEX, AND ALTITUDE

If I in my north room
dance naked, grotesquely
before my mirror
waving my shirt round my head
and singing softly to myself:
"I am lonely, lonely.
I was born to be lonely,
I am best so!"
If I admire my arms, my face,
my shoulders, flanks, buttocks
against the yellow drawn shades,—

Who shall say I am not
the happy genius of my household?

> -William Carlos Williams
> Danse Russe

In the fall of 2004, I landed my dream job directing the English Department Writing Center at the University of Washington. If I thought you were interested, I'd write chapters on the joys of working with brilliant, gifted students with a natural philanthropic bent – but I doubt you are. Briefly, then, I got to choose my tutoring staff based on writing samples and the capacity for empathy I detected in interviews, then teach them writing center pedagogy via my own class, and finally mentor them for years as they tutored in the center and grew up before my eyes. I learned so much from these students, who *wanted* to be of service to others, even though their lives didn't depend on it. I was "out" in the writing center as both a sober alcoholic and former lesbian, and from my desk I offered an "ask me anything" service much like

Lucy's psychiatry booth in *Peanuts*. They claim, to this day, to have learned as much from me as I did from them.

So… more about overcoming fear and sickness, but first, here comes a writing center Weird Thing.

Before I developed the online sign-up system, students used stop by in person to reserve tutoring appointments, which we scheduled on a clipboard. One day a girl came in requesting an appointment.

"Your name?" I asked, hovering my pen over the time slot.

"Wendy…" she said, and then paused for me to write it.

I *wanted* to write 'Wendy,' except something jammed up in my brain. I felt her waiting, but for the life of me, I could not *remember* how to make a 'W'! I pushed myself, but nothing happened. I *did* know how to make an 'L,' though, because my name began with L, so I just went ahead and wrote, 'Lee.'

The girl pulled back a bit. In a shocked voice she asked: "How did you do that?!"

"Oops!" I said, crossing it out. "I don't know why I wrote that!"

"No—! That's my last name," said the girl, her voice flat, "but I hadn't said it yet." She stared at me accusingly.

I felt as if I'd committed a social blunder. "I'm sorry!" was all I could think to say. "Lucky guess!" My primary feeling was not amazement that I'd just read this girl's thoughts, but embarrassment that I'd been caught doing so.

She pointed insistently at the crossed out 'Lee.' "That's how you spell it, too, with double E. I've never been here in my life!" She was clearly upset: "How do you know my name?!"

"I couldn't think how to make a 'W,'" I faltered, now hastily writing 'Wendy' after a comma and retracing the crossed out Lee letters, "so I just wrote 'Lee' instead!" I laughed uneasily as if to say, 'you know how it is!' and imagined if I could just get her appointment set, she'd let it go.

"*That makes no sense!*" She stared at me, incensed, as though I took her for a fool. She was searching as hard for a workable explanation as I was for an excuse for my 'rudeness.'

"I'm sorry! My mind must have just picked it up because you were about to say it!"

That answer – the truth – did not satisfy Wendy Lee. She argued more and left visibly angry. I told some of the tutors what had just happened and showed them the clipboard, but we could only laugh, shake our heads, and say things like, "That's crazy!" I emailed a few friends about it. When Wendy came in for her appointment a few days later while I was tutoring, she glared at me across the room as though I were either a witch or some kind of spy. I felt amused that someone could be so upset by a clear-cut case of telepathy, though, at Wendy's age, I'd have been equally insistent upon a logical explanation.

I still had no idea why so many Weird Things happened to me, but I was beginning to accept the fact that they did. It was just my lot.

~

Living a sober, healthy, god-centered life gave me guts. It opened the freedom to pursue all kinds of things I never would have tried pre-steps. It let me take risks and also make a few mistakes, though with minimal injury to others.

In terms of vanity, sex, and romantic love, being single in my mid-forties opened a whole new adolescence. I felt ashamed of my preoccupation with looking hot. Someone who said such spiritual things at meetings ought not to be caring how her ass looked while she said them – or so I felt. I told myself, at this phase of my life, that this vanity and sexuality ran counter to spiritual growth. I ought to be humbly celibate, wait for god to send a man with a large THE ONE arrow over his head, whom I would then marry and knit for. Anything else was self-will. What I believe now is that god wants us to bumble through exactly what we do in order to learn. All it ever asks of us is that we seek growth, even if that growth comes about in an awkward, ungraceful manner, as did mine. We can grow even as we maintain a concern about our asses' appearance. Humans are simple; we think stupid things.

I worked out consistently, five days a week at the university's gym. One day a Help Wanted sign in the locker room caught my eye, seeking part time fitness instructors. I "auditioned" well and, though the twenty-five-year-old hiring manager did pause a little over the fact that my last fitness teaching had been fifteen years ago (at a mostly-queer gym on Capital Hill), I soon found myself teaching an "Ab Lab" on my lunch hour twice a week. Instead of eating I'd dash down a 500-step hillside staircase to the gym, throw on workout clothes, crank up the gym's stereo, and start cueing our warm-up into the mic. Afterwards, I'd land back at my desk streaming with sweat. But if my son were with Jesse, I'd put in an extra workout before or after work. Weekends I ran. I shrank, I reclaimed my six-pack, and my shoulders actually got ripped – or at least stringy, pick your adjective. I got notes on my car again.

Still, two parts of my body refused to perk up: my breasts. Though they'd never been anything to write home about, nursing at forty when your skin lacks collagen is a definite "beauty don't." Deflated, they hung flat and dejected against my chest, mottled with crepe. All my push-ups and bench presses only made for a firm pectoral bulletin board on which these were two saggy bibs were tacked. I'd never forget the look on John's face when he first saw them, sort of like someone seeing a banana split with a big lugy on top.

For three post-nursing years I'd tried my best to love my *National Geographic* breasts. But, let's face it: if I were a guy, I'd want nothing to do with them. Even if I were a politically correct lesbian pretending to care nothing for conventional beauty, I'd be secretly bummed. If I wanted to date men well-preserved enough for me to find them attractive, I'd do so dreading that moment when the bra came off and gravity dropped the surprise of twin yo-yos. But worrying about this was so unspiritual! Like a shame-faced stalker I researched plastic surgeons on the web, prone to closing the windows with a sigh of dismissal. What would my mom say? What would my siblings think?

But in the sauna one day, I saw breasts exactly like mine hanging on a woman slumped over a newspaper. Realizing I would rather fondle a flaccid squid, I decided then and there to go ahead with surgery. My mom had gifted me ten thousand dollars in stocks a few years before. I could enjoy either the security of knowing I owned them, or the confidence of packin' perfect boobs. I chose to invest in my sexual future.

I found a woman surgeon at the UW School of Medicine who was also an instructor, meaning students would observe the whole process and I would pay slightly less. The surgeon proposed a combination of breast reduction and augmentation. I didn't want any augmentation, but she insisted I lacked adequate body fat to proceed otherwise. Without implants to absorb the corrugation of my ribs, I'd end up with bumpy boobs – a product she refused to sign her name to.

I did not want implants. Who wants packets of saline to become a part of their body? But she gave no ground, quite stern with her Slavic accent. She kept asking, didn't I secretly want bigger breasts? There was nothing to be ashamed of! This was for no one but me; I shouldn't consider what anyone else might think.

"Buy yourself a *Playboy*," she advised. "Clip out the what you want – being totally honest – and I'll create it for you."

I still had a bunch of girlie magazines left over from my Zoloft-wanking days, so I thumbed through the familiar images, this time boob shopping. I thought about hiking, running, jumping around. In the end I brought her photos of my own breasts pre-pregnancy and a small-breasted girl from a magazine. Finally, she agreed to use the smallest size shell and to fill it with the same volume as the fat she removed with my extra skin.

I went through with it – a choice I've never regretted. I woke post-op to a very gay male nurse saying, "You are going to look so cute in a tank top!" I couldn't think what he was talking about. But my surgeon was a master of her craft. Virtually every mammogram technician and female internist who sees me remarks, "That's the best work I've ever seen." What they mean is, they look entirely natural – for a woman half my age.

The biggest risk I took with this elective surgery was not a botched job or an infection, but the painkillers prescribed for my recovery. Since I'd stressed that danger to my surgeon, she prescribed me only five Vicodins and twenty Tylenol 3's. Normies can't imagine the excitement my addict felt bringing these drugs into my home. It was as if Al Pacino or a Madonna – someone I'd idolized in my youth as utterly cool – were sleeping a few nights on my couch. I knew the danger, though; I'd heard so many stories of relapses that dragged alcoholics to new lows, all begun with a doctor's blessings. My defense was to create a chart showing all the times I took each pill; I also had to call someone in AA and to swallow a pill only while on the phone. I never, even for a minute, relaxed my guard. I treated those pills as you would a known murderous cannibal joining you at the dinner table who says things like, "please pass the butter." Yes, you'd pass it, but with open eyes.

Still, it was hard to call my sponsor on the third day and admit I needed no more of either drug. "I want to hear flushing," she said (not yet considered a form of pollution).

"But what if I *need* them? What if I fall down the stairs and tear my stitches or Keno kicks me in the boob?"

"They have this wonderful thing called 'renewed prescriptions,'" she responded. "Let's go."

I dumped and flushed. Al Pacino and Madonna disdainfully left my house. The let-down was palpable. It was just me again, plus my dumb old ordinary reality. Five minutes later, though, I felt vast relief. They were gone! I was healing! And I had the boobs of my dreams.

Now I could date. Men.

~

I'm not real proud of this phase of my evolution, but here goes.

> 2/3/2005: "I'm realizing I'm a total shy scare-de-cat around guys. Two things:
>
> 1) I asked Billy to go see *Aviator* with me last night. Then I hugged him goodnight and went to give him a peck on the cheek. He tried to go for the mouth as I moved in, but that would've been *me* kissing *him*. I hope he's not PO'ed.
>
> 2) I made a dating profile on Nerve.com, and when men email me, I freak out. I answer, I mean, IM them back, but I am all freaked out.
>
> But I want something to happen with somebody. I want sex. I do. I'm really impatient! I'm restlessly wanting to feel desired & desirable & desiring. You can see, I'm in manic spaz-out mode, a lot like last spring.

I hadn't dated in high school. My college escapades were either pre-calculated strategies or drunken blurs. For fourteen years, excepting one neurotic night with Theo, I'd been a lesbian. Now I arrived at a second puberty, hetero and bumblingly naïve. How did my sexuality work? Was it bad and wrong? What was masculine desire all about? Were there right ways to explore what felt daring, like acting in the moment if both people wanted to? I did not know. And I couldn't find out without screwing up a bunch.

> 2/5/2005: "I had sex with Billy last night. I invited him over alone to watch *Kill Bill 2,* and we snuggled on the couch until he kissed me. Then I told him I needed his help. I said I wanted to be a slut, but I couldn't do it alone. I told him I hoped to date several men at once because I didn't know what I was doing. We joked about my breasts, about tonight being the grand opening. We laughed and were nervous the first time, but during the

night it was pretty hot. Though he's not right for me, somewhere in his kindness is a kind of intimacy, so I wonder about pain for both of us down the road.

The pain turned out to be greater for me than for Billy. He was a somewhat classic, emotionally unavailable alcoholic with at least sixty prostitutes in his past, by his own reckoning. Until you hit that barrier somewhere short of his inmost heart, he was a sweet, kind, and very funny man – though humor, also by his own admission, he used as a way to skirt intimacy. Only a week into it I abandoned all my slut resolve, shut down my Nerve account, and believed I was in love with Billy. He became, in essence, the new John. My need for his blessings was all-encompassing, while rejection would stamp my entire life BULLSHIT. Without the Other's admiration, I was still worthless.

Dinner dates and island trips and walks and lots of video movies interrupted by sex: it took us a few months to watch the entire *Lord of the Rings*. This was (and still is) the closest thing I'd had to a normal heterosexual dating. Billy was crazy about me at the outset and would often use such phrases as "all my life," "never dreamed," and "when we're old," which alarmed me internally. But as is standard for such dating relationships, after about four months Billy's interest began to wane. Never would he sit with me at an AA meeting: "It's nobody's business," he'd say. First an element of curt dutifulness entered his manner, then his calls became less and less frequent. A sort of constipated look of compliance haunted his face. I broke up with him after five months, almost as a strategy to win him back. Since we saw each other regularly at meetings, it was easy enough to take up again that fall. But as winter came on, he withdrew more and more.

My old ego support gizmo of the admiring partner was wearing thin. I knew, clear as day, what the problem was, but self-knowledge couldn't stop me from piling on love, surprise gifts, and hope. My self-worth, so full of holes and weak spots, was teetering on collapse yet again.

> 11/3/2005: "On a walk yesterday I passed the row of frat and sorority houses littered with the aftermath of Halloween parties – pumpkins drunkenly smashed, beer cups rolling about in the breeze among wet, fallen leaves. I could see into windows – faint lunchrooms with big, hand painted banners – and I felt envy, imagining ideal

lives in there filled with friends and excitement. I thought, 'My youth is over.' Over *and* wasted because it hadn't been fun enough.

"Then I asked god, 'God, is this Mountain Dew envy, *again*? [ads from the '70s set to raucous music and showing high-speed images of teens having fun, proving my life sucked.] Why does that stuff get me every time?'

"I passed the dorm where Jenna spent her first two nights at UW. I saw a muddy playing field and thought of Vassar, the Ultimate Frisbee games I watched from my lonely dorm window. I cried for a youth lost to envy and faking, for the beauty of Keno's precious childhood slipping away even now, lost in the stress of appointments and papers and chasing a social life. The pain spiked in yearning for *something* real – and I realized it was god's love.

"So I knelt, right there by the wet tennis court not caring who saw, and I cried, 'God, please help me feel your love, please let me love others until I lose this shell of aloneness! Teach me to love, to open my heart and trust you, so that I am free to be just human!'

"And I felt a little something. I stopped hurting. Back at work, in the break room, I ended up talking to a TA [graduate student] who also has a young child, about the preciousness versus stress. I managed to be a little more candid, a little more trusting that life is much the same for her, and to understand that I am never alone, even in my deepest pain."

Billy broke it off a few days later, an official statement I'd been waiting for. After a few days I bounced back and recommended searching for my dream-man. I read *He's Not That Into You* and *If the Buddha Dated*. I fired up the Nerve.com profile and started meeting scads of men – coffee, walks, lunch – so many men I was not one bit attracted to! Well, fourteen, to be precise. What if I was still gay? Internet dating was every bit as tortuous heterosexually as it had been gaily. In one case, I actually *timed* my nervously jabbering date to see how many minutes elapsed before he asked about me: thirty. Yet I couldn't enter a room without casing it for the guy I'd end up marrying. I played out a radically condensed love affairs extending into old age with every good-looking guy in the produce aisle. I started checking for wedding rings. When, during a meeting, I got a flattering series of texts from a buff, multi-racial 29-year-old across the room, I texted back and ended up sleeping with him – literally the *worst* sex of my entire life (nothing but doggie-style pounding that, by morning, had hurt my back). Enduring the morning hour while the boy drank his coffee, I tried to listen to his babble of nervous clichés. I felt like an old tycoon who'd brought home a bimbo. How did those old guys stand it?

That night cost me much of my sense of smell, as it turns out. To ward off an unsexy cold the night before, I used the cold remedy, Zicam, which burned away my exposed olfactory nerve in four excruciating hours. Only a small percentage of people have an exposed olfactory nerve, but for us the zinc in Zicam is caustic. For six months I was totally scent blind, and never did regain my original range of sensitivity. After many years, the class action suit brought only a few thousand dollars. I sometimes feel god was pointing out to me all I took for granted in my chase after what I thought would make me happy.

Over the course of that year I slept with a total of four men – my highest rate since college. Slowly, I began to learn the simple truisms most women learn in their teens and twenties: that sex without love is empty, and that trying to make things happen sexually was as fruitless as any form of desperate self-propulsion. If I were ever to find love, I'd need to let god find it for me.

Of John Church obsession, at least, I'd been cured. Our friendship stood as a rock not caught up in my Tasmanian Devil whirlwind of need, self, and sex. In fact, after he lost a girlfriend to his best friend, John took his turn at spinning out of control while I stayed sane. For a brief period of weeks, the tables of our relationship were turned.

> 2/18/2006: "John sent me an e-mail saying he's attracted to me and has trouble not flirting because I am beautiful, intelligent, sexy, and a bunch of other stuff – but I think he's really just curious about the new boobs. I replied saying that I feel it too, sometimes, but that what we have now is worth so much more, etc., that we need to stay on track with friendship. Crazy world!"

~

Some months before, I'd asked John if he would climb Mount Rainier with me. His response was that we should sign up together for the Glacier Climbing Course offered by a clean and sober mountaineering club called OSAT – One Step At a Time. I was loath. I thought I already knew enough about mountain climbing based on day hikes from the *101 Trails* books to somehow pull off an ascent of Rainier. When John pointed out the average of three deaths per year on the mountain, the need to master ice axe arrest, roped travel, and frickin' navigation skills, he seemed to me a wet blanket. But I agreed, mainly because the cost of a climb with OSAT was about $75, compared to $7,000 with Rainier Mountaineering, Inc. Besides, I might meet the man of my dreams in the course.

We attended seminars the first Monday of every month and went on conditioning hikes any weekend we could swing it. Keno was five, so I had to find sitters and ask Jesse for extra time, which she granted. There was a tremendous amount to learn, and a huge amount of gear to assemble. But because OSAT is connected to AA and run in the spirit of helping, I was able to borrow most of my gear. When, six months later, I finally stood atop the 14,410 foot summit of Mount Rainier, out of all my gear, including pack, crampons, ice axe, trekking poles, gaters, harness, goggles, ten essentials, and layers of clothing, the only things I actually *owned* were my socks, down jacket, helmet, and long underwear.

Conditioning posed the greatest challenge. As a fitness instructor, I'd considered myself in great shape until I took that course. Climbing for many hours to high altitudes with a heavy pack – it's a whole different game. The day before an April conditioning climb of Mailbox Peak, I'd had some glamour photos taken for my dating profile to show off the new boobs, so I'd eaten almost nothing all day. The morning of the hike itself, I was running late, so I didn't bother with breakfast. The pace of the climb seemed ridiculously brisk, and I started feeling faint almost instantly. My friend Cody loaned me a trekking pole, which I gripped with my long, glamorous acrylic nails. On our first break, I was fumbling to unwrap a granola bar when I looked up and saw, amid the speckles of near-faint, a little gnome with beard and pointed hat who tilted out from behind a tree like a metronome pendulum, waved hello, and tilted back out of sight.

This was no Weird Thing. It was straight up blood sugar depletion, which one or two granola bars weren't going to fix. Approaching the peak hours later, I was devastated to discover the falseness of the false summit; I still had five hundred feet left to climb. I hated everyone. With an unspoken 'fuck this,' I fell behind the group. That's when a shy man, already dismissed in that morning's marital bliss scan as just another graying male classmate, offered to hike behind me however slowly I needed to go. I thanked him and proceeded to huff my way up, every muscle dragging. At the summit, I dropped an earring that no one could find, then chatted some more with the nice, graying fellow on the way down – because the marital bliss indicator had blipped once or twice. But as soon as I learned he worked in electronics and had only six months' sobriety, I lost all interest. He struck me as an uncreative everyman, and besides, you're not supposed to date newcomers. For months I forgot all about him, including his name: Grayson.

I came a long way. Four months later, when my Rainier climb came up, I was in the best shape of my life at 46. I'd not only climbed many mountains, I'd also spent half an hour every day on an oldschool Stairmaster with a thirty pound pack, exhausting myself in intervals. The first time I climbed to Camp Muir, a base camp at 10,080 feet, I arrived far ahead of my classmates – includeing guys in their twenties and thirties. The second time, I arrived with the early birds though I was serving as a "sherpa," carrying forty pounds of the climbing party's gear.

Climbing Mount Rainier demanded more guts physically, mentally, and spiritually than any other undertaking of my life to date. It was also one of the most rewarding, a jewel of sober living and follow-through.

In case you don't know, Mount Rainier is an active volcano with twenty-six glaciers and a top crater encircled by steam vents. It's the most prominent peak in the contiguous forty-eight states, meaning it rises most from the surrounding landscape. Five hundred feet higher is Mount Whitney, which I can tell you is a walk in the park compared to the difficulty, hazards, and unpredictability of Rainier.

You can look up from Camp Muir and see avalanches of thunderous magnitude trickling down its cliffs, roaring in the air about you yet resembling a few sliding grains of sand. At dusk, John and I lay in our tent on the Muir snowfield trying to sleep before our 10PM departure time. Our ears would fill with the deep rumble of avalanches, our eyes would pop open, and we'd stared wordlessly at one another until the roar had faded away.

"What the fuck are we doing?" I said tonelessly, my heart pounding.

"I don't fuckin' know," he said, equally stricken.

Yet at 10:00 that night, when the frozen snow would best support our crampons, amid cold and wind, we suited up in the darkness. You just do it, even though you're terrified. I didn't yet know enough to keep whatever I didn't want to freeze in my sleeping bag with me, so my gaiters and gloves were stiff and uncooperative. Where were my crampons? How did snow get inside my helmet?

Our leader, Don't Follow Me Dave, had already designated rope teams, so we tied in four per rope, each climber thirty feet from the next. The first rope started off into the windy darkness like skein of yarn unwinding, each climber waiting for the rope to go taut in front of him before he took his first step. The only other girl in our party was Krista, just in front of me on my rope. I watched the orb of her headlamp shrink with distance, then there was a gentle tug at my harness. The rhythmic crunching of my crampons on the frozen snow began. I could see only a small circle of snow lit in front of me, with tracks leading into an all-encompassing blackness, yet I could sense the massive height of the volcano to my left.

"God help me. God help me. Please help me," I prayed over and over, interrupted only by fear's refrain: "What the fuck am I doing here?!"

> 7/28/2006: "OSAT had given me all the hard skills I needed, but my battle turned out to be with acrophobia – fear of heights. One thing I'd never done was climb in darkness, and I was unprepared for the way it amplified my vertigo. During our eight and a half hour ascent from Muir, I co-existed with a fear worse than any nightmare, as potent as seeing an oncoming car through your windshield, and found ways to exist beside it.
>
> "Any time I shone my headlamp toward the drop-off side of the trail, I saw a steep edge of ice vanishing into black obscurity. Thousands of feet down and yet almost directly below, tiny caterpillars of sparks appeared almost motionless – the headlamps of other climbing teams, each thirty feet apart.
>
> "Vertigo isn't rational; it's autonomic. Vertigo blared at me what was on the brink of happening: my whole rope team would tumble off a shelf into emptiness. I hyperventilated, became a quaking spastic with wobbly

legs and arms that shook like wind-up toys. Every so often I would lose my balance and jump like a yanked jumping-jack toy.

"As I got more physically tired, it got harder. The edge literally seemed to suck me toward it. We came to a place where the trail became a foot-wide shelf along an ice wall of shoulder height – nowhere to sink my ice axe handle. John, who was just behind me (first on his rope team, I last on mine), told me to swing the pick of my axe sideways into the wall, but swinging meant momentum, which swamped me in dizziness. I'd swing, surge in terror, and spit out: "Fuck!" Take another step, swing: "Fuck!" John's voice at my back sounded like meaningless monkey chatter in the face of death.

"By 2 AM, stumbling and sick with dizziness, I realized I would have to tell our leader I simply couldn't do this, so we would all have to turn back – although descent, I knew, is far more dangerous than ascent, especially on ice. I had no choice. What excuse would I use to destroy everyone's summit dreams? I'd tell them I was a mother, that my son needed me alive.

"But the instant I thought of Keno, something in me shifted. Maybe you've heard those stories of moms who've lifted cars off their children single-handedly. I tapped that power. No pain could touch my little Keno. I was strong. I was capable. I could jam that pick into ice hard enough to arrest my whole rope if Keno's happiness hinged on it.

"'Fear,' I said, 'go fuck yourself!'

"Right about then we came to a huge crevasse where we had to cross a snow bridge, then clip into a fixed line and shuffle along a narrow ledge above its gaping depths. The bridge couldn't hold two at once, so John coached me in advance: 'Don't shine your lamp down there, Weez.' But once I was halfway out, I heard his awestruck voice: 'Shit! Holy shit! That is fuckin' nuts!!' So I looked down. Giant ice formations and melted out shadows layered deeper and deeper into darkness. Not only the ice bridge but several houses could vanish down that thing without a trace. Damn you, John!

"On the other side John kept urging me to clip onto the fixed line, but I was shaking so violently, my karabiner bounced everywhere but over the rope. 'You want help?' he asked, and I snapped back: 'I don't need any fucking help!' I fuckin' clipped in and walked the ledge alone on my fuckin' jelly legs. Fear could shake its death puppet in my face all it wanted, and I would ignore it just like the hiccups.

"Dawn came and we reached the crater by about 6:00 AM, having ascended almost two vertical miles in two days. The crater is a snowfield about the size of twin football fields, rimmed in by rock so you can't see anything from its floor. John, with his crack-burned lungs, had dropped behind me by about two minutes. I waited for him to stagger over the brink and unrope, and when he swore he was too spent to climb to the crater rim's high point – the true summit – I actually linked arms and yanked him along with me. Still, he couldn't keep up, because his big muscles were sucking up the scant oxygen, so he begged off. That's how it happened that, as another party came down to get out of the wind, I reached Rainier's highest point alone.

"I'd always imagined this moment as my crowning glory, the ultimate 'I kick ass!' – but I felt none of that. Each step I advanced unfurled more of the Puget Sound valley, until its winding waterways and forested flatlands stretched out below me with a placid beauty I could hardly absorb. What I felt was my own fleeting insignificance. Rainier has stood there in its grandeur, overlooking that landscape, for almost a million years. For these brief moments, I looked with it. I began to cry in this weird nasal way, feeling love for the lifeblood of Nature that survives in the Pacific Northwest despite massive human assault. This green land was my England, my Shire, my home.

"I looked north toward the gray smudge that was Seattle, its scale too miniscule for my eyes. So many people I loved were in that gray! I wished them blessings. I realized I was standing at the point toward which I'd lifted my eyes countless times in my life, but now with the direction of vision reversed. I could see the island of our summer cabin, and Olympia where I'd gotten sober. I seemed to return the glances of Louisa at various ages, with various partners and hairdos and problems and hopes, all of them looking up here. 'We did it,' I told them.

"But because I'm an alcoholic, a loathing voice in me said, '*Down there you've lived all of your pathetic, fucked-up little life. It's more than half over now and amounts to nothing. Who cares if you've climbed all this way? You're as worthless up here as you are down there!*'"

"But because AA has taught me not to engage with that voice, but to seek god instead, I prayed. God told me, I'd done good. I'd done good in climbing and overcoming my fears, and I'd done the same thing day by day throughout all my life – choosing courage over fear, one little step at a time. I am just a person. I'm just here to love. All told, I've helped more than I've harmed. It is enough.

"Then John and everyone else came up and we yelled in the wind and took pictures, and I loved them all so much because we'd done this thing together. And I'm feeling like, man, really there's not much more to life than that! I have to remember that my fellows are with me, and we're here to help each other up. That's the climb of my life."

Clockwise from top left: Me on Mount Rainier above a f*cking huge crevasse; with John Church on Rainier's summit, 2006; brand new boobies at 45; with a few friends of Bill, 2005

28: LOVE MY WAY

*"I love you," she whispered, "only you, no one but you.
Oh! You have made me so unhappy with your
indifference. Oh! I have suffered, suffered! Now you are
here we shall love each other, my Robert. We shall be
everything to each other. Nothing else in the world is of
any consequence."*

-Kate Chopin
The Awakening, 1899

*"In Al-Anon, I had to unlearn a lot of romantic nonsense
in order to find a satisfying life in the here-and-now."*

-Courage to Change
October 12

I fell in love again that summer at the age of forty-six, when I didn't really mean to. I don't know that I was qualified to, since none of my past relationships had been founded on anything healthy. And though almost three years had passed since Jesse moved out, the fear of more pain like that still saturated me, partitioned off in a compartment where it wouldn't affect my chase after romantic adventure. I was lonely. I felt incomplete. But I also feared losing the small amount of true self I'd uncovered in three years on my own. As had happened with Billy, if I dated you five times, I'd toss my entire life in a storage closet and devote my every thought to pleasing you. I knew this was a problem. I just couldn't prevent it. The needed power wasn't there.

Over the course of the Glacier Climbing class, that shy guy who had walked behind me up to Mailbox Peak migrated gradually toward my "eligible male" target area. Grayson was six foot one and ruggedly handsome with distinctive, weatherbeaten features and hair once dark that was now graying and thinning at the temples. During field trips he tented with a friend of mine, Cody, so he was often forced, despite his quiet reserve, to overhear our goofy conversations. On our crevasse rescue field trip, for instance, I came crunching back from the camp's snow latrine and crouched beside their tent.

"Man, do I feel good!" I bragged to Cody, who'd had no luck there for two days. "I feel loads lighter! Just truckloads."

"Good for you. Tell the world."

"I am! You know, you need to relax a little – know what I mean? Be less uptight. Go with the flo-ow." I gestured groovily.

Grayson, sitting a few feet apart on his sleeping pad, smirked in another direction, unsure how much he was meant to hear. Later on that same trip, when we were taught to use our prusiks, set up snow anchors, and so on, I figured out that Grayson knew more about mountaineering than most of our instructors. A month later I volunteered as a sherpa for Cody's Rainier climb, carrying gear up to Camp Muir to condition for my own climb the following week. To pass the time, Cody and I invented an incredibly geeky game of "Finish the Big Book Quote!" which we played all the way from Panorama Point to Pebble Creek with Grayson yet again forced to overhear our jokes. I was getting a blister by the time we stopped at the creek to filter water, and there Grayson – notorious for carrying the world's smallest pack with absolutely everything in it – shyly offered me some moleskin. As he parceled it out, sitting beside me at the babbling creek, smiling too hard and blushing, I registered a palpable shift toward the target area.

At that time I was dating Damon, a thirty-nine-year-old play-boy finishing his BA who'd asked me out by sort of galloping sideways along the path beside me as I walked from the UW gym – a cute ploy I later discovered he used with many women. But he also happened to be ebony black and ripped from head to toe, and I to be exoticizingly curious, I'd taken the bait. Our dates thus far had consisted primarily of his overt lobbying for sex ("Pleeeaze? It's my *birthday*!") and my postponing it.

Damon was a confident, smooth operator. By contrast, Grayson's awkward sincerity seemed almost too tender for this world. He could only say what he meant and hope that you, too, would play by those rules. I had no inkling that day of his mountaineering feats or the crazily dangerous solo rock climbs he'd pulled off, but I did know he signed up for our course only because he'd lost his driver's license by refusing to blow for a DUI. As it turned out, he hiked faster than anybody I would ever meet and knew the wilderness like Daniel Fuckin' Boon, fine with no trail so long as he had a map and compass. All I saw now, though, was a shy man blushing and fumbling.

A few thousand feet higher, our group took a break at Moon Rocks, one of the last landmarks before Muir where climbers can sit down on rocks rather than snow to eat and drink, and, for some of the men, change their sweaty shirts. I had just turned with my mouth full to yell something at Cody when somebody beyond him – I didn't catch the face – pulled up his shirt to flash an eyeful of perfectly tapered and suntanned torso spanned with dark chest hair that narrowed to a seam through that somebody's six-pack. Jesus! The effect was so electric I turned away at once, embarrassed and scandalized. Why would someone *do* that? This was not the place!

When I looked again, cautiously, I could see no suspects in the vicinity besides Grayson. What – Mr. Shy-guy packing a bod like that?! Why was I so flustered? And what the hell was going on between my legs? It was years before it occurred to me that no other women on the climb had noticed anything remarkable. What hit me was some kind of chemistry, some energy of attraction almost as if a hint of the future had infiltrated my awareness.

A week later I summitted Rainier myself and posted online the account excerpted in the previous chapter. I sent out a link to the OSAT listserve, and among the congratulatory responses was Grayson's:

7/29/2006: FROM: Grayson Beaverton, TO: Louisa P.
"I've got to say your writing brought tears to my eyes. I've never read such a heartfelt/deep trip report before. Hope to see you in the class again next year. I really enjoyed climbing with you. Watch out for the little gnomes!

love ya,
Grayson"

I assessed it rapidly, noting a lack of grammar and spelling errors and, at the same time, experiencing a bodily memory of what came over me at Moon Rocks. But what a weird last name! Just as I'd been teased for the slang male part mine sounded like, he must have been teased for the female counterpart. Funny. And what about that "love ya" – ? I wrote back jauntily, and he responded with an answer which I answered. But the volley wound down to an inevitable close. Now that the course was over, I would probably never see him again.

About a week later, however, someone posted on the OSAT listserve that two OSATers and a friend from the Mountaineers had been attempting a difficult summit in the Cascades when one of them – a Glacier Climbing grad who helped out on many of our trips – had fallen to his death. Grayson was named as one of the companions.

Email didn't seem the right way to console someone for such a tragedy, so I got his number from Cody, who told me Grayson was holed up in his apartment and apparently ignoring his phone. So I decided to let it go. Who was I to him, after all? If he wouldn't even talk to his friends, he certainly wouldn't want words from some OSAT chick he'd exchanged a few emails with.

The following Thursday, however, working at my desk on campus, I got a weird intuition: *Call that shy guy. Do it now. He's in a lot of pain.*

I couldn't tell where this notion came from, but I acted on it straight away. Since I worked in a basement with no cell reception, I went into a break room across the hall and dialed from a wall extension, all the while fairly confident he wouldn't pick up.

He picked up. From the rusty, downcast slant of his voice, I could tell how long he'd been silent. I felt empty-handed. I had no answers. But I did know pain.

I felt my focus sharpen, that strange self-forgetting that happens when we choose to be of service. I asked him, not as a question but an instruction, to tell me the whole story, starting from before anything went wrong. To my surprise he began instantly, with that same trusting directness I'd noted before.

I listened, hearing his guilt for choices that had not been his alone to make. Whenever he reached such a juncture, I'd interrupt and, same as I do in fifth steps, ask the most uncomfortable questions. "Wait. So was it too hot for helmets? Who decided that?" Or, "Who decided you guys didn't need to rope up?" I was gambling, and I knew it, but in each case the choice had been unanimous.

When he described the fall itself, he began crying so hard he could hardly speak. Yet he kept on. He told me every visual, every comparison that entered his mind. He was doing what I'd asked, telling everything, to let me help him. He and the other survivor had climbed down a thousand feet, calling out, rushing, trying to plan a rescue. Then came that moment they spotted the body, sprawled and broken beyond any hope. "We just sat down with him and bawled. We cried for, God, an hour. There was nothing you could do but cry."

"Nothing," I echoed, my own eyes flooding. I waited while he cried.

"Louisa!" he burst out suddenly, "Louisa! Why did this *happen*?!"

My name – it shocked me to hear it sobbed from the depths of this man's heart. I became strangely aware of my own heart, the organ itself, which felt as though something had just struck it. *Pierced* it. Noisy people came into the break room; I plugged one ear. I tried shut out everything but his voice, speaking to him of god and all we can't know. The whole time, that strange sensation still zinged in my heart. What *was* it? When we'd hung up and I'd sat silent for a minute, I rubbed the spot on my chest.

A friggin' cupid arrow! Wrong time and place, but there it was.

I was still seeing Damon at the time, having succumbed to his coaxing twice for the second and third worst sex and of my life. When Grayson emailed to thank me for talking with him, his every phrase held a dozen times the intimacy of those copulations.

The following night I wrote in my journal, pausing, musing, surprised by each short, primer book sentence as it appeared on the page:

> 8/11/2006: "With Damon it doesn't feel like it can go anywhere. And for now, that's good. For now, it's good for me to experience a dead-end relationship that's mostly about sex.
>
> "I sort of love Grayson, though.
>
> "I talked to him yesterday about Ted Johnson's death. He told me how he fell and fell. He cried. I want to see him more. I think he is a simple man with a regular job. I know he is newly sober, but I like him. I think he is good. I could see having a real relationship with him, that was about love. Maybe I DO want love."

When Damon bailed on our Saturday plans without even bothering to cancel, I broke up with him. The fallen climber's memorial was that day, but I didn't know how to find it, so I caught a ride with Cody, having guessed correctly that Grayson would do the same. He remained silent during the drive, but somehow I ended up sitting next to him at the outdoor service. As friends shared memories of working or hiking with Ted, Grayson kept silent, declining to come forward. Only when the service had ended and the audience was rising around us did he begin to speak, his tear-filled eyes fixed on the grass beneath our feet.

"This one night Ted wanted to sleep out under the stars. We had all these goats hanging around our camp, and we warned him…"

He told several stories, all of them funny, touching. We laughed through tears. Somehow we'd ended up holding hands.

Later that afternoon I caught a ride home with John Church. He'd seen Grayson and me together and insisted I promise – actually *swear* – that I'd call Grayson and ask him out for coffee.

"I can't hit on a man who's in grief!" I protested.

John sighed. "Louisa, yes, he's grieving. But— there's no bad time for love."

I ended up inviting Grayson to my AA homegroup's annual picnic in the park. There he, I, and a few others tossed a Frisbee a while, at which I sucked, but as the event organizer and meeting secretary, I had a lot to do that kept us from talking. After the meeting broke up, I searched the crowded, noisy church basement and saw no trace of Grayson. My heart sank.

"Where is he?" John mouthed from across the room. When I signed, "I don't know!" he strode purposefully out the door to the parking lot, where he collared Grayson just short of a retreat into Cody's truck. "Get back in there and ask her out!" he told him.

Grayson obeyed. He waited, tortured with shyness, while I wrapped up another conversation. The first words he got out were about how awkward he felt.

"Whenever *I* feel awkward," I said brightly, "I just pretend I took an awkward drug on purpose, and then I'm like, 'Oh…. *man*! I'm startin' to feel pret-ty awk-ward!'"

He smiled bewilderedly. "I don't think I'd ever take that drug."

But he did ask me to coffee. Unfortunately, he lived twenty-some miles away and had only a bicycle, so I had to pick *him* up.

"No problem!" I effused. "I used to be a lesbian!"

Again, he looked bewildered.

So, after a long drive in bad traffic spent asking myself what the hell I was doing, I picked Grayson up in a bank parking lot across the highway from his apartment. We drove to a roadside

Starbucks where we perched at an absurdly tiny table amid a steady stream of beverage procurers. He seemed encased in awkwardness, his sincerity on hold. "How badly he must want to get laid!" I thought cynically.

When we moved to a quieter restaurant next door, he relaxed somewhat. He was three years younger than I and still married to a wife of nearly twenty years from whom he'd separated on and off for the past five. He was also in outpatient treatment, still on parole from the DUI, would not be driving for at least six months.

"Better and better!" I thought.

And yet I was drawn to stay longer, I couldn't say why, for what turned out to be a five-hour date winding up at IHOP. His past, I began to gather, had been marred by his mother's debilitating stroke when he was eleven, and his second daughter's severe and incurable genetic illness, leading up to a failed marriage and the loss of virtually every possession he'd worked to own. Both his parents had died years ago.

Yet he had resolved to be happy. Describing his 2,650-mile hike of the Pacific Crest Trail, he said, "So I'd find myself wondering, do chipmunks ever *walk*? I mean, when no one's looking? I can think about something like that for *hours* on the trail."

"Like a koan," I suggested, "a Zen koan?"

"No, not really," he shrugged. "I just don't need a lot to think about."

Did he even know what a koan was? It seemed so. Yet he used terms like "dandy," and "snug as a bug." He said "yard" to mean pull and pronounced certain words with an accent astoundingly similar to Zelda's and my old dumb talk, like "maysure" and "crick." At age sixteen he'd given up a hobby of hunting and trapping for beer money, only because his mother forbade it. And yet there was something about his presence, apart from anything he said, that drew me in. What was it?

Because I'd been on fifty million dates, when I dropped him off I was bold enough to ask whether, having *not* been on one for twenty years, he'd kissed a girl goodnight in that long –? He had not. Would he like to? Yes, he said simply, he would.

So from the passenger's seat he kissed me, his hand reaching across to cradle my jaw ever so gently. It was a classic goodnight kiss, just deep enough for the tips of our tongues to meet – totally sweet and guileless.

Then he hopped out of my car and I zoomed away. "God knows…" I muttered as I merged back onto the highway, shaking my head but grinning at the same time, "what the hell I'm doing!"

~

Grayson could not have been more unlike any of my previous partners. My modus operandi, except perhaps in the case of Jim Reilly, had been to go after popular, charismatic people. *Everyone* admired Kevin, Jenna, and Theo! Grayson, at the opposite extreme, was virtually friendless and incredibly awkward at socializing. Just incredibly. For our first few dates, he did that thing where a person in a car reads every frickin' sign aloud in some announcer-type voice.

He didn't know what to say, or how to be romantic. His hairdo was – let's face it – a mullet, a good 25 years out of date. I knew he'd grown up in a tiny town east of the mountains, but come on! He'd put himself through community college in Seattle, hitchhiking daily half an hour each way, living with a string of girlfriends, and occasionally Dumpster diving. Couldn't he have learned a little about modernity?

For our second date I invited him to a weekend party at the summer cabin. Over three days, many of my twenty- and thirty-something tattooed and pierced AA friends came and went; we had barbeques, swam in the lake, played charades around the campfire, and engaged in all kinds of immature belly-laughing. Grayson watched from somewhere inside himself, silent and incredulous at the degree of dorkiness these people could display stone cold sober. The first night, we took Kelsey and Sydney for a walk in the woods. Wanting to kiss me before we got back to the cabin, he bent his knees to get down to my level, which didn't work out at all.

The next night, though, he and I paddled kayaks along the shoreline and into a cove that filled with high tide. He was smoother in a kayak than a teen on a bike, finding ways to skirt the blow-downs that blocked our way and then coaxing me to follow him further and further back in the twilight. The shrills of killdeer spilled over the water's surface and fat drips from our paddles chimed like music; I felt as if we'd entered a different century. Gone was his awkwardness, though he preferred to point things out silently with a nod or the tip of his paddle. Back on our beach, in the midst of dragging the kayaks up the beach, we stopped and shared the hottest kiss of my entire life. The clatter from my dropped paddle went ignored, and when I bit his neck a quiver passed through his whole body. By the time we finally stopped, we were both in quite a state. He looked down for a moment at the kayak as if he had no idea what it was. Then he rearranged his shorts briskly and bent to pick it up again.

Later that night while my friends still hung around the campfire, I crawled into Grayson's tent to say goodnight. Somehow I managed to crawl out again ten minutes later, all out of breath. While I was in there, I felt a sense of a match tossed near a big stack of cartoon TNT, an intense force of chemistry. "I could eat... you... up!" he'd said through gritted teeth, just before I skedaddled out from under him and back to my own tent.

Our first time together, back at his apartment, I remember a strange sense that we were both quite young. His physique was swim team youthful, and he'd been without sex a long time, but there was something else – some spell or energy I couldn't place. We loved like two kids lost in a twilit desert, halfway through lives that hadn't turned out as we'd hoped. So I was thinking. And Grayson, meanwhile, was thinking: "Hot damn! Sex!"

~

Sex had been a lot of things to me over the years, but never before had it meant so much straight-up joy. Our joy had to do with knowing how lucky we were to have found something so sweet this late in life. For the first time since Kevin twenty years before, I could climax from plain ole' intercourse. Sometimes more than once, and in some positions more than others – Grayson kept tallies. There was no birth control to futz with – he'd been fixed. Some days and nights we could hardly stumble from the bed except to take turns chugging Gatorade naked.

During college, I'd had sex because that's what you were supposed to do. Now, over two and a half decades later, I was truly present and curious with a male partner. What was this mustache phenomenon? And how did things work around those super narrow hips? Grayson's skin was perfect. His scent, perfect. His, um, *shape* perfect and quite fulfilling. Quads carved of stone, so inhumanly hard they unnerved me. I'd rap on them with my knuckles. "This is *not* how people are made!"

I'd never known anything like this, to just lie there immersed, to want nothing but him. Kisses delving into hungry acres of sweetness. Warmth and smoothness that rendered touch tremendous.

Skimming sensations that kept awakening my every surface, while somewhere between brain and body, that poignant ache thickened. I could not get enough of him. Finally, drunk off each other, we'd wander to a restaurant to eat – but not too much – so we could resume later.

When it's like that, lack of sleep is your biggest problem.

Chafing is your second.

In the weeks that followed, we hiked and camped or played tourist around Leavenworth and Seattle. We made each other compilation CD's. He showed me wild plants and berries, traps of ant lions, how to read animal tracks, and I loaned him all my published stories. And so, very quickly and hard, we fell in love.

I felt terrified. I prayed in tears of dread and fear – please don't let me get hurt again this time! And the answer I got was always to calm down: *Trust this one. He is good.*

> 9/25/2006: "I went to kiss him goodnight before I turned on my side and there were tears running down his temples. I kissed them and asked what they were about. He said it had been so long since he'd felt love for someone and wanted to be loved, himself – that it was frustrating and frightening. I asked about the frustration part and he said it was from having to hold back so much. I said I knew he didn't want to push me too fast by saying 'I love you,' but that I had some of that for him, too.
>
> "The next day at the park, he said it all happened so fast, so intensely, that he wondered if it was just loneliness that made him fall so head over heels with a woman he 'hardly knew.' But he does know me! He delights in my zaniness, my bumbling, the eccentric idiosyncrasies of my [old VW] bus.
>
> "Later he lifted my bike from the bus like it weighed nothing and coasted it a hundred feet to my front gate. I couldn't believe the grace of motion when he swung off and stood on one pedal right up to the gate, everything fluid – a man so vividly alive, so attuned to his body in relation to the world. But his heart is so big, it's almost an encumbrance."

A few months into it, he emailed me at work saying he didn't know what he was doing. He wasn't even divorced yet. He couldn't support me or move in with me, so he didn't see where this thing was leading. He had promised himself he wouldn't marry or get tied down, and he didn't know what I expected.

I prayed a bunch. All my life, I'd lost myself in the other. Grayson and I were different and distinct enough, our magnetism jumping a wide gap, that I felt here was my chance to do everything differently. I emailed back that I had a full life of my own and that all I wanted from him was love – but without restraint. If he couldn't love me fully, he should go. I told him to take a month apart to think about it. Only an hour passed before he emailed again. He'd gone for a walk, cried, and realized he had no choice but to see where this led.

Our relationship never looked like love to a lot of people. Grayson lacked the social skills most people take for granted, which made socializing at best an uncomfortable chore and at worst a torturous obstacle course. He had no clue how to speak to a child, so he never got to know my son. For the first few years, we took part together in OSAT activities, but that stopped after he moved to a distant island. Most of my friends never even met my "imaginary" boyfriend. But every weekend when Jesse had Keno, I'd join him at his little country house and we would love each other. We were never what you'd call partners. I'd had a partner all my life, and I didn't really want one at this point. I liked mowing my own lawn and taking out my own garbage, raising my son by my standards alone. No, Grayson and I we were lovers in love – just the pure butter frosting without a lot of cake.

We were geeks together. I'd always win at Scrabble, but he'd beat me at practically everything else – especially "Fact or Crap." The man was a fact repository. We watched nature and science documentaries so he could soak up more, traded books and magazine articles, once even sat reading my huge dictionary together for hours, not to learn words, but to learn about them. Collaborating on crossword puzzles felt as fun as a picnic; I covered language and culture while he covered everything else. Every now and then, if he'd had way too much coffee, he'd talk up a storm about whatever was on his mind – then rue his indiscretion. But he was also a damn good listener. He'd listen so hard his lips would move a little with the words I spoke – one of countless little Graysonisms I adored without ever letting him know.

Almost every summer we took long trips through-hiking in the mountains, stuck in each other's pockets for more than three weeks and sometimes going days without encountering another person. In

2007 we hiked through Glacier National Park for a total of 175 miles. We almost got charged by a bull moose so tall he laced his antlers into a Douglas fir and rocked the whole tree to scare us away, then thundered past our camp; we spotted an adolescent grizzly whose overturned logs and stones Grayson had been reading for a mile; and we were once caught pretending to have backdoor sex on a flat rock slab in the midst of a roaring, white-water creek while our washed clothes lay drying in the sun (the hikers waved embarrassedly). We made love while a thunderstorm blasted and caromed about the surrounding mountains and rain battered our tent.

My attraction was constantly renewed because Grayson was so unlike anyone I'd ever met. At times he could be silent, impassive, and humorless as a warrior. Then when you least expected, he busted loose. There was a song on my iPod he loved, "Surround Sister," and when he cued it up and strutted ahead on the trail doing some sort of ridiculous chicken dance – he couldn't dance to save his life – I'd watch him picking up his knees and air-jabbing his trekking poles against the magnificent backdrop of the Rocky Mountains, his beard half grown-in and his do-rag tied on like a pirate – and feel I couldn't possibly love him more.

In 2008 we hiked 200 miles through the Eastern Cascades and two years later covered 250 miles along the John Muir Trail in the Sierra Nevada, tagging the summit of Mount Whitney. We skinny-dipped in pristine lakes, made love in nothing but tent netting amid a flower-filled alpine meadow ("But what if someone comes along and *sees* us?" "We'll jest show 'em our permit..."). Grayson could get so excited about the smallest treat, especially when we'd used up most of our supplies. Busting out a Lifesaver was a big deal. So was packaged salmon rolled up in an old tortilla with packet of mayonnaise, or a Kool-Aid snowcone in the blazing heat. We ate these like royalty, the boulders that made up our dinner table commanding stupendous views.

But Grayson's crappy communication skills often translated to relationship problems. To me it seemed he had next to no patience, while to him it seemed he extended reams of it. Fights erupted over his hiking speed, which left me in the dust for sometimes hours at a time, and his mechanically rapid packing speeds next to my morning pokiness. If he spoke sharply, I'd say nothing but would *seethe* for hours. When he went so far as to start without me from bug-ridden campground below Evolution Basin, I snapped – bigtime. All the times I'd said nothing when he failed to see what he *ought* to do, all the rights to chivalry I was sacrificing so gamely by roughing it, all the time alone on the trail – not to mention *off* it, since he played no role in my normal life – that entire load of stored resentment landed on the "asshole" side of the Grayson scales. I hit rage. As we climbed through some of the park's most breathtaking scenery, I yelled every accusation I could think of – "You abandon *everyone*, just like you leave me behind! You're completely selfish!" – and he did the same – "You're so goddamn insecure! That's why you're always chasin' attention from *anybody*, throwin' all those stupid parties, doing your Facebook crap!"

Fuck this! I resolved just like that to leave him, to hike out to the nearest town where I'd hitch or catch a bus to some city. When he left camp to filter water, I grabbed the maps from his pack to hastily plan my escape. Unfortunately, I saw that the nearest outpost of civilization, forward or back, was over forty miles away. I couldn't reach either with no tent and no water filter. I was stuck with this ass-wipe for two more days!

Somehow, though, he reeled me back in that night, camped at 12,000-foot Muir Pass amid the barren granite and thin air. "Let it go..." he whispered into the nape of my neck, his arms closing around me. "It feels," I whispered, crying, "like that would throw away my self-respect." "No... no..." he breathed. Although it seemed my heart weighed a ton, loaded with the pain of my whole life, I resolved to hoist it from the ground so that I could turn toward Grayson in the pitch dark. We kissed. And one more time, love survived.

When we did reach that next outpost of civilization, the tiny town of Independence about thirty miles west of Death Valley, we took a motel room and gorged at restaurants for two days before hitching a ride back to the trail, all dapper and restocked with food. We started walking toward the mountains before 9:00 AM while the air was still relatively cool. The bummer was that almost zero traffic traveled this dead-end route to Onion Valley. A lone utility truck passed our outstretched thumbs. By 11:00 the heat was brutal. High above the heat-wobbled cactus and scrub-dotted terrain, we could plainly *see* the lofty snowfields we longed to reach. Grayson stopped in the narrow shade of a 50 MPH sign and took a piss. I was doing the same across the road when I noticed he'd dropped his shorts to his ankles and was just standing there, contemplating the open desert.

"What-cha doin'?"

"Oh…" he said dopily, "just hangin' out. Enjoying a little cool breeze where I'm sweaty." He made no move to alter the situation.

Shorts around my own ankles, I waddled toward the yellow center line where we'd dumped our packs and went for the camera.

"Oh, no ya don't!" he said, spying me over his shoulder and grabbing his shorts up. "Those pictures are for *all my friends!*"

Which was absurd, because we both knew he didn't *have* any. Once I let the camera be, he dropped his drawers again, and we both continued to savor whatever breezes came along. Sunlight bounced off Grayson's white butt like it was phosphorescent. I don't know if you can imagine what a preposterous and magnificent freedom we enjoyed just standing in the wide-open space fishing for gusts. There was nothing else to do, nothing to lose.

Peering toward town, I thought I detected a tiny plume of dust. I squinted. My eyes aren't the best.

"Is that a car?" I asked.

Grayson looked. In an instant he snatched up his shorts and dashed for his pack. "For god's sake, woman!" he called out. "Pull up your britches and try to look respectable!"

There was much bustle of snaps and straps, but we were all put together, sunglasses off and pleading looks ready, when the car rounded a bend a quarter mile distant.

"Kiss me, quick!" I said. "Before they can see!"

He did – hard and fast.

The car pulled over on the dusty shoulder, and two hikers invited us in. And so, fifty years old and twice as strong as I'd been at twenty, with my hair in pigtails and blistered feet in trekking shoes with over two hundred miles on them, I threw my shit in the back and hopped in beside Grayson.

In moments like those, when my hide was tough, Grayson was the only man on the planet for me. An artesian spring of unexamined authenticity, he made every other man I knew seem a cow-poopy canal of conformity. Just when I felt sure he'd *never* sing the Beegee's "Tragedy" with me when things went wrong or let me do up his hair in elastics and barrettes by a shade-dappled stream, he'd prove me wrong. There was just no telling with him.

I remember when we hiked down from the summit of Mount Adams, second highest volcano in Washington at 12,326 feet, having climbed almost a vertical mile in snow that morning and descended 7,000 feet that afternoon. I'd not yet been treated for the amoebic dysentery I picked up a few months prior by drinking unfiltered stream water, so the climb had taken quite a toll on me.

The motel room we got had one of those big TV sets mounted just above the bureau. Not just once but *twice* I managed to bash my head on it when I stood up from putting something in the drawers. The second time, exhausted beyond restraint, I flung myself face down on the bed, caterwauling incoherently about my stupid fucking life. Whereupon Grayson, in the most tender display of our entire relationship, tucked my hair behind my ear repeatedly and said only, "Shhhh…" He had no idea what words might calm down a hysterical woman, but he did know how to calm a spooked horse – and it worked on me.

We'd just turned off that bastard TV and lain down showered and drowsy in the dark when Grayson began, to my astonishment, to put on the moves.

"Sweetheart, are you crazy?!" I protested. "It's after midnight and we – we just fuckin' climbed Mount Adams!"

"That's very true," he murmured between kisses with just a trace of Yogi Bear tones. "We've had a wunnerful day. Why not make it a wunnerful night?"

And so, long story short, we did.

Our first hike to the 3-Fingers lookout cabin – I nearly killed myself trying to impress him; on Kauai, New Year's 2007

29: CODEPENDENT SOME MORE

However, at the heart of most rescues is a demon: low self-worth. ...Just as a drink helps an alcoholic temporarily feel better, a rescue move immediately distracts us from the pain of being who we are.

> *-Melody Beattie*
> *Codependent No More*

Could've beens and if onlys are the stuff of self-will – not life. But I often indulge in thinking that if Grayson had only stayed sober, we could have shared our lives. The trouble is, he didn't want AA recovery. He felt confident he could beat alcoholism on his own, so it snuck up from behind and took over his life. Alcoholism is like that. It sucks into its gaping maw not only the drinker but all those close to him. In this case, me.

Early in our relationship when I still had trust issues, Grayson would call me almost every single day, no matter how tired or untalkative he felt – for five years. He'd learned that if he missed a day, I'd freak out and accuse him of not caring in a hysterical, virtually unintelligible bunch of sound effects rattling his phone. A logical man, he did what was necessary to prevent that.

Meanwhile I poured insecurities into my journal. Notice the span of years for these entries:

1/22/07: "Sometimes I feel like I just can't DO it, I just can't STAND it, this opening myself up and waiting for love to die and hurt me. Waiting for him to decide he doesn't love me."

3/8/07: "I keep imagining he finds me an annoying burden, a ball and chain. Then he does something incredibly sweet and I realize all the bad stuff was my projection."

1/24/08: "I have so much fear around loving and believing I'm loved. Grayson is a difficult man because he tells me so little; I have to feel it in the way he holds me and makes love to me. How easy to be a fool, supplying myself whatever I hope he feels, imagining."

1/11/09: "Our sex is soooooooo gooooooood, I stay high on it for days. Then as the vividness of the memory begins to fade, I go through withdrawal, unsure what we are to each other. Is that a bad thing?"

2/14/10: "Fooking Valentines Day and I'm lonely. Keno's at Jesse's. Grayson is working. Tonight I feel like I can't need him, can't expect anything from him. To-night, I don't know that he loves me."

Eventually, after enough of these freak-out episodes, I drew a comic strip detailing their stages and outcome. We went over it together, identifying ways to head off what we called, "The Thing." At that point I made a conscious decision to simply trust, despite any fears or insecurities, that Grayson loved me. And I learned to stand by it.

But a new problem developed. As soon as he didn't have to get his court slip signed anymore, Grayson quit attending AA meetings. Once he'd regained his driver's license and moved to a remote island with a three-hour work commute, he dropped out of OSAT, too, where he'd at least been doing service work by leading climbs of Baker and Rainier.

From that point on, we did everything alone – hikes, bike rides, kayaking, kite flying – just we two. I watched him grow increasingly listless. Nothing "wowed" him anymore, he said. We might be hiking and come upon some grand panorama of snow-slung peaks that a few years before would have blown him away. Now, he confessed, he felt nothing.

I vaguely recalled such numbness to be a symptom of "dry drunk" – physical sobriety with no psychic change – but kept the idea to myself. He grew increasingly dissatisfied with his work as well. One day, without so much as asking me how I felt about it, he applied for a job that would take him out of state about 80 percent of the time. Sacrificing, martyring, and mistaking compliance for love, I accepted this choice without a word: Grayson had always wanted to see the world, after all, and having put in 25 years with the same company, didn't he deserve to join its elite corps of travelling systems analysts? Wouldn't a supportive girlfriend grant him the freedom to experience this apex of his career?

Then, on his first trip abroad, it happened. I called him in his hotel room and thought once, then again, and yet again that I could hear him slurring his words. Fear struck in my gut, but my brain scrambled to deny it: "He must just be tired!" Same thing on the next trip. I mean, no! Probably he was just lying in bed and speaking carelessly.

After a few months of this, I was holding in so much fear that I grew physically ill with it. My stomach swelled with some painful mystery disease I feared to be cancer, and I consulted many doctors who ordered scans that all came back negative. Yet somehow I couldn't tell Grayson my fears – in part because acknowledging the truth would give me clear direction: I should leave him.

So matters stood when we left on our 1,100-mile bicycle ride from Seattle to San Francisco. The trip proved disastrous. Grayson wanted to cover 90 miles per day so he could reach his own goal of Baja within four weeks. I, on the other hand, had never so much as tried out clip-in pedals before we left, so I kept wiping out. I got a heavy period that slowed me down, then a bout of flu that gave me fever and chills and reduced my mileage, on our worst day, to a mere 35.

I slid into martyrdom: I suffered and pined and waited for Grayson to be overcome with remorse so he'd re-envision the trip on terms that suited me. Which never happened. When I tried to explain how difficult those 35 miles had been for me, being feverish and weak, he picked up a flyer from the café table and read it.

"Are you even listening?" I asked.

"I don't like whining," he said curtly, without a smile.

I martyred onward, cycling alone a vast majority of the time with countless eighteen-wheeler trucks blasting by within a yard of my shoulder. A day ahead of us, an older cyclist was killed when he wobbled over the bike lane's white line. Tunnels terrified me, the roar of an oncoming truck, the blast of air as it passed. Yet I refused to give up. After all, I'd told all my Facebook friends I was biking to San Francisco!

I did attempt several times to ask for what I wanted. Sitting by the ocean in the lee of a cliff, I put on a little puppet show using Grayson's do-rag and my neckerchief tied on my hands with little faces penned on them, where the Grayson puppet spoke sympathetically to the tired and discouraged Louisa puppet. "I'm sorry you feel so tired!" squeaked the Grayson puppet, while the real Grayson eyed me over the tops of my hands as though I'd gone mad.

Then came the night in our tent when he butted me in the back – hard! – for rustling too much after I'd gotten up to pee. I was dumbfounded. In fact, I'd been secretly hoping we might make love, my special sleeping bag protection kit at the ready by my side. Instead: *wham!*

I sat up and turned on my headlamp. "I don't want to be in a relationship where people treat each other this way!" I said.

He rolled his eyes with a sigh, switched on his own headlamp, and opened his paperback – some swashbuckling real life tale of a Mississippi to Amazon canoe venture. He seemed to wish he were off swashbuckling with the guys, not stuck in a tent with a bitching girlfriend.

"Did you just roll your eyes at me?" I said, furious. "Okay, fine! You can be right…*and* alone!"

This was our worst fight since the John Muir Trail. Seething, I turned off my headlamp and, just like that, resolved to leave him.

Neither of us had the guts to name the real problem: Grayson was absolutely dying for a drink, and the only barrier standing between him and that relief… was me. We'd even taken up with a group of normie cycling friends along the trail, so every time we ate out, Grayson would have to endure the view of their glistening pints just inches from his Pepsi.

At Samuel Taylor State Park, forty miles short of the Golden Gate Bridge, I was on my way back from the restrooms at 6:30AM when I sighted Grayson at a distance eating oatmeal from his Jetboil stove cap – never a good sign. That meant he lacked the patience to finish his coffee first so he could mix oatmeal in his one, all-purpose cup. Sure enough, at 7:00AM Grayson approached the picnic table where I sat chatting with other cyclists and, bristling with an almost palpable tension, announced he was going on ahead. I could catch up with him at a diner where he'd be charging his phone.

"Fine," I said, vowing silently to break up with him if he rode away. "Can I please have a map?"

We walked wordlessly to his bike, parked at our dismantled campsite where he'd heaped all my stuff on my sleeping pad as if with great disdain. The sight of it hurt me. He handed me his less favored map, and I thanked him solemnly.

"There's a name for what you have!" I called as he walked away.

Not turning around, he called back, "What is it? *Asshole*?"

"Untreated alcoholism!" I yelled.

That was as close as I could get to speaking the truth. I watched Grayson swing gracefully onto his bike and coast away down the slope below the campsite without a look back. We wouldn't see each other again for over a year.

Several hours later, friends and I reached the Golden Gate Bridge, which I ended up crossing alone amid throngs of tourists. As the outlines of San Francisco emerged through the fog, I blamed Grayson for *everything*. When I heard his voicemail inviting me to join him at a Marriott downtown, I returned it with a blasting tirade accusing him of having no heart— and now no girlfriend, either.

I spent just one night in San Francisco, staying with my friend Meghan from the old Dancing Goats days. Now in recovery herself, she took me to an AA meeting where strangers heard my story and hugged me after. They assured me I was being led and promised things would get better, words comforting if not helpful.

The next morning, armed with nothing but a crappy tourist map, I set out to bicycle across San Francisco to the airport in Oakland. Along the way, strangers of all ethnicities, orientations, and walks of life took the time to give me directions or sometimes even walk me to places or carry my loaded bike down subway stairs; at the airport a kind maintenance man disassembled and boxed up my bike for me, listening as he worked to my tale of woe. "Your boyfriend," he told me in parting, "he stupid."

Once I got to Seattle, John Church met me at the airport with his truck. I felt vindicated: my world seemed full of goodness, whereas Grayson's was riddled with selfish disease. I'd be better off without him – I saw that clearly. Except for one little problem: beneath all that anger, I still loved him.

~

Codependence is subtle stuff. I mean, it's fairly easy to tell whether I've taken a drink. It's a lot harder to know whether I'm living in my own truth or projecting fears. First off, I have to know my truth. I need some clarity on what I truly think, value, and feel – and for me that's quantum physics. Having grown up in a family that never spoke of what was really going on, I learned to shift the outlines of my perception to whatever story would best keep the peace. My truth got determined by the people around me.

We hear a bit about codependency in AA, and I'd been to a few Al-Anon meetings around issues with Jesse. But until I went through the steps in Al-Anon, I couldn't see the extent to which that addiction – and it *is* an addiction every bit as powerful as substance abuse – ruled my life.

Clearing out my stuff from Grayson's house before he returned, I left a ten-page letter enumerating all things he needed to change about himself. Most important was that he work the steps of AA and bring me a Ninth Step amends reviewed by a sponsor. Otherwise, I refused to see him.

I was betting the house this time, that Grayson loved me enough to do what I asked. This is the delusion untreated codependents always fall for, that we can use love as a fulcrum to leverage alcoholics into doing what we think best. Unfortunately, alcoholism has a mass far greater than Archimedes' earth. Could I have stopped drinking for Kevin or Jenna's sake? Ha!

I started attending Al-Anon meetings with the confused sense that they might help me to reform Grayson. Like a wet drunk in an AA meeting, I babbled on about the bike trip until even I was sick of it, though I often felt annoyed at how others failed to reciprocate with horror stories about their qualifiers. No – instead they hogged up the meeting time yacking on about self-care and how much they loved their own lives.

Gradually, I began to realize there might be some sort of boat I had missed, something involving the steps. I asked a woman I knew to take me through them in Al-Anon. Since she had all the sponsees she could handle, she referred me to one of them – a woman she'd worked with years before.

I liked Glenda immediately, and working with her brought me a whole new experience of the Twelve Steps' power. As I listened in Al-Anon meetings, I felt amazed to hear others telling parts of my story, just as I had in my early AA days. Like them, I suffered the pain of intrinsic unworthiness that drove all my actions. Like them, I could avoid looking at it by focusing all my attention on others – what they did to me and what they ought to do.

Around this time my practical life was also in turmoil. I'd been laid off from the writing center in 2009, and now, two years later, my unemployment insurance had run out. Despite hundreds of applications, the only job I could land was working for $9 per hour as seasonal temp at Crate & Barrel. And one day when I came downstairs to leave for work, my car had been stolen right out of my driveway. In the midst of this, I heard from Grayson.

12/27/11 "Grayson sent me an Xmas card signed, *still loving you.* I emailed that I was ready to talk and would like to meet. He responded, 'As much as I'd to see you, I think it's best if we not. These last few months have been hard. I want you to forget about me and find a better man, one who will make you happy.

Always,
Grayson'"

To me this was an unforeseen disaster. I'd meant to leverage Grayson into doing what I wanted – not drive him away! Had he deleted the word "love" and put nothing its place? Because he *did* love me! I wanted to shout at him: You'll do anything to keep me – even getting sober! Yet, at the same time, enough Al-Anon had seeped into my head enough to suggest the selfish underside of such thinking.

1/6/12: "What am I kidding myself about now, god? I see I was *always* planning to change and improve Grayson, just as I was with Jesse and Jenna. Except instead of enlightening him with my education, I was going to do it with my wisdom in AA. I willed him to become like me. I felt superior, yet again.

"What are those four M's? Managing, manipulating, martyrdom, and mothering?"

The only problem was that giving up on fixing Grayson's alcoholism meant giving up on seeing him, too. I was torn. In my car I'd scream at him until I lost my voice. I came close to emailing half a dozen times, long lecture-essays that filled the screen before I finally clicked delete. I came close to calling, but somehow, each time, I managed to call Glenda instead.

It was also around this time that I became aware of what Glenda did for a living. She was a therapist who specialized in treating "gifted" individuals – people with extraordinary left-brain abilities who had difficulty navigating the world of emotion and social interaction. It didn't take her long to peg Grayson. A master of electronic systems analysis, eh? Held schematics the size of phone books in his head? Sped through stacks of library books? Chess whiz? Finished *New York Times* crossword puzzles on his lunch break? Hmm, she said. Hmm…

"Grayson's left-brain gifted," she told me matter-of-factly one day. "He has an extraordinary ability to absorb information and manipulate it cognitively." She explained that, while gifted people are often dumb as a stump about their emotions, they still *have* them as much as anyone. What they can't do is slice and dice them to recognize what's going on, so they often learn to suppress them instead out of sheer frustration.

"It hurts," Glenda told me, "when they can't interpret the signs from others. They know they're different. When someone they love turns away because of something they can't even perceive, it *hurts*. It's not that they don't care. It's that they can't navigate."

I've often wondered if my Al-Anon experience might have brought a different outcome if I'd had a different sponsor. Though Glenda never advised me directly, Grayson was a lot like her husband, so her loyalty occasionally slipped out. "You'd probably be better off finding some-one who can interact normally. On the other hand, if Grayson didn't give you what you needed, I don't think it was for lack of love. It was because you didn't tell him."

That's all I needed to hear: *If I could show up in a different way, I could fix us!* I felt sure god had sent Glenda to act as Grayson's interpreter, to express the muddled love behind his apparent indifference. What I needed was simply to open my mind to the "differences" of Grayson's emotional "language."

I began to think about getting him back – sober or not.

By the time the next summer rolled around, I'd done a lot of work on myself. I'd written a 4th Step with the Blueprint for Progress as well as a four-column inventory, read it to Glenda, and prayed my way through Steps 6 and 7. But I'd also taken my son on a trip to Hawaii – a healing adventure for us both that proved I could do anything I wanted without a partner.

And in August I followed through on my dream of hiking the 100-mile Wonderland Trail around Mount Rainier – solo. For the first two days of that week-long hike, I cried. I couldn't say why but I also couldn't stop. Though I'd pull it together whenever I encountered fellow hikers, the tears kept resurfacing as soon as I was alone. I wept my way through breathtakingly dramatic landscapes, praying non-stop for I knew not what.

I missed Grayson! I missed my youth! I missed the illusion of knowing what the fuck my life was about or where it was going. Hiking alone, I felt every emotion I'd pressed down surge up into my throat – and much of it was simply mourning. But on the third morning, my eyes stopped leaking. Instead, they showed me an amazingly bright orange and convoluted fungus growing on a log. How remarkable! I thought, peering – and realized the pain had left me. A lone, bright yellow flower bobbed at me from underneath a huge fallen tree as I sat having my lunch beside it. "Life renews!" the flower piped to me in earnest. "God works with what's here now – not what used to be!"

So I became whole. Or at least, closer to whole than I could remember ever having felt. I hiked with joy in my own company. The persistent little critter that was Louisa – god loved her. And I thanked god every step for this beautiful, abundant life.

~

Not long after returning home, I emailed Grayson the list 9th Step amends that Glenda and I had worked out. They acknowledged, among other things, that I'd thought I knew what was best for him, kept him a prisoner of my neediness, made mountains of molehills, and over-managed the relationship. Did he want to meet to discuss them, or just talk over the phone?

We'd actually started exchanging texts back in July, when I was training for my solo hike and he was bicycling from San Francisco to Baja, mostly light exchanges about snow depth or road conditions. Then, just before I left for the Wonderland, I had called him. But instead of the Grayson I longed for, I got a dull-witted stranger on the line. His voice had shifted to a callow, nasal sort of drone. Allusions and jokes whizzed over his head.

He was drunk.

8/5/2012: "He didn't remember reading the dictionary together on the couch. He didn't even remember Dwayne! I'm so disappointed! Al-Anon is about loving the alcoholic whether he's drinking or not. But in some ways, the man I fell in love with no longer exists."

Realizing he was sick, I'd given up my hopes of reuniting – part of what I mourned on the Wonderland. Meanwhile, Grayson emailed that he'd prefer to discuss my amends list over the phone. When he called – sober this time – I was all business. Together we reviewed each item, Grayson commenting on moods or actions of mine that he'd noticed and weaving in apologies of his own. We finished.

9/5/12 "Then there was a long, long silence which I didn't break. I just waited on the line. And when he finally spoke, it sounded like he'd been crying for some time with the mic covered. He told me he'd relapsed two years ago. Exactly as I'd thought, it happened on his first trip abroad. He'd tried to stop, but he couldn't. He sobbed, 'It felt so awful to deceive you!'"

I felt tremendous compassion for him – it tore at my heart. But I also spoke what I knew to be true: we simply couldn't be together. I was a sober alcoholic and he was an active one: I'd constantly want to 'help' him get sober, and he'd constantly feel guilty for drinking. Worse, I might feel tempted to drink *with* him.

Grayson concurred, saying I deserved better. But then, his voice torn with violent sobs, he almost shouted, "I still love you!" I actually had to ask him to repeat it twice – then he hung up abruptly.

I remember where I was standing in my house. I looked out the window, grounded in the fundamental fact that alcoholics deceive themselves every time they take a drink – a baseline lie that breeds dishonesty in all things. As much as I loved Grayson, I knew that love, no matter how strong, cannot fix alcoholism, and that alcoholism, no matter how recognized, wields power enough to corrupt both sides of even the most pure relationship. Over the past 17 years I'd built a life of integrity. Painful as it was, I knew the only right thing to do was to hand Grayson over to god, to let him find his own path.

~

This chapter might have ended right here if Grayson hadn't blurted out those final words, "I still love you!" But he did. Over the next two weeks as I struggled for closure, they kept coming back to me. Grayson *loved* me! Fantasies of loving and wanting and having him again flitted into my thoughts. Why couldn't that be? Didn't Al-Anon teach that we could love the alcoholic *whether he is drinking or not*?

Relapse in love addiction can strike every bit as suddenly as it does in drinking or drugging. Two weeks after that amends call, I reached a point of wanting Grayson so much I couldn't stand it. Having arrived half an hour early to chair a board meeting of OSAT, I was driving around in the dark to kill time while the longing for Grayson churned through me. Abruptly, I pulled to the side of the road and got out my phone.

Everything I knew about alcoholism went flying out the window. Everything Al-Anon had taught about self-care, detachment, emotional sobriety – whatever! Integrity? Screw it! I didn't give a shit what was good for me. I knew only one thing: I couldn't live without Grayson – I just *couldn't*.

I texted him: "I can't stand this. I have to see you." He texted back, "What do you want me to do?" He followed with, "I mean that literally. Tell me what you want me to do."

We talked on the phone the next day. I told him I hadn't so much as dated during the year apart. What about him? Had he gotten into a relationship? "Nothing," he said, choosing his words, "of a lasting nature." I took that to mean he'd had a few one-night stands, which I could accept. Soon after, he read me the most romantic speech you can imagine, all about how hard he'd tried to forget me and how impossible it had proven. At least, I'm pretty sure he read it, because his delivery sounded stiff, almost monotone. But from Glenda I'd learned this made the words not less sincere, but more so, because every word cost him effort: "Whenever I see something beautiful, I want to show you. When I hear new music, I wonder if you'd like it. I've tried everything I know to stop thinking about you. And I can't."

Ten days later, we met at a farm-like park near his house. On a hilltop bench among the fields, I laid out my conditions for trying it again: 1) that he develop a relationship with my son and 2) that I see no signs of alcohol whatsoever. He agreed to both. Afterwards, as we walked on the beach holding hands, I asked why he hadn't kissed me yet. He was silent for several paces.

"Because," he said, "I wouldn't know how to stop."

In a little glen of alders near my car, we stood face to face. His eyes searched my neck. "Your mole's gone?" he said, confused and nervous.

"Yeah," I said. "I got it removed. It was poking out and I thought I was gonna be dating new people and it might gross them out." I had to shut myself up from babbling. I asked what he was feeling.

His eyes ricocheted between mine, full of fear. "Well... my heart's goin' t' town," he confessed. "I tried *so hard* to forget you."

Then he kissed me, his arms closing around me, squeezing me so tight I literally couldn't breathe, lifting me so my toes barely touched the ground and my spine flexed into him. Our kiss itself opened like a portal to that world we both knew, my whole body reacting with arousal, floodgates open.

He stopped with a jolt. He set me down.

"Well!" I muttered, breathless. "Everything still works!"

"I know," he said. "You better go."

Swiftly he walked me to my car and helped me into it. We didn't say I love you. We just knew, trading flashes of our eyes, that we'd unlocked something potent and both needed time to absorb it.

A week later, Grayson came to Seattle and we rode our bicycles along the bluffs of Magnolia. But again, when we stopped at an overlook, he didn't touch me. Back at my house, instead of sweeping me upstairs, he sat in my living room staring into space. I asked what was wrong.

"Oh, sweetheart," he said unhappily. "I should just go home!"

"What do you *mean*?" I asked, puzzled.

"I can't…" He gestured as if words were beyond him.

What could possibly be holding him back? Maybe we'd been apart so long, he felt awkward about jumping straight into bed? Maybe he feared getting hurt again? Silly reasons, both of them! Nothing could possibly keep us apart. So I said simply, "Sure you can!" and, taking him by the hand, I pulled him toward the stairs to live out my fantasy.

> 10/5/12: "How do I write about the fact that Grayson was with me night before last, and that we made love, and that he was here, here, here…? How can I tell with words how alive and real his skin, how clear his vulnerability, how surreal the realness of doing what we'd both dreamed of alone so many times? I cried tears on his neck and the side of his face. I said, 'Oh, it's *you*. It's really you. I don't ever want to be apart from you again!'"

And I was deliriously happy with him. Deliriously, as if he were cocaine. We took a vacation trip to the Yukon, riding a ferry several days along the Alaska Marine Highway and sleeping out on the deck in our tent, then riding a train along the old gold rush route to Whitehorse, YK. From there, Grayson set off alone to bicycle 1,700 miles through the Canadian Rockies to his own doorstep – a trip he'd planned while we were apart. He'd invited me to come along, but I knew better. Instead I used the time to hike a section of the Pacific Crest Trail alone. I wished he'd been willing to scrap his plans to do something with *me* – but maybe that was selfish?

Glenda thought so. Love, I told myself, lets people fulfill their dreams, and Grayson had long dreamed of this trip.

There was just one little problem. Actually, there were many. For one thing, the connection with my son never materialized. I set up a few activities for the two of them, but Grayson seemed to check them off without any feeling for Keno. As for signs of alcohol, there were plenty. Several times when I called in the evening, he either answered drunk or just didn't pick up. And then there was this little fact of his being gone 80 percent of the time. Sometimes he'd go days without so much as texting or emailing. Twice when I got upset about this, Glenda reminded me I'd made amends about my freak-outs and therefore couldn't indulge in them. I should focus on my *own* life, not my fears about Grayson. "If he doesn't contact you, it's because his work is intense and consuming – which has nothing to do with you. Louisa, this man *loves* you!"

Yes. I grabbed at those words: Grayson *loved* me. I would trust him to focus on work while he was working. I'd wait months to see him, and if I found him gruff, shaky, and restless when our weekends together finally came around, I'd understand that he was the sort of man who calmed himself with tasks. He'd tinker for hours with the old Karmann Ghia he'd bought his daughter or reorganize some cupboard in his spotless house or mow his huge lawn. But those shakes, that task tension – they didn't *have* to be signs of alcohol withdrawal, did they?

The problem that concerned me far more was this: Grayson didn't seem to *want* me anymore. On the boat to Alaska, we never made love. And increasingly when we did, he'd just lie there entirely passive so I had initiate everything. Maybe this was his way of avoiding the sex headaches he sometimes got from exertion or – let's face it – just a symptom of age? He'd turned fifty, after all. Could he suddenly be losing his drive?

Finally came nights of apparent dysfunction – for instance, at our hotel in Winthrop for a romantic weekend. Astoundingly, these flops caused Grayson no concern whatsoever. "Must be getting' old!" he'd quip cheerily, lying back on the pillow with his hands behind his head. Internet research convinced me that the Benadryl he took for hay fever must be the culprit, but Grayson didn't even care – he kept buying the stuff! He had nothing but contempt for coworkers who relied on "little blue pills," so I didn't dare even mention Viagra.

For him, sex just seemed to have lost all importance. For me, it certainly had *not*: I spent the months alone fantasizing about him, but our passionate reunions now proved anything but. Plus there was this new business of his being so exhausted. He'd greet my arrival by sleeping for hours in an easy chair rather than lying down in the bedroom with me – because of jet lag, he explained. We took an eight-day hike through the Olympic Mountains with no sex at all, and during our otherwise dream vacation in Costa Rica, he seemed to prefer TV. One night there, he straight up asked me to stop.

I consoled myself with the reassurance that in all other areas of life, we'd grown closer than ever. "That year apart," I journaled, "brought us so much more love and commitment. We know now that we belong together, bonded to survive these long stints apart." He also started giving me stuff – a laptop, a Kindle, fancy dinners out. Sure, I'd occasionally find a six-pack stashed in the back of some cupboard, but I never nagged him about it. No, I was giving him room to work out his own relationship with alcohol, though it seemed to me – dared I hope? – he was actually learning to moderate.

Except he *wasn't*. Because, you know what? Alcoholism doesn't work that way. Once it's taken root it grows like a cancer, rotting a person from the inside, corroding every fiber of character until nothing remains but sheer ego – ego and the show it puts on to get what it wants. Prolonged alcohol abuse actually *atrophies* centers of the brain that register emotion, so the addict needs more and more stimulation just to *feel* something. He seeks out higher highs. He becomes reckless. And having lost all compassion, he turns into a selfish, heartless monstrosity.

I dreamed one night of a bedroom just crawling with giant black spiders. In the dream I thought, "This is scary, but giant spiders mean my life will change soon!" I somehow skewered one of them on a shish kabob stick – a scrabbling, crab-like thing – and tried to pull it off like a burnt marshmallow. The revolting carcass stuck to my fingers like black tar. There was nothing I could do, it seemed, to get it off me.

~

When, about two years after getting back together, Grayson and I returned from a week in Costa Rica, I came down with some horrible tropical virus: I ran a fever of 103 for three days and experienced a slew of rashes and sores. When my doctor suggested some of these symptoms might be due to a sexually transmitted disease, I was incensed: How dare he even insinuate such a thing!

He didn't know my honest, sincere Grayson! Finally, just to prove him wrong, I took the blood test.

The result came back positive. Thunderstruck, I texted Grayson in Australia: "All I need to know is that you've been true to me since we got back together. Have you been?"

He replied, "I won't lie to you, Sweetie. There was this chick in Boston I was seeing a coupla times. But it meant nothing and I wore a condom the whole time." Boston had been just six months after we got back together.

My world imploded. I sobbed, I keened, I wailed. Over the next few weeks I e-railed at Grayson in rage, anguish, and disbelief. As soon as he was in town, he called to say he was coming to see me and "spill his guts." He presented me with a single red rose, as on every visit. We sat on a park bench overlooking the Sound.

In his youth, he explained nervously, he'd once gotten a voicemail from a girl who claimed he'd given her the disease – but since his wife never caught it, he'd assumed she was wrong. The Boston fling was unrelated, because he'd worn – like he said – a condom. That woman, Kimberly, had propositioned him in a hotel elevator, so he'd gone to her room and then found her again in the bar the following evening. But no such thing would ever happen again.

"No more secrets!" he promised.

Still absorbing his story, I showed him a number line I'd drawn of all our years together. Holding it as the breeze flapped it, I pointed to each year and asked him specifically, "Were there any women *here*? Any women *here*?" Each time, he replied, "No," except for that year we'd been apart, where he put his finger. "In Dubai—" he began. I interrupted: what he'd done while we were broken up was his business. But with me, he could be *only* with me.

Next I asked if I could look at his phone. "Why?" he scoffed, almost laughing. "We never even exchanged phone numbers!"

So I didn't look at it. I trusted. And I resolved to forgive him.

From the park we went to a local farmers' market bustling with spring flowers and hawkers offering samples, where we strolled hand in hand. But Grayson said he felt close to vomiting. Why, I wondered, if he'd just spilled his guts, would his stomach still be in knots? But there it was – maybe some kind of virus? He left for home after only half an hour.

Before he took off for Japan a few days later, he spent a night with me and finally – to my joy – came alive in bed. Apart, we chatted over Skype, which Keno set up on our phones, every other day. I still sent him anguished emails on occasion, and to one of these he replied as if insulted: "So I fucked up. Don't rub my face in it. I told you, I won't lie to you again."

Finally, he came home for a long break. When the weekend finally rolled around I picked him up from his work, my hair and nails freshly done, wearing a new sweater. Unfortunately, he'd "not slept well" the night before, so when we arrived at his house he dozed in the easy chair for an hour or so while I read.

"Poor thing!" I thought, looking up from my book. "Always messed up from jet lag!"

The next weekend, however, was close to perfect. Out for lunch, we talked of countries to visit next, places we'd retire someday. We climbed Mount Pilchuck, where for some reason I sang the whole of "On Top of Old Smokey" (all about a false-hearted lover) as we lay sunning on the snowy summit. The next day we took a hillside walk above the beach and took off our shirts lying in the tall grass, where he tickled me with a long stalk but snatched mine away when I tried to get even. I put my combs in his chest hair and on the walk back invented a dumb shell-finding game that made me laugh so hard I wet my pants a little. Grayson squeezed me tight to his side.

But in the midst of this, something happened. While making our Saturday breakfast, I'd noticed a fun refrigerator magnet from Australia – an aborigine mask with a tuft of hemp hair. "That's so cool!" I remarked. "I wish you'd gotten one for me!"

"I did!" said Grayson sleepily. Then, when I stared at him, "Didn't I give it to you?"

"No, you didn't." I wanted to joke, "must've given it to your *other* girlfriend," but the words wouldn't come out. They just wouldn't.

Then, while Grayson was taking a shower, I did something I'd never done in all our years together. I searched his phone contacts. Up came the name Kimberly and a Boston number. But he'd *said* they never exchanged numbers! With shaking hands, I searched for texts, but none came up. I don't recall what I was looking for later that day when I noticed Grayson's old iPhone in the back of a drawer. What made me slip it into my computer bag, I can't say either. It also happened that on Sunday, for the first time ever, I asked Grayson for the code to unlock his iPad so I could look up a movie time. He hesitated, shaving, and seemed to remember "No more secrets!" before reluctantly naming the numbers.

Those same digits, switched around, unlocked the old iPhone back at my house. When I found no texts from Kimberly, I rejoiced. I stuck the phone back in my computer bag and even made fun of my fears at an Al-Anon meeting. But this particular iPhone had a problem: it wouldn't turn off. The next day as I was driving to meet a client, it seemed almost to call to me from my bag: "Run a search for the words, *see you*. Right now. Just do it."

This time, a text queue came up. My entire life changed in a matter of seconds.

What I stumbled on in that phone was not a mere affair. It was an entire secret life, a long-term relationship of recurring drunkenness, near daily porn-style sexting, and countless sexual hook-ups with a girl half my age – 26 when they started. Grayson had been seeing us both for the entire two and a half years we'd been back together.

The phone's window opened a chasm straight down to a hellish scene of writhing, copulating figures: "Got me all horned up thinkin' bout your shaved pussy," Grayson texted. "Wish I was eatin it." Then, "Wish I was doin' somethin nasty to ya!" "Me too!" she responded. My hands shaking wildly, I took pictures of those two texts with my own phone and messaged them to Grayson at work.

iPhones hold a lot of memory. This one contained hundreds of sex texts from a six-month span the year before. I saw arranged in every possible configuration the words pussy, cock, fuck, fucking, fucked, eat, suck, wet, shaved, blow, spank, rounds, wanna, gonna, make you, brains out, ass, hard, sexy, sore, mouth, hot, nasty, tie down, tie up, and, of course, cum. Strangely, not a word about tits.

When I got home, I asked Keno to connect the phone to our Wi-Fi so I could see the dates. By cross-referencing with my calendar and journal, I was able to piece together a history of their romance, in part because KC (her real name – hell if I'm changing it!) loved to reminisce about great fucks of the past.

She and Grayson's daughter were five years apart. Two photos showed a broad-faced, thick-necked blond with pudgy hands – and nothing of her body. She worked with Grayson as an electrician and clearly worshipped the ground he walked on. Little mentions she dropped let me know they'd hooked up originally during the year he and I were apart ("nothing... of a lasting nature"). Then he'd gotten her admitted to his prestigious international program so her pussy could travel the world with him: "You fucked me hard every night in Chile," she recalled fondly of her first assignment. Chile, my journal indicated, had been a 60-day trip.

"Thanks for the good hard fuckin," she'd text from the ferry on a day I was headed out to Grayson's. "Pleasure's mine," he'd respond perhaps an hour before kissing me hello.

Their growing romance poured from the phone. I'd eaten the fancy Danish cheese she forgot in his fridge. They drank at the bars of the same restaurants we frequented. She used *my* shish-kabob (spider) sticks to cook on the barbeque he got from *my* neighbor. And they'd screw for many "rounds" until dawn – hence his exhaustion. Now I recalled how *consistently* I'd seen sets of sheets wadded atop Grayson's laundry basket, and that *every time* I took out his recycling, the outdoor bin was empty. Was it trust or denial? I'd seen text arrivals from "KC Snow" at least three times.

She gushed, "After you've fucked me a good few rounds I go around for days with a stupid smile on my face. I love taking a shower at your place because then I smell like you and turn myself on all day long."

Whenever together, they got shitfaced, and whenever parted, shared how hungover they'd been at work and who noticed, who was a dick. She was the confidant from whom he hid nothing. I, by contrast, was the goody-goody from whom he hid most of himself, the one who shamed him by the very fact of my sobriety.

I gathered KC was a fan of *Fifty Shades of Grey,* which I've never read. It was she who did all the tying up and fucking out of brains – or at least, texted promises to do so. "I have some other things I'd like to try out on you," she mused. I could almost see her consulting the novel. Plain and chunky as she was, she pulled off a dominatrix role outside my repertoire. And that, it seemed, was what Grayson craved.

I was, once again, the obstacle that made these meetings so enticingly forbidden. "Kinda cramped in style cuz Gf is here," Grayson wrote. She responded, "I hear yas. Hit me up when you can, sweetcheeks!" (his name for *me* in the past). "K prolly tonight! :)" he answered.

KC, like Barbara, had won.

Again, I had lost.

To the photos I'd sent him, Grayson made no reply. Two days later I mailed the phone back to him with a sticky note that said only, *Please do not contact me.*

So ended our nine-year relationship.

~

Since then, I've had plenty of days when I've looked back and felt just plain pissed. It's disgusting to think how often I had sex with that liar just one shower apart from KC. Truthfully, I'd rather use someone else's shit-on toilet paper – at least then I wouldn't have a goddam disease to show for it. And I'd rather have licked the underside of a dozen public toilet seats than his greedy little double-dippin' weenie.

Then there are days when texting itself – a perfectly innocent phrase sent by a friend – still flares panic through my body. The trauma of seeing those first sex-texts resurges, my heart pounds, and I remember that gaping chasm to hell. Back comes the pain of knowing Grayson craved KC's shaved pussy and plagiarized thrills over my sincere, vanilla love-making – and I feel like I'm falling.

We were doomed from his first relapse. Recovered from alcoholism, I couldn't drink with him, and cured of my bondage compulsion, I got no kinkier than high heels, so he concealed his swelling corruption from me like a submerged pustule.

Still, I can't help feeling amazed at how life comes full circle. Discovering those texts, I was Jenna reading my journal. Shocked at Grayson's bondage exploits, I was my mom stumbling on the dark secrets of my childhood drawings. Except for one big difference: I've been there – a pawn of that tyrant, addiction. I can feel compassion for Grayson even as I realize his selfish arrogance has him every bit as removed from my pain as I was from Kevin's and Jenna's. He had a great thing going with two adoring women, but then Louisa had to go fuck it all up by snooping in his phone. Alcoholics can be that inhuman. I certainly was.

At the same time, as time passes, I gain more perspective on *my* part in what happened. "Fool me once, shame on you; fool me twice, shame on me." Sure, Jesse and Grayson are different foolers, but I'm the common denominator. I'm the one who told Grayson,

Oh, you don't care for my son? That's okay; I'll still love you.
So you don't want to know my friends? Okay, I s'pose.
You're gonna move an hour and a half away? Interesting.
What? You plan to be gone 80 percent of the time?
Oh, now you've relapsed and don't intend to quit?
It's all okay – I love you *unconditionally*!

As deeply as Grayson was enmeshed in sex addiction with KC, I was enmeshed in love addiction with him. I'd built him up and whittled myself down. I invented a fictional character for him that I chose over reality. I scrambled for crumbs and stocked the gaps between with fantasy. Why? Because his ever-inaccessible love and his gorgeous body were my drugs of choice.

What's so hard to believe is that all those happy feelings I had in Grayson's presence came from *me*. *I* made the little things we shared a joy; *I* felt pretty when I went to meet him. He gave me next to nothing. Really, I still have everything in the world I ever had with him except whatever pings of self-esteem I manufactured by reflecting my worth off a not-very-nice man.

On my darkest days, all those years seemed wasted. Not just the ones I spent duped in a blind three-way, but the whole ill fated relationship. And yet, *something* happened over those years, because my reaction to betrayal was so changed. This time, even losing Grayson to a scenario far more gruesome than Jesse's, I intuited from the start that god had arranged the whole seeming catastrophe for my benefit. Really. My will had left few alternatives. Given my stubbornness with certain character defects around relationships, god had no choice but to drop a frickin' piano on me.

"Wake up!" That was the message.

Even the acknowledgement that *I betrayed myself* has value as I face what I most dislike in myself and become willing to change it. The past, with all its pain, is my teacher, my gift. That's the difference made by following a spiritual path. For Grayson, it's all just shit that happened, water under the bridge.

Yes, I've cried away many nights and often fear I'll never find a vibrant, lasting love with someone I want as much as I did Grayson. I feel guilty for caring so much about physique and all that superficial stuff – but I *do*! But at least this time I've walked through every one of these feelings awake, calm, and celibate. I have faith that god will arrange my next relationship if I just do the things I love and stay out of the way.

Lastly, this time I feel no desire to punish anyone even if I could. Grayson? He's a late stage alcoholic screwing a confused girl from his work! KC? She's one of us – a mess. I hope she finds sobriety before suicide. Alcoholism's four horsemen will eventually encircle them both – maybe ruthlessly enough to goad them toward the rooms. In fact, I still pray every day for Grayson to find peace and healing, whatever they may look like for him.

He has a god, too.

Clockwise from top left: Hiking 250 miles in the Sierra Nevada at 12,000-foot Glenn Pass; bicycling 1,100 miles on the Pacific Coast Trail, 2011; selfie I sent Grayson to keep him honest on the road – not bad for 51; mean Grayson on the bike trip.

.

30: LAST WEIRD THINGS AND WHY THEY KEEP HAPPENING

> Freeman: *And did you believe in God?*
> Carl Jung: *Oh, yes!*
> Freeman: *Do you* now *believe in God?*
> Carl Jung: *Now?! Difficult to answer. (pause)*
> *I know. I don't need to believe – I*
> *know."*
>
> -Carl Jung
> *Interview with John Freeman, BBC's*
> *Face to Face, 1959*

Weird Things continued to happen as the years rolled by, most of them involving low-stakes clairvoyance and telepathy. By low-stakes I mean, I didn't know someone would die or get saved from death, myself. Three of these knowings were completely unremarkable except for the fact that they defied all logical explanation. The other was a series of mystical dreams I channeled from my father as he approached the threshold to the other side.

WEIRD THING # 11

This one happened in 2007 while Grayson and I were working on a statement to overturn the divorce agreement he'd signed during the early months of our relationship. Head over heels and on a pink cloud of early sobriety, he'd waltzed in and signed the papers without so much as reading them. They held him to twenty percent more child support than the state required and for five years longer than required, while forbidding him to claim either child on his taxes.

The mistake devastated him financially. He was outraged by his own naïveté and that stupid myth of spiritual freedom he'd bought into. To make the first payment, he had to hock his father's Civil War rifles.

When Grayson had told me he was going to sign without reading, I'd said nothing, minding my own business, so now I felt as guilty as he did stupid. Only years later would it become clear to me that this arrangement was actually just and good, given that Grayson's ex-wife sacrificed her freedom to keep their daughter, who couldn't speak or practice any self-care, out of an institution. But I didn't see that yet. All I saw was Grayson living in a tiny box apartment while she got the whole three bedroom house with its acreage and barn, and Grayson driving a beater truck while she drove a new Chrysler Cruiser – all on his dime. So I was using all my writing skills to write him the most convincing challenge statement I could compose so he could take her to court.

During these weeks in 2007, I was reading on my sofa one evening when, out of nowhere, a vivid image of a high school classmate came to mind: David Soluck. I hadn't given David Soluck a thought in the thirty years, and I'd hardly known him even while we went to school together, so why now was I seeing this strikingly intimate close-up of his youthful face, with that sandy long hair parted in the middle? Even the pubescent down on his upper lip came to mind. "What innocence!" I thought. "I should have been kinder to him. And to think he's a grown man now, aging as I am!"

Then I went to bed.

The next morning on my Myspace page was a message from... David Soluck. He'd stumbled on my page, he said, and thought it might be nice to reconnect. He was indeed a grown man. He lived east of the mountains now, divorced, with two sons. The message had been sent at the hour when I was reading. I told him about having pictured him, which we agreed was cool.

About a week or two later, Grayson handed me a letter from his ex-wife's goddamn lawyer. It was signed, Jim Soluck – an unusual name. I messaged Dave and asked if he had a brother named Jim. He did, he said. Jim was a divorce lawyer in the county where Grayson used to live.

At the time, I saw only a Weird Thing that somehow vaguely pricked my conscience, but today I think I see what that was about. The strongest feeling to accompany Dave's youthful, downy face, was regret for my loveless dismissal. What if Dave's brother wasn't just a damn lawyer, but someone protecting a girl who couldn't speak for herself and the mother who gave her a safe, stable home? In other words, what if I was fighting on the wrong side?

In the end, Grayson consulted a lawyer himself, who convinced him that, supporting a teen so helplessly disabled, he didn't stand a chance in court.

WEIRD THING # 12

This was another of those skeptic-killer Weird Things. I have no idea why it happened. But if I understood my Weird Things, they wouldn't be weird.

I was driving up Olive Way one day when I suddenly *knew I was about to see my friend, Tim Smith*. How nice! We hadn't seen each other for several years since I'd quit going to his AA homegroup. Tim Smith! Come on, Tim! I felt happy and excited, knowing without a doubt I was on the verge of a Weird Thing. At the same time, my logical brain questioned what made me presume Tim was even living in Seattle, much less walking west on Olive Way. For whatever reason, though, his face was fairly dancing in front of my eyes as I drove.

And – oh my god – there he *was*! On the right-hand sidewalk, a handsome, bearded man came striding down Olive toward Summit; Tim Smith, it had to be! Until I got close enough and saw …wait a minute. No, that *wasn't* Tim, after all. It was just some guy who vaguely resembled him. In my excitement, I'd made the face fit. What a disappointment.

"Oh, Louisa!" I shook my head at myself. "Why are you *so* silly, always so sure you've got these woo-woo premonitions? Probably *all* of them have been just as false as if you'd driven on convinced you'd actually *seen* Tim Smith! Granted, a few inexplicable things have happened to us, but it's time to hang up the whole woo-woo trip, don't you think?"

Just then, this time on the left-hand sidewalk, the real Tim Smith strode into view, heading down the steep hill of Olive Way. Was it *really* Tim this time? Holy shit – it *was*, really *was,* and no mistake! Tim! In my flustered excitement I honked my horn too late, when I'd already passed.

My cynic shriveled in defeat. I felt triumph. Weird things *happened*! They were real! Joy filled me – a buoyant confidence at the undeniable fact that there truly *is* more to this world than our five senses report. God is real, god can read me, I knew it as a fact.

"Thank you, god, for my Weird Things! And what about showing me that not-Tim first? – you're such a jokester!"

When I got home, I Facebooked Tim (Myspace being *so* over) and asked if he'd been walking down Olive Way at about 1:00. Yes, he replied, he was in school now and had been heading home for lunch. A horn, he'd heard it. I told him about knowing I would see him, then seeing the "fake" Tim first. He was totally down with that. But aside from a resounding kick to the curb for my skepticism, neither of us could figure out what to make of it. At least, not *yet*.

WEIRD THING # 13

My father was a brilliant man who built a successful career despite an upbringing that caused him to reject all spirituality and a disease that only spirituality could cure. His small town family had been Catholic. Their priest had a fondness for altar boys and my father, overweight and slow to escape, was often given wet, lingering kisses. Before he left home for Harvard, he informed his father during an argument that he did not believe in God, that science had proved there was none. The story goes that that same night, the crucifix fell from above his bed and either narrowly missed or hit his head – I forget which. Anyway, he adopted the mixed view he kept throughout his life: There is no God, and He's a mean bastard.

For most of his life, Dad's strong work ethic hemmed in his drinking til after hours. But every evening, weekend, and holiday, he drank wine to relax, to silence the restless, irritable self-loathing that told him he was never good enough. One bottle, two bottles, maybe start a third, and finish off the night with a multi-shot nightcap. But because he knew so much about winemaking, he was not an alcoholic. I got bombed with my parents many times. Those were fun nights of silliness and daring candor. Bacchus was always a welcome guest in our home and wine a symbol of the good life.

As soon as he was forced to retire at seventy, however, Dad lost his defense against the constant pull of drink. His career became news monitoring, performed from his post across from the TV and next to the fridge. About once per hour he rose and toddled, with increasing difficulty as his back pain worsened, over to the fridge door to refill his coffee mug (pre-noon) or glass (post-noon) with wine. Though at retirement he'd been a robust bicyclist who could still trounce a law student at handball, by age eighty-five his doctors had long since diagnosed him with wet brain and an enlarged liver. Whether they had also diagnosed alcoholic cardiomyopathy – a weakening of the heart as a result of long-term alcohol abuse – I don't know. If they had, it was nothing Mom spoke of.

Because in our family, these were fuddy-duddy doctors! What they failed to get was that wine made Dad happy, which was, of course, why the family continued to drink with him at every gathering. It's the reason Mom smuggled wine into him at the hospital and family members continued giving him liquor for holidays. He himself constantly forgot I was sober and made jokes about drunkenness as a good thing. I have no doubt that, deep down, he was aware of his addiction and tortured by it, especially as alcohol worked less and less to alleviate his self-loathing. By the end, alcoholism had left very little of the man I loved and respected so intensely. It rendered him childlike and selfish.

I lacked the gumption to speak to him candidly about his alcoholism. I lacked the gumption to write this book until after his death. When I spoke to a caller from Seattle AA Intergroup who, by chance, turned out to be a former student of Dad's, he urged me to go ahead and offer Dad his phone number. I never did. It's still written in my Big Book. I think part of me had internalized the whole family myth – that Dad's alcoholism was special – or simply couldn't face the conflict I'd stir up if I spoke truthfully. So I participated in the family lie; I enabled his disease; I chose fear and safety over faith and honesty.

Eventually, the damage to his heart caught up with him and his lungs began filling with fluid. Even when doctors had sent him home from the hospital for hospice care, he would not or could not recognize his terminal condition.

"Did I really almost *die*?" he asked Zelda and me with squinting incredulity at what would prove his last meal with us – toasted cheese and tea on a Sunday afternoon. In the safety of his kitchen, with a daughter on either side of him, the prospect seemed ludicrous. Zelda and I only looked at each other. Neither could say, "You're dying now, Dadda."

Overnight Dad was left in the sole company of Tonn, a Fijian caretaker I'd not met, who shared my father's final conversation. They got up at midnight so Dad could venture out to the kitchen with his walker, where the two of them watched TV with coffee and cookies, my father considerately asking permission each time he changed the channel. I don't know what they watched. Coffee finished, Tonn helped my father back to what would prove his deathbed. After that, Dad went under, slipping into a delirium from which he never fully surfaced.

I'd gone home to bed hours before.

6/15/2008: "First I dreamed I was sitting at his usual seat by the fridge and he came in looking very young. He sat across from me and teased me somehow, though without words. I felt so happy but then I remembered and said, 'Dad, I think this might be just a dream and really you're *dying*!' He heard me and his image faltered a bit like a broken transmission, horizontal lines buzzing across it, but then he was still teasing me, pouring out more love, and looking younger than ever.

"Then I was outside at nightfall near a house set up on a bank above a big lake [Michigan?]. I was starting down a trail to go swimming when a woman came out of the house and called to me. She looked old-fashioned in her dress and apron and reminded me of my dad's mother, Grammy, though I couldn't quite see her features. She called to me that she was looking for her little boy, that it was time for him to come home. As I neared the beach I met a man and a boy coming toward me. The man was Jamaican and the boy, reaching up to hold his hand, only about three. Yes, the kindly man assured me, they were heading for the house right now."

In the morning I reached my parents' house in time to meet Tonn, who spoke earnestly of my father's politeness and grace. "Hmm. Fijian, not Jamaican," I thought.

All that day Dad spoke to us urgently, reflectively, and humorously in fluttering phrases that made no sense. We would smile, agree, and laugh if he seemed to think he'd made a joke. But now and then his mind cleared. At one point he lifted his hand and clinked wedding rings – fifty-nine years – with my mom. At another, his eyes focused on me where I stood at the foot of his bed. "You're beautiful," he said simply. Those were his last words to me.

6/15/2008: "On Monday night, my dreams were filled with anguish and regret for all I had not done or loved in this precious life. I can't describe the intensity of loss, of mistaken waste. I was driving through a desert where the banks of dry earth had formed into church bells, bulging out in smooth curves. Now they rang, they filled the open desert air with a beautiful clang full of longing, and I wished with all my heart I had embraced the Catholic Church! I loved it! I knew it! The bells' airs were so pure and transporting, but I could not embrace the sound because I, stupidly, misguidedly, had turned away.

"Then a white roadside guardrail – I was driving fast – eclipsed them from sight. Was it too late, I thought, to make up for my choices? Yet it hadn't been a choice, I thought in my own defense: I had *wanted* to respect the church but I *couldn't*. It simply did not mesh with my scientific understanding of the world, which I loved as much as anyone loves church.

"I deeply regretted never having answered emails from my friends Jerome and Carolee, to let them know I did love them [Dad had never made up with his brother, Jerome]. I came to the monastery where I'd once lived, but all my belongings had been cast out by an angry nun. "Take your stuff and get out of here!" she commanded. I stooped to gather what was mine from the dust and saw, as a final insult, that they had stepped on my reading glasses and crushed them. My heart ached with rejection."

I woke from this dream at 4:00 AM, knowing full well it was Dad's. I threw on my clothes and drove in the predawn light to my parents' house. Mom was sleeping elsewhere and only Tonn awake. I asked to speak to Dad privately, though he was unconscious. I took his hand in both of mine.

"God loves you, Dadda. God loves you so much, and god is *not* the Catholic Church! People made the church. No one is angry. No one is disappointed. You've filled your life with love and goodness and that's all god wants from any of us. Let go the church! Let god love you! You are a good, good man!"

He didn't open his eyes, and his squeezes of my hand were tremulous and erratic, but I felt part of him heard me. The thing was, I sensed the battle raging on inside him regardless of whatever I said. He was busy; he had much work to do by himself, all the years of alcoholic denial to slog through. Whereas Adelyn had embraced Jesus in her final years and stood on the brink of free-falling faith, my father had let conflicts with god pile up for a lifetime. That was for him the work of dying, to reconcile his mind's empiricist life with his spirit's divine destination – and there was nothing I could say to help him along. I remembered the woman on the path to the house. She'd find him. I'd trust that she would call him home.

That afternoon a social worker from hospice came and turned Dad from his left side to his right, which – I *knew* – would kill him rapidly. There was something wrong; his fluid-filled left lung weighed too heavily on his heart. I felt guilty deciding whether or not to speak up, because part of me wanted him to just go. What harm could there be to let this change of position do its work, since everyone else thought one side just as good as another?

But I sat with Dad and Tonn's cousin, Sara, while the rest of the family moved into the kitchen to talk with the social worker. It's hard not to feel privileged when you know stuff no one else does. They were talking away in there. If I'd joined them and Sara had gone on reading her magazine, Dad would have died alone.

I felt even more guilty for secretly hoping to sense the Light again. "Look at you, Louisa!" I shamed myself. "Here your sweet, devoted father is dying – how can you be thinking of the Light like some carnival ride? You're heartlessly callous!"

At that point god (or some attending spirit) told me pretty directly to knock off the guilt. Self-centered callousness is part of the human condition, it told me. You're stuck with it. Your father is passing, and that's a beautiful, holy thing. So quit wasting energy beating yourself up and just call your family, because it's time.

I asked Sara to bring the family in – Dad was going now. She protested slightly, reminding me the social worker had just advised us he might well linger on for several weeks.

"No," I said with a simplicity unlike me. "It's happening now. Go get them."

The Light didn't reveal itself this time, maybe because I was so much anticipating it or because too much time had passed since my NDE; this time my Light receptors, or whatever, brought me nothing. Instead I experienced a profound peace in knowing Dad would make his journey soon.

Family encircling him, he breathed slower... and slower. I knew all we had to do to "save" him was turn him back to his left side, and he'd breathe just fine for hours. But nothing told me to intervene. I stayed silent and let it happen.

Zelda and I described for him the times he'd taken us out on the Sound in the little motorboat at the summer cabin. We'd fly across the water, wind roaring in our ears. "We'd shout, 'Go faster, Dadda! Faster!' And then you would, and we'd love it!'"

He stopped breathing.

Though I tried to sense my father's joy in the room, as I had Adelyn's, I picked up none. He may still have been reconciling. As his draped corpse was carried from the house he'd lived in fifty years, I felt a draught of bitterness, though it may have been only my own sense of how his earthly personality would view that moment. I do wonder. Like me at the time of my NDE, Dad only *thought* he was atheist because he rejected a monotheistic figure of God. He did unwittingly love god in nature, in science, in human compassion. Why should he suffer any more obstruction from the Light than I had? I don't want to believe my father had to work through purgatory to reach the Light. I prefer to assume I was just too dense with worldliness to pick up his spirit's energy.

That night I dreamed a huge, powerful grizzly reared up so high on its hind legs that it burst through the ceiling of our living room, then paced ferociously outside the house. It was Dad – his spirit fighting, fighting, not willing to leave! Months later, though, on a night when I'd prayed to him for relief from a particularly dark fit of self-loathing, he came to me in another dream as his young, teasing self. He made me know, without words, that I was the apple of his eye and could do no wrong: he loved me absolutely.

Not a lot: absolutely. His love felt like a shaft of the Light.

WEIRD THING # 14

This last one's about intruding on your friend's sex life.

So I'm looking for a parking space at Home Depot one morning in 2010, when quite suddenly, into my mind pops my friend, Joel. I'd known him over nine years, since Jesse first sponsored his wife, Wyly. My thoughts ran like this:

"I like Joel a lot. He's a great guy, great artist, and – oh, that's right! He works construction, so I bet he comes *here* a lot. He and Wyly are such a rad couple. You know, I bet they still have a damn good sex life, those two, even after all these years and having kids and all. I bet they still really enjoy sex. In fact, I bet it's *hot!*"

Next thing I knew, into my thoughts popped a visual of Wyly stretched out naked and curvaceous on a fancy bed, her blond hair tousled enticingly in her face as I'd never seen it: that was one damn desirable woman!

"Holy shit!" I pulled back. "I can't believe I just pictured that! What's *wrong* with me? I don't think of Wyly that way!"

Shaking off my thoughts, I went into Home Depot. First I went the wrong way for something and had to double back. Then, as I strode past aisle after aisle at the front of the store, I recognized someone coming the opposite way: it was Joel.

We exchanged happy hellos and hugged.

"Gosh, that's so funny!" I said, guiltily. "I was just thinking of you." I asked how things were going.

"Rea-ally good," he said with a slow, grinning nod. "Wyly and I just got back from a weekend away. We dropped the girls off at Grandma's so we could have a night at a bed and breakfast, just us two. Yeah..." he nodded again, smiling at something I could no longer see. "It was *much* needed!"

"And *hot!* Who knew Wyly was so babe-a-licious?!" That's what I kept to myself. What I did say aloud, maybe even blushing, was, "Oh, how nice for you guys! That sounds great."

We chatted a little more. I felt oddly embarrassed for having snooped in Joel's private thoughts flustered by the knowledge that Weirdness had happened *again*. Once I'd told Grayson and John Church about it, though, the whole scene became funny. Earlier this year, I told Joel and Wyly themselves. Unlike Wendy Lee, they were delighted.

What do you do with unintended telepathy like that, dipping into a friend's private thoughts as, unbeknownst to you, they pull into the opposite end of the same parking lot? All I can do is acknowledge that thoughts are, undoubtedly, something more than chemical synapses. Rather, they're bits of the same energy that, in total, makes up god.

WHY WEIRD THINGS HAPPEN TO ME

I don't watch TV. In all my life I've seen one *Seinfeld*, one *Cheers*, and two DVD episodes of *Gray's Anatomy*. During my period of depression during the late '90s I did watch *Friends* and *The Simpsons* regularly, but that was about it. *Oprah* I've also watched one time. So Oprah's coverage of Near Death Experiences, which I've heard tell of since, never appeared on my radar.

I do, however, listen to NPR now and then if I'm stuck in traffic, which happened to be the case en route to Grayson's one

Friday evening. I tuned in during an interview with author Jeff Long, MD, about his bestseller, *Evidence of the Afterlife.* You can imagine how my ears pricked up when I heard him explain that millions of people around the globe have Near Death Experiences (NDEs), and thousands had responded to an NDE survey on his website. Their tabulated data formed the basis of his book.

I'd given up on the NDE movement after reading a friend's copy of Betty Eadie's *Embraced by the Light,* which made me feel almost sick. I cringed at the Christian imagery and bureaucratic organization that dominated "Heaven" in her account. "I can't consort with these loony people," I thought. "I need to keep my own experience pure."

This Jeff Long, however, was no loony. He was an oncologist by trade whose extensive research into NDEs had revealed that each of these thousands of people tended to perceive god relative to their own imagery in vital experiences distinguished by an array of hallmarks – nine, in fact, that he had isolated – while their bodies were clinically dead.

"Hunh!" I thought. Maybe specific imagery was relative, while its import – the power of love and the spiritual dimension of existence – was consistent. Old Betty Eadie could be a bureaucracy-respecting Christian who thus met Jesus and a huge staff of angels, while I had been an atheist who saw the sun and the life-evolving sea. Maybe I didn't have to veer away from other people's experiences to safeguard my own.

Nevertheless, it took me nearly a year to Google Near Death Experiences and discover the International Association for Near Death Studies (IANDS) had a Seattle group. Unfortunately, they met only one Saturday per month, and, as we know, my Saturdays were always devoted to either Grayson or Keno.

But when Grayson and I parted ways, I resolved to attend the next Seattle IANDS meeting. For almost thirty years I'd carried the experience of my NDE privately, sharing it with only a few people, usually when drunk. Now I wanted to find out if there were others like me.

As soon as I entered the room, I knew I was home – in the same way I'd found a home in AA. I could feel it in the room, an energy. Light traces hummed collectively around a dozen people who, like me, had all crossed over. The other thirty people, as raised hands would later reveal, were attending out of interest often sparked by inexplicable experiences other than NDEs.

Kimberly Clark Sharp likes to open the meetings with a freely garrulous preamble explaining what an NDE consists of and why we meet – to share our memories from the other side and our conviction that it does in fact exist. She defines an NDE as a memory or a collection of memories from a period when the body was clinically dead, without pulse or breathing, for a substantial period of time. At that first meeting, two things she said blew me away.

1) NDE memories do not fade with time, as do normal ones. I'd assumed that by this time, the bulk of my vivid NDE memory *had* to be an accretion of imagination layered over the scaffold of memory. How else could a journey of thirty years ago persist in my memory more vividly than yesterday's lunch? Imagine how I felt to learn that so it goes for all of us.

2) An NDE often leaves survivors with psychic after-effects, including prescience, telepathy, hearing spirit "voices," and, most often in children, the ability to see spirit forms. During a given meeting, she might call out, "How many have seen a spirit?" or "How many have known of a specific occurrence before it happened?" Hands go up – of half a dozen or more slightly uncomfortable but defiantly certain people.

I was not crazy! I was not a delusional egomaniac! "I'm just an ordinary, garden-variety Near Death survivor," I told my Al-Anon sponsor delightedly, "the same way I'm an ordinary, garden variety alcoholic!" The more meetings I attend, the more I continue to identify.

Some of our speakers have described NDEs much longer and more detailed than mine, often had in the company of various spirits. When I listen to them relating their stories, especially trying to put into words the overwhelming love of the Light, I travel with them toward that bliss. I remember the Light. I get greedy for it. I want them to keep describing it *forever*. Other NDEers have told me they do, too. I want to hear more about the spirit who guided someone's life review and bathed him in unconditional love, about the reception of knowledge via wordless telepathy. During IANDS meetings, this earthy, body-encased experience becomes only one aspect of my spiritual being.

In AA, we sometimes use the expression "god shot" to describe a moment when, like a shot of whiskey, a wave of god-consciousness warms our awareness with wellbeing. Well, I get so many god shots at an IANDS meeting, by the end I'm pretty well plowed. Love, Light, and joy all around!

I soon read *Evidence of the Afterlife*, recognizing dozens of parallels to my own experience. Of particular interest to me was the survey question: "Did you have any psychic, paranormal, or other gifts following the experience you did not have prior to the experience?" To this, 45% answered, "Yes," meaning they, too, had experienced Weird Things.

Can you imagine going all your life not knowing why certain things happened, and then finding out the reason?

I told my story to the group in January 2012 – or at least all I could fit of it into 90 minutes. Tim Smith was in the audience, as well as Joel the artist and several other AA friends. That my 14 Weird Things were so varied – a ghost, foreknowledge of death, warning voices, extreme serendipities, a clairvoyant dream and serendipitous explanation, anticipating a stranger's name, anticipating contact with friends, and picking up deathbed emotions and mental images from others – made me feel like I was all over the map. I have no particular "gift." But so it goes for countless NDE survivors. For instance, while describing my sense of Adelyn's spirit hovering in the hospital room, I was suddenly overcome with self-conscious apology.

"I know this sounds like something from TV," I faltered.

Kim, who was moderating, stopped me right there.

"How many people in here have hovered?" she asked of the room. Hands went up, perhaps eight. "And how many people have sensed hoverers?" Different hands, perhaps five, went up. The faces on these people were resolute. They knew their truth, and they were standing by it. Either we're all damn good at deluding ourselves, or these things really do happen.

During the break, a woman came up to me in the restroom. "Don't feel bad for not telling your brother about his baby's death," she said, referring back to my talk. "We can't. I knew my two friends were going to be in a terrible car accident, and I felt so guilty when it happened. But there's no way to warn people if we don't know when or why or how."

I thanked her. It felt just like AA: *I've been there, too. It's okay.*

Since attending IANDS, I've made more note of the little woo-woos I get every few weeks or so. These are too many to tell. More than once I've known in advance the speaker for an AA meeting. I was mopping my worn out kitchen floor recently when I sensed that Wyly (of the bed & breakfast babe-ness) hated her equally worn-out kitchen floor so much she'd recently decided to get it replaced. Five minutes later, Wyly called to ask if I could help her finish painting her kitchen before the new floor arrived in the morning. Even more recently, a young friend from IANDS popped into my mind as I drove to an AA meeting, and I resolved to email him since we'd had no contact for months. Minutes later at a red light, something drew my attention to the homeless guy who always hangs out on a particular median. Crouching to talk with him was... my IANDS friend. He ran over to my window – "I thought of you, too! Five, seven minutes ago, right?" – before the light changed. Lots of people have little woo-woos of this kind but discount them as coincidence. We don't.

I'm greedy for more woo-woos, big and small. All of us NDEers are, and we admit it. There's no knowing whether I'll get another major Weird Thing. I wait and hope, but I don't embellish. Weird Things, like orgasms, are no fun if you fake them.

CHAPTER 31: PROGRESS, NOT PERFECTION

The point is, faith affects... our relationships and aspirations in everyday life by enabling us to see them against the backdrop of a more comprehensive image of...the meaning of life.

> *- James W. Fowler*
> *Stages of Faith*

Much as we would like, we cannot bring everyone with us on this journey called recovery. We are not being disloyal by allowing ourselves to move forward. We don't have to wait for those we love to decide to change as well.

> *- Melody Beattie*
> *The Language of*
> *Letting Go*

Over a year has passed since I wrote most of this book, during which some pretty heavy stuff has gone down. I have nineteen years of sobriety now, for which I'm more grateful than I can say. Vicissitude – a fancy word for scary, disturbing shit – has indeed shaken it, but my faith and program have kept me sober through all. At this point I'm grateful for everything that's happened.

What kinds of vicissitude are we talking? The short version is, I told my siblings about this book, and within days my email was overrun with their outrage. The book was narcissistic, full of lies, and shameful to the family. For weeks the flamer emails kept arriving, characterizing me as an AA-brainwashed, selfish twit – and at the height of this storm, I learned I had breast cancer. The ground seemed to split open beneath me. Everything I had counted on was giving way.

Writing the book, I'd taken for granted the mindset it was based on, steeped in nearly twenty years of give-and-take sharing in the rooms of AA and Al-Anon. I knew my siblings didn't understand alcoholism or recovery; they'd never been interested in coming to meetings or even hearing about them. Like many people, they seemed to envision strangers droning on about drinking and trying not to rather than a community exposing the inner challenges of being human or the courage of living by faith. Actually, I have no idea what they envisioned. All I know is the wine flowed freely throughout all our family functions and any conversation I started about AA seemed to strike a sour note.

I honestly hadn't foreseen that the book would enrage them. To call our father an alcoholic, to talk publically about the inner dynamics of our family as *I* experienced them – these were extreme trespasses. My mother I'd asked not to read, as I knew the account of my various mental illnesses would hurt her. But I'd been foolish enough to imagine that, learning for the first time of my obsessive compulsion disorder, or maybe the suicidal depths addiction took me to, my siblings might feel empathy. I even imagined they'd understand the good I meant to offer by sharing my story with fellow alcoholics. I couldn't have been more wrong.

Walter accused me of out-and-out lying. He said I invented our sister's fatal hemorrhage because, while my book already featured plenty of "lurid sex," it was lacking blood and gore. Whatever sick behaviors I'd developed as a child and teen had *nothing* to do with our upbringing – they were just some kinky fluke of mine. By registered mail he sent a two-page list of passages he wanted cut, then ended by urging me to "just take the turd down." Zelda's emails virtually quivered with fury: I was a narcissist. She instructed me to read the description of narcissism in Thomas Moore's *Care of the Soul* so I would see how the narcissist is incapable of loving anyone. Over time her emails hit deeper: I'd polluted my son's innocence by bringing him to meetings and I was a sadist – which was why I'd been attracted to masochism. By the end, she was hurling everything in arm's reach: "You stupid, selfish, blind idiot!"

I, meanwhile, couldn't understand the degree of panic these messages triggered in me. My rational mind knew their words couldn't hurt me, but my body reacted chemically as though each email were a mushroom cloud on the horizon. I developed a fear of my laptop. Glenda, my sponsor, advised me to *pause* before responding. A hasty apology, she said, is never heartfelt; I should allow everyone time to process feelings and calm down before trying to sort things out. Her mistake was assuming my siblings would calm down. Instead, they assumed the lack of reply reflected my contemptuous indifference and amped up their rebukes accordingly.

After a week of this, I responded by doing everything they asked. I apologized earnestly, removed our last name from the book, and began the process of making all the cuts requested – but none of it helped. Cached Google and Amazon sites take time to show changes, so again, they assumed I was lying and had done nothing. The angry emails proliferated, coming now from my niece and Walter's wife Betsy, both of whom had already ridiculed the book on Facebook and posted mocking "reviews" on its Amazon page – each now demanding personalized apologies.

Meanwhile, I received a callback on my yearly mammogram. Those images led to my being called in for a biopsy, and eventually to the news that I had breast cancer. At that point, I sort of lost my mind.

This is what it looked like. I found myself carrying on intense thought conversations with my siblings and sister-in-law during *every* unoccupied moment. That is, if I wasn't totally absorbed by some mental effort, I'd imagine defending myself against their charges. I held forth convincingly whenever I was washing dishes, feeding the chickens, driving anywhere, buying groceries, or chucking a tennis ball for our dog. Seconds after resolving to *stop thinking about it*, I made crystal clear how grossly they'd misinterpreted my book and how deeply they'd hurt me, the words filling my mind while I got ready for bed or poured water in the tea pot.

These thoughts took up far more of my attention than, say, my having been diagnosed with a life-threatening illness. Why? I think somewhere in my confused brain, the two threats had merged. And yet, of the two, there seemed something far more lethal about my family's attacks. Sure, cancer wants to kill you, but it's nothing personal. It's just doing what any disease does. Malignancy doesn't single you out and, having speed-read an account of every pain and adversity you've undergone, berate you as a worthless fraud. It was my family's *intent* to hurt me, to shove my face in my wrongness and punish me, that felt almost like assault or rape: their satisfaction in skewering me far outweighed any concern for my heart. And yet the principles by which I lived left me no option of striking back.

I called my symptom compulsive narration. I *could not stop* myself from narrating. I made fun of myself in shares at meetings, forced myself to recite bad poems about it, wrote flashcard mantras, and of course, journaled reams because I thought if I could just set my arguments down, I'd be able to let go of them. But within seconds of banishing them from my mind, my critics pooled back like liquid to a low point, and I'd resume defending myself.

So I conceded, eventually, that I was frickin' nuts. I took a First Step on this thing: I was powerless. I could not fix my broken mind with my broken mind. I'd need to go back to therapy to understand what was going on.

Finding a good therapist who'd accept my poor folks' insurance wasn't easy. But Elsa had fourteen years in Al-Anon and had grown up in a rigid Chinese family that now viewed her as quite the black sheep, so we were able to build off that shared foundation. Still, any time you see a new therapist, there's that enormous mural of your entire life to sketch in. Where do you start? What do you tell?

I decided to begin by sharing with some of the online messages that had brought on this compulsive self-defense, because I'd lost all ability to gauge whether my family members were behaving responsibly. Obviously, they didn't have to like my book. My question was, were these fair and acceptable ways to say they didn't, or were they, in fact, mean bitches? At our second session, I handed Elsa a printout of the following Facebook queue – the exchange my niece and sister-in-law posted about thirty hours after I'd phoned my brother to say I'd written a book.

Oh, one more random thought . . . it's kind of hilarious when someone who works as a professional writer, tutor, and editor publishes something that is absolutely chock-full of typos and misspellings. Yep, that's who I want proofing my essays, for sure . . .

20 December at 22:51 · Like

I'm up to 28 typos so far...

20 December at 23:10 · Like · 1

29!

20 December at 23:22 · Like · 1

30!

20 December at 23:42 · Like · 1

I really like this game. It's like I-spy, but better.

20 December at 23:44 · Like · 1

They're like Easter eggs.

20 December at 23:58 · Like

I think I found my favorite one: "Until I could identify my elf-destructive reflexes." Yes, it is difficult dealing with those reflexes to destroy elves, that sucks . . .

21 December at 02:41 · Like

Elsa sat reading in her armchair, her face registering confusion. She shook her head as if to clear it. "I'm sorry – *how old* is Betsy, again?"

"Forty-nine. It's a grade school photo."

"Okay. A bit ironic. And your niece is...?"

"Twenty-three."

What had my response to this been, she wanted to know.

Did she mean besides shaking, beginning to sob, and dashing upstairs so my son wouldn't have to see me bawling my eyes out? I'd done what I always did – tried to turn the other cheek. I didn't respond online, but armed with phone support from several Al-Anon friends, I chose to show up a few nights later to the family Christmas Eve celebration acting as if I hadn't even seen the posts. I helped cook dinner, gave everyone their gifts, and wished them a sincere merry Christmas. Elsa took copious notes.

Only many months later would I realize this had been my own form of insanity. I'd imagined that if I responded with enough kindness, I might foster love and tolerance for our differences. In other words, I hoped to *change* and *manage* my family members. Instead, three days later my niece and sister-in-law Betsy posted their sarcastic, ridiculing book reviews on Amazon. And those demands for individual apologies were yet to come.

The weeks I worked with Elsa pretty much exactly overlapped my six weeks of radiation therapy. While the latter intended to eradicate any remaining cancer, the former attempted to get at the shame I felt in my family.

Elsa helped me to recognize two key insights: first, that my family had ceased knowing or supporting me years ago, in part because they operated by an entirely different view of the world; and second, that their shaming something that exposed my deepest vulnerabilities had triggered Post Traumatic Stress in me, based in the primary trauma of having my sexual drawings discovered as a child.

Back when I was drinking, my family and I got along fine. We valued academia and tacitly scorned the ignorance of average Americans. God was a crutch for the weak-willed, and church communities were herds of conformists. Most of all, though, we lived by self-propulsion, convinced that our judgments were accurate. AA – that cult of brainwashed nobodies giving each other creepy hugs and sharing dramatic confessions – was a world apart from us.

When I became one of those cultish dolts, my siblings felt I'd fallen off the deep end. We no longer saw each other outside family celebrations of Christmas and the occasional birthday, gatherings which always involved half a dozen bottles of wine with glasses occasionally ending up at my place setting. "Sorry about that!" We knew nothing of one another's real lives, so we filled in the gaps with assumptions. I'd known for some time that Betsy and Walter ridiculed me privately and with other family members. Glenda had helped me see how they were trying to knock some sense back into me. *Change back!* they were essentially saying. *Don't you remember what's right and good?*

I'd never tried to describe for them the changed perspective of an alcoholic who's surrendered. All active addicts operate with a vision of how our lives are supposed to turn out, much as my siblings do. All of us have tried our damnedest to steer toward it, much like them. The split happens when we're forced to admit total defeat – that we're helpless puppets of that invisible master, addiction. The *last* thing any of us wanted to be was helpless. The *last* place any of us wanted to go was AA. We fought both like death. But in the end, our lives, our realities, and our hopes were destroyed.

From that rubble of defeat, we slowly rebuilt lives founded on the very things we used to loathe: a Higher Power, intimate fellowship, and fidelity to a program. As we found happiness via everything we'd ridiculed in the past, we developed a more complex view of life – an understanding that our own perceptions were limited, that we were frequently wrong, and that we had no right to judge others.

What happens in AA is the opposite of cultism: life loosens. Sick newcomers, we know, have far more to offer than their current behavior indicates. Once they "come alive" through the psychic change, we get to see the rich beauty buried inside them. Some of the greatest wisdom I've ever heard has come from people who can barely read. That's why I began to associate with people who, to my family, were contemptible.

For example, there was the time I went down to the family summer cabin with half a dozen lesbians (me a post-lesbian), one of them a sponsee of my friend Tiffany – a homeless girl with a shaved head who was on Day 1 of sobriety. She smelled of B.O. We all kept hoping she'd take a shower, and while we swam at the lake we called out to her a ridiculous number of times how great the water was, but she held off. Back at the cabin, my friends begged me: "We can't ride back in the car with her, we just *can't!*" So, carrying two towels, I approached her as she sat on the deck.

"Five," I said evenly (she was part Native American and had adopted a number name), "you can take a shower *before* me, or *after* me. Which would you rather?" At first Five responded politely that she'd take one later. But when I repeated the two options, she gathered my meaning.

Within seconds, she was on her feet and getting in my face. "What the fuck are you *saying*?! You saying I *stink*?!" Wordlessly, my heart full of compassion, I held out a towel. She wheeled on the others sitting out in the field and yelled in disbelief, "She's fuckin' sayin' I *stink*! What the fuck?!"

In one of the most priceless moments of my entire sobriety, none of the women looked up. Eventually the girl nearest, who suffered from advanced rheumatoid arthritis, met Five's glare and shrugged uncomfortably.

Five seized the towel and stormed away. Afterwards, freshly showered, she strode past the lot of us and headed for the beach trail, followed by my coyote mix, Kelsey. For several hours, my friends and I let her be. That night, Five shared at our campfire meeting about her new understanding of humiliation versus humility – the latter being an acceptance of what *is*. And after years of floundering in hopeless alcoholism and drug addiction, on that day Five founded a lasting sobriety. I saw her years later at a meeting, her hair grown out and styled, wearing fashionable clothes and jewelry, and building a career in marketing. She thanked me yet again for my directness, kindness, and loaning her my coyote. That was the bottom she'd needed to hit, she said, in a safe and spiritual place – an experience that saved and transformed her life.

I made the enormous mistake of telling my mother that story. The next time I went to the cabin, I found several tall stacks of folded linens on the table along with a bill from a cleaning service: "Launder all linens; disinfect premises: $250." Never mind that Five had slept under the stars in her own sleeping bag – she must have contaminated the entire cabin with her vermin and filth.

The incident showed my family, and Walter in particular, that Louisa lacked any kind of responsible judgment for who should be allowed at the cabin. My family could only theorize that I must *so* desperate for a clan of admirers, I'd round up any scumbag, even a homeless girl or ex-con, to show off our cabin to. These low-lifes, Walter said, would return to rob or squat – a reason I should never post any photos of the cabin on Facebook. He rallied to put a cap on the number of guests I could invite, citing the septic tank's limitations (I doubt any of my family can imagine the candor with which alcoholics discuss optimal peeing and pooping strategies), and forbid me to allow any but "close friends." Despite my guests' service commitment to always leave the cabin cleaner than we found it, Walter found cause to complain: "Your friends may 'love' the cabin," he emailed sternly, "but when I'm cleaning their old toothpaste scum out of the drain, I'm not feelin' the love!"

Walter's scoldings were all gentle compared to his wife's. No one on the planet has flung more poo at me than Betsy, the vast majority of it e-poo. I was almost nine months pregnant when her first flamer accused me of being more concerned about my own "woo-woo birthing experience" than the safety of my unborn child. (I didn't reply and still allowed her in my birthing room.) Another time I had "savored" a description of my sister's death as a tale about how spiritual I was, so that Betsy's blood ran cold thinking how much I'd delight in describing *her* death. With my huge ego, I traipsed (or something like that) through life oblivious to the harm left in my wake.

I'd convinced myself that responding with nothing but prayer and kindness followed the AA advice of "restraint of pen and tongue," so it must be best. I was wrong. Years ago an LA Fitness locker room, I overheard an African American mom and her coltish teenage daughter talking about some bullying the girl had suffered at school. The mother said clearly, "Do you see what's going on here? You *teach* these people how to treat you. You're the one who taught them this was okay."

Her words struck me – one of the ways god guides us. I had "taught" my family that Louisa would passively absorb any kind of insult. Even when Betsy condemned me as a parent, invoking Child Protective Services because I'd left my eight-year-old son in the lobby of the Lake Quinault Lodge for ten minutes, I replied only, "So report me!" A long email dispute ensued between Zelda and Walter. I didn't participate, but my heart sank when Zelda forwarded me Walter's Louisa-bashing messages. A mother's love runs deep, and so do words that undercut it.

By some kind of backward management strategy, I thought my refraining from any self-defense would throw their assault into such clear relief that they'd *see* it for what it was. In other words, I was once again managing through martyrdom.

The point is, for years I'd been teaching my siblings that Louisa fought back no more than a leaky punching bag. I'd believed I did this from love, but it was really from fear. I lacked the courage to establish boundaries, so I opted for sainthood and the quiet consolation prize of a holier-than-thou ego.

Cancer taught me that I *had* to draw boundaries. When your life is threatened, you realize that you're its sole caretaker, responsible for all the thoughts and energy you invite into it. Cancer *forced* me to create a haven where love concealed no malice.

When I called Walter to tell him I had breast cancer, he responded skeptically, "Oh? And how did *this* come about?"

"From a biopsy," I said.

He backpedalled immediately, assuring me he and Betsy wanted to be "a support."

"All I want from you," I said clearly, "is for you to leave me alone. I want to be left in peace. Most of all, I want to hear *nothing* from Betsy." My adrenaline shot up and I repeated many times, voice shaking, "Nothing. *Nothing!* Not a word! I *do not* want her in my space!"

Sure as shit, a card arrived from Betsy within two days, a flowery Hallmark thing with a scrolly "Thinking of you" penned above her signature. I stuck it in the recycling. Then, sensing it still in my house, I took it out to the recycle bin. I wheeled the recycle bin to the curb. And when at last I saw the truck come, I breathed a sigh of relief. It was gone.

Zelda, too, wanted to reverse everything. She sent a weekly gift delivery of organic produce. Unfortunately, the sight of those big purple bins left on my doorstep had the effect of a flaming cross: they triggered the PTSD almost as badly as email. Phone texts caused a similar reaction, so I blocked them. I'd already blocked Facebook and email.

To make it through cancer, I leaned on my *chosen* family.

~

I'd just parked in Fremont prior to a tutoring session when the phone call came. "Are you driving?" asked an upbeat woman, not a solicitor but a nurse from some kind of lab. "Well, there's good news and there's bad news. The good news is, one of your tumors was benign!"

I'd gotten out of the car and was walking along a cyclone fence, diamond shapes of gray wire fanning past me on the right. Through those wires was a parking lot with some weeds and garbage. The sidewalk beneath my shoes was wet. None of these factors could change what I'd just heard. My dumbstruck brain formed the question, "Do I have cancer?"

Yes. Details to follow.

In an altered state I wandered into the café, told my client the news, and received her awkward hug and kind words – that I had taught her so much about writing – which seemed weirdly funereal. I headed home. What else could I do? You don't drive well absorbing news like that. You tend to mistake stop signs for stoplights and vice versa.

My plan was to crawl into bed, curl up in fetal position, and cry – but I felt an urging from outside me to do the opposite. Okay, okay, god! But it won't help! Reluctantly I pulled over dialed one friend after another, hanging up at each voicemail, until I reached a live person. Matt had been one of those newcomers I'd met nine years ago at Stanley's March AA birthday's party when, "among some who knew me and some just coming to know me," I'd prayed for god to transform my life. Of late he'd been going through a rash of drug relapses and brief stints of sobriety, so I wasn't even sure if he was clean. But I called him anyway.

"Get your ass over here," he said immediately. "I don't care. No, I don't care. Yes, you do. You need to be here and I won't hear different."

Arriving at his house, I felt shocked at first to see he had a *girl* over, someone I didn't know. But what should I care about social awkwardness? I introduced myself to Liz: "Hi, I'm Louisa, the one with breast cancer." Since Matt lived only a few blocks from my house and was dog-sitting, he ordered me to go get my dog we'd all take a walk to a nearby dog park.

The January air felt cold and dry, reminding me of childhood walks with my family on holidays, except that today every aspect of my awareness seemed tinged by dread of dying. What stage of cancer, what lay ahead for me, I didn't know. My siblings' emails echoed in my thoughts as if my addled brain were flinging them about in some futile effort to clear space: *cancer! being despised! death! a liar who cannot love! dishonored our father! malignant growth!* The afternoon sky hung gray with depression; I couldn't tell what was real and what projected. We walked past houses – they wouldn't save me. I spoke to my dog – he couldn't, either.

But then something magical did happen. Crossing a street, I was unsure whether a car would stop for us, so I held back cautiously, then dashed across to catch up with Matt and Liz. Matt looked back at me.

"Jesus, Louisa!" he called out before I reached the curb. "First you go and get breast cancer, then you almost get mowed down –

what the hell's next?! Are aliens going to zap us from the sky?" He did a flinching double take overhead, hands shielding his head.

Excuse me. What did Matt just say?? First you *go and get breast cancer*?! Had he really just yelled that word "cancer!" into the afternoon air? As a *joke*? Did he not realize I could *die*?

I walked a few steps, head down. "They might," I said tersely, referring to the aliens. But then I cut him a look and smiled. Not laughed, but smiled, not just in my face, but in my heart. Because Matt loved me. And I loved Matt. And I knew that encircling us was the love of our whole tribe of AA, where we disarm life's suffering, darkness, and terror by naming the worst directly and making fun of it. In that moment, everything shifted just a little bit: Cancer became a part of life; I understood that I was loved, throughout my life, by friends who would walk beside me one day at a time. Maybe they couldn't save me, but they could surround me with a love that was safe.

Believe it or not, I had fun at that dog park, knowing I had cancer and laughing at all kinds of stupid things – my dog's repeated attempts to mount another and talk of whether Matt's sexual finesse resembled his – that seemed to insist life was humble, that even though we were enclosed by skin and separated by empty air, the love behind our dumb jokes linked us all to god. Liz became my friend.

Earlier that morning I'd begun drafting individual notes of apology for Betsy and my niece in my journal, but had to leave for work before I finished. The instant I got home, I sat down at the computer and typed out two apologies. I prayed, tears streaming down my face, for the happiness and healing of each. Then I hit send.

When I rose from the computer, I was done.

Done.

From this time forth, I promised myself, I would allow into my circle only those people who acknowledged and lived by the sanctity of kindness. No more mean-ass bitches!

My friends Rosemary and Jesseca came along to my surgery consult, where we learned my cancer was likely Stage 1, so that a lumpectomy was favored over mastectomy.

Since I'd already invited scads of people to my 18th sober birthday party a few days later, instead of cancelling I just changed the name to a "Get to Keep my Boob!" party. Thus it came to pass that eighty former drunks and lowlife drug addicts converged on my house three days before my cancer surgery bearing bouquets, gifts, cards, and food, food, food – loving me, hugging me, the lot of them singing Happy Birthday off key. I was cornered by the cake as they sang, my son at my side, and terribly embarrassed by all the attention when a voice said to me (as if from my left), "Louisa, this is *as good as it gets*! Don't resist. Let them love you."

I realized the voice spoke truth; all they wanted to do was love me, and all I had to do was let them. At that very moment, two photos were taken of me, shot by two different people and from two different angles, one a second after the other.

In both photos, an orb is hovering to the left of my head, and close examination shows features on it that have rotated in the interim. Many people believe orbs like this represent the presence of a spirit. Call me wacky, but I believe these photos caught some image of the voice I'd just heard. It's the energy of my guardian angel – the presence that greeted me decades ago on the other side and has warned and prompted me throughout my life.

On the morning of my surgery, which just happened to fall precisely on my 18th sober birthday, a former crackhead and ex-con rang my doorbell before dawn to drive me to the hospital. (A year before, he'd texted me "NEED HELP" as I shuffled through Safeway in slippers and a bad hair hat, so I'd picked him up across town and driven to a clinic for psyche meds.) We were met at the hospital by Rosemary, my friend of thirty years and a breast cancer survivor, who waited through my surgery. Another crack addict and alcoholic, now a chemo nurse (with whom I'd talked almost daily as she walked through a painful separation from her husband), took over to drive me home, having filled my prescriptions and brought along a double order of hot vegetarian pho. Meanwhile, John Church and his fiancé were hanging out with Keno at my house, having stocked our fridge with groceries.

I'd barely sat down when the doorbell rang: in bopped Matt with two pints of ice cream – exactly what tastes good post-narcotics! (He oughta know, he said.) My phone, meanwhile, was blowing up with well-wishing texts and voicemails, people asking if I needed anything. We were laughing, but in my friends' eyes I kept noticing a strange look I didn't understand until later that night when I saw my own eyes in the mirror, cloudy and at half-mast. They were worried about me.

This was love. This was shelter – what true family feels like.

Two cameras, two angles, two moments – same orb, same place, slight drifting. The less distinct image on the right was posted on Facebook by a friend, yet close inspection shows the same features on the orb have rotated slightly. Another friend who sees spirits has told me mine travels "above and to your left."

~

"What if it's just ego?" I asked Elsa about my lack of voice. "What if the reason I can never tell my siblings to leave me the fuck alone is that I'm too worried about my spiritual image?"

"Do you think it's that?" she asked, all therapist-y. "What else might it be?"

"I don't know," I pondered. "Fear, maybe. Not just *of* them, but of being *like* them."

As Elsa often said, "Anger rises up in defense of something sacred." We'd already covered the fact that Betsy, Walter, Zelda, and my niece all sincerely believed they were defending sacred memories from my accusations of family alcoholism and imperfect parenting. By their ethics, to inflict painful punishment on another, whether by mockery, insult, or accusation, was fully justified in order to teach that transgressor a lesson. AA maintains the converse – that we judge no one because we've not walked in their shoes, that love and tolerance be our code, that we practice the St. Francis Prayer in any way we can.

"Their way isn't a way I want to live," I told Elsa, "not even in counter-attack."

Elsa explained the difference between counter-attack and laying firm boundaries. Years ago I could have said, "You need to stop." I could have told them, "If I want your advice, I'll ask for it," or even "Please don't insult me." She also tried to explain justified distancing. "If people keep coming at you with knives," she said, "that puts the onus on *you* to step aside to safety."

Elsa worked with me via EMDR (Eye Movement Desensitization and Reprocessing) to revisit the original trauma around my childhood drawings and the new instance of the hate-emails. My psyche had been overflowing with self-defense to make up for my lack of voice in real life. Anger, Elsa told me, has a place – even for recovering addicts.

This last bit of advice, though, I doubt. Anger is never the answer, at least for me. Here's why:

After six weeks of daily radiation, I was at the end of my rope both physically and emotionally, but still had half a week to go. My mother had asked if I weren't making "an awfully big deal" of radiation, since I was largely unavailable to take care of her after she suffered a fall. Walter had told her that Betsy "hardly noticed" radiation after six rounds of chemo. Was I maybe overdramatizing this whole breast cancer thing? By that final week, the flesh of my armpit had begun to break down as if decomposing. I looked old as the hills. I'd wake each morning utterly exhausted with a headache just as severe as the one I'd gone to bed with – a pain that no rest, medicine, or massage could alleviate – and feel overwhelmed by the reality that I had to get up to keep earning a living, caring for my son, and keeping up my home.

I'd just absorbed my thirty-first radiation dose when I came home to discover a new review of my book – this book – on Amazon. It seemed odd. I'd suspended all marketing back when my siblings demanded rewrites, so there had been no sales for months. Nevertheless, "Hawks Fan" testified that he'd bought the book hoping it would be about recovery, but had found it to be nothing but a sordid monologue of all the twisted things the author had ever done – certainly a waste of time and money.

I lay on my bed sobbing my guts out for about an hour. This felt like the last straw. Here I'd poured out my story in hopes that my fellow addicts would identify, but now one of my own was going out of his way to inform the world my work was crap. I despaired. The book sucked. I must have been wrong after all, imagining my story could help anyone. I should give up. I should just chuck it, after all these years' work. Yet I *loved* my book, and the pain of abandoning it made me howl out loud.

"God," I wailed to the skylight above me, where god-as-the-clouds inched serenely past, "God, I'm lost! I thought you wanted me to write this thing, but it turns out Walter was right! It's nothing but a sordid monologue of every twisted— a... a sordid monologue of, of— "

I sat up. Hold the phone—! What kind of Hawks Fan said *that*? The review started off with a thuggish, unpunctuated diction and suddenly spiked to... the very words of Walter's emails! I grabbed my laptop for a second look. Walter playing a role, every word of it. Even the title, "Not Feeling It," was a '90s phrase he often used when trying to sound like an average Joe. A little more investigation showed me that a single book had indeed sold – one day prior to this review. So this *wasn't* a real review by an alcoholic: Walter and Betsy had just bought a new Kindle! Betsy couldn't post another withering review, so Walter had obliged.

I texted him: "Funny, I never knew you were so into football."

He responded almost instantly: "??? Who isn't?!"

I smiled sadly. Poor dude. Such a shitty liar.

On my second to last day of radiation, I felt the machine conveying me into its tube and waited while, behind me, the eighteen-ton leaden door slowly sealed off the room. First came the chest X-ray – my thirty-second – to help the beams of radiation avoid my heart. Lying as still as I possibly could, I listened to the TomoTherapy machine's emitter begin to circle me and fire radiation – click! click! click! click! – shooting billions of sub-atomic particles through my upper chest.

"That fucker!" I thought. Hadn't I whittled the book down in every way he'd asked, editing and rewriting even through my diagnosis and treatment? And he hadn't even bothered to read it! When I left the building into the angled sunlight of early morning, I sat down on a curb in the parking lot and called up Walter at work. He answered.

"What the hell do you mean," I said, "posting that thing on Amazon in my last week of radiation?!" I said. "Why would you *do* that?! When I'm the most exhausted? When all I asked from you was to be left in peace!"

"We didn't know…" he faltered.

"Bullshit!" I said. They knew I was getting radiation. I told him to write his own fucking book and leave mine the hell alone. "Betsy is a sick, sick woman!" I began. As soon as he heard that, Walter hung up.

I stared a few seconds at the asphalt, my heart pounding and the phone trembling in my hand, but not with fear. Exhilaration. Man, did that feel *g-o-o-d!* Did I tell him, or what? "God," I prayed, "this might be fucked up, but that felt right. It felt like courage." I stood up and saw my own shadow in the early morning light. For the moment, I didn't care about my headache or exhaustion. I felt free and righteous. I also noticed feeling skinnier, cooler, and more bad-ass than I'd felt in years. "Crawl before no-one," I quoted. I blew smoke from the barrel of my virtual six-shooter.

The next day Amazon pulled the review because Walter shares my last name and their policy prohibits immediate family from reviewing books. I told Elsa about the incident, giddy with excitement. My voice! I'd finally found it! And the compulsive narration – gone at last!

Except you know what?

A few weeks later, after I'd come down off that high, I saw it for what it was: a high. A self-righteous one, exactly like my siblings'. Not much different from an alcohol or cocaine high in that it felt absolutely terrific in the moment but improved nothing of substance. I saw now how that same old pal from drinking days – my puffed up ego – was what made me feel skinny, cool, and bad-ass afterwards. Because in truth I'm none of those things. I'm just Louisa, as god made me, trying to do her best.

I'm not here to harm others, not even if they've harmed me. My brother was doing the best he could, placating a wife who must suffer. If I pretend my anger will ultimately benefit anyone by teaching them what *I* think is right, I'm dishonest. True, I didn't insult Walter directly, but I spoke with an insulting blare of hostility. I felt he deserved no respect because he'd shown me none – but an eye for an eye makes the world blind. Anger is not the only alternative to martyrdom.

I decided to release mine and simply add this part of my story – about family and cancer – whether they'd like it or not. What's wrong with my family is the family disease of alcoholism, where truth telling is forbidden as high treason. Walter and Zelda are likewise at odds with one another. It's nobody's fault.

The great irony here is that, if you'd asked me any time between Adelyn's death and that first wave of flaming emails, I'd have told you I'd never let a day go by estranged from my siblings. I'd have said life is too fleeting and too precious to waste in conflict. As it stands, I've forgiven my family, but I'm still working on the readiness to invite them back into my life. I am no saint. I'm a work in progress.

Taking care of myself is my god-given right and responsibility. When the time comes to reconcile with my siblings, I'll need to redefine those relationships. As I keep attending Al-Anon and ACA, I keep learning more ways that dysfunctional alcoholic homes resemble each other. I realize my family is classically warped, but even so, I don't want "loved ones" who talk shit about me. If people aren't willing to speak both of me and to me with a basic respect, then I don't want them in my circle. That's an axiom. And I don't have to attend those wine-soaked family functions anymore. Maybe we can have family breakfasts instead.

~

Why is it that some people can know god and sense its calling even without experiencing an NDE or any Weird Things while others remain deaf to it all their earthly lives? When I left my body during my NDE, having spurned god all my life, why did I walk a beautiful beach to a familiar house and get pulled by the setting sun into the ultimate love of the Light? I didn't deserve it, not by moral standards, at least. Why did friends of mine who left their bodies, one of them only a child at the time, suffer the terrors of a dark, lonely, despairing hell?

It's frustrating to have no answers and to be incapable of reaching any. Our brains are fantastic little balls of cellular circuitry that are amazingly adept at navigating our paths on this earth, having co-created intricate cultures over hundreds of generations. But for understanding life outside our bodies, they ain't worth shit. That's not what they're designed to do.

Even so, mine carries in it this splinter of the inconceivable enormity of the other side. Our life in matter is only part of the big picture. Unlike my friend who's so bent on regaining heaven she can hardly wait to die ("You'll be fine either way," she assured me when we talked about my breast cancer), I cherish this side all the more for that knowledge. We abide here, sparks of god. We inhabit exquisitely complex bodies, collaborative projects of trillions of cells that grant us five portals to the physical world. What a glorious privilege! I get to eat toast. I can talk to you, a stranger, see the spark of god in your eyes and your movements, and my brain can generate a model of you-ness that I love. Both of us sense this connection despite the fact that you're on your way to Jiffy Lube and I'm headed back to a café where I forgot my keys, and all we exchange is a smile. And that, I believe, is the expression of god.

I don't know anything, but my sense is that god loves a challenge. Love is love is love on the other side, but in the realm of matter, loving others involves a reaching, an art, a creation unique to each person. For some of us, learning to love as a way of life is hard work – a slow, painful shedding fear and selfishness, a spiritual evolution motivated by each slight decrease in pain, each hint of new joy.

But what rewards come along as we start to get there: my life is so sweet, I can hardly stand it! I'm rich in everything but money. I write. I have my son, a miracle of conception and the joy of my life. I'm healthy and active, with the strength to climb volcanoes and the skills to thru-hike alone amid the sublime beauties of mountain wilderness. Most important, because it's the foundation for everything else, I haven't taken a drink for nineteen years, and with god's help, I'll never be drunk again. My life is full. Okay, I've got no partner, no lover, it's true. But I have love. Friends and acquaintances, sometimes women I scarcely know, call me to ask advice – *me*, that flailing, compulsive addict of yore – because they trust me. Or they tell someone else to call me; a few times I've spent half an hour on the phone unable to place the person I'm talking to, except that they're in tears and have asked for my help.

And life keeps growing. The year I turned fifty, I took up ballet again after a twenty-four year break. At first all I wanted was to not injure myself, but gradually, to my amazement, dance came back to me. Now in an advanced intermediate class I dance alongside women a fraction of my age, pulling off pirouettes, battements, and grand allegro jumps. Sure, when I was young I had better balance, but I never used to weep with joy at the sheer privilege of interpreting music. When I was young I could pull off an entrechat-six, but I never walked into the studio after missing two weeks for cancer surgery and saw the whole room of dancers stretching out on the floor rise to their feet to applaud.

But the greatest development in my life, I'd say, is the muscle of compassion. It's lookin' kinda ripped. When I see someone hurting – an addict, a normie, or anyone struggling with the trials of daily life (in other words, all of us) – my briefest "What's with *them*?" reflex (if I even feel it) gets kicked out of the ballpark by compassion. I give change and a bit of friendly conversation to every panhandler who asks. I'm quick to joke with strangers of all kinds – about a stray owl in a downtown tree, the fact that we both jumped out of our cars at an intersection, or some dumb thing I just did in the grocery store. In the laughter and camaraderie of strangers, you'll hear the song of god.

As we say in meetings, the Twelve Steps are *not* a save your soul program, they're a save your ass program. And yet ironically, to save our own asses, we have to focus on service to others. A thing works best when doing what it's designed to do, and we're designed to love and help each other. That's why AA is my church, my medicine, and my source of joy. Meetings keep me connected to the lives and emotions of others who are likewise hurting and healing. If I were to stop going, my head would get sucked up my ass again and I'd become consumed with my own problems, plans, and fears. I'd become again the selfish, confused, blind parasite I was for so many years. That Louisa, I'm certain, wouldn't need long to decide a drink might fix things.

In other words, I remain humbled by the lethal power of alcoholism. Humility before this cunning, baffling, and powerful disease is the not so secret secret to racking up nineteen years of sobriety – even while shit keeps continuously hitting the fan: I *get it* that it's always god, not Louisa, keeping me sober.

Dear reader, I'm grateful to you for the compassion that led you to read on and stay with me through this book despite its many flaws. Like me, it's far from perfect! You read because you love human beings, because you understand that we share the same inner struggles, and because you sense at some level that we are all one, all charged with an energy passed down from the same origin.

Whatever you saw of yourself in here, let it give you permission to be more loving toward everyone who enters your life even briefly. Bust out your kindness despite shyness and inhibition and help others at every opportunity: your life will bear the fruit of inner joy. If you're in too much pain to attempt it, ask your god for the willingness to work the Twelve Steps. Amazing things will follow, I promise!

Clockwise from top left: at Camp Muir, 10,000 feet with group I co-led there, 2012; at one of my sober parties, taken by John C.; dancing one month after finishing six weeks' radiation therapy, 2013; filming my YouTube video, "How to Turn 50, Bitches!" at Pike Place, 2010.

Made in the USA
San Bernardino, CA
26 June 2015